MONTAIGNE IN TRANSIT
ESSAYS IN HONOUR OF IAN MACLEAN

LEGENDA

LEGENDA is the Modern Humanities Research Association's book imprint for new research in the Humanities. Founded in 1995 by Malcolm Bowie and others within the University of Oxford, Legenda has always been a collaborative publishing enterprise, directly governed by scholars. The Modern Humanities Research Association (MHRA) joined this collaboration in 1998, became half-owner in 2004, in partnership with Maney Publishing and then Routledge, and has since 2016 been sole owner. Titles range from medieval texts to contemporary cinema and form a widely comparative view of the modern humanities, including works on Arabic, Catalan, English, French, German, Greek, Italian, Portuguese, Russian, Spanish, and Yiddish literature. Editorial boards and committees of more than 60 leading academic specialists work in collaboration with bodies such as the Society for French Studies, the British Comparative Literature Association and the Association of Hispanists of Great Britain & Ireland.

The MHRA encourages and promotes advanced study and research in the field of the modern humanities, especially modern European languages and literature, including English, and also cinema. It aims to break down the barriers between scholars working in different disciplines and to maintain the unity of humanistic scholarship. The Association fulfils this purpose through the publication of journals, bibliographies, monographs, critical editions, and the MHRA Style Guide, and by making grants in support of research. Membership is open to all who work in the Humanities, whether independent or in a University post, and the participation of younger colleagues entering the field is especially welcomed.

ALSO PUBLISHED BY THE ASSOCIATION

Critical Texts
Tudor and Stuart Translations • *New Translations* • *European Translations*
MHRA Library of Medieval Welsh Literature

MHRA Bibliographies
Publications of the Modern Humanities Research Association

The Annual Bibliography of English Language & Literature
Austrian Studies
Modern Language Review
Portuguese Studies
The Slavonic and East European Review
Working Papers in the Humanities
The Yearbook of English Studies

www.mhra.org.uk
www.legendabooks.com

Portrait of Ian Maclean (2016) by Elizabeth Mortimer.
By kind permission of All Souls College, Oxford. Photography: Colin Dunn.

Montaigne in Transit

Essays in Honour of Ian Maclean

EDITED BY NEIL KENNY,
RICHARD SCHOLAR, AND WES WILLIAMS

LEGENDA

Modern Humanities Research Association
2016

Published by Legenda
an imprint of the Modern Humanities Research Association
Salisbury House, Station Road, Cambridge CB1 2LA

ISBN 978-1-909662-96-4 (HB)
ISBN 978-1-78188-303-7 (PB)

Printed in Great Britain

Copy-Editor: Rebecca du Plessis

CONTENTS

NOTES ON THE CONTRIBUTORS

Chimène Bateman is Career Development Fellow in French at New College, University of Oxford. Her research focuses on issues of gender, sexuality, and rhetoric in both medieval and early modern French literature. She has published articles on gender and women's writing, on erotic literature, and on the rewriting of Ovid's *Metamorphoses* and other texts from classical antiquity. This work has appeared in journals such as *Modern Language Notes* and *Romanic Review*. She is currently completing a book entitled 'Address to Women in Medieval and Renaissance Love Literature: The Ethics and Poetics of Desire'.

Warren Boutcher is Professor of Renaissance Studies in the School of English and Drama, Queen Mary University of London. He has published numerous studies of Montaigne's English reception and of the transmission of other European authors' works in the late Renaissance. His two-volume monograph on *The School of Montaigne in Early Modern Europe* (vol. 1: *The Patron-Author*; vol. 2: *The Reader-Writer*) will be published by Oxford University Press in the first half of 2016.

Colin Burrow is a Senior Research Fellow at All Souls College, Oxford. His publications include *Shakespeare and Classical Antiquity* (Oxford University Press, 2013), 'The Poems' in *The Cambridge Edition of the Works of Ben Jonson* (Cambridge University Press, 2012), *The Complete Sonnets and Poems* for the Oxford Shakespeare (Oxford University Press, 2002), *Edmund Spenser* (Northcote House, 1996), and *Epic Romance: Homer to Milton* (Clarendon Press, 1993). He is presently completing a monograph on literary imitation, and is writing the Elizabethan volume for the *Oxford English Literary History*.

Terence Cave CBE, FBA is Emeritus Professor of French Literature, University of Oxford, and Emeritus Research Fellow of St John's College, Oxford. His publications include *The Cornucopian Text: Problems of Writing in the French Renaissance* (Clarendon Press, 1979), *Recognitions: A Study in Poetics* (Clarendon Press, 1988), *How to Read Montaigne* (Granta, 2007), and *Mignon's Afterlives: Crossing Cultures from Goethe to the Twenty-First Century* (Oxford University Press, 2011). His latest book is *Thinking with Literature: Towards a Cognitive Criticism* (Oxford University Press, 2016).

Timothy Chesters is University Lecturer in French, University of Cambridge, and a Fellow of Clare College, Cambridge. He is the author of *Ghost Stories in Late Renaissance France: Walking by Night* (Oxford University Press, 2011), as well as of a number of articles on early modern French demonology, Ronsard, and Montaigne. Other research interests and publications bear on attitudes to the French Renaissance among nineteenth-century writers and thinkers (with a particular emphasis on

Flaubert), and on cognitive approaches to literature, especially in Renaissance contexts.

Ingrid A. R. De Smet is Professor of French and Neo-Latin Studies in the School of Modern Languages and Cultures at the University of Warwick, where she directs the interdisciplinary Centre for the Study of the Renaissance. Her research concerns the intellectual culture of sixteenth-century and early seventeenth-century France and the Low Countries, with particular attention to the Latin writings of the period. She has published widely on such topics as the classical tradition and the history of scholarship; satire and polemics; Jacques Auguste de Thou, Montaigne, and their contemporaries; and, in recent years, the history of falconry.

Kathy Eden is Chavkin Family Professor of English and Professor of Classics at Columbia University. Her books include *Poetic and Legal Fiction in the Aristotelian Tradition* (Princeton University Press, 1986), *Hermeneutics and the Rhetorical Tradition: Chapters in the Ancient Legacy and its Humanist Reception* (Yale University Press, 1997), *Friends Hold All Things in Common: Tradition, Intellectual Property and the 'Adages' of Erasmus* (Yale University Press, 2001), and *The Renaissance Rediscovery of Intimacy* (University of Chicago Press, 2012).

Emma Herdman is Lecturer in French at the University of St Andrews. She has published articles on the literary and artistic representations of the atrocities committed during the religious wars, on attitudes to alcohol in the early modern period, on Marguerite Yourcenar, and on Renaissance obscenity. She is currently working on a book entitled 'Flights of Fancy: Avian Themes in Renaissance France'.

Neil Kenny is Professor of French at the University of Oxford and a Senior Research Fellow at All Souls College. His publications include *The Uses of Curiosity in Early Modern France and Germany* (Oxford University Press, 2004), *Death and Tenses: Posthumous Presence in Early Modern France* (Oxford University Press, 2015), and *La Librairie de Montaigne* (Cambridge Research Colloquia, 2012; co-edited with Philip Ford).

Frank Lestringant is Professor of Sixteenth-Century French Literature at the Université Paris-Sorbonne. His many books include *Le Huguenot et le sauvage: la controverse coloniale, en France, au temps des guerres de Religion (1555–1589)* (Klincksieck, 1990), *L'Atelier du cosmographe, ou, L'image du monde à la Renaissance* (Albin Michel, 1991), *Cannibals: The Discovery and Representation of the Cannibal from Columbus to Jules Verne* (trans. Rosemary Morris; Polity, 1997), *Le Livre des îles: atlas et récits insulaires de la Genèse à Jules Verne* (Droz, 2002), and, as editor, *Le Brésil de Montaigne: le Nouveau Monde des 'Essais' (1580–1592)* (Chandeigne, 2005). He is also the author of a substantial two-volume new biography of Gide, *André Gide l'inquiéteur* (Flammarion, 2011–12).

Kathryn Murphy is Fellow and Tutor in English Literature at Oriel College, Oxford. She has published several articles on early modern literature, especially on the interaction of style and philosophy in Robert Burton, Thomas Browne, and

Thomas Traherne, and co-edited *The Emergence of Impartiality* (Brill, 2013; with Anita Traninger) and *A Man Very Well Studyed: New Contexts for Thomas Browne* (Brill, 2008; with Richard Todd). Work in preparation includes editions of Francis Bacon's *Sylva Sylvarum* and Browne's *Urne-Buriall* and *Garden of Cyrus* for Oxford University Press, and a book entitled 'The Tottering Universal: Metaphysical Prose in the Seventeenth Century'.

John O'Brien is Professor of French at the University of Durham. He is the author of *'Anacreon' Redivivus: A Study of Anacreontic Translation in Mid-Sixteenth-Century France* (University of Michigan Press, 1995), the editor of *(Ré)interpretations: études sur le seizième siècle* (University of Michigan, 1995) and *La familia de Montaigne* (*Montaigne Studies*, 13, 2001), and the co-editor of *Montaigne et la rhétorique* (Champion, 1995; with Malcolm Quainton and James J. Supple), Remy Belleau's *Les Odes d'Anacréon* (in *Œuvres poétiques*, Champion, 1995; with Keith Cameron), and *Distant Voices Still Heard: Contemporary Readings of French Renaissance Literature* (Liverpool University Press, 2000; with Malcolm Quainton). Despite a recent foray into the world of Gargantua and Pantagruel as the editor of the *Cambridge Companion to Rabelais* (Cambridge University Press, 2011), the epicentre of his research remains Montaigne, and he is currently carrying out research on readers of the French text of the *Essais* in early modern England and Germany.

Richard Scholar is Professor of French and Comparative Literature at the University of Oxford and a Fellow of Oriel College. His books include *Montaigne and the Art of Free-Thinking* (Peter Lang, 2010), *The 'Je-Ne-Sais-Quoi' in Early Modern Europe: Encounters with a Certain Something* (Oxford University Press, 2005), and, as co-editor, *Pre-Histories and Afterlives: Studies in Critical Method* (Legenda, 2010; with Anna Holland).

Rowan Tomlinson is Lecturer in French at the University of Bristol and works on the cultural, literary, and intellectual history of Renaissance France. She has published on Rabelais, Montaigne, and Pliny the Elder, and co-edited *The Culture of Translation in Early Modern England and France (1500–1660)* (Palgrave Macmillan, 2015; with Tania Demetriou). Her monograph, *Inventive Inventories: Lists, Literature, and Natural History in Renaissance France* (Oxford University Press, forthcoming), examines the relationship between natural history and literature across the long sixteenth century. Her new project is concerned with vernacular poetry's relationship to other disciplines — most notably philology and *historia* — from the 1480s to the 1560s.

Kate E. Tunstall is University Lecturer in French at the University of Oxford and Fellow of Worcester College. She mainly writes about the literature, aesthetics, art, and philosophy of the French eighteenth century, Diderot in particular, whose work she has also translated. She is the author of *Blindness and Enlightenment* (Continuum, 2011), the editor of *Self-Evident Truths? Human Rights and the Enlightenment* (Continuum, 2012), and co-translator of a multimedia edition of Diderot's *Rameau's Nephew* (Open Book Publishers, 2014; with Pascal Duc, Marian Hobson, and Caroline Warman). One of her current projects is, in collaboration with Katie

Scott and Elena Palaccios Carral, a new edition, translation, and interpretation of Diderot's *Regrets sur ma vieille robe de chambre*.

Wes Williams is Professor of French Literature at the University of Oxford and a Fellow of St Edmund Hall. His publications include *Pilgrimage and Narrative in the French Renaissance: 'The Undiscovered Country'* (Clarendon Press, 1999) and *Monsters and their Meanings in Early Modern Culture: Mighty Magic* (Oxford University Press, 2012). His current projects include a study of the changing shapes of Voluntary Servitude from early modernity to the present.

Valerie Worth-Stylianou is Professor of French at the University of Oxford and Senior Tutor of Trinity College. Her main research areas include translation in early modern Europe, women writers of the French Renaissance, and Montaigne. She was one of the team of international specialists that produced the two-volume critical edition of the *Œuvres complètes* of Marie de Gournay (Champion, 2002). She has recently authored the chapter on translations from classical Latin to French in the sixteenth century for the *Histoire des traductions en langue française XVe et XVIe siècles*, ed. Véronique Duché (Verdier, 2015).

REFERENCES AND ABBREVIATIONS

Unless otherwise stated, references to the *Essais* are to the following edition: Michel de Montaigne, *Essais*, ed. Pierre Villey, rev. V.–L. Saulnier (Paris: Presses universitaires de France, 1965); 2nd edn (retaining the original pagination) in the PUF series Quadrige (1992). Villey–Saulnier's indications of the chronological layers of the *Essais* are sometimes provided within quotations, with [A] designating the 1580 edition, [B] the 1588 edition, and [C] Montaigne's handwritten interventions in the Bordeaux Copy of the 1588 edition. Unless it is stated that the English translations (including Montaigne's chapter titles) are the author's own, they are taken, sometimes with slight modification, from Michel de Montaigne, *The Complete Works: Essays, Travel Journal, Letters*, trans. Donald M. Frame (1957; London: Everyman's Library, 2003). This means that Montaigne's chapter titles vary in translation as much as the rest of his text. Where John Florio's 1603 translation is used instead, the edition used is specified within the relevant chapter below.

V = Villey–Saulnier edition

F = Frame translation

Fl. *or* Florio = Florio translation

INTRODUCTION

Neil Kenny, Richard Scholar, and Wes Williams

Literary criticism has often posited, explicitly or implicitly, a key moment at which a work is completed by an author and sent out into the wider world. Writers, too, often mark the moment with a gesture of farewell, or, perhaps, of greeting to their anticipated readers. The moment may be thought to gain its worth and authority from being distinctive, or singular; and yet it can also be repeated, for example if the work in question is revised by its author, and sent forth once again. Positing the existence of such moments organizes the coming-into-being of literary works in terms of a 'before' and an 'after', in ways that tend to give the former priority over the latter. On the 'before' side are the work's genesis and production, including for example the author's reading of 'sources' and his/her composing of the text; on the 'after' side are the work's diffusion and reception, including for example its potential entry into print and its being read in different times and places.

This model has often been deployed more subtly than this bald outline suggests, and has produced profound insights. However, it has come under pressure in recent years from approaches that place less emphasis on that real or imagined authorial 'signing off' as the crux that structures the coming-into-being of literary works. The critical theory that entered literary studies from the 1970s onwards sometimes contributed to that pressure: for example, 'intertextuality' challenged the notion of 'sources' as essentially prior to the composition of a text, and in so doing brought the work of author and reader into the same orbit. Since the 1980s, studies in the history of the book have contributed even more to that pressure (especially strongly in the early modern field) by eroding the distinction between authors and readers (constituted as 'prior to' and 'post' publication) in favour of a single 'communications circuit'.[1] More recently still, a range of new critical approaches inspired by the cognitive sciences have begun to argue for what amounts to a rethink of the same distinction by emphasizing a continuous act of communication that encompasses the thinking of both authors and readers: not so much before and after, as together in concert and in time.

To our knowledge, the peculiar pressures that can be brought to bear on the before-and-after model of much literary criticism have not been tested in a concerted way in relation to one canonical author. That is what the present volume seeks to do. Michel de Montaigne lends himself particularly well to the task because he drew explicit attention to the coming-into-being of his most famous work, the *Essais*, and clearly considered it to be a continuous process that he did not think of as ever quite stopping — not even at the point of his own, future, death. On this and other levels, in both matter and manner, the *Essais* communicate a distinctive preoccupation with movement through time and space. That preoccupation has inspired landmark studies such as those of Jean Starobinski and Michel Jeanneret,[2] which have tended to emphasize what is immaterial about the writing, and a certain ease of movement in Montaigne, by focusing on the saturation of his work in the thematics of metamorphosis (Jeanneret) or on his appeal to reader response (Starobinski). Another landmark volume, the collection of essays edited by Ian McFarlane and Ian Maclean in memory of Richard Sayce,[3] also tackles a number of the themes and processes in which we are interested here: from the genesis and evolution of the text, by way of problems of reading and the art of transition, through to human psychology, virtue, and philosophical speculation. Such themes and questions are fundamental to any reading of the *Essais*, but their true interest might be seen to lie in the ways in which they are re-described and reconceived over time and in different critical contexts.

Our own volume, focusing explicitly on the material circumstances — the specificities and the vagaries — of movement in Montaigne, understands it as the 'transit' of his work through time, space, language, discipline, and genre. Mobilizing a variety of techniques for the study of early modern culture, including the recently developed methods of cognitive criticism and book history, *Montaigne in Transit* also makes new sense of more established techniques such as those of philology and intellectual history. The concept of 'transit' is here seen as a complex of processes, ranging from 'genesis' and 'production' to 'diffusion' and 'reception'. These four critical concepts are used as provisional starting points for analysis rather than as givens; still less as rigid categories. While they have their origins in the before-and-after model of literary communication alluded to in opening, the pressure applied to that model by the present volume will make them seep somewhat into each other, albeit not necessarily in ways that dissolve entirely the distinctions between them.

This project of rethinking Montaigne's communications circuit in the light of book-historical and other approaches is designed to honour someone who, as well as being a Montaigne specialist of international renown,[4] is also one of the world's leading historians of the early modern European book.[5] Given the unparalleled range of Ian Maclean's influential contributions to our understanding of early modern intellectual and literary culture,[6] it was decided to focus in a cohesive way on one of the numerous areas he has investigated, rather than to attempt in one volume to embrace that extraordinary range. While taking its cue from his work, the volume nonetheless goes beyond it, since Montaigne and book history have so far been largely non-intersecting lines within Ian Maclean's work.

No single method is proposed by the volume; but it begins with two essays that are paradigmatic in that they show Montaigne being in transit in ways that defy any neat distinction between genesis, production, diffusion, and reception (Part I). Firstly, a cognitive approach traces an arc from Montaigne's own reading to his forging in the *Essais* a mode of embodied thought that, by enacting what it describes, can still touch readers today (Terence Cave). Secondly, a story of a man prone to trances is tracked from late antiquity to the eighteenth century, partly via Montaigne in the sixteenth, to explore the connections between Montaigne as both imitator and imitated (Kate Tunstall). In other words, Montaigne's work reveals itself in Part I to be perpetually in motion not within one communications circuit, but within a potentially infinite series of them.

The volume then focuses on how Montaigne might be seen to be operating in transit both at and between each of the four phases of the communications circuit: 'genesis' and/or 'production' (Part II); 'diffusion' and/or 'reception' (Part III).

Part II's focus on 'genesis' and 'production' takes various forms. The relation between Montaigne's reading and writing is explored through investigation (by Rowan Tomlinson) of his relation to an earlier major Renaissance writer. Montaigne's understanding of communication is shown to associate a personal writing style with a necessarily unique face (Kathy Eden). Two essays further analyse the movement of the writing, by demonstrating the rich instability of established themes such as marriage (Chimène Bateman) and vanity (Frank Lestringant) in the *Essais*. All the contributions to Part II have profound implications for an understanding of the reception of Montaigne, even if that is not the contributors' immediate focus. Part II ends with an essay that explicitly stretches across from 'genesis' and 'production' to 'diffusion' and 'reception' (Warren Boutcher). By analysing the punctuation used by Montaigne, and by both the earliest and the most recent editors and translators of the *Essais*, Boutcher demonstrates that there is no clear moment at which Montaigne's responsibility stops and his successors' starts — in other words, no definitive distinction between 'before' and 'after'.

In the same spirit of bridging, Part III's examination of 'diffusion' and 'reception' begins with an analysis (by Emma Herdman) which is primarily of the expectations Montaigne had of different contemporary readers (especially women as opposed to men) and yet which also gives careful consideration to 'genesis' and 'production' (especially in respect of Montaigne's own reading and quoting of Juvenal). The subsequent essays on 'diffusion' and 'reception' branch out beyond the immediate context of late sixteenth-century France to explore dimensions of Montaigne's transit to France, England, and Germany at different moments, from the seventeenth to the nineteenth century. The aim is not to provide systematic coverage but to explore through case-studies different ways in which editings, readings, and imitations of Montaigne further complicate the before-and-after model. For even as these later moments direct our attention as readers to the diffusion and reception of Montaigne's work, they also loop back to its genesis and production: in other words, they further illuminate the writing itself.

Those ensuing essays in Part III of this volume respond to a tension always present in the *Essais* — between Montaigne's French prose and his Latin quotations (Valerie Worth-Stylianou) — and highlight dimensions of the *Essais* that Montaigne's early French readers and modern exegetes neglect (John O'Brien); they respond to the fragmentariness of how the *Essais* were mediated (Ingrid De Smet), and encourage us to reassess the acuity and the impact of Montaigne the travel writer in the *Journal de voyage* (Timothy Chesters). They sharpen our awareness of the specificity of Montaigne's meditation of the relation of the particular to the universal (Kathryn Murphy); and they illuminate how the *Essais* could (and can) make readers — and in particular Shakespeare — *think* (Colin Burrow).

The connections between essays indicated by the above pairings are certainly not the only ones the reader will find in this volume. Others are based on Montaigne's practice of quotation (Worth-Stylianou, Boutcher, Bateman, Cave, and Herdman), on genre and author (Cave and Herdman both consider poetry and Montaigne's relation to the Roman poet Juvenal, while Tunstall and Tomlinson consider his relation to St Augustine), on rhetoric (Eden, Boutcher, and Tomlinson), on translating the *Essais* (Worth-Stylianou and Boutcher), on typography and layout (the same two again), on women reading and/or editing Montaigne (Bateman, Herdman, and Worth-Stylianou), on the problematic notion of 'source' (Tomlinson, O'Brien, De Smet, and Burrow), and so on.

What matters above all throughout the volume is the process whereby specialists in very different areas offer distinctive contributions to an evolving discussion about a single major early modern writer in transit. In his Afterword, Ian Maclean responds to these contributions, continuing a discussion he has done so much to inspire and inform.

That discussion started life in one panel of a larger conference, in honour of Ian, which was entitled 'Transforming the Early Modern Republic of Letters: Literature, Learning, Logic, Books' and took place in Oxford from 31 March to 2 April 2014. The discussion continued in a planning workshop, held in Oxford on 15–16 September of the same year, when the present volume took shape. It is fitting that it should appear with a publisher whose very name was first proposed some twenty years ago by Ian, after he had served as first Director of the University of Oxford's European Humanities Research Centre. (Legenda started life as the EHRC's imprint.) We are most grateful to Graham Nelson of Legenda for his encouragement and support, and to Rebecca du Plessis for superb copy-editing, provided with patient good humour.

We have incurred many further debts of gratitude in the course of editing the volume and organizing the workshop and conference: to the Warden and Fellows of All Souls College, the Maison Française d'Oxford, and the Oxford University Press John Fell Research Fund, for making the events and this volume possible; to Alexis Tadié, for securing additional funding from the Frontiers of Modernity programme; to the Faculty of Medieval and Modern Languages at the University of Oxford, for its kind assistance; to two (then) postgraduates in the Faculty, Emma Claussen and Jennifer Oliver, for their help during the conference; and to Humaira Erfan-Ahmed at All Souls, for doing an enormous amount of organizational work over many months.

We wish to thank all those who participated in the conference and workshop: Chimène Bateman, Ann Blair, Warren Boutcher, Robin Briggs, Colin Burrow, Terence Cave, Timothy Chesters, Richard Cooper, Nicholas Cronk, Nicholas Davidson, Marie-Luce Demonet, Ingrid De Smet, Cristina Dondi, Kathy Eden, Frédéric Gabriel, Ian Gadd, Emma Herdman, Howard Hotson, Jill Kraye, Frank Lestringant, Christophe Lüthy, Jan Machielsen, Noel Malcolm, Scott Mandelbrote, Alexander Marr, Michael Moriarty, Kathryn Murphy, Paul Nelles, David Norbrook, John O'Brien, Richard Parish, Martine Pécharman, William Poole, Lyndal Roper, Richard Serjeantson, Alexis Tadié, Rowan Tomlinson, Kate Tunstall, Helen Watanabe-O'Kelly, and Valerie Worth-Stylianou.

Special mention must go to Pauline Maclean, who supported the events held in Ian's honour with all the warmth and wry good humour that Ian's colleagues and pupils know to be characteristic of her.

Our final and warmest expression of gratitude must go to Ian Maclean himself, who supervised us during our doctoral work and has been a colleague and friend for many years. His interventions in our work have invariably been bracing in their rigour, but also profoundly wise, positive, and generous. To have benefited from them has been an uncommon privilege. It has also been a lot of fun, thanks to his capacity for communicating the pleasure and sheer excitement of intellectual enquiry, whenever and wherever it may lead. If we take this chance to record our gratitude to Ian for his inspiration and support, as well as for the challenge he sets us by his example, we do so in the certain knowledge that we also speak for many others.

Notes to the Introduction

1. The famous formulation is Robert Darnton's, in his 'What Is the History of Books?', *Daedalus*, 113.3 (1982), 65–83.
2. Jean Starobinski, *Montaigne en mouvement* (Paris: Gallimard, 1982), and Michel Jeanneret, *Perpetuum mobile: métamorphoses des corps et des œuvres, de Vinci à Montaigne* (Paris: Macula, 1997).
3. *Montaigne: Essays in Memory of Richard Sayce*, ed. I. D. McFarlane and Ian Maclean (Oxford: Clarendon Press, 1982).
4. See *Montaigne*, ed. McFarlane and Maclean, including Ian Maclean, '"Le païs au delà": Montaigne and Philosophical Speculation', pp. 101–32; Ian Maclean, 'Montaigne, Cardano: The Reading of Subtlety/The Subtlety of Reading', *French Studies*, 37 (1983), 143–56; 'The Place of Interpretation: Montaigne and Humanist Jurists on Words, Intention and Meaning', in *Neo-Latin and the Vernacular in Renaissance France*, ed. Grahame Castor and Terence Cave (Oxford: Clarendon Press, 1984), pp. 252–72; 'Montaigne et le droit civil romain', in *Montaigne et la rhétorique: actes du colloque de St Andrews (28–31 mars 1992)*, ed. John O'Brien, Malcolm Quainton, and James J. Supple (Paris: Champion, 1995), pp. 163–76; *Montaigne philosophe* (Paris: Presses universitaires de France, 1996); and 'Montaigne on the Truth of the Schools', in *The Cambridge Companion to Montaigne*, ed. Ullrich Langer (Cambridge: Cambridge University Press, 2004), pp. 142–62.
5. See Ian Maclean, *Learning in the Marketplace: Essays in the History of Early Modern Books* (Leiden: Brill, 2009), and *Scholarship, Commerce, Religion: The Learned Book in the Age of Confessions, 1560–1630* (Cambridge, MA: Harvard University Press, 2012).
6. To add but a few examples: Ian Maclean, *Woman Triumphant: Feminism in French Literature 1610–52* (Oxford: Clarendon Press, 1977); *The Renaissance Notion of Woman: A Study in the Fortunes of Scholasticism and Medical Science in European Intellectual Life* (Cambridge: Cambridge University Press, 1980); *Interpretation and Meaning in the Renaissance: The Case of Law* (Cambridge: Cambridge University Press, 1992); *Logic, Signs and Nature in the Renaissance: The Case of Learned Medicine* (Cambridge: Cambridge University Press, 2001); and Girolamo Cardano, *De libris propriis*, ed. and intro. Ian Maclean (Milan: FrancoAngeli, 2004).

PART I

Opening Moves

CHAPTER 1

The Transit of Venus:
Feeling Your Way Forward

Terence Cave

L'Histoire, c'est plus mon gibier, ou la poësie, que j'ayme d'une
particuliere inclination.[1]

[History is more my cup of tea, or poetry, for which I have a
special fondness.][2]

Nothing could be more casual, more 'cool', than the delivery of this sentence, given
that it encapsulates a good deal of the intellectual mode of the *Essais*. When, a few
lines later, Montaigne cites Plutarch on the power of the imagination, he completes
a trio of subjects that was central to the humanist educational programme —
history, poetry, and moral philosophy — as opposed to the logic-based scholastic
syllabus on the one hand and the professional disciplines on the other. All three,
in Montaigne's day, belonged to the realm of the imagination; all three proposed
particular, contingent examples of human behaviour, thoughts, and feelings; all were
open to the informal, improvised exploration of cognitive space that is designated
by the word, and the title, 'essai'. The *sprezzatura* of the sentence — the everyday
metaphor, the off-hand syntax — is very precisely in its place here. Montaigne is
enacting in words and style the intellectual *habitus* that will hold good not only for
this chapter, explicitly concerned with education, but for the whole book.[3]

It is entirely in keeping with that *habitus* that the procedural term 'ou' doesn't
impose a choice ('either history or poetry'): it marks a casual shift from one topic to
another, as if the very naming of intellectual preferences were contingent.[4] Once
poetry has been named, history will in fact be left aside in favour of an evocation of
the specially penetrative power of verse. This new sentence is marked by a change
of tone, register, and syntactic organization:

> Car, comme disoit Cleantes, tout ainsi que la voix, contrainte dans l'étroit canal
> d'une trompette, sort plus aiguë et plus forte, ainsi me semble il que la sentence,
> pressée aux pieds nombreux de la poësie, s'eslance bien plus brusquement et me
> fiert d'une plus vive secousse.

> [For, as Cleanthes used to say, just as the voice, when forced through the narrow
> passage of a trumpet, sounds sharper and louder when it comes out, so too,
> it seems to me, a thought, when constrained by the rhythmic feet of poetry,
> comes across more powerfully and strikes me a livelier blow.]

The change begins already with the conjunction 'car', which (unlike that 'ou') imposes a logical connection: it announces an explanation. It continues with the allusion to what looks like a classical authority. As it happens, the authority here is not Cleanthes, but Seneca, who himself claims to be citing the opinion of Cleanthes on poetry.[5] Most readers are likely to be fooled by this little trick; those who are not may read it as an ironic gesture, a feint of the kind to which Montaigne's practice of *imitatio* is prone. It's sometimes notoriously hard, in the flow of his prose, to know what is a quotation and what is not.[6] In the most benevolent possible sense, Montaigne is manipulating his reader, and my choice of that word isn't random: the fingers of the conjuror are at work behind his cloak. What matters is that this praise of the power of poetry should be endorsed, however nominally, by an ancient authority: despite the personal tone of the preceding sentence, Montaigne's 'special fondness' must be seen to have a recognized guarantor.

The distancing effect created by the naming of Cleanthes is maintained throughout the sentence. It is apparent above all in the use of a formally structured simile that displays a marked symmetry, accompanied by an elegant broadening of the phrasal rhythm as the sentence comes to a close (compare 'sort plus aiguë et plus forte' with 's'eslance bien plus brusquement et me fiert d'une plus vive secousse'). The symmetry is in fact more marked than it is in Seneca's version; one might even say that it is more *Ciceronian* than anything one normally finds in the prose of the *Essais*. So why this alienation, just when Montaigne was talking about his own personal tastes? A deep structure emerges here to which others have drawn attention:[7] the *Essais* evoke ideal paradigms of behaviour, virtue, modes of life, literary excellence, and the like, in an apparent movement of self-deprecation ('I can't match them, my own abilities are too feeble') which then mutates into a kind of self-affirmation.[8] That is exactly what happens quite explicitly in the next segment of the passage we are looking at. Montaigne says that he found in Plutarch a much more powerful account of the imagination than he is capable of, but he still claims to have had his ideas on the subject first, and points out that, unlike 'les escrivains indiscrets de nostre siecle' (V, p. 147), he knows the difference between his writing and that of the ancients. So it is too with the poetry sentence. Poetry is itself an ideal paradigm, a beautifully structured thing that has an irresistible force. Montaigne can't do it (he tried once, without success),[9] but he does the next best thing: as everyone knows, he gives poetry a special place in his own writing. And although he (apparently) can't do it, he is capable momentarily of enhancing the symmetry and rhythmic impetus of a sentence of classical Latin as he renders it into French, so that it looks and sounds something very like poetry. This passing skill is, again, an act of prestidigitation. And we need here to note that the distancing effect is itself mitigated by a first-person modalizing expression ('ainsi me semble il'): Cleanthes's claim is replaced by the writer's own, after which the first person reappears in the concluding clause of the sentence ('me fiert'). The formality is not broken, but the conjuror can't resist showing his hand.

Immediately after, at any rate, we are back in the mode of the sentence we began with: 'Quant aux facultez naturelles qui sont en moy, dequoy c'est icy l'essay, je les sens flechir sous la charge' [As for my own natural faculties, which I'm putting to the test here, I feel them giving way under that pressure]. We are back in the mode of the *essai*, in the 'here' and now of the first person, the place that is proper to the writer himself and his native skills.

I have elsewhere characterized the movement of this passage — a movement that can in fact be traced back to the very beginning of the chapter — as an oscillation between tension and relaxation.[10] The 'poetry sentence', with its references to constraint, pressure, the channelling of sound in a confined space, affords a powerful moment of tension that is felt in the writer's (and arguably the reader's) body: he it is who is 'struck' by the shock, the lively blow, of the emerging trumpet blast. The relaxing movement which is explicit in 'je les sens flechir sous la charge' is entirely muscular, priming the reader for the metaphor that takes over in the following sentence, where the prose enacts the movement of a body walking unsteadily,[11] groping its way forward through the mist:

> Mes conceptions et mon jugement ne marche qu'à tastons, chancelant, bronchant et chopant; et quand je suis allé le plus avant que je puis, si ne me suis-je aucunement satisfaict; je voy encore du païs au delà, mais d'une veuë trouble et en nuage, que je ne puis desmeler.

> [My conceptions and my judgement can only grope their way forward, staggering, tripping, and stumbling; and when I have gone as far as I am able, I am still in no way satisfied; I can see further terrain in the distance, but with a murky, cloudy vision which I'm unable to resolve.]

This sensorimotor imagination and the sound-world of the poetry sentence could hardly be more sharply contrasted: poetry is something one listens to, albeit with the inward ear; thinking ('Mes conceptions et mon jugement') is conducted with the rhythm of the moving body.

★ ★ ★ ★ ★

I shall return later to this groping sentence, but I want first to move from a passage which represents in graphic form the openings Montaigne contrives for himself in the 1580 edition to a famous late passage where the dialogue between poetic tension and the dexterous relaxation of prose is noticeably more intimate:

> Mais de ce que je m'y entends, les forces et valeur de ce Dieu se trouvent plus vives et plus animées en la peinture de la poesie qu'en leur propre essence,
>
> > *Et versus digitos habet.*
>
> Elle represente je ne sçay quel air plus amoureux que l'amour mesme. Venus n'est pas si belle toute nue, et vive, et haletante, comme elle est icy chez Virgile[.][12]

> [But from what I know of it, the powers and strength of this god [Venus] are more alive, more animated in the painting of poetry than in their own essence,
>
> > *A line of verse, too, has fingers.*
>
> Poetry represents some indefinable air that is more amorous than love itself. Venus is not so beautiful all naked, alive, and panting, as she is here in Virgil[.]]

The single line (or part of a line) quoted from Juvenal's *Satires* is only barely recognizable, out of context, as verse.[13] In fact, it is Montaigne himself who has added the first two words. The original only has 'digitos habet', and refers to the Greek terms of endearment used by Roman concubines to excite their ageing clients; these words, and the woman's voice (*vox*), are identified with another form of erotic action (fingers caressing).[14] Montaigne's sleight-of-hand transfers the caress to erotic poetry. It is integral to the much-studied manoeuvre by means of which he links his intimate, first-hand knowledge of ancient poetry to a quasi-confessional account of his own sexuality and thence to a powerfully transmitted sense of the trajectory of his inwardly felt life from youthful arousal to reflective old age. The link is advertised — albeit obliquely, not explicitly — in the title of the essay, where the reader is primed to look out for these lines of Virgilian poetry that prove so erotically to have fingers.

This is a complex chapter, which I discussed at some length many years ago, in another context and according to a different mode of reading; for good reason, 'Sur des vers de Virgile' has in fact frequently attracted the attention of Montaigne specialists in the last few decades.[15] Let me pick out here one or two central strands that will be familiar to anyone who has studied the chapter and its topics. The first of these is the extraordinary way in which Montaigne manages to couple a sense of his whole life and its energies, imagined in sexual terms, with a lifetime love of poetry, especially Latin poetry. It takes a long time for this coupling to take effect, but it is already there, hidden in the implicatures of the title.[16] And when the lines of Virgil finally come to the surface in the passage I have just quoted, the delayed action effect is by no means over. We have to wait for many pages before a parallel passage from Lucretius is quoted and subjected to a close reading. But then we come to the heart of the matter. After the Virgil passage and its brief commentary as quoted above, the discussion had shifted to a different topic (the tepid sexuality of marital relations). The Lucretius parallel, however, takes Montaigne deep into a version of one of the master-themes of the *Essais*: *imitatio*, as something much more deeply grounded than a pedagogical or technical practice, proves to have been a further implicature of the title.[17]

What stands out above all else in this remarkable passage is the reciprocal, even chiastic, relation between poetic language and thought:

> Quand je voy ces braves formes de s'expliquer, si vifves, si profondes, je ne dicts pas que c'est bien dire, je dicts que c'est bien penser. C'est la gaillardise de l'imagination qui esleve et enfle les parolles. [C] '*Pectus est quod disertum facit*' [B] Nos gens appellent jugement, langage; et beaux mots, les plaines conceptions.

> [When I see those bold forms of self-expression, so alive, so profound, I don't say 'That's well said', I say 'That's well thought'. It is the joyful vigour of the imagination that raises and swells the words. [C] '*It is intuition*[18] *that makes the speaker eloquent.*' [B] Nowadays people call judgement language; and fine words, full conceptions.]

Montaigne uses the verb 's'expliquer', literally 'explaining oneself', but he may well have in mind the etymology of 'expliquer', 'to unfold' or 'unwrap'. The choice of verb is in any case clearly connected to the theme of the priority of thought over language. Poetry thinks: people call it language, rhetoric, but it's a mode of cognition, or more specifically *imagination*. But this assertion of the cognitive force of fine poetry is no denial of the embodied life of poetic language, on the contrary. The ensuing passage on the relative poverty of the language of French poets in comparison with the ancients makes it quite explicit that Latin poetry draws on a powerfully physical, sensual language. And thought is always expressed here in the language of the body:

> Plutarque dit qu'il veid le langage latin par les choses; icy de mesme: le sens esclaire et produict les parolles; non plus de vent, ains de chair et d'os. [C] Elles signifient plus qu'elles ne disent.

> [Plutarch says that he saw the Latin language in terms of things;[19] here it's the same: the sense illuminates and produces the words; no longer made of wind, but rather of flesh and bone. [C] They signify more than they say.]

At such moments, Montaigne's prose speaks for itself; and it signifies more than it says. What that last claim implies is that embodied language is not prior to thought, nor is it a code. The life that is inherent in Virgil's and Lucretius's lines is a mode of thinking that communicates itself to the reader by means of sensorimotor imagery and sentence rhythms; the body, when it speaks, uses a language which, despite or perhaps because of its immediacy, is intrinsically open to further possibilities of meaning.

Throughout this whole development, Montaigne's own language strives for embodiment of the most directly erotic kind. What has happened, it seems, is that the opposition in I.26 ('De l'institution des enfans') between the paradigmatic 'poetry sentence' and Montaigne's confession of relative laxity ('je les sens flechir sous la charge') is raised here to a higher pitch of reflective intensity. Instead of a prose sentence describing poetry, he gives us two quotations from the very best of Latin verse. Instead of a low-key (though already quietly positive) meditation on the cognitive powers of his own prose, he composes a passage of French that draws on the latent power and immediacy of the vernacular to fashion a unique mode of embodied thought that is entirely his own.[20] In order for this to happen, the 'opposition' itself (the formal tension of the poetry sentence versus the relaxation of muscular tension in the sentences that follow) is also dissolved or transcended. The quotations from Virgil and Lucretius are haptic, erotic; they come to life, become bodies. And their life flows palpably over into Montaigne's prose: 'Venus n'est pas si belle toute nue, et vive, et haletante, comme elle est icy chez Virgile'; 'C'est la gaillardise de l'imagination qui esleve et enfle les parolles.'

★   ★   ★   ★   ★

The trajectory that led from I.26 ('De l'institution des enfans') to III.5 ('Sur des vers de Virgile') (and we are here speaking, of course, of just one strand in a more complex weave) was remarkably swift. 'De l'institution des enfans' was almost certainly written in the months before the 1580 edition went to press, while the key passages of 'Sur des vers de Virgile' that I have quoted were present in the 1588 edition. The perspective which seems to encompass a whole life, from childhood to the retrospective meditations of old age, is thus in fact a mirage. Already close to the age of 47 when he wrote I.26, he was perhaps no more than 54 when he wrote III.5. And one needs to remember that in those seven years he both went on a long journey and assumed the position of Mayor of Bordeaux. During that short and busy period, some subterranean maturation process was taking place. In the hijacked Senecan sentence of I.26, poetry is imagined as something that is heard but also felt epidermally: the acoustic properties of the trumpet channel the air and turn it into a blast of sound that 'strikes' the listener, like a blow from a weapon. In the hijacked sentence of III.5 from Juvenal, as we saw, poetry is haptic; its fingers reach out across a temporal span of many hundreds of years to touch and arouse us. There is an evident continuity between these two ways of imagining poetry, yet in the later passage Montaigne knows exactly how to bring poetry to life, and, with it, the sound and feel of his own writing.

In such a context, the second dominant metaphor from the opening of I.26, the sensorimotor enactment of a stumbling movement forward into the unguessable landscape of the future, begins to resemble something like an intuition of the trajectory of the *Essais* over those next seven or eight years. What we are observing here is something very rare and beautiful: an utterance that begins gropingly, hesitatingly, in fragments, then gains momentum ('Viresque acquirit eundo')[21] and a marked assurance, while always somehow expressing, clarifying, and rephrasing its own initial implicatures, the things that it left partially unsaid.

These latter remarks are intended as a contribution to the way one might understand Montaigne's claim 'Mon livre est toujours un'.[22] Montaigne in transit is not a dismembered postmodern 'effect' of neutral texts; nor is he a fragmentary self, existing only in the moment of transition between one point and the next, a challenge to our naïve (but robust) sense that individual persons have continuity.[23] The coherence and continuity of the *Essais* is historical: it wears the colours of its day. But it is also enduring. It arises from the particular ways that an individual thought and felt, and from the remarkably potent ways he found to communicate those thoughts and feelings. As I have remarked elsewhere,[24] Montaigne's book has the character of a single extended sentence, full of parentheses and exploratory clauses, but always held in a kind of suspended control.

You can speak of these questions in thematic terms, or as an instance of Renaissance *imitatio*, but however you do it, your reading will be fed by the cognitive-somatic infrastructure, the sense in which Montaigne's essays as a whole are an act of extended cognition that is still astonishingly available for us to explore. Why do people continue to read them more than four hundred years after they were written (they seem especially popular in our own day)? Not because they contain certain kinds of knowledge, or philosophical wisdom, although there is no doubt a lot of that too, but because they reach out to us like fingers, transmitting the thoughts and feelings and sensations of a living person.

This 'reaching out' is already a potential implicature of the haptic metaphor Montaigne uses in I.26 as he attempts to demonstrate how his thoughts grope their way forward through a mist (a metaphor that Ian Maclean used long ago in his contribution to the Sayce memorial volume).[25] It seems appropriate to juxtapose these two metaphors, one early, one late, to illustrate the key role of embodied thought in the *Essais* as it moves through space and time and between author and reader.

★   ★   ★   ★   ★

What I have tried to do, then, as a contribution to this opening section of *Montaigne in Transit*, is to observe the transit of the *Essais*, as one might observe the transit of Venus. The conceit might seem a little strained. After all, Venus is only present, alive and panting, in III.5; she wasn't there in I.26, and the poetry sentence offers trumpet blasts instead of fingertip touches. A possible first defence, 'weak', but still in my view valid, would read the relaxed bodily mode of Montaigne's groping amble through uncertain territory as equivalent in some sense to the haptic mode. They both belong to that cognitive-somatic continuum which Montaigne progressively explores and elaborates, that is to say to imagination (in all the senses that Montaigne gives to this word) as an embodied, enactive process. They belong to the same cognitive ecology. And in another register, the way the poetry sentence of I.26 is delivered is continuous with the reiterated 'showing off' of the powers of poetry that runs through the whole book and reaches a sumptuous high point in III.5. There are of course many other high points, not least the valedictory final quotation of III.13 ('De l'expérience' [On Experience]),[26] which is both a quotation like those from Virgil and Lucretius, and a self-reflecting 'poetry sentence' like the disguised quotation from Seneca; without them, the continuity would look suspiciously patchy.

But the clinching argument for the notion of a 'transit of Venus' in Montaigne's *Essais* is that apparently redundant phrase 'la poësie, que j'ayme d'une particuliere inclination'. We can if we like read the verb *aimer* here in its lighter sense ('to like', 'to be fond of'). But Montaigne has high standards where friendship is concerned: I.28, 'De l'amitié' [On Friendship] is also a moment in the transit of Venus. And perhaps we are entitled, if only with a retrospective gaze, to project into that verb some of the erotic force of 'Sur des vers de Virgile'. Montaigne does indeed seem to have loved poetry with a kind of erotic intensity.[27]

Transits of Venus are among the rarest of predictable astronomical phenomena: a cosmic object becomes visible in the very act of passing. So it seems to be with Montaigne's record of his passing imaginations. Seen in the light of our common human cognitive resources, those tiny objects — a quotation, a stumbling, groping sentence, a conjunction even — acquire a distinct shape and character. We see them not only for what they are, but also for what they *were*, moments from a historical past and from a remarkable individual's experience, consigned to a language that knows inimitably how to think.

★   ★   ★   ★   ★

Perhaps it is not inappropriate, given that Ian Maclean's career has run parallel with mine since the 1960s and that we have worked in the same university since 1972 (as it happens, the four hundredth anniversary of the putative beginning of the composition of the *Essais*), to evoke that double trajectory here. Like a latter-day Plutarch, Ian has acquired a vast syncretic knowledge of Renaissance and medieval theology, law, philosophy, science, and much more; in addition, he early mastered the intricacies of literary theory, which have incontestably inflected both of our careers. I have learnt a great deal from him, and I often feel that I have only scribbled arabesques in the margin of his learning, like the 'grotesques' that Montaigne speaks of in the opening pages of 'De l'amitié'. This essay is just one such. But I hope he will agree that somehow, as the end of the road comes closer, the underlying vigour of our friendship and collaboration, emerging as it were out of the mist, has again become palpable.

Notes to Chapter 1

1. V, p. 146 (I.26, 'De l'institution des enfans' [On Educating Children]). This page reference is valid for all the ensuing quotations from this chapter except where otherwise indicated.
2. All translations in the present essay are my own. I have not been able to capture here both the informality of the phrasing and the insistence, bordering on redundancy, of 'que j'ayme d'une particuliere inclination'. A more literal version would be 'which I love with a particular fondness'.
3. See my essay 'Chiastic Cognition: Kinesic Intelligence between the Reflective and the Pre-reflective', in *Kinesic Intelligence: Rethinking Movement in Renaissance Literature*, ed. Kathryn Banks and Timothy Chesters (forthcoming 2017). These two pieces are intended to be complementary.
4. Procedurals are the large class of words and expressions that inflect (or frame) the listener's (or reader's) reception of the conceptual content of the utterance. Its borders are porous: it may arguably be expanded to include modalizing expressions ('perhaps', 'arguably', 'it seems to me'), scalar expressions ('almost', 'partly'), and others. The point of using the word here is to show that 'ou' is not just a logical operator; it communicates the speaker's attitude and even her posture (try reading Montaigne's sentence aloud and you'll find yourself *performing* the permissive gesture implied by 'ou' as a kind of hinge between 'histoire' and 'poësie'). For a technical account of the conceptual/procedural distinction, originally proposed by Diane Blakemore in her *Semantic Constraints on Relevance* (Oxford: Blackwell, 1987), see Robyn Carston, *Thoughts and Utterances: The Pragmatics of Explicit Communication* (Oxford: Blackwell, 2002), pp. 160–64. The broader frame of reference for the distinction is provided by the theory of communication known as relevance theory; see Dan Sperber and Deirdre Wilson, *Relevance: Communication and Cognition* (1986; Oxford: Blackwell, 1995).
5. Seneca, *Letters to Lucilius*, 108.
6. This kind of effect is closely related to the blurring of boundaries between quotation and surrounding text that was admirably captured by Mary McKinley's seminal *Words in a Corner: Studies in Montaigne's Latin Quotations* (Lexington, KY: French Forum Publishers, 1981).
7. Jean Starobinski's *Montaigne en mouvement* (Paris: Gallimard, 1982) proposes a three-phase dialectic which is not the same as, but is arguably related to, the one I am speaking of here; see also Marcel Gutwirth, *Michel de Montaigne, ou Le pari de l'exemplarité* (Montreal: Presses de l'Université de Montréal, 1977).
8. The paradigms are often personified: Plutarch (as here), Socrates, Epaminondas, Estienne de La Boëtie, and many others. Whole essays can display such structures: II.12 ('Apologie de Raimond Sebond') is a notable case, but so is III.5 ('Sur des vers de Virgile' [On Some Lines from Virgil]).
9. V, p. 875 (III.5, 'Sur des vers de Virgile').
10. See my 'Chiastic Cognition'.
11. It should be admitted that some of the verbs Montaigne uses ('bronchant', 'chopant') are often used of the gait of horses rather than humans; perhaps he was so familiar with their gait that the human and the animal become indistinguishable for the purposes of the metaphor.
12. V, p. 849 (III.5, 'Sur des vers de Virgile').
13. Juvenal, *Satires*, VI. 197. For an overview of Montaigne's quotations from Juvenal, see Bénédicte

Boudou, 'La présence de Juvénal dans les *Essais*', *Montaigne Studies*, 17 (2005), 119–33. On this specific line, see Marc-André Wiesmann, 'Verses Have Fingers: Montaigne Reads Juvenal', *Journal of Medieval and Renaissance Studies*, 23 (1993), 43–67. Wiesmann notices the change from voice to verse, and emphasizes the erotic intimacy of Montaigne's writing, comparing the elderly Montaigne to Juvenal's inappropriately lusty old woman still trying to seduce in Greek. I am indebted to Emma Herdman for this and the following note; see also her 'Montaigne and Juvenal: Intertextual Recognition and the Readership of the *Essais*', Chapter 8 in this volume.

14. In II.26, 'Des pouces' [On Thumbs] (V, p. 691), Montaigne quotes two lines from Martial (XII. 97. 8–9), in which the joint action of seductive words (*vocibus blandis*) and an erotic thumb are not sufficient to produce sexual arousal. Although these two *loci* are quite remote from one another in the spatial and temporal flow of the *Essais*, they perhaps inhabit adjacent domains in Montaigne's pre-reflective memory. At all events, they show yet again how interconnected the fabric of the *Essais* is: as Montaigne himself puts it somewhat later in III.5 ('Sur des vers de Virgile'), 'les matieres se tiennent toutes enchesnées les unes aux autres' (V, p. 876).

15. See my study *The Cornucopian Text: Problems of Writing in the French Renaissance* (Oxford: Clarendon Press, 1979), pp. 284–97. This is not the place to compile even a short list of other contributions.

16. I have borrowed from relevance theory the term 'implicature', which is, broadly speaking, an intended but unspoken element of the meaning of an utterance. More generally it will perhaps be helpful to indicate here that my account of these passages is 'cognitively inflected': it draws on the notion that literature (like all forms of human communication) may be mapped on to the openings and constraints afforded by cognition itself. My references to procedurals and other such features belong to this methodology, the overall sense of which will emerge more clearly in the course of this essay. See also my book *Thinking with Literature: Towards a Cognitive Criticism* (Oxford: Oxford University Press, 2016).

17. V, pp. 873–76.

18. The Latin word used here (*pectus*, literally 'breast', 'heart') refers to the seat of an intuitive understanding (intelligence afforded by feeling) as opposed to acquired or technical thought. Montaigne is quoting Quintilian (x. 7. 15).

19. Montaigne's word 'choses' notoriously has a range of meanings that cannot be captured by a single English word. He is thinking of Latin *res*, which can mean 'thing', but also 'subject matter', even 'thought'. Thought in this domain is always something material, not an ideal abstraction.

20. It is true that Montaigne says a moment later that French is lacking in 'estoffe' (substance, material); he even echoes the verb *fléchir* from the earlier passage: '[nostre langage] languit soubs vous et fleschit'. Yet any reader will feel the mature energy of the writing here: this is arguably why Montaigne has been read over and over again, regardless of the varying intellectual and aesthetic cultures of his readers.

21. 'It gathers strength as it goes on' (literally 'by going/walking'). This motto appeared on the title page of the 1588 edition of the *Essais*; it is taken from Virgil, *Aeneid*, IV. 175, where it refers to Fama, the rumour goddess, who gathers momentum as she goes.

22. V, p. 964 (III.9, 'De la vanité' [On Vanity]).

23. Among contemporary philosophers, Galen Strawson has made Montaigne a paradigm of the 'episodic' as opposed to the 'diachronic' (narrative) presentation of the self; see his essay 'Against Narrativity', *Ratio*, 16 (2004), 428–52, reprinted in *Real Materialism and Other Essays* (Oxford: Oxford University Press, 2008), pp. 189–207.

24. *How to Read Montaigne* (London: Granta Books, 2007), p. 26.

25. Ian Maclean, '"Le païs au delà": Montaigne and Philosophical Speculation', in *Montaigne: Essays in Memory of Richard Sayce*, ed. I. D. McFarlane and Ian Maclean (Oxford: Clarendon Press, 1982), pp. 101–32.

26. V, p. 1116: 'Frui, paratis et valide mihi,/ Latoe, dones, et, precor, integra/ Cum mente, nec turpem senectam/ Degere, nec cythara carentem' [Grant me, Apollo, that I may enjoy the fruits of my life's labours in good health and, I pray, with a sound mind; that I may not fall into a shameful old age; and that I never be deprived of my lyre]. The quotation is from Horace, *Odes*, I. 31.

27. I am grateful to Elizabeth Guild for drawing my attention to the implications of this phrase and suggesting that it had a deeper import than I had suggested in an earlier (oral) version of these remarks. For her extensive exploration of such questions, see her book *Unsettling Montaigne: Poetics, Ethics and Affect in the 'Essais' and Other Writings* (Cambridge: Brewer, 2014).

CHAPTER 2

A Case in Transit:
Reading Diderot (Reading Montaigne)
Reading Augustine

Kate E. Tunstall

The story of 'le prêtre de Calame' [the priest of Calama] is one that the Enlightenment *philosophe*, Denis Diderot, was particularly fond of telling and retelling.[1] It involves a priest who would pass out, fall to the ground, and lose all feeling, such that nothing, not even extreme physical violence, would bring him round; and yet, though not breathing, he had not passed away and would later return to his senses, reporting that he had felt no pain. If this intriguing little tale will be the focus here, it is not or, at least, not only because it stages a man who is 'transit' [in a state of transport]; rather, it is because this is a tale that is itself in transit. Diderot knew the version of it that appears in Montaigne's chapter I.21, 'De la force de l'imagination' [Of the Power of the Imagination],[2] itself a retelling of the version told by Augustine in *The City of God*,[3] which Diderot knew too, both directly and, perhaps, also as quoted in Arnauld and Nicole's *Logique* (1662).[4] To say the story is 'in transit' should not, of course, be taken to mean that it turns up unchanged in different texts and contexts; far from it. This is a tale that transitions as different contexts confer different meanings, and certain details come into sharper focus, are tweaked, changed, misremembered, or misread by different writers at different historical moments and for different ends. In fact, it would be more accurate to speak of the '"case" of the priest of Calama' since, unlike 'story' or 'tale', the term 'case' more obviously foregrounds the writer's work of framing his material, assembling and staging the elements in a particular way with a view to proving a particular point, be it theological, medical, or legal. And so, despite the risk of conjuring up an image of lost luggage, this essay is entitled 'a case in transit'.[5]

In exploring the transit of this particular case, which has not to date received any scholarly attention, this essay seeks both to expand the minimal existing scholarship on Diderot and Augustine,[6] and to contribute to the substantial body of existing work on Diderot and Montaigne.[7] There is ample evidence that Diderot knew the *Essais* well; indeed he was clearly fond enough of them for his lover, Sophie Volland, to leave him her seven-volume edition in her will,[8] and he often quotes the *Essais* with a degree of inaccuracy that suggests the familiarity of someone so secure in his knowledge of the text that he has no need to check his quotations.[9] Moreover, although Diderot's liking for 'la parole des autres' [speaking other people's words] is well known,[10] Montaigne is a privileged 'other' for Diderot, whose words he speaks in particularly frequent and intense ways, notably in his literary self-portrait in the *Salon de 1767*, which is so saturated with Montaigne as to produce the rather paradoxical object that is the literary self-portrait that sounds like someone else.[11] In the instance under consideration here, Diderot's use of Montaigne is not simple, however, but, rather, triangulated since he also quotes Augustine, whom Montaigne was likewise echoing, and he does so in ways and for purposes that require some careful teasing out.

Of Diderot's various reworkings of the case, the focus here will be on that found in the *Pensées philosophiques* (1746), an early work, which, though published anonymously, can be said to have made Diderot's name, for it was widely read across Europe and condemned to be burned by the Paris Parlement in 1747.[12] Modern scholarship has tended to neglect it, however, for, although an incendiary Diderot is a figure that philosophers and historians of ideas and science have been keen to promote, they have invested most in Diderot the materialist, the natural philosopher, and scientist, a figure that is absent from the *Pensées philosophiques*, the concerns of which are primarily politico-religious.[13] Moreover, in their efforts to present Diderot as a formally innovative writer, literary historians and critics have tended to focus their attention on his later dialogues, such as *Le Rêve de d'Alembert* [D'Alembert's Dream] and *Le Neveu de Rameau* [Rameau's Nephew], his highly self-reflexive novel, *Jacques le fataliste* [Jacques the Fatalist], and his invention of the new genre of literary art criticism in the *Salons*, rather than on his early use of 'pensées', despite (or perhaps because of) the interpretive challenges raised by the disjointed genre.[14] The present essay seeks, then, to restore the early political Diderot to view by examining the *Pensées philosophiques* — the title recalling both Pascal's *Pensées* (1669) and Voltaire's *Lettres philosophiques* (1734) — and the way in which it stages the case of the priest of Calama, via both Montaigne and Augustine.

At this point, Montaigne scholars might well be wondering what is going to be in it for them: what will this essay tell them, if anything, about Montaigne or the *Essais*? (Montaigne's name does, after all, only appear parenthetically in my title.) There are two answers to that question. The first is that, insofar as the *Pensées philosophiques* offers instances of the ventriloquization of certain passages from the *Essais*, this study sheds light on a moment in the history of their reception, as well as a particular mode of their reception. We know that certain chapters of the *Essais* have been read with particular attention at different historical moments, as well as in different social and political milieux,[15] and this study of the *Pensées philosophiques* offers some further evidence of what the Enlightenment chapters were, how they were read, and how the Enlightenment's selective readings enabled a construction of Montaigne as an Enlightenment *philosophe*.[16] The second answer is that attention to Diderot's presentation of the case of the priest of Calama reveals something of the way in which Montaigne read Augustine, and something of the essayist's role in the history of the reception of the Church Father. To date, scholarly interest in the role of Montaigne in the Enlightenment's reception of Augustine has been focused on Rousseau's *Confessions* (1782), which played such a significant role in the crystallization of the notion of the self.[17] Yet Montaigne was much more familiar with *The City of God* than he was with Augustine's *Confessions*, although his reading of it has received comparatively little attention;[18] and the Enlightenment Augustine was as much the author of *The City of God* as the *Confessions*, if not more so.[19] The present essay argues, then, by way of an analysis of the case of the priest of Calama, as it is presented in the *Pensées philosophiques*, that Diderot read Augustine both by way of Montaigne and in direct contrast to the way Montaigne read Augustine. It demonstrates that what was, in Augustine, a theological case of the power of the will, becomes, in Montaigne, a pathological case of the power of the imagination, and that, in Diderot, the quotation of the Augustinian case in a Montaignian frame, taken from another chapter of the *Essais*, III.11, 'Des boyteux' [Of Cripples], enables Diderot to put a political case. (Being in parentheses, then, may turn out to be more interesting than, at first, it might look.)

1. Reading (Montaigne reading) Augustine

Montaigne's 'De la force de l'imagination' opens with the essayist confessing to the power of his own imagination — he has only to hear someone else cough and he starts to get a tickle in his throat (V, p. 97; F, p. 82). This admission of suggestibility is the cue for a series of interrelated anecdotes, some more striking than others, in which the imagination is said to be what made the bodies behave in the uncontrollable ways they did. The best known is, no doubt, the case, originally reported by Paré as a medical case,[20] of a man called Germain, who had been known by the name of Marie until the age of 22, when she jumped over a ditch and sprouted male genitalia;[21] but the series also includes cases of men condemned to death who are so afraid of the moment of execution that they are already dead by the time they arrive on the scaffold, of a mute so impassioned that he acquired the power of speech, King Dagobert's mysterious flesh wounds, St Francis's stigmata, levitating bodies (V, pp. 98–99; F, pp. 82–83) — and a priest mentioned by Celsus who would remain for long periods of time 'sans respiration et sans sentiment' [with no breathing and no sensation].[22] It is following this reference to Celsus's priest that Montaigne observes, 'Saint Augustin en nomme un autre' [St Augustine names another one], and goes on to present his case.[23]

Before we explore what Montaigne says, it must be observed that anyone familiar with Augustine's version may be rather surprised to find it included by Montaigne in a chapter about unruly bodies,[24] for Augustine had presented the case in *The City of God* as being that of a man who was, on the contrary, able to make his body submit to the rule of his will.[25] And so in order to grasp the significance of Montaigne's reframing and re-relating of the case (and, in due course, the significance of Diderot's re-reframing and re-re-relating of it), we must begin by examining the case as presented by Augustine.

2. The case of the 'presbyter of Calama'

Augustine relates it in Book 14, Chapter 24, in which he makes the theological claim that man, before his fall into a state of sin, had perfect control over his body. The chapter is, no doubt, best known for its claim that Adam's willpower was so perfect that he could even control the movements of his penis, which had since become post-lapsarian man's most unruly member (a point seemingly confirmed by Marie/Germain's surprise growth), but the chapter also contains a series of anecdotes or cases of modern men who, fallen though they are, are able nonetheless to exert some quite remarkable control over their bodies.

Augustine's series begins with men who can wiggle their ears, swallow and then regurgitate an amazing number and variety of items, and fart both musically and without making any smell. It culminates in a case that would, he says, be thought quite 'incredible', had the events not recently been witnessed by members of the local church:[26]

> Presbyter fuit quidam Restitutus nomine in paroecia Calamensis ecclesiae: qui quando ei placebat (rogabatur autem ut hoc faceret ab eis qui rem mirabilem coram scire cupiebant,) ad imitatas quasi lamentantis cuiuslibet hominis uoces, ita se auferebat à sensibus, et iacebat simillimus mortuo, ut non solùm uellicantes atque pungentes minimè sentiret, sed aliquando etiam igne ureretur admoto, sine ullo doloris sensu, nisi postmodum ex uulnere: non autem obnitendo, sed non sentiendo non mouere corpus, eo probabatur, quod tanquam in defuncto nullus inueniebatur anhelitus: hominum tamen uoces, si clarius loquerentur, tanquam de longinquo se audisse postea referebat.

> [There was a presbyter, named Restitutus, in the parish of the church of Calama. Whenever he pleased (and he was often asked to do it by people wanting to witness so remarkable a phenomenon), at/to[27] the sound of voices pretending to wail in grief, he could make himself so insensible and lie in a state so resembling death that he could be pinched and pricked and even exposed to fire and burned without his feeling a single thing, until afterwards when his injuries would hurt. That his body was not motionless owing to an effort of resistance on his part but owing, instead, to a loss of sensitivity is proved by the fact that he would no more breathe than a dead man. And yet he would report that if people spoke particularly clearly, he could hear their voices though they sounded as if they were a long way off.][28]

Whereas some people are special because they can fart an odourless tune, the special gift possessed by the presbyter of Calama is that he could make his body completely lifeless, and he did so, according to Augustine, not by holding his breath, which the reader might have thought would be the ultimate act of willpower, but, rather, by departing his body, leaving it behind, as is made clear in the reference to his reporting that the voices he could hear seemed to be a long way off. These seem, then, to be cases of post-lapsarian men demonstrating quite remarkable degrees of control over their bodies. What are we to make of them? Is Augustine suggesting that such cases offer some evidence of what man's pre-lapsarian willpower might have been like or, even, that they are cases of men possessing some vestige of that power?

Certainly that would be one way of reading Augustine's assertion, 'Sic ergo et ipse homo potuit oboedientiam etiam inferiorum habere membrorum, quam sua inoboedientia perdidit. [...] Nam et hominum quorundam naturas nouimus multum ceteris dispares et ipsa raritate mirabiles' [Then man himself may also have once received from his lower members an obedience which he lost by his own disobedience. [...] We do in fact find among human beings some individuals with natural abilities very different from the rest of mankind and remarkable by their rarity].[29] However, in the cases of the ear-wiggler and the melodious, odour-free farter, there is something of the fairground about their powers, which not even the addition of a penis-puppeteer to the series could make appear Adamic, with the result that their cases are easier to read as comic or ironic rather than as serious signs of man's amazing potential.[30] But is the same true of the case of the presbyter, a man who wills his own fall and his return? Is his case comic and ironic too?

Some sense in which he might be somewhat different to the other cases is suggested by the fact that he alone has a name, and that the name he has is significant. 'Restitutus' is likely to be a name taken by a convert to signal his status as such, and, moreover, in this instance, his name evokes the events that make up his case, which is to say that 'Restitutus' is the name of a man restored to feeling and consciousness, as well as to the Christian Church. Of course, such referential duality may, precisely, allow for comedy and irony: perhaps the name is a joke (although quite whom the joke is on, is not quite clear), and while it would, no doubt, be too much to suggest that the name implies that the case is a hoax, 'Restitutus' might, despite (or perhaps because of) the assurance of its authenticity supplied by Augustine's reference to the credible witnesses, be read as the name of a character in a comic tale. And yet a further twist is also possible for, although it is unlikely that this is the same Restitutus, also known as Possidius, Bishop of Calama, who was kidnapped and assaulted for having converted,[31] it is nonetheless possible that the pinching, pricking, and burning, to which Augustine's Restitutus was exposed, might, although he exposed himself to them perfectly willingly, be read as recalling the acts of violence to which converts were exposed in Augustine's time. The ironic possibilities of the case seem to be counterbalanced or held in check by the symbolic politico-religious associations of his name. What exactly Restitutus is a case of thus seems to be rather less easy to determine than that of the ear-wiggler, although even his case can be read either as an amazing sign of man's potential or as an ironic indication of quite how far he has fallen.

That it is, at least, in part, Restitutus's name that makes the significance of his case harder to stabilize than the others in the series may also be indicated by the fact that Montaigne draws attention to Augustine's act of naming. He states, we recall, 'Saint Augustin en nomme un autre', and yet he omits the name himself. Perhaps Montaigne decided that 'Augustine' was the more important name of the two; perhaps he wished, on this occasion in the *Essais*, to avoid any allusion to religious conversion or to violence done to converts, or to avoid the possibility of any such allusion having anything comic about it, especially given recent events in France. All three are possible, at once. Yet the name is not the only unstable element in the case related by Augustine. A more detailed examination raises the question:

just how much control does Restitutus really have over his body, over his fall, his transit, and his return?

When read as one of the series, the case of Restitutus, regardless of the symbolic significance of his name, would appear to be that of a man able, entirely at will, to perform a pretty extreme kind of trick, one that requires quite extraordinary levels of self-control. Indeed the trick is so remarkable that people would come and request him to perform it for them; Augustine parenthetically tells us, we recall: '(rogabatur autem ut hoc faceret ab eis qui rem mirabilem coram scire cupiebant)' [(and he was often asked to do it by people wanting to witness so remarkable a phenomenon)]. Doubtless we can assume that Restitutus would indeed perform it at their request if he so pleased (and that he wouldn't if he didn't), but it is not obvious that he would actually ever do it if nobody wanted him to — after all, although it might not hurt at the time, the wounds he receives clearly do afterwards: 'nisi postmodum ex uulnere' [afterwards when his injuries would hurt]. True, Restitutus's self-command is not called into question by the implication that he would only ever actually perform it at other people's request, but it might be by the fact that the performance itself relies on audience participation.

There are two different kinds of audience participation in the story, and they have different implications and serve different ends. What we might think of as extreme audience participation (the pinching, pricking, and burning) functions to guarantee the extraordinary nature of Restitutus's ability, but, insofar as the presbyter subsequently reports hearing other people's voices as though they were a long way off, it also suggests that he may be dependent on others in order to prove, perhaps even to himself, that he has gone into transit, once he has. (He does not say, for instance, that he observed his own body as if from afar.) Another kind of audience participation is found slightly earlier in the story, in the second of the two phrases that stand either side of the parentheses, and, though less extreme, its consequences for the case are far-reaching since it suggests that the presbyter may be dependent on others to go into transit in the first place. Whereas in the first phrase, we are told that Restitutus would do his trick 'quando ei placebat' [whenever he pleased], in the second, we read that he would do it 'ad imitatas quasi lamentantis hominis voces', a phrase in which much hinges on how we read the preposition 'ad', which introduces 'the sound of voices pretending to wail in grief'. If we take it to imply a merely temporal relationship, then the presbyter's ability to perform his trick 'whenever he pleased' is not compromised, and we understand that the feigned lamentations were performed either in anticipation of the trick, setting it up in the manner of a drum roll (albeit a strangely mournful one), or coinciding with it, playing along. However, if we take the preposition to imply logical precedence, that is to say, if we take the feigned lamentations to be a pre-condition for the presbyter to be able to perform his trick, then the earlier claim that he could do it entirely at will is called into question. Indeed Restitutus even starts to seem a little vulnerable — when the impersonators did their trick of sounding grief-stricken, was he able *not* to do his trick, if he didn't want to?

That the feigned lamentations introduce further ambiguity into Restitutus's case (in addition to that introduced by his name, which had already made it more ambiguous than the others in the series) is confirmed by Vives, Augustine's most important commentator. In his commentary, first published in 1522, Vives reports that a copy in the Carmelite library in Bruges gives a variant (not of the preposition but of the verb form following it) that would make it possible to ascribe the impersonation of the lamentations to the presbyter himself, placing him firmly in control of every element of the trick.[32] Vives does not himself adopt the Bruges variant (and nor will Montaigne, although we know he read Augustine in an edition containing Vives's commentary)[33] — but some later commentators would,[34] though not uncontroversially.[35] A more drastic solution to the ambiguity over the strength and independence of the presbyter's will is offered by Arnauld and Nicole, who simply omit any reference to the feigned lamentations from their vernacular gloss on the passage in the *Logique*, which reads, 'toutes les fois qu'il vouloit, [il] s'aliénoit tellement de sens, qu'il demeuroit comme mort' [every time he wished, [he] would withdraw from his senses as if he were dead],[36] ensuring that Restitutus can be read as having acted entirely of his own will, as having been in complete control of the proceedings.[37]

Yet another way of resolving the ambiguity is offered by Montaigne. In contrast to Vives and to Arnauld and Nicole, who, in different ways, bolster the case for Restitutus's willpower — which may or may not be quasi-Adamic — over his body, over his fall, his transit, and his return, Montaigne instead further weakens it. And it is to that representation of the case that we now turn.

3. The case of the priest named by Augustine

Given the title of the chapter and the string of anecdotes with which 'De la force de l'imagination' opens, we are primed to understand that the 'other' priest, not the one in Celsus but 'another one', named by Augustine, did not voluntarily transit any more than Montaigne coughs and Marie/Germain grew a penis. Montaigne tells the story as follows:

> Sainct Augustin en nomme un autre, à qui il ne falloit que faire ouir des cris lamentables et plaintifs, soudain il defailloit et s'emportoit si vivement hors de soy, qu'on avoit beau le tempester et hurler, et le pincer, et le griller, jusques à ce qu'il fut resuscité: lors il disoit avoir ouy des voix, mais comme venant de loing, et s'apercevoit de ses eschaudures et meurtrissures. Et ce que ce ne fust une obstination apostée contre son sentiment, cela le montroit, qu'il n'avoit cependant ny poulx ny haleine. (V, p. 103; F, pp. 82–83)

> [St Augustine names another one, who had only to be made to hear mournful and wretched cries, and suddenly, he would collapse and transport himself out of himself in such a lively manner that there was no point shaking him and shouting, and pinching him, and burning him until he came round, whereupon he would say he had heard voices, but as if coming from afar, and notice his burns and bruises. And that this was no obstinate refusal to feel pain was evident from the fact that, throughout, he had no pulse, nor was he breathing.][38]

Here the priest — or, rather, the man, for in addition to the omission of his Augustinian name his profession is elided in Montaigne's formulation — enters a state like that which Augustine's presbyter had entered, and in which he appears to be dead. As in Augustine, he was not holding his breath, and in Montaigne's version, he didn't have a pulse either, which we might imagine to be even more difficult to control than one's breathing. And, again as in Augustine, the fact of his having left his body behind is conveyed by reference to his having heard distant voices. There is, however, no ambiguity here regarding either the sequence of events or their logical relationship to one another. Whereas Arnauld and Nicole will later avoid referring to other people feigning cries and will thereby downplay the possibility that Restitutus is not in complete control, Montaigne here proceeds in the opposite manner and simply cuts Augustine's opening phrase, 'whenever he pleased'. Moreover, the verbal construction, '[lui] faire ouir des cris', has the priest clearly subjected to the sound,[39] which the restrictive formulation 'ne ... que' ensures we understand him no sooner to hear than he involuntarily falls to the ground. This is not a case in which the protagonist could be read as exhibiting any vestige of Adamic willpower.[40]

As Montaigne's narrative progresses, however, it appears to gain in similarity to Augustine's, and, as a result, Montaigne's presentation of the man's agency, or lack of it, gains in complexity. Where a preposition in Augustine could unsettle the case, in Montaigne it is the pronouns that perform unsettling work. What they register are shifts in agency, in its presence, absence, and location.

Montaigne states, we recall, that 'il defailloit et s'emportoit si vivement hors de soy', a curious phrase involving a intransitive verb with a subject pronoun, followed by a reflexive verb without a subject pronoun and qualified by an adverb, and a preposition, followed by a third-person impersonal object pronoun. The man's transition from agent to inanimate object is conveyed here in the shift from 'il' to 'soy', and though 'soy' is no doubt not as strange in early modern French as it would be in modern (where one would expect 'lui'), the impersonality allows for a striking presentation of the lifelessness of the priest's body. Peculiarly, however, the agent of that transition would seem to be the man himself, for the reflexive verb ('s'emporter') and the adverb ('vivement') ascribe agency to the man, who effects his own transit in a lively manner, leaving a lifeless body behind. This would seem to undercut Montaigne's framing of the story as one about a man who is not in control. So, is it, in fact, as Augustine might have been saying it was, the case of someone able, at will, to transport himself out of his body? And are the sounds not causal after all?

The answer to both questions is 'no'. Although there is no grammatical reason to repeat the subject pronoun, its disappearance halfway through 'il defailloit et s'emportoit' is not without significance. Of course, there can be no doubt that the reflexive verb is governed by the same subject pronoun as that governing the preceding verb, and yet not only is it difficult to imagine the man being the agent of his self-transport given that he has just been the subject of the verb 'défaillir', but also, in the absence of a contiguous subject pronoun, the only marker of subjecthood in 's'emportoit' is the reflexive object pronoun, which appears to be a kind of halfway house between the subject pronoun, 'il', and the impersonal object, 'soy'. And so the apparently banal disappearance of a subject pronoun, in fact, performs the disappearance of the agent; and the gap between subject and verb, ('il

[...] s'emportoit'), is one into which another agent inserts itself, namely the man's imagination.

Another ellipsis, indicated by a colon,[41] marks the moment when the man's imagination relinquishes its control and his will returns. Montaigne states, we recall, 'on avoit beau le tempester et hurler, et le pincer, et le griller, jusques à ce qu'il fut resuscité: lors il disoit avoir ouy des voix', a curious phrase insofar as the list of verbs referring to actions that it was futile to perform because they would not have caused him to come round culminates in a statement that he would come round nonetheless, the causal explanation for which is, however, withheld. The colon, located at the moment of transition between transit and return, is a kind of pivot that transforms the phrase, 'il fut resuscité', from being a counterfactual into an actual. Before the colon, it is part of an assertion that the man would not come round, but the colon has the effect of retrospectively dissociating the phrase from 'on avoit beau [...] jusques à ce qu[e]' and transforming it into the positive condition for him to become the subject of a verb of action once again: 'lors [qu'il fut resuscité], il disoit'. It is undoubtedly significant that at the very point at which his imagination gives way to his will again, the word 'resuscité' is to be found, for when his will is restored, so is an echo of his Augustinian name.

The question remains, however, as to why it was that the man's imagination ran away with him or, rather, what it was about those 'cris lamentables et plaintifs' that caused his imagination to afford him a near-death experience.[42] While Montaigne's ticklish throat seemed to be a straightforward case of suggestibility, this man's suggestibility is of a different order, for his imagination does not make him identify with the mourner and begin to feel grief too; rather, the mournful cries cause his imagination to make him identify with the person being mourned. He passes out as he imagines himself passing away, and his case thus gestures ironically back to the previous chapter, which stages another way of responding to mortality, one so different that, in the light of it, the man's response appears comic. That chapter is, of course, I.20, 'Que philosopher, c'est apprendre à mourir' [That Doing Philosophy Teaches You How to Die] (V, pp. 81–96; F, pp. 67–82), and the Stoic contemplation of death thus gives way in 'De la force de l'imagination' to (what might today be referred to as) a 'hysterical'[43] death.

Having re-related the case in we might call 'non-voluntarist' terms, Montaigne interrupts his series of cases to consider the belief that extraordinary behaviour, such as that exhibited by various people in his list, has a supernatural cause. This consideration, wholly foreign to Augustine, requires our attention here, for it is crucial to understanding the story's subsequent transit.

4. Transit (de)mystified

Immediately following the case of 'the other one Augustine names', Montaigne makes the following statement:

> Il est vray semblable que le principal credit des miracles, des visions, des enchantemens et de tels effects extraordinaires, vienne de la puissance de l'imagination agissant principalement contre les ames du vulgaire, plus molles. On leur a si fort saisi la creance, qu'ils pensent voir ce qu'ils ne voyent pas.[44]

[It seems to be the case that the principal credit afforded to miracles, visions, enchantments, and other such special effects is due to the power of the imagination pressing principally against the souls of common people, which are softer. Their credulity is so forcibly seized upon that they think they see what they do not see.][45]

Here the implicit disagreement with Augustine over whether bodies behaving in extraordinary ways do so under the influence of human willpower or under the power of the human imagination has been replaced by an explicit disagreement with 'common people', who are said to believe that such extraordinary behaviours are caused by a superhuman power. Montaigne's counter-claim is that just as a powerful imagination can wreak all kinds of havoc on the body, so a weak soul is powerless when confronted with the imagination, which can impress on it all kinds of unfounded beliefs. For Montaigne, the beliefs in question relate to demonological activity, in particular, also the subject of the later chapter 'Des boyteux',[46] in which Montaigne will again enlist Augustine:

> Il me semble qu'on est pardonnable de mescroire une merveille, autant au moins qu'on peut en destourner et elider la verification par voie non merveilleuse. Et suis l'advis de sainct Augustin, qu'il vaut mieux pancher vers le doute que vers l'asseurance és choses de difficile preuve et dangereuse creance. (V, p. 1032; F, p. 961)

> [It seems to me that we might be forgiven for not believing in a marvel, at least when we can come up with an alternative, non-marvellous way of explaining it away. And I am of the same opinion as St Augustine, which is that it is better to lean towards doubt rather than assurance when it comes to things that are difficult to prove and dangerous to believe in.][47]

Of course, with respect to the presbyter of Calama, Augustine had nothing to say of any belief, popular, unfounded, or otherwise, that the events had a supernatural cause. However, by juxtaposing the case of the 'other [priest] named by Augustine' and the belief in the supernatural, Montaigne effects a mystification of the events, which he then demystifies. This process of mystification and demystification will have lasting consequences for the ways in the case will subsequently be read and re-related.

5. The case of 'the priest of Calama'

Over a hundred years later, in Diderot's *Pensées philosophiques*, the phenomenon to be demystified by means of a comparison with the case of the priest of Calama is not demonological, but thaumaturgical. The context is the second wave of Jansenist miracles, the first being that of 'la Sainte Épine' [the Sacred Thorn], which cured Pascal's niece and goddaughter of an eye infection,[48] and established miracles as a significant part of Jansenist culture. By the late 1720s and early 1730s, particularly in the poorest areas of Paris, Jansenism had become a kind of popular movement, sparked by the papal bull, 'Unigenitus', of 1713, which had condemned as unconstitutional many of the Jansenist beliefs, notably those regarding grace and predestination. A key element in that movement was the high incidence of reported miracles in the cemetery of the Paris church of Saint-Médard, where the prominent Jansenist magistrate, François de Pâris, had been buried in 1727; by early 1732, the frequency of miraculous cures, states of ecstasy, and convulsions was so high that the police took the decision to close the cemetery.[49] When the *Pensées philosophiques* were published in 1746, the affair had not entirely gone away: Carré de Montgeron, a notable convert, lawyer, and Parlementarian who had undergone a transformative experience on Pâris's tomb, had just published the third volume of his *La Vérité des miracles démontrée* [*The Truth of Miracles Demonstrated*] (1745),[50] a work containing witness statements and other documents, presented as proofs in a legal case for the miraculous nature of the events.[51] It is in discussing or, rather, debunking the 'miracles of Saint-Médard' that Diderot relates the case of a man he calls 'le pendant du prêtre de Calame' [the modern-day equivalent of the priest of Calama].[52]

Where the case had appeared in Augustine and Montaigne as one in a series, in Diderot it appears as one of a pair:

> Un homme est étendu sur la terre, sans sentiment, sans voix, sans chaleur, sans mouvement. On le tourne, on le retourne, on l'agite, le feu lui est appliqué, rien ne l'émeut: le fer chaud n'en peut arracher un symptôme de vie; on le croit mort: l'est-il? Non. C'est le pendant du prêtre de Calame. *Qui, quando ei placebat,*[53] *ad imitatas quasi lamentantis hominis voces, ita se auferebat a sensibus et jacebat simillimus mortuo, ut non solum vellicantes at que pungentes minime sentiret, sed aliquando etiam igne uretur admoto, sine ullo doloris sensu, nisi post modum ex vulnere,* etc. (Saint Augustin, *Cité de Dieu*, Liv. XIV, chap. xxiv.) Si certaines gens avaient rencontré, de nos jours, un pareil sujet, ils en auraient tiré bon parti. On nous aurait fait voir un cadavre se ranimer sur la cendre d'un prédestiné; le recueil du magistrat janséniste se serait enflé d'une résurrection, et le constitutionnel se tiendrait peut-être confondu.[54]

> [A man is lying on the ground, he can't feel anything, he's not saying anything, he's stone-cold and stock-still. We roll him over one way and roll him back, we shake him, we hold a flame to his skin, but nothing brings him round, not even a hot iron can induce a sign of life. We believe he's dead, but is he? No. He's the modern-day equivalent of the priest of Calama. *Who whenever he pleased, to/ at the sound of voices pretending to wail in grief, could make himself so insensible and lie in a state so resembling death that he could be pinched and pricked and even exposed to fire and burned without his feeling a single thing, until afterwards when his injuries would hurt etc.* (St Augustine, *City of God*, Book 14, Chapter 24.) If certain people were to have encountered such a subject today, they would have put him to good use. We'd have been made to see a corpse come back to life on the ashes of one of the elect; the magistrate's casebook would have expanded to include a resurrection, and the constitutionalist might find himself rather perplexed.][55]

The designation, 'le prêtre de Calame', suggests the figure's dual genealogy: it combines the geographical location given by Augustine with the job description suggested by Montaigne, but made much more audible. What we witness here is a demystification and a hypothetical mystification: while the quotation from Augustine (minus the parentheses containing the reference to the fact that he would do his trick on request) makes it clear that the priest's case involves no supernatural intervention, Diderot also makes it clear that, were the priest of Calama alive today, the magistrate, Carré de Montgeron, would mystify his case by representing it as one of a man who had died and come back to life.[56] Clearly Diderot is mobilizing Montaigne's reframing of the case in anti-marvellous terms here in order to undercut the legal and theological case being made by the Jansenist magistrate — but what are the implications of his quoting Augustine?

The Church Father is, of course, a major Jansenist authority, and one obvious reason for citing Augustine is to be able to turn him against the popular neo-Augustinians. Yet this is not the only reason. The question of the will is fundamental to the case with which Diderot compares that of Restitutus: it is one in which not only is the man's performance a willed act, but its reception by the onlookers is wilful too — Diderot observes, we recall, that if the man had been alive today, 'certaines gens [...] en auraient tiré bon parti' [certain people [...] would have put him to good use]. The question raised by Diderot is thus not, as it was in Augustine, whether the man could play dead whenever he pleased or whether he needed other people to play at being grief-stricken first, but rather whether or not, were he alive today, he would willingly accept to play a role in someone else's politically motivated trick, involving the pretence that he was the subject of a miracle. Would a modern-day priest of Calama be someone who was just having some (somewhat masochistic) fun (with some sadists) in the graveyard at Saint-Médard, but who found himself unwittingly used as Jansenist pro-miracle propaganda? Or would he, in fact, be a willing participant in the pro-miracle propaganda, either by claiming himself to be the subject of a miracle or by allowing others to claim it for him? In both readings, what is important is that charlatanism is involved, and Augustine's version of the case is amenable, in a way that Montaigne's is not, to what we might call a 'voluntarist' reworking, one in which the protagonist subjects his body to his will.[57] Moreover, the Montaignian framing enables not simply the mystification and demystification of the case; it also enables Diderot not only to present the charlatan as a priest, but also to suggest that it is precisely because he is a priest that he is a charlatan.

That the Jansenists are indeed viewed as charlatans is made clear a couple of pensées later, in which we can also hear further echoes of the case of the priest of Calama. The sounds of voices, which had been absent, now return, albeit in the form of cheering rather than wailing, and we read: '[u]n faubourg retentit d'acclamations: la cendre d'un prédestiné y fait, en un jour, plus de prodiges que Jésus-Christ n'en fit en toute sa vie. On y court' [a suburb rejoices as the ashes of a chosen one perform more miracles in one day than Jesus Christ performed in his entire life. People rush along to see].[58] The voices function not so much to set the priest off, as they did in Montaigne, as to pull the crowd in, as perhaps they did in Augustine. However, drawing on the Montaignian frame, while the crowd cheers 'Miracle!', Diderot's penseur, now abandoning the third-person pronoun 'on', and speaking in the first-person, recounts:

> [J]'arrive à peine, que j'entends crier: miracle! miracle! J'approche, je regarde, et je vois un petit boiteux qui se promène à l'aide de trois ou quatre personnes charitables qui le soutiennent [...]. Où donc est le miracle, peuple imbécile? Ne vois-tu pas que ce fourbe n'a fait que changer de béquilles?

[No sooner do I get there than I hear cries of 'Miracle! Miracle!' I move closer, take a look, and see a little cripple walking with the help of three or four kind people who are holding him up [...]. Where is this miracle then, you silly people? Can't you see that this conman has simply swapped one set of crutches for another?][59]

And in a further twist, the *penseur* asserts that those who see miracles are not, as they were in Montaigne, victims of their over-active imaginations; rather they too are voluntarists since they willingly fall for the tricks: 'tous ceux qui voyaient là des miracles, étaient bien résolus d'en voir' [all those who saw miracles in such events did so because they had firmly decided to].[60] Just as Diderot's priest of Calama willed himself not to feel anything, so the onlookers willed themselves not to see anything other than evidence of the workings of a power beyond their control.[61]

★   ★   ★   ★   ★

This, then, is a case that undergoes a number of transformations as it transits from Augustine to Diderot via Montaigne, from theology to law and politics, via medicine and pathology. Indeed one might even compare the case in transit to its own protagonist, whom 'on [...] tourne, on [...] retourne'. Moreover, like the protagonist in the cases related by Montaigne and Augustine, who, on coming round, reported hearing voices in the distance, each version of the case echoes with earlier versions.[62] Yet the context for each version is different, and each both calls for and confers new meanings and frames. In fifth-century North Africa, Augustine related a case involving a performance that replayed the violence done to a convert and which, even as it offered a cathartic outlet for that violence, revealed it to have no effect because Restitutus, precisely because he was a convert, had a strength of will that enabled him to feel no pain. In late sixteenth-century France, in the aftermath of a bloody civil war fought between Catholics and Protestants, Montaigne presented a case in which the protagonist needed only to hear the sounds of people grieving their loss for his imagination to seize control, distance him from such unbearable sounds, and close him off from feeling any pain. And in early to mid eighteenth-century Paris when the popular Jansenists were protesting against the Papal bull, Diderot quoted Augustine's case in a Montaignian frame, presented its protagonist as being unambiguously in control of his body, and suggested he was performing a politically orchestrated spectacle — one that only someone who was wilfully blind would not see through. A case of a man in temporary transit, then, but also a case in both transit and transition across time.

Notes to Chapter 2

1. Diderot relates it at least three times between 1746 and 1769; see his *Pensées philosophiques*, ed. Jean-Claude Bourdin (Paris: Garnier-Flammarion, 2007), p. 85; 'Impassibilité', in *Encyclopédie, ou Dictionnaire raisonné des sciences, des arts et des métiers, par une Société de Gens de lettres*, ed. Denis Diderot and Jean Le Rond D'Alembert, 28 vols (Paris: Braisson, David, Le Breton, and Durand, 1751–72), vol. 8 (1765), p. 584; and *Le Rêve de d'Alembert*, ed. Colas Duflo (Paris: Garnier-Flammarion, 2002), p. 145.

2. V, p. 99; F, pp. 83–84.

3. St Augustine, *The City of God*, trans. Henry Bettenson, intro. G. R. Evans (London: Penguin, 2003), p. 588.

4. Antoine Arnauld and Pierre Nicole, *La Logique, ou L'art de penser*, ed. Pierre Clair and François Girbal (Paris: Vrin, 1981), p. 73; *Logic, or, the Art of Thinking*, ed. and trans. Jill Vance Buroker (Cambridge: Cambridge University Press, 1996), pp. 50–51.

5. 'Case' might also be thought the most appropriate term given the nature of the events involved, for 'case' is etymologically linked to the Latin 'cadere' [to fall]. Diderot refers to the priest of Calama when he is in transit as a 'cadavre', and the implications of the Christian story of the Fall are an important part of Augustine's framing of the case.

6. See Kate E. Tunstall, 'Eyes Wide Shut: *Le Rêve de d'Alembert*', in *New Essays on Diderot*, ed. James Fowler (Cambridge: Cambridge University Press, 2011), pp. 141–57 (p. 154, n. 26), and Colas Duflo, 'Prêtre de Calame', in *Encyclopédie du Rêve de d'Alembert*, ed. Sophie Audidière, Jean-Claude Bourdin, and Colas Duflo (Paris: CNRS, 2006), pp. 321–22. The literature on Diderot and Pascal is a little more voluminous, but still fairly thin: see Robert Niklaus, 'Les *Pensées philosophiques* de Diderot et les *Pensées* de Pascal', *Diderot Studies*, 20 (1981), 201–17; Hisayasu Nakagawa, 'Trois Pascal dans la pensée de Diderot', *Recherches sur Diderot et l'Encyclopedie*, 7 (1989), 23–41; and Kate E. Tunstall, *Blindness and Enlightenment: An Essay. With New Translations of Diderot's 'Lettre sur les aveugles' and La Mothe Le Vayer's 'Of a Man Born Blind'* (New York: Continuum, 2011), pp. 122–24.

7. See Jerome Schwartz, *Diderot and Montaigne: The 'Essais' and the Shaping of Diderot's Humanism* (Geneva: Droz, 1966); Michèle Chabanon, 'Présence de Montaigne dans la pensée ultime de Diderot', *Recherches sur Diderot et l'Encyclopedie*, 21 (1996), 51–67; Philip Knee, 'Diderot et Montaigne: morale et scepticisme dans *Le Neveu de Rameau*', *Diderot Studies*, 29 (2003), 35–51; and Kate E. Tunstall, 'Portraits and Afterlives: Diderot and Montaigne', in *Pre-Histories and Afterlives: Studies Towards a New Cultural History*, ed. Anna Holland and Richard Scholar (Oxford: Legenda, 2008), pp. 95–105.

8. See Emmanuel Boussuge, 'Le testament de Sophie et autres documents concernant Louise-Henriette Volland aux Archives nationales et dans les registres paroissiaux de la Marne', *Recherches sur Diderot et l'Encyclopedie*, 47 (2012), 299–313 (p. 302). It seems likely that the edition in question was that in seven volumes, printed in London by Jean Nourse in 1745.

9. See, for instance, Diderot, *Pensées philosophiques*, p. 72. The corresponding passage from Montaigne is V, p. 1030; F, p. 959.

10. Jean Starobinski, 'Diderot et la parole des autres', *Critique*, 296 (1972), 3–22.

11. See Tunstall, 'Portraits and Afterlives'.

12. Robert Morin, *Les 'Pensées philosophiques' de Diderot devant leurs principaux contradicteurs au XVIIIe siècle* (Paris: Belles Lettres, 1975).

13. The standard view is that the *Pensées philosophiques* is the work of a sceptic or a deist, and that Diderot's more interesting atheist materialist writing begins with the *Lettre sur les aveugles* [*Letter on the Blind*] (1749); see Aram Vartanian, 'From Deist to Atheist: Diderot's Philosophical Orientation, 1746–1749', *Diderot Studies*, 1 (1949), 46–63. For another reading of the *Lettre*, see Tunstall, *Blindness and Enlightenment*.

14. Such a challenge is taken up, to a degree, by the philosopher Jean-Claude Bourdin in his Introduction to the *Pensées philosophiques* (pp. 20–24; 51–56). Given the relatively scarce attention given to the text these days, it is ironic that Diderot gave the work two epigraphs: the declaration, 'Piscis hic non est omnium' [This fish is not for everyone], and the question, 'Quis leget hæc?' [Who will read this?].

15. See, for instance, Dudley M. Marchi, *Montaigne among the Moderns: Receptions of the 'Essais'* (Providence, RI: Berghahn Books, 1994).

16. The most comprehensive work remains Maturin Dréano, *La Renommée de Montaigne au XVIIIe siècle, 1677–1802* (Angers: Éditions de l'Ouest, 1952).

17. See, for instance, Charles Taylor, *Sources of the Self: The Making of the Modern Identity* (Cambridge: Cambridge University Press, 1992).

18. Surprisingly, the only full-length study of Montaigne's use of *The City of God* is the recent doctoral thesis, Takeshi Kubota, 'Montaigne et Saint Augustin: lectures de la "Cité de Dieu" à la Renaissance', doctoral thesis, Bordeaux 3, 2009. Kubota notes the borrowing in his table

of concordances (p. 63), but offers no analysis. For a study of the presence of the *Confessions* in Montaigne, see Gisèle Mathieu-Castellani, 'Absence et présence des *Confessions*', in *Montaigne, ou La vérité du mensonge* (Geneva: Droz, 2000), pp. 107–27. For more on Montaigne and Augustine, see Nigel Abercrombie, *Saint Augustine and French Classical Thought* (Oxford: Clarendon Press, 1938), pp. 40–56; Elaine Limbrick, 'Montaigne et Saint Augustin', *Bibliothèque d'Humanisme et de Renaissance*, 34 (1972), 49–64; Andrée Comparot, *Augustinianisme et Aristotélisme de Sebond à Montaigne* (Lille: Atelier national de reproduction des thèses, 1985); Élisabeth Caron, 'Saint Augustin dans les *Essais*', *Montaigne Studies*, 2 (1990), 17–33; Alain Legros, 'Les *ombrages* de Montaigne et d'Augustine', *Bibliothèque d'Humanisme et de Renaissance*, 55 (1993), 547–63.

19. See Jean-Louis Quantin and Scott Mandelbrote, 'Augustine beyond Theology and Back: Augustine in the Seventeenth and Eighteenth Centuries', in *The Oxford Guide to the Historical Reception of Augustine*, ed. Karla Pollmann, 3 vols (Oxford: Oxford University Press, 2013), vol. I, pp. 83–96.

20. Ambroise Paré, *Monstres et prodiges* (1585), ed. Jean Céard (Geneva: Droz, 1971), pp. 28–29.

21. V, p. 99; F, p. 83. See, among others, Stephen Greenblatt, 'Fiction and Friction', in *Shakespearean Negotiations: The Circulation of Social Energy in Renaissance England* (Berkeley: University of California Press, 1988), pp. 66–93; Thomas Laqueur, *Making Sex: Body and Gender from the Greeks to Freud* (Cambridge, MA: Harvard University Press, 1990), pp. 126–27; and Edith J. Benkov, 'Re-Reading Montaigne's Memorable Stories: Sexuality and Gender in Vitry-le-François', in *Montaigne after Theory, Theory after Montaigne*, ed. Zahi Zalloua (Seattle: University of Washington Press, 2009), pp. 202–17.

22. V, p. 99; F, p. 83. My translation.

23. V, p. 99; F, p. 83. My translation.

24. I have borrowed the word 'unruly' from Richard Regosin; see *Montaigne's Unruly Brood: Textual Engendering and the Challenge to Paternal Authority* (Berkeley: University of California Press, 1996).

25. This might itself be thought rather surprising, given Augustine's well-known hostility to Pelagianism, which leaves open the possibility, also to be discussed in this essay, that the case may be read as ironic.

26. For a study of Augustine and testimony, see Peter King and Nathan Ballantyne, 'Augustine on Testimony', *Canadian Journal of Philosophy*, 39 (2009), 195–294. No mention is made of this particular case.

27. The Latin preposition 'ad' will be the subject of commentary below.

28. Augustine, Bishop of Hippo, *De civitate Dei: collatione & fide castigatissimi facti Lodovici Vivis, eruditissimis commentariis* (Lyon: S. Honoratum, 1570), pp. 97–98. My translation. I have consulted the following translations: *The City of God*, trans. Bettenson; *The City of God against the Pagans*, ed. and trans. R. W. Dyson (Cambridge: Cambridge University Press, 1998); *The City of God*, ed. Philip Schaff, trans. Marcus Dods (New York: Modern Library, 1993 [Edinburgh, 1871–72]); *Sainct Augustin, De la Cité de Dieu: Contenant le commencement et progrez d'icelle cité, avec une deffence de la religion chrestienne* [...] *illustré de commentaires de Jean Louys Vives* [...] *le tout faict en françoys par Gentian Hervet* [...] *et enrichy de plusieurs annotations par François de Belle-Forest*, 3rd edn (Paris: chez Michel Sonnius, 1585).

29. *De civitate Dei*, p. 97; *City of God*, p. 588.

30. Kate Cooper and Conrad Leyser argue that the series of anecdotes is aimed at undermining the moral claims of contemporary ascetics by presenting them and their ability to control their bodies as the stuff of fairground performances; 'The Gender of Grace: Impotence, Servitude, and Manliness in the Fifth-Century West', *Gender and History*, 12.3 (2000), 536–51. They make no distinction between the ear-wiggler and Restitutus in this regard. I suggest in what follows, by contrast, that such a distinction might be made, and argue that Montaigne and other early modern readers did, in fact, make it.

31. See Erika T. Hermanowicz, *Possidius of Calama: A Study of the North African Episcopate in the Age of Augustine* (Oxford: Oxford University Press, 2008), pp. 106–07. R. W. Dyson says of the Restitutus who appears in *The City of God* that he is not known from any other source; Augustine, *City of God*, trans. Dyson, p. 1223.

32. See *De civitate Dei*, p. 99. Hervet observes: 'si ainsi est, il signifie que luy-même avait coutume de se contrefaire, et ainsi se départit de ses sentimens corporels' [if that is so, it means that he

was himself in the habit of imitating himself, and that that was how he took leave of his bodily feelings]; *De la cité*, trans. Hervet, p. 412.

33. Kubota persuasively demonstrates that Montaigne read the text in Latin in one of the Erasmian editions, accompanied by Vives's commentaries and printed between 1550 and 1570; see Kubota, 'Montaigne et Saint Augustin', pp. 136–37. Montaigne mentions Vives by name on one occasion in the *Essais* (V, p. 87; F, p. 87).

34. See, for instance, Louis de Bonnaire, *Examen critique, physique et théologique des convulsions, et des caractères divins, qu'on croit voir dans les accidens des Convulsionnaires* (n.p.: no pub., 1733), p. 49.

35. See Bonnaire, *Suite des Observations apologétiques de l'auteur de l'examen critique, physique et théologique des convulsions* (n.p., no pub., [1733]), pp. 74–76, in which he responds to those who had criticized him for having adopted the Bruges variant. For more on Bonnaire, see Catherine Maire, 'Les querelles jansénistes de la décennie 1730-40', *Recherches sur Diderot et l'Encyclopédie*, 38 (2005), 71–92.

36. *Logique*, p. 73; *Logic*, p. 50. My translation. Their gloss is followed by the complete lines in Latin from Augustine.

37. There is not room here to explore what the stakes of such readings and commentaries are, although they should be read in conjunction with the debates over Pelagianism, for which, see Conrad Leyser, 'Semi-Pelagianism', in *Augustine through the Ages: An Encyclopedia*, ed. Allan Fitzgerald and John C. Cavadini (Grand Rapids, MI: Eerdmans, 1999), pp. 761–66, and Irena Backus and Aza Goudriaan, '"Semipelagianism": The Origins of the Term and its Passage into the History of Heresy', *Journal of Ecclesiastical History*, 65.1 (2014), 25–46.

38. My translation.

39. Perhaps it is not insignificant that the preposition 'à', though not performing quite the same function here as it does in Augustine's, occupies such a prominent position in Montaigne's sentence: 'un autre, à qui il ne fallait que'.

40. Later in the same chapter, Montaigne makes it clear that he is not convinced by Augustine's claim that if Adam had not disobeyed God in paradise, modern man's body would do his bidding (V, p. 103; F, p. 87).

41. For a study of punctuation in Montaigne, see Warren Boutcher's essay in this volume.

42. There is no room here to explore the ways in which the case of 'the other [priest] named by Augustine' points to Montaigne's story about his own fall in II.6, 'De l'exercitation' [Of Practice].

43. Of course, Montaigne does also discuss the female imagination in the chapter; see Wes Williams, *Monsters and their Meanings in Early Modern Culture: Mighty Magic* (Oxford: Oxford University Press, 2011), pp. 15–22.

44. V, p. 99; F, p. 84. My translation.

45. My translation.

46. See, for instance, Emily Butterworth, 'The Work of the Devil? Theatre, the Supernatural, and Montaigne's Public Stage', *Renaissance Studies*, 22.5 (2008), 705–22. For early modern demonology more generally, see *Voyager avec le diable: voyages réels, voyages imaginaires et discours démonologiques (XVe–XVIIe siècles)*, ed. Grégoire Holtz and Thibaut Maus de Rolley (Paris: Presses de l'université Paris-Sorbonne, 2008).

47. My translation.

48. See Henri Gouhier, *Blaise Pascal: commentaires* (Paris: Vrin, 1984), pp. 131–40.

49. See Dale Van Kley, *The Religious Origins of the French Revolution: From Calvin to the Civil Constitution, 1560–1791* (New Haven, CT: Yale University Press, 1996); Monique Cottret, *Jansénismes et Lumières: pour un autre XVIIIe siècle* (Paris: Albin Michel, 1998); and Brian E. Strayer, *Suffering Saints: Jansenists and Convulsionnaires in France, 1640–1799* (Brighton: Sussex Academic Press, 2008).

50. Louis Basile Carré de Montgeron, *La Vérité des miracles de M. de Pâris démontrée contre M. l'Archevêque de Sens* (Cologne: Lib. de la Comp., 1745). The first two volumes had appeared in 1737 and 1741.

51. Jean-Robert Armogathe, 'À propos des miracles de Saint-Médard: les preuves de Carré de Montgeron et le positivisme des Lumières', *Revue de l'histoire des religions*, 180.2 (1971), 135–60.

52. Diderot, *Pensées philosophiques*, p. 85.

53. Diderot omits the parenthetical statement about how people would come and ask Restitutus, whose name he also omits, to perform the trick. The same is true of Arnauld and Nicole, which may suggest that Diderot is quoting from the *Logique* rather than directly from the *City*, despite the parenthetical citation.

54. Diderot, *Pensées philosophiques*, p. 85.

55. My translation.

56. For a study of eighteenth-century practices of mystification, see Reginald McGinnis, *Essai sur l'origine de la mystification* (Saint-Denis: Presses universitaires de Vincennes, 2009).

57. Diderot also strips the case of any theological implications. For the eighteenth-century French discussions of original sin, see, for instance, Mark Hulliung, 'Voltaire, Rousseau, and the Revenge of Pascal', in *Cambridge Companion to Rousseau*, ed. Patrick Riley (Cambridge: Cambridge University Press, 2001), pp. 57–77.

58. Diderot, *Pensées philosophiques*, pp. 85–86. My translation.

59. Diderot, *Pensées philosophiques*, p. 86. My translation.

60. Diderot, *Pensées philosophiques*, p. 86. My translation.

61. Diderot will later tend to consider the question of free will from a philosophical perspective rather than from the polemical, political one adopted here, and, when he does, he presents it as an illusion; see, for instance, 'Lettre à Landois' (29 June 1756), in Denis Diderot, *Œuvres complètes*, ed. Herbert Dieckmann, Jacques Proust, and Jean Varloot (Paris: Hermann, 1975–), vol. 9, pp. 243–60.

62. The wording of this point was inspired by the title of John O'Brien and Malcolm Quainton's *Distant Voices Still Heard: Contemporary Readings of French Renaissance Literature* (Liverpool: Liverpool University Press, 2000).

PART II

Genesis and Production

CHAPTER 3

'No Book Was So Bad':
Montaigne and Angelo Poliziano

Rowan Tomlinson

'C'est folie de rapporter le vray et le faux à nostre suffisance' (I.27) is conventionally presented by editors of the *Essais* as a testing ground for materials — ideas, anecdotes, and textual borrowings — that will be deployed and developed at length in the vast 'Apologie de Raymond Sebond' (II.12). For Pierre Villey, proponent of a doggedly influential linear view of Montaigne's philosophical allegiances, it bears the traces of the 'intellectual prudence' that will, in time, 'lead him to Pyrrhonism'; Bénédicte Boudou points to the chapter's concern — influenced by both St Augustine and Plutarch — with the urgency of coming to terms with the limits of human knowledge, while Jean Balsamo's description of it as 'the first apologetic chapter' places it firmly in a foreshadowing role.[1] And yet at the heart, formally and genetically, of this apologetic chapter is an apologia that looks not forwards to the extended reflections of II.12 but backwards: a carefully constructed defence of a triumvirate of the classical canon. Montaigne here begins with his professed favourite, Plutarch, and then moves on to Caesar. The climax of the apologia, though, is not an encomium to the sceptical sensation — and favourite of Montaignistes — that makes its first substantial appearance in I.27: Lucretius's *On the Nature of Things*. It is, instead, a paean to the practice of judgement by a less celebrated sceptic and more longstanding reference, Pliny the Elder, the polymathic compiler whose *Natural History* fifteenth- and sixteenth-century humanists would carefully repair, and then translate, rather than dramatically rediscover:

> Est-il rien plus delicat, plus net et plus vif que le jugement de Pline, quand il lui plaist de le mettre en jeu, rien plus esloingné de vanité? je laisse à part l'excellence de son sçavoir, duquel je fay moins de conte: en quelle partie de ces deux là le surpassons nous? Toutesfois il n'est si petit escolier qui ne le convainque de mensonge, et qui ne luy veuille faire leçon sur le progrez des ouvrages de nature.

> [Is there anything more delicate, clearer, and more alert than Pliny's judgement, when he sees fit to bring it into play, or anything further from inanity? Leaving aside the excellence of his knowledge, which I count for less, in which of these qualities do we surpass him? However, there is no schoolboy so young but he will convict him of falsehood, and want to give him a lesson on the progress of nature's works.] (V, p. 181; F, p. 162)

In line with the central preoccupation of I.27, Montaigne's defence of Pliny's judgement is an attack on its opposite: namely, presumption; his target is the smug schoolboys of his day who are taught to dismiss the Roman's compilation as worthless because the ancient knowledge it offers cannot match up to their modern understanding of the 'faits de nature'. The sniggers of these schoolboys run counter to the generous approach to reading for which the Roman was famous. In his *Letters*, Pliny the Younger recalls how his uncle was wont to declare that 'no book was so bad' (III. 5) that it couldn't prove useful, and this declaration became a Renaissance favourite, adopted regularly to promote the eclectic reading that is a prerequisite for eclectic imitation. Erasmus uses it, unattributed, in his prefatory letter to the 1533 edition of the *Adagia*, partially though ironically to salvage the reputation of the two-a-penny compilers he has just attacked and who are set in opposition to the philologist readers whom he addresses; the bibliophile Conrad Gesner marks its ubiquity in his 1545 *Biblotheca universalis* by adding an 'etcetera' to his paraphrase; and in his 1559 *Variae lectiones* Marc-Antoine Muret, at one time a tutor at Bordeaux's Collège de Guyenne, asserts that Pliny's omnivorous approach to reading should apply also, and especially, to manuscripts.[2]

The superciliousness of Montaigne's *escoliers*, who resolutely fail to practise this generosity when it comes to the *Natural History*, mimics contemporary questioning of Pliny's authority. This was intensified from the mid-century onwards by the growing body of medical and natural-historical literature, in both Latin and the vernacular, in which the discoveries of practitioners of learned empiricism queried the ancient and modern hierarchy.[3] But the critique of Pliny, along with the defensive position that Montaigne takes, has longer-standing precedents. Montaigne upbraids his contemporaries for their poor reading of an ancient whose work should be celebrated not for its provision of facts, accurate or otherwise, but for the less quantifiable practice of judgement. In so doing, he is in implicit conversation with an earlier generation of humanists, whose convictions of Pliny's book as good or bad — insofar as it is textually corrupt and/or factually reliable — prompted a series of published quarrels in the late quattrocento.[4] In these polemical disputes over Pliny's errors, the most prominent defender of the Roman author was the prodigious and exuberant Florentine poet, *grammaticus*, legal commentator, and renowned letter-writer Angelo Poliziano. Tutor to Lorenzo de' Medici's children before he was appointed in 1480 to a chair in poetry and rhetoric at the University of Florence, Poliziano was a vocal proponent of the encyclopaedic model of learning, which enabled eclectic imitation; he was another promoter of Pliny's generous attitude to reading and a stubborn thorn in the side of his philosopher contemporaries.[5] It was Poliziano's radical approach to ancient texts, influenced by a classical model, Aulus Gellius, who was himself influenced by Pliny the Elder, that would see the traditional pedagogical commentary replaced by a scholarly genre which allowed more space for idiosyncrasy and which Montaigne would go on to make his own: the miscellany.[6]

The influence of Poliziano's brand of humanism on the first generation of French humanists was considerable.[7] If, as Franco Simone suggests, these early humanists 'durent connaître le *Panepistemon* (1492)' (ibid.), Poliziano's introductory lecture to his course on Aristotle's *Ethics*, his reach went beyond — and is both less concrete and less measurable than — the availability of particular works. Nor was it limited to the first half of the sixteenth century. Anthony Grafton argues for longevity as well as breadth, observing that Poliziano is the earliest humanist whose prose style and philological skill are 'still taken seriously'[8] at the end of the sixteenth century: his epistolary exuberance earned him praise from as prominent a figure — and admiring a correspondent of Montaigne — as Justus Lipsius, while the younger Scaliger would later report his father's esteem for the Florentine.

Tell-tale markers on the title-pages suggest that Montaigne inherited from La Boëtie the mid-century reprints of the 1528 Gryphius edition of Poliziano's complete works that carry Montaigne's signature.[9] How much Montaigne (or La Boëtie) read of these, though, or how closely, we don't know. The copies, now held in Bordeaux, give us no hints. The *Essais* themselves make no direct reference to Poliziano and offer next to nothing in the way of watertight proof of borrowings since the transmission of any suggestively shared arcana or examples is almost impossibly muddled by the ubiquity of intermediary compendia and florilegia. Perhaps Montaigne simply wasn't much taken with Poliziano? This is what Villey concludes in his classic study, where generic resemblances between the *Miscellanea* and the *Essais* are proposed, only to be discounted for the most part: Montaigne surely 'avait peu de chose à prendre' in what Villey characterizes as 'surtout des éclaircissements grammaticaux'.[10]

Villey's description plays down the brio and polemic of the *Miscellanea*, charismatic traits most notable in the provocative preface — which Martin McLaughlin describes as Poliziano's literary manifesto — but also regularly woven in to the individual chapters.[11] This said, it is certainly credible that the painstaking erudition proudly displayed in Poliziano's ingenious philological excursions might have fallen foul of Montaigne's proclaimed anti-intellectualism, and they hardly fit with his stated preference for 'des livres ou plaisans et faciles, qui me chatouillent, ou ceux qui me consolent et conseillent à régler ma vie et ma mort' [pleasant and easy books, which entertain me, or those that console me and counsel me to regulate my life and my death] (I.39, 'De la solitude' [Of Solitude]; V, p. 246; F, p. 220). The optimism of the programmatic, polymathic summary of knowledge presented in the *Panepistemon* may appear naïve, hubristic, in the wholly different cultural, philosophical, and political context of late sixteenth-century France. And if the Frenchman might have commended the audacity of Poliziano's *praelectio* to his course on Aristotle's *Prior Analytics*, the *Lamia*, in which he attacked the rigid disciplinary and institutional expectations which held that a chair of poetry and rhetoric should stay well away from philosophy, Montaigne's dislike of the 'subtilitez espineuses de la Dialectique' [those thorny subtleties of dialectics] (I.26, 'De l'institution des enfans' [On Educating Children]; V, p. 163; F, p. 146) and his mockery of the procedure that lay at the heart of the text on which Poliziano was claiming the right to work — the syllogism — might seem to augur differences more than sympathies.[12] If so, this could put Poliziano among the 'livres morts' that Villey suggests may make up a substantial part of Montaigne's library, books possessed yet rarely, or even never, consulted, let alone actively or visibly used; and it might then go some way to explaining the minimal interest shown by Montaigne scholarship in the Florentine, symbolized by the lack of an entry for Poliziano, or even for philology, in such benchmark reference tools as the *Dictionnaire de Montaigne*.[13] Or is the lack of attention paid to Montaigne's relationship to the Italian humanist a case of a tendency bemoaned (albeit also demonstrated) by Villey as far back as his 1908 study and yet — owing in part to the tools of digitization and searchable databases, which bring dangers as well as triumphs — alive and very well today? Namely that, spoilt by the legion proofs we *do* have of Montaigne's reading and writing, we too happily overlook potential intertexts which in the case of any other author would take pride of place in a study of sources.[14]

If Villey concluded that Montaigne would find Poliziano's philological purpose off-putting, proposing the *Miscellanea* as a generic model for the *Essais* is not uncommon in more recent scholarship. Richard Cooper does so, for example, in his account of the Italian share of Montaigne's library, while John O'Brien has drawn our attentions to Poliziano's role in the culture of commonplacing out of and against which Montaigne works.[15] Suggestive links have also been made, if largely in passing, in Perrine Galand-Hallyn's treatment of Poliziano's pupil and fellow miscellany writer Pietro Crinito, and, more implicitly still, in Pierre Laurens's revealing, though uncommented, choice to translate extracts from Poliziano's preface to his *Miscellanea* with terms taken directly from Montaigne.[16]

The beguiling question that hangs over these momentary meetings of the philologist and the essayist — can we prove that Montaigne read Poliziano? — is in the end less productive than the question of how far such encounters might throw into relief our understanding of the cultural-historical particularity of the *Essais* and hence help counter stubborn tendencies that can lead us, in part due to Montaigne's own transitions between open and hidden, deliberate or osmotic borrowing, to prefer certain intertexts over others. In this sense, I am working in the tradition of those scholars who have looked to trace the processes (rather than the objects alone) of imitation, transfer, and influence, explicit and implicit, in a bid to reconstruct, as far as possible, the *outillage mental* of the period. To do so is to build a more detailed picture of what, to borrow Gisèle Mathieu-Castellani's terms, we might call the 'polygenesis' and the 'autogenesis' of the *Essais*, always with a view to both the benefits and the methodological challenges that analysis of a commonplacing culture holds as a historical exercise.[17] More specifically, my approach is informed by the resistance to linear or proof-hunting models of source and reception that is voiced in Ian Maclean's study of Montaigne's 'Des vaines subtilitez' (I.54 [Of Vain Subtleties]) and Girolamo Cardano, and, under a different complexion, in John O'Brien's idea (which, as O'Brien points out, complements André Tournon's concept of 'la lecture à distance d'examen') of 'la lecture à proximité', or 'à contiguïté'. This is a conception of reading that allows texts 'an imaginative empathy with each other, to take liberties with each other, swap characteristics, spill over, intrude, comment on each other'.[18]

My business here is not, then, to offer up proofs of movement between texts; and I take as a premise not as an endpoint the likelihood that Montaigne had read at least parts of the complete works of Poliziano. Rather, in what follows I seek to revive

Thomas Greene's statement that 'the unconfessed genealogical line may prove to be as nourishing as the visible',[19] a suggestion that, three decades later, takes on a new, and perhaps more urgent, resonance in a scholarly world where the digitally searchable and quantifiable hold increasing sway. As readers and as fund-seeking researchers, we are coaxed to leave behind the less manageable realms of the re-said, half-said, or unsaid; characteristics, as we shall see, of the kinds of writing favoured by both Poliziano and Montaigne, and which demand of us the kinds of slow reading and resistance to the 'fuite hors du texte' and the 'pulsion d'accumulation des références' that, Frédéric Tinguely has recently argued with great conviction, risk sacrificing the singularity of works in the name of contextualization, categorization, or theorization. His promotion of 'slow reading', Tinguely explains, is by no means a return to the self-sufficient textuality of structuralism, nor yet is it to dismiss the fundamental importance of historical and cultural context. It is a call to resist the temptation to rank attention 'à la lettre', which offers a privileged means of understanding works in their particularity, lower than other approaches.[20] I also sidestep a temptation of a different kind: the choice to focus, for enticing generic reasons, on the *Miscellanea centuria prima* (1489) to the neglect of other of Poliziano's writings.[21] This is natural given clear parallels in the terms the two use to describe their writing. When Poliziano says, for example, that he won't take umbrage if the *Miscellanea* is considered as 'a kind of disordered, confused and muddled heap', since it was written not 'in continuous style' but 'in leaps and bounds', his terminology inescapably brings to mind Montaigne's reference to his admiration for a style that operates 'à sauts et à gambades' [by leaps and gambols] (III.9, 'De la vanité [On Vanity]; V, p. 994; F, p. 925), or else his mode of reading 'sans ordre et sans dessein, à pièces décousues' [without order and without plan, by disconnected fragments] (III.3, 'De trois commerces' [Of Three Kinds of Associations]; V, p. 828; F, p. 762), or his open disregard for order (II.12, 'Apologie de Raymond Sebond'; V, p. 465; F, p. 414).[22] Yet Montaigne's curiosity as a reader, coupled with the layout in each of the three volumes of Gryphius's edition of the Florentine's collected works, makes it hard to believe that he wouldn't have looked beyond the *Miscellanea*. Moreover, if we move out from the specifics of Montaigne's late-Renaissance library, and consider the earliest phases of French humanism, we find evidence of clear conventions for reading, but also for collating, Poliziano's works, which might well have influenced their consequent reception.

The appeal and the complicity of three texts that vividly express the Florentine's charismatic form of humanism — the *Miscellanea centuria prima*, the *Lamia: praelectio in priora Aristotelis Analytica* (1492), and the *Panepistemon* (1492) — were recognized in 1511 by the Parisian publisher Josse Bade, who anticipated his 1512 and 1519 editions of Poliziano's collected works with an anthology that grouped these together, alongside epistles and commentaries by other Italian humanists.[23] For the purposes of this essay, and to make a pragmatic choice among Poliziano's prolific output, I therefore take Bade's grouping as a ready-made corpus, complementing this triptych with a fourth, earlier text: his 1480 inaugural lecture, the *Oratio super Fabio Quintiliano, et Statii Sylvis* [Oration on Quintilian and the 'Silvae' of Statius]. My aim is to show that Montaigne's explicit sympathy for Pliny, voiced in I.27, is the most visible of a number of resonances that invite us to bring into contact the professional humanist and the amateur essayist, living and writing a century apart, in vastly different institutional, cultural, and professional contexts; shared interests which suggest that the pursuits and allegiances of Poliziano's singular practice of philology are more actively in dialogue with the forms of self-expression, creative imitation, and generic and disciplinary idiosyncrasy for which the *Essais* are famed than either Montaigne, or his modern readers, conventionally allow.

★   ★   ★   ★   ★

The reader who comes to Poliziano with knowledge of the *Essais* will find it hard not to write in the margin, in defiance of the coincidences bred by commonplace culture, 'Montaigne!' The most obvious point of comparison is their stance on that central concern of humanism (and of Montaigne scholarship), imitation, and in particular the touchstone of imitation that is Ciceronianism. Both the Italian and the Frenchman make extensive use of Cicero in their works and at times rehearse conventional praise for him: Poliziano refers to 'the sacred glory of Cicero', while Montaigne observes that his eloquence 'est du tout hors de comparaison', concluding that 'jamais homme ne l'egalera'.[24] This hyperbole, however, is countered by a declared antipathy for the kind of obsessive imitation of a single author epitomized by the Ciceronians whom Erasmus, himself influenced by Poliziano, mocked so viciously in his 1528 *Ciceronianus*.[25]

In around 1485, Poliziano notoriously replied to Paolo Cortesi's gift of a set of letters in the Ciceronian style with a bluffly dismissive treatment of those who refused to sign up to his commitment to eclectic imitation.[26] He had, though, made his anti-Ciceronianism public before this famous, much-quoted letter: his decision, in 1480, to teach rhetoric through lectures on Quintilian and Statius rather than on Cicero was controversial enough for him to include an anticipatory defence in his *praelectio*. Here he argues the case for lecturing on these two authors from the purportedly corrupted Silver Age by suggesting that they provide perfect material for boys to practise on before they move on (or back) to the complexities of Cicero: 'What prevents us from not immediately offering to the young the highest of authors but those (so to speak) of lower, and, as it were, second rank whom they should learn, with the intention of making it easier for them to imitate the greatest writers?' (*Oratio super Fabio Quintiliano*, p. 870). Poliziano nods, in this rhetorical question, to standard hierarchies of author, but the broader argument operates, as Peter Godman observes, through 'careful ambiguity'.[27] The *praelectio* is filled with stylistic features that nudge the reader to look more closely: in the quotation just given, a parenthesis and a concession, but also affirmation through denial, double negations, and circumlocutions. With the result that the apparent defence starts to look like an argument of convenience, a sop to any hastier readers scandalized by the boldness of his challenge to the hierarchy of ancient texts, an interpretation encouraged by the surfeit of familiar metaphors that follows and that protests just a little too much: young vines start out with only low props; novice riders avoid frisky horses; landlubbers train in ports on quiet seas before venturing in to their first sea battle.[28] A century later, Montaigne makes clear on the one hand how scornful he is of those who abuse the practices of imitation in laboriously aping Cicero's characteristics and, on the other, that Cicero's status as an ancient does not make him immune to criticism. On the contrary, the *Essais* repeatedly attack the Roman orator's style and person: in I.40 ('Consideration sur Ciceron'), Cicero is convicted of wrongly prizing eloquence over action, losing out to Seneca because the latter provides models for moral as well as verbal conduct, while in II.10 Montaigne dismisses him as the stuff of school syllabi.[29] More significantly, both authors make links between their stance on this long-running imitation debate and their view of writing as having the capacity — where not the duty — to communicate the particularity of a writing self. Poliziano's mercilessly anti-Ciceronian letter famously includes a Horatian-style imagined dialogue of the kind Montaigne deploys intermittently in the *Essais*: a conversation between him and a nameless interlocutor.[30] In its rejection of the conventions of imitation, this provides material for Erasmus in his *Ciceronianus*, as McLaughlin has suggested.[31] But it also seems neatly to foreshadow certain of Montaigne's most memorable declarations on imitation: 'Non exprimis, inquit aliquis, Ciceronem. Quid tum? Non enim sum Cicero! Me tamen (ut opinor) exprimo' ['You do not write like Cicero', someone says. So what? I am not Cicero. Yet I do express myself, I think].[32] Even with our ears attuned to teleology, there is a compelling resemblance between the sentiments here and Montaigne's declaration in his final chapter that 'J'aymerois mieux m'entendre bien en moy qu'en Ciceron' [I would rather be an authority on myself than on Cicero] (III.13, V, p. 1073; F, p. 1001), all the more since Cicero is a 1595 addition, replacing the 'Platon' of the 1588 version. The convergence moves beyond shared sentiment into style in another C-layer addition, a celebrated declaration by Montaigne, which was added to his famous chapter on pedagogy: 'Je ne dis les autres, sinon pour d'autant plus me dire' [I do not speak the minds of others except to speak my own mind better] (V, p. 148; F, p. 131; I.26, 'De l'institution des enfans' [On Educating Children]). As Terence Cave notes, this quotation silently refers to, rephrases, and recontextualizes Seneca in his *Letters to Lucilius* (1. 16. vii).[33] But Montaigne's statement, in keeping with his commitment to eclectic imitation, doesn't only rework Seneca; in the way it gains much of its clout through its concessive structure it also seems to echo Poliziano's simultaneously concessive and assertive parenthesis. In both examples, the particularity of the self is called on as an explanation for the writers' irreverent attitudes to the role of quotation in composition, and the intricacies of their respective citation practices deserve comparative study. What concerns me here, though, is the way both writers also use their singularity to justify their overturning of convention when it comes to subject matter and their departure from existing genres.

In his *Oration on Quintilian and the 'Silvae' of Statius*, Poliziano boasts about the unprecedented character of his decision to teach the little-known author Statius in place of Cicero, silently appropriating the very author whose authority his text is challenging in order to make his argument: his claim that 'novas tamen quasique intactas vias ingrediamur, veteres tritasque relinquamus' [we are trying new and virtually untrodden paths, leaving behind the old and already well-worn ones] (*Oratio super Fabio Quintiliano*, p. 870) ironically uses terms that strongly recall without directly quoting a famous statement in Cicero's *Orator*, so that the imitative act, to use Greene's typology, moves well beyond respectful citation into something closer to parody.[34] A similar claim is made in the preface to the *Panepistemon*, which Poliziano heralds as surpassing standard summaries of knowledge in casting its net wider than philosophy to include liberal and mechanic arts as well as 'vile arts and artisanal trades'.[35] Here, though, the image of newly forged paths comes cheek by jowl with a distinctly more personal statement. Poliziano asserts the bold originality of his work by pointing to its difficulty and its lack of precedents. His willingness to take on this seemingly rebarbative task is then explained by his revulsion for the familiar and quotidian, his apparent failure to pick up the knack of following the example of others, and — in a statement that is as striking for its defiance as it is for its staccato simplicity — by his nature. He tackles what others won't, he tells us, because that is just the kind of man he is; such undertakings may or may not succeed, but to be willing to have a go is in itself laudable:

> Nec autem me fallit quam sit operis ardui, quam nec ab ullo temptatum hactenus, quam denique obtrectatoribus opportunum quod polliceor. *Sed ita homo sum.* Sordent usitata ista et exculcata nimis, nec alienis demum vestigiis insistere didici, quoniam in magnis etiam voluntas ipsa laude sua non caret, et vilissimos hominum Plato existimat imitatores, meritoque ob id a vate Horatio servum pecus appellati sunt.

> [And it hasn't slipped my attention that this is an arduous task, which has been tried by nobody before now, nor that what I promise is favourable to my detractors. *But that is the kind of man I am.* What is too commonplace and well-trodden disgusts me. I have never learned to follow in the footsteps of others, since when it comes to great undertakings, the will itself is not devoid of merit, and Plato reckons imitators to be the most base of men while they are rightly called by the poet Horace a servile herd.][36]

The explicit, authorizing references to Plato and Horace brought in as backup at the close of this statement are far from the only references at play.[37] To talk of well-trodden paths and following (or avoiding) predecessors' footsteps is to write yourself into classical tradition: Cicero, for sure, but also Seneca's *Letters to Lucilius*, and Quintilian, who remarks in his *Orator's Education* that he has sought 'to avoid going along the beaten track and finding myself merely treading in other's footsteps'.[38] However, the *Panepistemon*'s concern with an exhaustive presentation of knowledge recalls yet another work, generically distinct from these predominantly rhetorical or epistolary models: that stalwart of Renaissance commentaries from the earliest days of humanism, the *Natural History*.

In Pliny's prefatory letter, the image of the untrodden path is used to press home the work's ambitious scope and its lack of precedents.[39] A little further on, though, after a passage in which he boasts of the vast and varied reading necessary to produce the '20,000 noteworthy facts' that his history offers, Pliny excuses what he pitches as inevitable lacunae. His defence is rooted not in failed method or faulty sources, which would become standard scapegoats for the apologies (and invectives) of humanist prefaces, nor else in arguments about the obsolescence of knowledge over time, which Pliny will enlist elsewhere. The justification — which hinges on the bald statement 'homines enim sumus' — is that he is human, a man busy with duties. It is only therefore in the small hours that he has found the time to write, so that the work is set up as part of the genre of *lucubrationes* (night-work), writing carried out away from the pull of *negotium* and which turns profit from leisure: 'Nec dubitamus multa esse quae et nos praeterierint; homines enim sumus et occupati officiis, subsicivisque temporibus ista curamus, id est nocturnis, ne quis vestrum putet his cessatum horis' [Nor do we doubt that there are many things which have escaped us: for we are but human and busy with public duties, and we pursue this in our spare moments, namely at night, lest any of you think the night hours have been given to idleness] (*Natural History*, p. 13).

Pliny's defence of his original undertaking is rooted in the particularity of his circumstances yet operates on a universal level when he appeals to the reader through their shared humanity, presented in the most basic statement of general truth. Through its use of the deictic determiner 'ita' ('so, such, of this nature, of this kind'), by contrast, Poliziano's sentence 'sed ita homo sum', which acts as explanation for his rejection of convention and as a springboard to further definition of his nature, occupies a mid-ground between singularity and types; it relies on a certain recognition by the reader of what the 'ita' is pointing us to — which places the reader alongside Poliziano, with a shared viewpoint — and/or of a *type* of man with which the reader is familiar and into which category Poliziano fits, which therefore assumes a reader with a shared frame of reference. Montaigne's version of Poliziano's 'ita homo sum' statement, found in II.17 ('De la praesumption' [Of Presumption]), imagines, on the other hand, a reader whose viewpoint differs from the author's. But this anonymous reader's potential criticisms of Montaigne and objections to his project, presented via faceless 'on' pronouns (rendered more personal in the Frame translation), are answered by a sentence in which the vernacular version of 'ita', 'tel', is surrounded by verbs that place the emphasis on the author rather than the reader; the reader who might think up criticisms to Montaigne's detriment is effectively silenced by a sentence whose reflexive verbs claim interpretive authority and so muffle the impact of any negative readings:

> Par ces trains de ma confession, on en peut imaginer d'autres à mes despens. Mais, quel que je me face connoistre, pourveu que je me face connoistre tel que je suis, je fay mon effect. Et si ne m'excuse pas d'oser mettre par escrit des propos si bas et frivoles que ceux-cy. La bassesse du sujet m'y contrainct. [C] Qu'on accuse, si on veut, mon project; mais mon progrez, non.

> [From these lines of my confession you can imagine others at my expense. But whatever I make myself known to be, provided I make myself known such as I am, I am carrying out my plan. And so I make no excuse for daring to put into writing such mean and trivial remarks as these. The meanness of my subject forces me to do so. Blame my project if you will, but not my procedure.] (V, p. 653; F, p. 602)

The *Essais* are of course repeatedly presented as an undertaking without precedent, as possessing an originality which is guaranteed by the singularity of their subject, Montaigne himself, and the image of the pathway plays a role in this. In II.6, 'De l'exercitation' [Of Practice], near the start of a C-layer addition that extends to the end of the chapter, and a few lines down from a re-contextualized paraphrase from the *Natural History* which casts Pliny as a proponent of self-study, the image features in close proximity to a claim that the 'extraordinaire' pursuit of the *Essais* has drawn Montaigne away from the 'occupations communes du monde', from *negotium* (V, p. 377; F, p. 331). The uncommon nature of his project does not mean, however, that his route is entirely without precedent: a good humanist, Montaigne concedes that he and his generation *have* had word of one or two ancients who wrote about themselves. These are, feasibly, the three authors mentioned at the start of II.17 — Lucilius, Rutilius, and Scaurus (V, p. 632; F, p. 582). Yet only the names and not the works have survived and Montaigne chooses to withhold even these, the anonymity serving the broader purpose of the passage. It moves through clauses whose restrictive and negative structures chip away at his period's fragmentary knowledge of the classical past and salvage singularity by negating the possibility of comparison, before ending with Montaigne's confident announcement that the more immediate past, the centuries between these enigmatic writers and his own, have seen nobody at all attempting to follow the vestiges of their early efforts: 'Nous n'avons nouvelles que de deux ou trois anciens qui ayent battu ce chemin; et si ne pouvons dire si c'est du tout en pareille maniere à cette-cy, n'en connoissant que les noms. Nul depuis ne s'est jetté sur leur trace' [We have heard of only two of three ancients who opened up this road, and even of them we cannot say whether their manner in the least resembled mine, since we know only their names. No one since has followed their lead] (V, p. 378; F, p. 331).

Donald Frame's translation of this sentence gives 'mine' for 'cette-cy'. To insert a first-person singular possessive pronoun, however, is to overlook the seemingly studied insistence of the 'nous' and the conspicuous absence of the 'je'. This continues as Montaigne turns from the opacity of the more distant cultures of the past, of external knowledge, to the obscurity of the internal, describing how demanding enquiry into the mind is, this 'espineuse entreprise' which looks to 'penetrer les profondeurs opaques de ses replis internes'.[40] It consequently sets up a strong contrast with what follows: that well-known, intensely self-reflexive passage, which, in a move from collective and universal claims to individual experience, claims that for several years now Montaigne has focused entirely on himself and has annexed externals — 'autre chose' — to the aim of exploring interior knowledge, the interiority emphasized by his amending the preposition 'sur' to 'en'.[41]

The claims for originality made by Pliny, Poliziano, and Montaigne would seem, then, in their move from general truths to recognized types to the hidden space 'en moy', to fit with the familiar narrative of an increasing interiorization of identity which is essential to accounts of the formation of modern conceptions of the self favoured by some histories of ideas.[42] In such narratives, the *Essais* are frequently attributed with the role of threshold between the pre-modern and the modern and are seen, in their renegotiation of the practices of humanist culture and the use they make of scepticism, to point forward. Gisèle Mathieu-Castellani has shown, however, that Montaigne's declaration of his interest in the 'replis internes' of his mind (II.6) and his commitment to making himself known 'tel que je suys' (II.17), are among a series of statements that bear really very strong resemblance to passages in a work which upsets Montaigne's claim that 'nul ne s'est jetté depuis' and which is a touchstone for the methods that Montaigne scholars use to move between the

Essais and their intertexts: St Augustine's *Confessions*, in which the Church Father speaks, for example, of a 'knot of difficulties, so labyrinthine and so complicated' (II. X. 18) and states his desire to portray himself 'not as I was but such as I am' (X. IV. 6).[43] Mathieu-Castellani's avowedly speculative but wholly convincing findings challenge a shibboleth of Montaigne scholarship, which dates back to Villey: the 'commonly held conviction', to quote Wes Williams, that Montaigne can't have read the work, an assumption driven by the absence in the *Essais* of explicit reference to the *Confessions* and, Williams suggests, by scholars' 'over-literal reading' of an apparent lacuna in Montaigne's knowledge about St Augustine, namely the fact that he had a son.[44]

In convicting Montaigne of ignorance of Augustine through this supposed factual lapse, scholars risk recalling the *savants* from whom Montaigne distances himself in II.17, those who, he claims, 'ne connoissent autre prix que de la doctrine, et n'advouent autre proceder en noz esprits que celuy de l'erudition et de l'art: si vous avez pris l'un des Scipions pour l'autre, que vous reste il à dire qui vaille?' [admit no other procedure for our minds than that of erudition and art. If you have mistaken one of the Scipios for the other, what is there left for you to say that can be worth while?] (V, p. 657; F, p. 605). At the same time, are we not taking Montaigne too easily at his word if we read his rejection of those models of confession that are, he claims, concerned with opinion rather than with morals as an indication of a broader dismissal of Augustine?[45] All the more since the generically explicit mode of confession in the *Confessions* isn't the only paradigm of confession that the Church Father demonstrates in a varied corpus which was widely available thanks to three editions of his complete works, as well as publications of individual works (including a 1515 edition of the letters by Bade), Augustinian anthologies, epitomes, and florilegia, and inclusion of excerpts in compilations, such as Vincent de Beauvais's *Miroir hystorial*, which we know Montaigne owned.[46] Nor is Augustine, and the theological, by any means the only paradigm of avowal and self-exposure available to Montaigne. Pliny consistently confesses to his reader the fallibility of his knowledge in his *Natural History*, with an insistence that reaches beyond modesty tropes. There is playful precedent in classical poetry: following his reference to the 'trains de ma confession' in II.17 (V, p. 653; F, p. 602), for example, the essayist points us, through direct quotation, to the intimate style of Martial's epigrams, works in which the Roman poet confesses his own inconsequentiality and with which the *Essais* share self-deprecating moves. And Montaigne would of course be familiar with legal examples and procedures of confession in court both through classical works, including Cicero's accounts of legal cases, and through his training and subsequent work in the law.[47] Yet another paradigm for the admission of error, however, is found in a contemporary genre to which the *Essais* are related even as they are (and explicitly seek to be) distinct: the meeting of the activities of reader and writer that is the philological commentary, a form of writing which, as Jean Céard demonstrated some time ago, is far less impersonal than our view of commentaries — overly influenced by nineteenth-century conceptions of philology, as Jean-Marc Mandosio has argued — can lead us to conclude.[48]

This is certainly the case in the preface to Poliziano's *Miscellanea*. Here we find an energetic tirade against exegetes of bad faith, whom he convicts of 'crimes against letters', of 'contaminating, forging, soiling, encrusting, distorting, mixing up, damaging, and turning upside down the meaning of everything, without any sense of responsibility, with no shame, with no judgement', casting himself, by contrast, as a free and committed exposer of the truth in an annexing of authority whose confidence — and whose apparent conception of the singularity of the truth — would seem to contrast with the insistence on subjectivity that characterizes the *Essais*.[49] This attack on dishonest interpreters is followed, though, by a passage in which Poliziano, prompted by an imagined interlocutor, qualifies his claim to authority. The verb 'fateor', a synonym of 'confiteor', introduces an admission that, being human, he is of course far from infallible, but his fallibility is then partially compensated for by his introduction of the idea of sincere error: 'Dicat his aliquis: Quid tu autem: Fateor equidem, possum falli, ut humanus, sed neminem profecto sciens fallo, et ut mendacium fortasse dico, sic certe non mentior' [Someone may well say: And are you immune from all this? And I admit: I can make mistakes, human as I am, but I don't knowingly mislead anyone, and even if I do say something mistaken, it's because I believe it to be true not because I'm lying].[50] From this reflection on unintended error Poliziano next turns to the idea of self-knowledge, voicing a comment by 'Mevius', a type featured in Gaius's *Institutes of Roman Law*, where he is named in examples of cases of mistaken identity, and whom Poliziano could have encountered in his work on the *Pandects*. Under the variant 'Maenius' he is also a stock character with roles in Lucilius, Juvenal, Martial, and Horace; in the last's *Satires* (I.3), his slander of one Novius behind his back leads someone to ask him, 'Do you not understand yourself [ignoras], or do you think you can deceive us as though we don't know you [ignotum]?'[51] To this he replies, 'I *am* understanding to myself' [mihi ignosco], a quip that Poliziano borrows directly: 'Tum egomet mi ignosco: Mevius inquit, imo autem (extra iocum) nec egomet mi ignosco, et sui quid indoctius incautiusque protulero, refutari a quovis cupio, refutaturus ipse me, si fuero admonitus' [So I'm understanding to myself, says Mevius. No, on the contrary (joking aside) it's not entirely true that I'm understanding to myself, and, if I've produced something that isn't cultivated or careful enough, I wish that to be rejected by anyone, I myself will reject it, if I have heard about it].[52] Mevius's purpose here is to allow Poliziano to show his willingness to confess his errors, to admit when his judgement has faltered, whether such instances of error are pointed out by others or spotted by him subsequently. This commitment to self-correction is then served up as proof of Poliziano's refusal to deceive others and of his disavowal of self-love. These traits enable him to claim membership of a group who use writing less as a means of self-promotion or glory-hunting than — through the repeated verb 'profiteor', which carries the sense of advancing, accomplishing, but also being of service, or contributing — as a means of making progress in the field of letters which he is defending so vehemently: 'Non enim sic me perverse amo, ut errare alios malim, quam innotescere quod errem. Sed ex eorum sum numero et ipse, qui proficiendo scribunt, et scribendo proficiunt' [So I don't love myself so perversely as to prefer to deceive my fellow man or to not make it known that I have erred. I am therefore among those who write making progress and who make progress writing].[53]

For the reader of Montaigne, the terms Poliziano uses bring to mind on a broad level the essayist's commitment to self-exposure and his openness to his own fallibility; and, on the level of individual utterances, his insistence in his pedagogical chapter, I.26, that the schoolboy must show sufficient judgement and sincerity to admit any errors that he discovers for himself,[54] the idea, in II.17 and II.37 ('De la ressemblance des enfans aux peres' [Of the Resemblance of Children to their Fathers]) of his writing as a record of his progress,[55] or his admission in I.10 ('Du parler prompt ou tardif' [Of Prompt or Slow Speech]) that in his writing he has been known to lose the train of what he is trying to say to such a degree that somebody else discovers it before he does.[56] This confessional mode, however, comes hand in hand for both writers with a preference for a mode of imitation that fits firmly with what Mathieu-Castellani describes as the Renaissance penchant for mixing the 'marqué' with the 'masqué'.[57] Poliziano might talk insistently in his preface of openness and sincerity and lay the emphasis, repeatedly, on the first person as guarantor of what he is saying. The interlocutor Mevius's words are not, though, the only words that he borrows from elsewhere. In this climate of confession, what Poliziano does not declare is that both of the sentences quoted above are virtual calques from St Augustine's *Letters*, letter 143:

> Ego proinde fateor me ex eorum numero esse conari: qui proficiendo scribunt: et scribendo proficiunt.[58]

> [I therefore admit that I try to be among that number who write while progressing and progress while writing.][59]

> Nam nimis perverse seipsum amat: qui et alios vult errare, ut error suus lateat.

> [For a man loves himself far too perversely if he wants others to err so that his error may remain hidden.] (Ibid.)

Fervent enemy of slavish imitation, Poliziano doesn't make these borrowings without some small but significant changes, alterations that seem to be more than the accidents of half-remembered quotation. The order in which the sentences appear is inverted and the two statements made consecutive, suppressing an involved reflection by Augustine on how and by whom errors in his writing are recognized, the sentiments of which Poliziano condenses into the earlier sentence that followed the Mevius reference.[60] The third-person 'amat' is made more personal with 'amo' and Poliziano dispenses with the slight caution contained in Augustine's 'conari', so that he positively includes himself rather than *hoping* to be included among those for whom writing and making progress are mutually dependent and productive. Such active yet undeclared borrowing and adaptation conforms neatly to the model of good imitation that Montaigne offers in C-layer additions to III.12, 'De la phisionimie' [Of Physiognomy]; it meets his preference for 'l'honneur de l'invention' over the parading of flagged quotations that constitutes 'l'honneur de l'allegation' and fulfils his ideal of putting borrowings to new use and giving them a particular and personal stamp, as opposed to concocting what he scornfully describes, in an echo of Poliziano's consistent critique of poor imitators, as 'pastissages de lieux communs' [concoctions of commonplaces].[61]

Confounding our thirst as researchers for neatly visible narratives of influence,

Augustine's pithy statements do not make their way into further service in the *Essais* in any irrefutably recognizable form. Ideas contained in that same letter, however, whether read directly by Montaigne or filtered through Poliziano, may, I suggest, add a different hue to some of what we have come to see as peculiarly Montaignian interests, characteristic of Montaigne's response to the late Renaissance *crise de l'humanisme*: Augustine challenges the hierarchy of author and reader, for example, separating authorial intention and reader interpretation, and defends his position with the bald justification that it is *his* viewpoint; he shows an interest in the inconsistencies of an individual's readings; and he reveals both concern with and a certain insouciance over misreadings by others of his authentic self.

There is not space here to explore these possible resonances in detail. Even if there were, we must concede, as with all work on the 'polygenesis' of the *Essais*, that the nature of Renaissance imitation culture — the processes of disguise and deformation that both Poliziano and Montaigne promote and embrace — will always (indeed, must always) keep us in the realm of speculation rather than proof, even where the findings of research into dissemination and book ownership take us closer to reconstructing a particular reader's environment. This is in part the result of our distance from our objects of study: however much, however widely, and however hard we read, we cannot read ourselves into the head of a Renaissance reader, even were this desirable. But nor should we blanch the variety of Renaissance readers or else overplay the idea that Poliziano and Montaigne's peers wished, were able, or were meant to spot every one of their references, borrowings, or allusions. As Shane Butler has observed, some of Poliziano's prose is so dense with allusion as to amount to an erudite game that the author must surely be playing partly for his own satisfaction and in which, moreover, authorial intention vies with unknowable processes of memory, recollection, and association.[62] As early as 1613, Jean-Pierre Camus is, in his *Diversitez*, both admiring of and frustrated by the *Essais'* layers of borrowing, bemoaning his generation's comparative poverty of references and regretting that his disciplinary affiliations prevent him from writing (and reading) as Montaigne does.[63] Would Montaigne and Poliziano judge Camus and us as harshly as we do ourselves when we lack the erudition or experience to identify a possible allusion? Are we to take Montaigne's threat to return from the grave to correct any errant readings as an expression of his commitment to the primacy of authorial intention?[64] Or should we give priority to those statements where he seems to evince a more liberal view of the interpretive activities of his readers? I want to conclude by suggesting that the ideal reader of the *Essais* — that *suffisant lecteur* who has been read as a symbol of the increasing autonomy of reader interpretation in the late Renaissance — looks backwards at the same time as looking forwards; that in their imagined readers both Poliziano and Montaigne balance exclusionary criteria with more generous conceptions of the work of reading that are rooted in a shared resistance to disciplinary compartmentalization and are informed, explicitly and implicitly, by a broad understanding of that central humanist activity, philology.

★   ★   ★   ★   ★

Poliziano and Montaigne describe very clearly those readers who firmly do not fit their ideal: pompous exegetes who seek out obscurities where there are none, or who fill their books with elaborate 'trifles' and indulgent neologisms;[65] impractical philosophers who don't know the way to the forum and whose purported wisdom is tripped up by common-sense serving-maids;[66] readers — fellow humanists included — who doggedly force interpretations onto texts driven by narrow disciplinary affiliation or, baser still, by motives of profit.[67] The readers whom they cultivate, by contrast, are those who are actively independent in their judgement: in his *Oration on Quintilian*, Poliziano urges his students 'not to be content only with what I put before you' (p. 881), while Montaigne borrows from Lucretius to encourage his readers to make discoveries for themselves; he will point the way and then let the material speak for itself, leaving such interpretive crutches as 'paroles de liaison et de cousture' to those writers happy to indulge more passive minds.[68]

Disdain for professional interpreters might seem misplaced given Poliziano's official role as professor of rhetoric and poetry and his fervent promotion of the value of philology; he does not possess the gentleman status that allows Montaigne to tread his nonchalant, idiosyncratic path, distancing himself from the 'babil' of those 'qui en font profession expresse'.[69] In the preface to his philological tour de force, however, Poliziano both works hard to position his interpretive explorations outside formal categories of writing and circumscribed public roles and rejects binary models of divisions between *otium* and *negotium* inherited from classical culture.[70] His philological work occupies both and neither category: he devotes himself to it, 'as though I were passing not from leisure to study but from study to leisure [...], without design, by chance, free from care, like taking a relaxed stroll along the beach, gathering seashells in the meantime';[71] and, like Montaigne, who, as Mawy Bouchard argues, views withdrawal from the world, literal or metaphorical, as an act contradicting *honnêteté* and smacking of the pedant, Poliziano projects for his writing a space *between* the public and the private.[72] What kind of reader will this work, situated in this in-between space, satisfy? Neither the 'coarse, foul-smelling people' who will be excited by Poliziano's occasional use of 'rough-hewn' words, nor those delicate readers who will at instances be dazzled by what the author describes as the mosaic-like characteristics of certain of the miscellany's chapters. Rather, Poliziano predicts that the *Miscellanea* 'will satisfy the middling sort among these, who aren't to be placed in either column'.[73]

Poliziano's division of readers into types and his reference to a middling reader resonates with a passage that closes the brief but complex chapter, I.54, 'Des vaines subtilitez', in which Montaigne speculates that the *Essais*, misunderstood by vulgar minds and over-interpreted by those rare, excellent *esprits*, might most aptly occupy a space 'en la moyenne région' (V, p. 313; F, p. 276). This vivid comment has drawn much attention: for Tournon, Montaigne's reader in the middle is another way of speaking to (or imagining at least) the select few who, rightly, lean on their own judgement rather than on received systems of thought;[74] Maclean, reminding us how frequently the *Essais* resist programmatic reading, shows the capriciousness of this middle region, which seems to invite the intimacy of identification but to prompt at the same time a negative and an indeterminate reading;[75] while Richard Scholar has suggested that Montaigne's call to the reader to 'come and join me in the middle region' is dampened by that region's being 'all but empty'.[76] Unlike Montaigne's chapter, Poliziano's consideration of readership does not stop short with this enigmatic middle region; instead, he goes on to explain *why* his work will appeal to this category of reader: namely, that 'there is no one thing in which it excels, and it partakes of everything' (*Miscellanea*, p. 214). The first clause here could be a standard humility topos but the statement of mediocrity is redeemed by the second, which casts his philological work as participatory, intensely sociable, willingly diverse. As such, it runs directly counter to the image of the philologist which Poliziano contests in his provocative *Lamia*, where he both bemoans that 'we have brought this name low by reducing it to a grammar-school game, enclosing it in a backroom workshop' and mourns the loss of the ideal of the encyclopaedic circle of learning, declaring that 'our age, knowing little about antiquity, has fenced the philologist in, within an exceedingly small circle'.[77]

Montaigne is well known for his studied rejection of the kind of 'fencing in' he associates with professional or disciplinary affiliation; he has a horror of being attached to 'un seul train', tells us loudly that he is not a *philosophe*, and mocks himself when he seems to be doing the etymological work redolent of a *grammaticus*.[78] What, then, should we make of the categorization of his *Essais* in the French section of Georg Draut's 1610 bibliographical compendium of vernacular publications, the *Bibliotheca exotica*, where they are listed under 'Libri philologici', alongside a motley collection of the paradoxical, philosophical, bibliographical, poetic, and the utopian, of *sommaires*, *specula*, and compendia?[79] On one level, it is hardly surprising that the generically amorphous *Essais* should be placed under 'philologici': where else could they go? All the more since the French catalogue offers no category of 'libri philosophici', which conventionally provided a handy portmanteau label for works otherwise resistant to generic classification.[80] The capaciousness of the category looks more significant, however, when we see that it is mirrored in the breadth of a definition of philology found at a mid-point between Poliziano and Montaigne, in the Swiss bibliophile Conrad Gesner's 1548 *Pandectae*.[81] Gesner's philology is a broad school: more than one kind of author works under its auspices and, if some of these operate methodically, tidying nomenclatures into neat categories and working according to the demands of particular disciplines, others are described with a far more capricious vocabulary: they toss together varied topics under a single cover, criteria of inclusion being neither order nor reason but the hazard of whatever comes to mind, the result being miscellaneous in form and various in subject matter.[82] Gesner's aspiring philologist, far from operating in the constraints of a narrow circle, is urged, in the same terms as the polymathic ideal poet of the Pléiade, to move freely like a honeybee, wandering this way and that through a varied corpus. And in contrast to the fields of law and theology, where philology has a fixed aim of contributing to the removal of doubt that is essential to the establishment of the certain knowledge of *scientia*,[83] the philologist is here characterized as being free and independent of purpose; if his wide reading is fundamental to any attempts to unearth the *sensus germanus* of ancient texts, he is at the same time given only the broad aim of *seeking* to 'procure knowledge [cognitio] and pleasure [voluptas]', not of 'meeting any precise purpose or use'.[84] He is free, we might say, along with Montaigne, Poliziano, and Pliny before them, to declare loudly that for their purpose as readers, writers, and independent interpreters, no book is too bad.

Notes to Chapter 3

1. V, p. 178; Montaigne, *Les Essais*, ed. Denis Bjaï, Bénédicte Boudou, Jean Céard, and Isabelle Pantin (Paris: Librairie générale française, 2001), pp. 274–75. Balsamo, 'Notes et variantes', in Montaigne, *Les Essais*, ed. Jean Balsamo, Michel Magnien, and Catherine Magnien-Simonin (Paris: Gallimard, 2007), p. 1408.

2. Erasmus, 'Érasme de Rotterdam à tous les philologues, salut', in *Les Adages*, ed. Jean-Christophe Saladin, vol. 1 (Paris: Les Belles Lettres, 2013), pp. 22–25 (p. 25); Conrad Gesner, *Bibliotheca universalis* (Zurich: Christoph Froschauer, 1545), fol. *3v. and p. 157; Marc-Antoine Muret, *Variae lectiones*, II.16, quoted in Jean-Eudes Girot, 'Muret ou l'otium du philologue', in *La Philologie humaniste et ses représentations dans la théorie et la fiction*, ed. Perrine Galand-Hallyn, Fernand Hallyn, and Gilbert Tournoy (Geneva: Droz, 2005), pp. 526–44 (p. 533). Ian Maclean notes the appearance of the commonplace in Cesare Baronio's *Annales ecclesiastici* (Venice: Apud Haeredem Hieronymi Scoti, 1600), where its status as a *sententia* is remarked upon ([fol. a6v.]); Maclean, *Scholarship, Commerce, Religion: The Learned Book in the Age of Confessions, 1560–1630* (Cambridge, MA: Harvard University Press, 2012), p. 52, n. 32. Ann Blair has considered the relationship between Pliny's saying and the encyclopaedia in its compiling sense; Blair, 'Revisiting Renaissance Encyclopaedism', in *Encyclopaedism from Antiquity to the Renaissance*, ed. Jason König and Greg Woolf (Cambridge: Cambridge University Press, 2013), pp. 379–97 (pp. 382–91).

3. On learned empiricism, see Gianna Pomata and Nancy Siraisi's Introduction to *Historia: Empiricism and Erudition in Early Modern Europe*, ed. Pomata and Siraisi (Cambridge, MA: MIT Press, 2005), pp. 1–38 (pp. 17–31).

4. For an account of the quarrels, see Brian Ogilvie, *The Science of Describing: Natural History in Renaissance Europe, 1490–1620* (Chicago: University of Chicago Press, 2006), pp. 30–34 and 121–33.

5. See, for example, his *Praefatio in Suetonii expositionem*, in *Angeli Politiani opera* (Basel: Apud Nicolaum Episcopium Juniorem, 1553), pp. 499–509 (p. 503): 'any kind of writing (as Pliny says) pleases: because men are by nature curious' (my translation).

6. On Poliziano and the commentary tradition, see Anthony Grafton, *Joseph Scaliger, A Study in the History of Classical Scholarship*, vol. 1: *Textual Criticism and Exegesis* (Oxford: Clarendon Press, 1983), pp. 9–44.

7. See Grafton, *Joseph Scaliger*, pp. 71–100, and Franco Simone, 'La notion d'Encyclopédie: élément caractéristique de la Renaissance française', in *French Renaissance Studies, 1540–70: Humanism and the Encyclopedia*, ed. Peter Sharratt (Edinburgh: Edinburgh University Press, 1976), pp. 234–62.

8. Grafton, *Joseph Scaliger*, p. 10.

9. That is, *Angeli Politiani operum tomus primus, epistolarum libros XII ac Miscellaneorum centuriam I complectens* (Lyon: S. Gryphe, 1550), and a second volume which contains *Angeli Politiani operum tomus secundus* (Lyon: S. Gryphe, 1545), followed by *Operum Angeli Politiani tertius tomus, ejusdem Praelectiones, orationes et epigrammata complectens* (Lyon: S. Gryphe, 1546). See Alain Legros, 'Dix-huit volumes de la bibliothèque de La Boétie légués à Montaigne et signalés par lui comme tels', *Montaigne Studies*, 25 (2013), 177–88 (p. 186).

10. Pierre Villey, *Les Sources et l'évolution des 'Essais' de Montaigne* (Paris: Hachette, 1908), vol. 1, p. 201.

11. Martin L. McLaughlin, *Literary Imitation in the Italian Renaissance: The Theory and Practice of Literary Imitation in Italy from Dante to Bembo* (Oxford: Oxford University Press, 1996), p. 196.

12. See, famously, I.26, 'De l'institution des enfans' [Of Educating Children] (V, p. 171; F, p. 154).

13. *Dictionnaire de Michel de Montaigne*, ed. Philippe Desan (Paris: Champion, 2007).

14. Villey, *Les Sources et l'évolution*, p. 57. Villey doesn't himself resist the temptation to create hierarchies of Montaigne's reading, consigning texts that appeal less to post-Renaissance sensibilities — compendia, florilegia, compilations, miscellanies — to his juvenile tastes.

15. Richard Cooper, 'La bibliothèque italienne de Montaigne', in *La Librairie de Montaigne: Proceedings of the Tenth Cambridge French Renaissance Seminar, 2–4 September 2008*, ed. Philip Ford and Neil Kenny (Cambridge: Cambridge French Colloquia, 2012), pp. 39–57, and John O'Brien, 'Wounded Artifacts', *Modern Language Notes*, 127 (2012), 712–31 (p. 730).

16. Perrine Galand-Hallyn, 'Les miscellanées de Pietro Crinito', in *Ouvrages miscellanées et théories de la connaissance à la Renaissance*, ed. Dominique de Courcelles (Paris: École de Chartes, 2003), pp. 57–77, and Pierre Laurens, 'Les *Miscellanea* de Politien dans la lumière du premier centenaire', *Euphrosyne* n.s. 23 (1995), 349–67.

17. Gisèle Mathieu-Castellani, 'L'intertexte rhétorique: Tacite, Quintilien et la Poétique des *Essais*', in *Montaigne et la rhétorique: actes du colloque de St Andrews (28–31 mars 1992)*, ed. John O'Brien, Malcolm Quainton, and James J. Supple (Paris: Champion, 1995), pp. 17–26 (p. 25). For an insightful essay on this challenge, see Terence Cave, 'Thinking with Commonplaces', in *Retrospectives: Essays in Literature, Poetics, and Cultural History*, ed. Neil Kenny and Wes Williams (Oxford: Legenda, 2009), pp. 38–47.

18. See Maclean, 'Montaigne, Cardano: The Reading of Subtlety/The Subtlety of Reading', *French Studies*, 37 (1983), 143–56 (p. 152), and O'Brien, 'Montaigne's Anacreon', in *La Librairie de Montaigne*, ed. Ford and Kenny, pp. 141–55 (p. 151).

19. Thomas Greene, *The Light in Troy: Imitation and Discovery in Renaissance Poetry* (New Haven, CT: Yale University Press, 1982), p. 19.

20. Frédéric Tinguely, 'Conclusion: pour une lecture topographique', *Le Voyageur aux mille tours: les ruses de l'écriture du monde à la Renaissance* (Paris: Champion, 2014), pp. 221–23.

21. The *Miscellanea secunda* remained unpublished until Vittore Branca's discovery of its manuscript in the 1960s.

22. 'Praefatio' to the *Miscellaneorum liber*, in *Angeli Politiani opera*, pp. 213–17 (p. 213). Translations from the *Miscellanea* are mine unless otherwise stated. I am grateful to Fabrizio Martello for his invaluable advice on Poliziano's densely playful Latin. See also Poliziano's explanation for the variation in chapter lengths, where his claim that a new work should always be 'limping with dissimilitude' (*Miscellanea*, p. 214) uses the same striking image, albeit with a different inflection, as Montaigne does when he states 'tout exemple cloche' [every example is lame] (V, p. 1070; F, p. 997).

23. See *Annotationes doctorum virorum in grammaticos, oratores, poetas, philosophos, theologos et leges* (Paris: Josse Bade and Jean Petit, 1511), catalogued in *Imprimeurs et libraires parisiens du XVI᷂ siècle* (Paris: Service des travaux historiques de la ville de Paris, 1969), vol. 2, p. 76, no. 145.

24. *Oratio super Fabio Quintiliano et Statii Sylvis*, in *Prosatori latini del Quattrocento*, ed. and trans. Eugenio Garin (Milan: Ricardo Ricciardi, 1952), pp. 869–85 (p. 877), with English translations mine; II.10, 'Des livres [Of Books]; V, p. 415; F, p. 367.

25. On Montaigne and Erasmus, see Margaret Mann Philips, 'From the Ciceronianus to Montaigne', in *Classical Influences on European Culture*, vol. 2: *1500–1700*, ed. R. R. Bolgar (Cambridge: Cambridge University Press, 1976), pp. 191–97; Mary McKinley, 'La présence du *Ciceronianus* dans "De la vanité"', in *Montaigne et la rhétorique*, ed. O'Brien, Quainton, and Supple, pp. 51–65; and Michel Magnien, 'Montaigne et Erasme: bilan et perspectives', in *Montaigne and the Low Countries (1580–1700)*, ed. Paul J. Smith and Karl A. E. Enenkel (Leiden: Brill, 2007), pp. 18–45.

26. See Book 8, Letter 16 of *Epistolarum libri duodecim*, in *Angeli Politiani opera*, pp. 113–14 and, in translation, *Ciceronian Controversies*, ed. Joann DellaNeva, trans. Brian Duvick (Cambridge, MA: Harvard University Press, 2007), pp. 2–5. On the role of the letter in the Ciceronianism quarrels, see Marc Fumaroli, *L'Âge de l'éloquence: rhétorique et 'res literaria' de la Renaissance au seuil de l'époque classique* (Geneva: Droz, 1985), pp. 81–83; and Jean Lecointe, *L'Idéal et la différence: la personnalité littéraire à la Renaissance* (Geneva: Droz: 1993), pp. 321–23.

27. Peter Godman, *From Poliziano to Machiavelli: Florentine Humanism in the High Renaissance* (Princeton, NJ: Princeton University Press, 1998), p. 40.

28. *Oratio super Fabio Quintiliano*, p. 870.

29. The question of Montaigne's attitude to Cicero has received substantial attention from Villey onwards. See M. Gutwirth, 'L'anti-Cicéron de Michel de Montaigne', in *Montaigne et les Essais, 1580–1980: actes du Congrès de Bordeaux (juin 1980)*, ed. Pierre Michel (Paris: Champion, 1983), pp. 48–53, and Michel Magnien, 'Un écho de la querelle Cicéronienne à la fin du XVI᷂ siècle:

éloquence et imitation dans les *Essais*', in *Rhétorique de Montaigne*, ed. Frank Lestringant (Paris: Champion, 1985), pp. 85–99 (p. 95), an essay that ranges rather more broadly than its title suggests. On Montaigne's style, see Kathy Eden's essay in this volume.

30. See, for example, III.13, 'De l'expérience' [On Experience]; V, p. 1108; F, p. 1036, and III.9; V, p. 995; F, p. 926.

31. McLaughlin's point about Erasmus (*Literary Imitation*, p. 203, n. 45) adds Poliziano to Terence Cave's seminal 1979 account of Renaissance imitation, the later French edition of which acknowledges Poliziano's influence: *Cornucopia: figures de l'abondance au XVIe siècle*, trans. Ginette Morel (Paris: Macula, 2004).

32. Letter 1 (Angelo Poliziano to Paolo Cortesi), in *Ciceronian Controversies*, ed. DellaNeva, trans. Duvick, p. 3.

33. Cave, 'Representations of Reading in the Renaissance', in *Retrospectives: Essays in Literature, Poetics, and Cultural History*, ed. Kenny and Williams, pp. 10–19 (p. 16).

34. Compare Cicero's 'inusitatas vias indagemus, tritas relinquamus' [leaving the well-worn paths and hunting for new ones] (*Orator*, 11). For the different modes of imitation, see Greene, *The Light in Troy*, pp. 38–48.

35. *Angeli Politiani Praelectio, cui titulus Panepistemon*, in *Angeli Politiani opera*, pp. 462–73. Jean-Marc Mandosio offers a substantial extract of this, with French translation, in *Poétiques de la Renaissance: le modèle italien, le monde franco-bourguignon et leur héritage en France au XVIe siècle*, ed. Perrine Galand-Hallyn and Fernand Hallyn (Geneva: Droz, 2001), pp. 76–79.

36. *Panepistemon*, in *Angeli Politiani opera*, p. 462. My italics. Translation adapted from the French translation by Mandosio and from McLaughlin, *Literary Imitation*, p. 199.

37. McLaughlin, *Literary Imitation*, p. 199, n. 37.

38. Quintilian, *The Orator's Education*, Books 1 and 2, ed. and trans. Donald A. Russell (Cambridge, MA: Harvard University Press, 2001), Book 1, Prooem. 3.

39. 'The path is not a beaten highway of authorship, nor one in which the mind is eager to range: there is not one person to be found among us who has made the same venture, nor yet one among the Greeks who has tackled single-handed all departments of the subject'; Pliny, *Natural History*, trans. Harris Rackham (1938; Cambridge, MA: Harvard University Press, 1979), vol. 1, p. 9. For more on the significance of Pliny's implicit presence in the *Panepistemon*, see the Introduction to my *Inventive Inventories: Lists, Literature, and Natural History in Renaissance France* (Oxford: Oxford University Press, forthcoming).

40. V, p. 377 (II.6, 'De l'exercitation'). The full sentence reads: 'It is a thorny undertaking, and more so than it seems, to follow a movement so wandering as that of our mind, to penetrate the opaque depths of its innermost folds, to pick out and immobilize the innumerable flutterings that agitate it' (F, p. 331).

41. 'Il y a plusieurs années que je n'ay que moy pour visée à mes pensées, que je ne contrerolle et estudie que moy; et si j'estudie autre chose, c'est pour soudain le coucher sur moy, ou en moy pour mieux dire' [It is many years now that I have had only myself as object of my thoughts, that I have been examining and studying only myself; and if I study anything else, it is in order promptly to apply it to myself, or rather within myself] (V, p. 378; F, p. 331).

42. On the dangers of this *grand récit*, see Cave's Introduction to his *Pré-histoires: textes troublés au seuil de la modernité* (Geneva: Droz, 2001), pp. 1–22, and Chapter 4, 'Fragments d'un moi futur: de Pascal à Montaigne', *Pré-histoires*, pp. 109–27.

43. See Gisèle Mathieu-Castellani, 'Absence et présence des *Confessions*', in *Montaigne ou la vérité du mensonge* (Geneva: Droz, 2000), pp. 107–26, and 'Les *Confessions* de Saint Augustin dans *Les Essais*', in *Lire les 'Essais' de Montaigne: actes du colloque de Glasgow 1997*, ed. Noel Peacock and James J. Supple (Paris: Champion, 2001), pp. 211–26. See also Elizabeth Caron, 'Saint Augustin dans les *Essais*', *Montaigne Studies*, 2.3 (1990), 17–33.

44. Wes Williams, *Monsters and their Meanings in Early Modern Culture: Mighty Magic* (Oxford: Oxford University Press, 2011), p. 148.

45. 'S. Augustin, Origene et Hippocrates ont publié les erreurs de leurs opinions: moy, encore, de mes meurs' (III.5, 'Sur des vers de Virgile' [On Some Lines from Virgil]; V, p. 847; F, p. 780).

46. On editions of Augustine, including Erasmus's complete works, which, unlike the 1505–06 Amerbach Basel edition, incorporated the letters, see Arnoud S. Q. Visser, *Reading Augustine*

in the Reformation. The Flexibility of Intellectual Authority in Europe, 1500–1620 (Oxford: Oxford University Press, 2011).

47. On the influence of his legal training on his writing, see André Tournon, *Montaigne: la glose et l'essai* (1983; Paris: Champion, 2000); see also Ian Maclean, 'Montaigne et le droit civil romain', in *Montaigne et la rhétorique*, ed. John O'Brien, Malcolm Quainton, and John Supple (Paris: Champion, 1995), pp. 163–76 (p. 167).

48. Jean Céard, 'Les transformations du genre du commentaire', in *L'Automne de la Renaissance, 1580–1630*, ed. Jean Lafond and André Stegmann (Paris: Vrin, 1981), pp. 101–15; and Jean-Marc Mandosio, 'La représentation de la philologie dans *Les Pandectae* de Conrad Gesner (1548)', in *La Philologie humaniste et ses représentations*, ed. Galand-Hallyn, Hallyn, and Tournoy, pp. 565–98. For Montaigne's critique of commentaries, see, for example, III.13 (V, p. 1067; F, p. 995).

49. *Miscellanea*, p. 215.

50. *Miscellanea*, p. 215. According to Lewis and Short, the verb *confiteor* ('acknowledge', 'confess', 'own', 'avow') carries the strongest moral sense of confession, suggesting a sacrifice of will or a change of conviction, but Latin also offers *fateor*, which expresses a simple acknowledgement ('confess', 'own', 'grant', 'acknowledge'), and *profiteor*, a voluntary avowal ('declare publicly', 'own freely', 'acknowledge', 'avow', 'confess openly', 'profess'); C. T. Lewis and C. Short, *A Latin Dictionary* (Oxford: Clarendon Press, 1945).

51. Horace, *Satires*, Book 1, ed. Emily Gowers (Cambridge: Cambridge University Press, 2012), 1. 21–23, pp. 38 and 119.

52. *Miscellanea*, p. 215.

53. *Miscellanea*, p. 215.

54. '[A] Qu'on luy face entendre que de confesser la faute qu'il descouvrira en son propre discours, encore qu'elle ne soit aperceue que par luy, c'est un effet de jugement et de sincerité, qui sont les principales parties qu'il cherche' [Let him be made to understand that to confess the flaw he discovers in his own argument, though it be still unnoticed except by himself, is an act of judgement and sincerity, which are the principal qualities he seeks] (V, p. 155; F, p. 139).

55. V, p. 653; F, p. 602 (where Frame offers 'procedure' for 'progrez'), and V, p. 758; F, p. 696.

56. V, p. 40; F, p. 31.

57. Mathieu-Castellani, 'L'intertexte rhétorique', p. 19. See also McKinley's idea of hidden borrowings as an 'acquis'; 'La présence du *Ciceronianus*', p. 64.

58. *Liber epistolarum beati Augustini* (Paris: a Johannes Parvus [= Jean Petit] and Jodocus Badius Ascencius [= Josse Bade], 1515), fol. VIIIr.–fol. VIIIv.; the letter is here listed as no. VII. A modern edition of the *Letters* is available at <http://www.augustinus.it/index.htm> [accessed 22 September 2015].

59. English translation from *The Works of St Augustine*, ed. Boniface Ramsey (Charlottesville, VA: InteLex Corporation, 2009), p. 302, no. 2.

60. Augustine writes: 'Hence if I said something that is either lacking in caution or lacking in learning, which is rightly reprehended not only by others who can see it but also by myself, because I ought to be able to see it, at least afterwards if I am progressing, it should come as no surprise, nor should I be saddened over it. Rather, it should be pardoned, and I should be grateful, not because I made a mistake but because it has been criticized' (ibid.).

61. III.12 (V, p. 1056; F, p. 984).

62. Shane Butler, 'Things Left Unsaid' (forthcoming). I am grateful to the author for letting me see this article pre-publication.

63. Jean-Pierre Camus, Letter CVII ('Jugement des Essais de Michel Seigneur de Montaigne'), in *Les Diversitez: Tome Huictiesme* (Paris: Claude Chappelet, 1613), Livre XXIX, pp. 409–60.

64. III.9 (V, p. 983; F, p. 914).

65. For Montaigne's mockery of the penchant for obscurity, see, for example, III.9, V, p. 995, F, p. 926; for Poliziano's vehement critique, see *Miscellanea*, p. 215.

66. See *Angelo Poliziano's 'Lamia': Text, Translation, and Introductory Studies*, ed. and trans. Christopher S. Celenza (Leiden: Brill, 2010), p. 53, and V, p. 538; F, p. 488.

67. II.12 (V, p. 586; F, p. 538), and *Miscellanea*, p. 215 and passim.

68. V, p. 983; F, p. 913; and V, p. 995; F, p. 926.

69. I.26 (V, p. 168; F, p. 152).

70. 'I haven't supplied works for the forum or the meetinghouse, but for the private room and the schoolhouse'; *Miscellanea*, p. 214.

71. *Miscellanea*, p. 286; translation by Godman, *From Poliziano to Machiavelli*, p. 83.

72. Mawy Bouchard, 'Pour une philosophie "illustre": l'honnesteté cardinale des *Essais* de Montaigne', *Tangence*, 84 (2007), 63–86 (p. 80).

73. *Miscellanea*, p. 214: 'Mediis autem inter hos, et neutro notandis, quasi quidam diversorum Cinnus (ut ait Cicero) satisfaciet, non uno aliquo excellens, et omnium tamen particeps.'

74. Tournon, *Montaigne*, p. 295.

75. Maclean, 'Montaigne, Cardano'.

76. Richard Scholar, 'The Middle Region', in *The 'Je-Ne-Sais-Quoi' in Early Modern Europe: Encounters with a Certain Something* (Oxford: Oxford University Press, 2005), pp. 249–55 (pp. 254 and 250).

77. *Lamia*, p. 71; translation adapted. A 'pistrinum' was a mill or bakery, but became metonymic for a place of punishment or drudgery.

78. III.3 (V, p. 818; F, p. 753); III.9 (V, p. 950; F, p. 881); I.48, 'Des destries' [Of Warhorses] (V, p. 287; F, p. 254).

79. Georg Draut, *Bibliotheca exotica* (Frankfurt: Pierre Kopf, 1610), pp. 136–41 (p. 138). On Draut, see Ian Maclean, 'English Books on the Continent', *Learning and the Market Place: Essays in the History of the Early Modern Book* (Leiden: Brill, 2009), pp. 339–51 (p. 343).

80. See Ian Maclean, 'Scholarly Books and Conceptions of Genre', *Learning and the Market Place*, pp. 9–24 (p. 22). 'Libri philosophici' could be made broader still by the addition of 'et libri miscellanei'; Maclean, 'The Readership of Philosophical Fictions in France', in *Learning and the Market Place*, pp. 25–37 (p. 28).

81. *Pandectarum sive partitionum universalium Conradi Gesneri Tigurini, medici et philosophiae professoris, libri XXI* (Zurich: Christoph Froschauer, 1548), fol. 15r. See Mandosio, 'La représentation de la philologie', p. 572.

82. *Pandectarum*, fol. 18v.

83. See Ian Maclean, 'The Other Philology: Resolving Doubts about Textual Meaning in Early Modern Law and Theology', forthcoming in *The Marriage of Philology and Scepticism: Uncertainty and Conjecture in Early Modern Scholarship and Thought*, ed. Anthony Grafton and Jill Kraye (London: Warburg Institute). I'm grateful to Ian for allowing me to see this pre-publication.

84. *Pandectarum*, fol. 15r.

CHAPTER 4

Facebook *avant la lettre*: Communicating Renaissance-Style in Montaigne's *Essais*

Kathy Eden

... or moy, je suis tout face.

(I.36, 'De l'usage de se vestir' [Of the Habit of Wearing Clothes], V, p. 226)

It has become a commonplace of newspapers, magazine articles, and even academic journals to compare the current revolution in communication technology to the age of printing in the early modern period, to draw out the symmetries, real or imagined, between the transition from the manuscript to the book and from the book to Facebook. In keeping with this trend, the distinguished editor of a recent volume of *Montaigne Studies* has attributed the first essayist's renewed popularity in the age of social networking both to his 'willingness to bare his soul' and to the 'style of writing' this literary laying bare engendered.[1] Without questioning either the success of Montaigne's transition as a stylist into the twenty-first century or the manifold differences between his communication revolution and our own, this essay takes as its point of departure one particular commonality between these two revolutions: a shared investment in the power of the face. For Michel de Montaigne is like Mark Zuckerberg in having successfully exploited the status of the human face as a stand-in for — a substitute or short-hand for — the singular identity that each of us believes we possess.

Even where the face is concerned, however, there are differences between these two communication visionaries. The substitution or metonymy (as I will call it) of the human face was so central to Zuckerberg's vision that he trademarked it.[2] And it is under his innovative trademark that users of all ages serialize their unique life stories punctuated by photos. Montaigne, in contrast, enjoyed no such trademarking opportunity. If he had, however, chances are he would not have exercised a claim on the bookishness of the human face, not because he was reluctant to broadcast how innovative his work was but because he would have considered the metonym itself thoroughly traditional — a part of the intellectual commons.[3] On the other hand, as I hope to show, he may have underestimated just how important a role he would play in its transition from Latin literature to the vernacular. For Montaigne embeds the metonym of the human face into his French in a way that succeeds in linking him ever more intimately to his style — so intimately, in fact, that the two, the self and its style, could seem to readers then as now to go gadding about together (III.9, V, p. 994: 'Mon stile et mon esprit vont vagabondant de mesmes'). Without explicitly labelling it so, in other words, Montaigne conceives of his *Essais* as a facebook — one that presents him in all his singularity (at least in part) by deploying a metonym inherited from some of his favourite Latin authors.

Chief among these favourites is Erasmus, whom Montaigne echoes everywhere in his essays but mentions only once.[4] And chief among Erasmus's discussions of style that leverage the metonym of the human face is the *Ciceronianus*, a provocative intervention in the hottest literary controversy of his day, the so-called Ciceronian controversy. This heated public debate pitted members of the republic of letters who upheld Cicero's style as the only model for imitation against those who considered Cicero one among a number of acceptable ancient models.[5] Subtitled *De optimo dicendi genere* or *On the Best Style*, the *Ciceronianus* stages the case against the strict Ciceronians as a satirical dialogue, a conversation between the frustrated Nosoponus, whose unremitting labours to imitate Cicero have cost him his health without fulfilling his aspirations, and his more open-minded friend Bulephorus, who undertakes not only to cure Nosoponus of his fixation but to enlighten him about what it really means to write and speak well. In the interest of Nosoponus's enlightenment, Bulephorus assumes the Socratic mantle of backing his interlocutor into a logical corner where he cannot escape the incoherence of his position. In this case, the *aporia* or logical contradiction concerns the paradoxical relationship between sameness and difference, likeness and unlikeness. For the more Nosoponus strives to be *like* Cicero, the more *unlike* him he becomes.

And why not, Bulephorus asks, unpacking the paradox: Cicero himself imitated multiple models, while Nosoponus imitates only one; Cicero himself accommodated his style to the particular circumstances of the case at hand, including the time, the place, and the people involved, while Nosoponus continues to ignore changing circumstances and clings instead to a fixed set of stylistic standards established by an extant but incomplete Ciceronian corpus. 'You say that no one can speak well unless he reproduces Cicero', Bulephorus rebukes Nosoponus, 'but the very facts of the matter cry out that no one can speak well unless he deliberately and with full awareness abandons the example of Cicero.'[6] The only way to become *like* Cicero, in other words, is to be *unlike* him. 'Now anyone who copies Cicero in the detail of all this, doing exactly what he did', Bulephorus repeats (*CWE*, vol. 28, p. 450), 'will finish up quite unlike Marcus Tullius, but the person who does something equivalent or similar to what Cicero did, will in fact turn out someone to whom we can give the title "Ciceronian".' For the ultimate aim of communicating, and especially of communicating in the best possible style, is self-expression, and you cannot express yourself, Bulephorus famously warns, if you are preoccupied with sounding like Cicero:

> But if you want to express the whole Cicero you cannot express yourself, and
> if you do not express yourself your speech will be a lying mirror. It will be
> just as ridiculous as painting your face [*coloribus oblita facie*] and pretending to

be Petronius instead of Nosoponus. (*CWE*, vol. 28, p. 399; *ASD*, I-2, 649, ll. 24–27)

In recent years, renowned readers of Erasmus such as Terence Cave and Jacques Chomarat have reminded us not only that this call to self-expression is key to the early modern communication revolution but that Erasmus, as one of its most influential advocates, was actually raising the volume of earlier calls to audible levels.[7] Without losing sight of these important reminders, I would like to shift the focus from the injunction itself to the analogy Erasmus invokes to drive it home. For he compares the wrong kind of imitation, the kind that hinders self-expression, to disguising one's face with paint: to using *colores*, as we see in the ablative absolute above, to cover up or conceal one's *facies*. Here and throughout the *Ciceronianus*, the human face serves as a stand-in not only for the whole person but for personal style.

In keeping with this comparison, Erasmus has Bulephorus earlier in the conversation feature another kind of face-painting, the portrait-painting of the ancient artist Zeuxis. As an example of the right kind of imitation, Zeuxis's portrait of Helen combines the best features of a number of Croton's women to create an image of beauty that excels any of its models (*CWE*, vol. 28, p. 357; *ASD* I-2, 616–17). Bulephorus's sidekick Hypologus later reinforces this lesson by satirizing the wrong kind of portrait painter — the one who keeps altering the face of his sitter [*mutavit faciem*] because some small detail, like the length of the sitter's beard or his pallor, has changed since their last meeting (*CWE*, vol. 28, p. 376; *ASD* I-2, 631; cf. *CWE*, vol. 28, p. 399). At the end of the dialogue, when the time comes for Bulephorus to wrap up his argument for the best style, he appeals yet again to the prominence of the human face. Even someone whose features lack comeliness, Bulephorus claims, wants his portrait painted to represent rather than belie his face. Similarly, any author worth his salt hones his style, here his *stilus*, to express himself rather than Cicero (*CWE*, vol. 28, pp. 440–41; *ASD* I-2, 704, ll. 10–11).

So Bulephorus chides those misguided stylists who will settle for nothing less in their writing than the face of Cicero's style — in Erasmus's Latin, Cicero's *tota dictionis facies* (*CWE*, vol. 28, p. 397; *ASD* I-2, 648, ll. 19–20). For the human soul, like style itself, has a face that style reveals as if in a mirror: 'Habet animus faciem quondam suam in oratione velut in speculo relucentem' (*CWE*, vol. 28, p. 441; *ASD* I-2, 704, ll. 10–11).[8] When Nosoponus balks at Bulephorus's charge against slavish imitation as metonymically taking on someone else's face [*faciem alienum assumere*], Bulephorus redoubles his reliance on this metonym:

> If you should take it into your head to try to make your face [*tuam faciem*] look like someone who doesn't resemble you at all, you will waste your time. But if you observe someone not at all that unlike yourself making his face [*formam*] hideous with a gaping guffaw of extravagant laughter, or spoiling his looks by frowning, wrinkling his brow, turning up his nose, drawing back his lips, rolling his eyes, and similar behavior [*aliisque similibus minus decentem reddi faciem*; or, more literally, 'and other similar things that render his face unbecoming'], you can improve your own appearance [*tuam formam*] by avoiding such tricks, and you will not then be borrowing another's face [*vultum alienum*], but getting your own under control [...]. On the other hand, if you observe how attractive a person is made by an unassuming cheerfulness of expression, modesty of eye,

a set of the whole face [*totusque vultus habitus*] that expresses integrity, with no sign of ill temper or arrogance, frivolity or indiscipline, it will be no cheap deception to model your face [*tuum vultum*] on the pattern of his. For you yourself can ensure that your mind corresponds to the face [*ut et animus vultui respondeat*]. (*CWE*, vol. 28, p. 442; *ASD* I-2, 704, ll. 35–705, l. 11)[9]

Just as there is something to be gained from observing others' faces, Bulephorus insists, so there is something to be gained from studying others' styles, including Cicero's. Featuring the face with its physical capacity for expressiveness as the counterpart to — and even the stand-in for — the psychological expressiveness enabled by style, Bulephorus also insists that it is the writer's or speaker's soul, in both cases, that is being expressed. Bulephorus's own expressive style here, moreover, provides a good illustration of the lexical variety that Erasmus himself advocates in *De copia* and elsewhere, for Bulephorus alternates *facies* first with one of its synonyms, *forma*, and then with another, *vultus*.[10]

But the *Ciceronianus* is far from the only Erasmian work that recruits the power of the human face to set in high relief the communication capabilities of style. In his singularly popular manual of letter-writing, the *De conscribendis epistolis*, Erasmus combats the rigidity of those epistolary theorists who insist on fixing a compositional standard, warning them that 'those who try to impose a single form and style [*formam ac faciem*] on this branch of writing are taking on a task that is both fruitless and absurd' (*CWE*, vol. 25, p. 20; *ASD* I-2, 224, ll. 1–3).[11] Like the satirical dialogue, in other words, the textbook champions stylistic variety not only with the help of lexical variety but with the same key lexical pair, *forma* and *facies*. This recruitment of the face for matters of style, moreover, pertains not only to composing letters but to interpreting them.

In his edition of Jerome's letters, Erasmus defends his editorial choices on the grounds of his deep familiarity with Jerome's style, which is, he claims, as recognizable as the saintly father's face.[12] 'The surest sign and truly the Lydian stone', Erasmus explains,

is the character and quality of speech [*character orationis & habitus*]. As each individual has his own appearance [*facies*], his own voice, his own character and disposition [*mos & genius*], so each has his own style of writing [*stilus*]. And the quality of mind is manifest in speech even more than the likeness of the body is reflected in a mirror. (*CWE*, vol. 61, p. 76)[13]

Here the analogy between one's face and one's style serves to bolster the even greater expressiveness of style as the mirror of the mind [*mens*]. The analogy also empowers Erasmus to refute the most damaging charge of his opponents, namely that Jerome's style is unrecognizable because it has inevitably changed over time and in response to different occasions and genres. To address this charge, Erasmus first assures these opponents that he has taken all these changes into account — 'as if indeed we were not aware', he retorts impatiently, 'that there is some variation in a writer's use of language, the variation arising either from his time of life or from the nature of his subject or from his predilections or from an advantage sought or an attitude of mind' (*CWE*, vol. 61, p. 77). Erasmus then strengthens this assurance with the counter-argument that we recognize the face of those we knew in former days even though they have aged, just as we recognize the same face regardless of its changes in mood (*CWE*, vol. 61, p. 77; *Hieronymi opera*, vol. 4, p. 9):

> The countenance [*vultus*] of an angry man is unlike that of a man of kindly spirit; the countenance of a sad person unlike that of a cheerful one; and yet this is no bar to the recognition of an acquaintance [*& tamen ea res non obstat, quominus agnoscas hominis tibi noti faciem*; or, more literally, 'it doesn't keep you from recognizing the face of a man known to you']. A person whom you knew in his younger days you recognize in his old age, though everything is changed by the passage of time.

Here as in the *Ciceronianus*, Erasmus not only links style to the human face on the grounds of its expressiveness but leverages the incontrovertible differences and therefore recognizability of the face to buttress his claim regarding the stylistic individuality of different authors.

Erasmus may deserve more than a little credit, then, both for tightening the link between style and the face and for extending this linking to interpretive as well as compositional matters — to style-conscious reading as well as style-conscious writing. The link itself, however, is not his forging. On the contrary, some of Erasmus's most influential predecessors — both ancient and modern — pay particular attention not only to expressiveness in successful communication but to the face as communication's reigning metonym. In the *Institutio oratoria*, for instance, Quintilian concludes his discussion of the traditional three kinds of style by rejecting them on the grounds that eloquence has many — not just three — faces ('plures igitur etiam eloquentiae facies', XII. 10. 69).[14] As part of his treatment of delivery in Book 11, he draws an analogy between the face and the orator's voice. Just as the *facies* itself remains constant despite changes in *vultus*, Quintilian argues, so the orator uses his voice, which is ever one and the same, to effect the appropriate modulations (XI. 3. 47). Earlier in Book 11, he similarly insists on the interplay of sameness and difference as it affects the sound of the voice. Here again, the mode may change from fast to slow or from high to low, but the voice itself, like the face, remains the same. '[T]here are many intermediate gradations between the two extremes', Quintilian explains,

> and just as the face [*facies*], although it consists of a limited number of features, yet possesses infinite variety of expression, so it is with the voice: for though it possessed but few varieties to which we can give a name, yet every human being possesses a distinctive voice of his own, which is as easily distinguished by the ear as are facial characteristics by the eye. (XI. 3. 18)[15]

Whereas Erasmus, as we have seen, enlists the individuality of the face to make the case for every stylist, like Jerome, having his own style, Quintilian applies the analogy to the orator's voice — although Quintilian does concede elsewhere (XII. 10. 10) that 'if we turn our attention to the various styles of oratory [*in oratione*], we shall find almost as great variety of talents [*ingeniorum*] as there are of personal appearance [*corporum formas*]'. For Quintilian as for Erasmus, then, physical appearance, and especially the face, epitomizes difference.

During his discussion of rhetorical figures, moreover, Quintilian warns against indiscriminate crowding and compares the inartistic effect of too many figures to a face that shifts jarringly from one expression to another:

> But even perfectly correct figures must not be packed too closely together. Changes of facial expression and glances of the eyes are most effective in pleading, but if the orator never ceases to distort his face [os] with affected grimaces or to wag his head and roll his eyes, he becomes a laughing-stock. So too oratory possesses a natural mien [Et oratio habet rectam quondam velut faciem; or, more literally, 'style has, as it were, its own face'], which while it is far from demanding a stolid and immovable rigidity should as far as possible restrict itself to the expression with which it is endowed by nature [quam natura dedit]. (IX. 3. 101)

It is at least in part on Quintilian's authority, in other words, that Erasmus puts a face on style. In doing so, he, like Quintilian, stresses that one's style, for all it may be enhanced by art, is, like one's face, endowed by nature.

For a more contemporary authority on matters of style, Erasmus turns to Angelo Poliziano. Roughly forty years earlier in a letter to Paolo Cortesi (mid-1480s), the Florentine humanist countered the strict Ciceronians of his own day with the provocative quip that his writing did not sound like Cicero's because he was expressing himself. In the Ciceronianus, Erasmus has Bulephorus lavishly applaud this brief in favour of self-expression (CWE, vol. 28, pp. 444–45; ASD I-2, 706–07), judging its stylistic elegance and argumentative acumen more Ciceronian than the efforts of Poliziano's opponent, a self-proclaimed imitator of Cicero who prides himself on his so-called 'Ciceronian features' — his liniamenta Ciceronis. To combat this misplaced pride, Poliziano in response puts some pressure on Cortesi's version of the metonym, first questioning his slavish admiration for these liniamenta or facial lines and then contrasting the face of a bull or a lion with that of an ape. 'For you generally do not approve of anyone, as I understand it', Poliziano writes to Cortesi, 'unless he copies the features of Cicero [liniamenta Ciceronis]. To me the face [facies] of a bull or a lion seems far more honorable than that of an ape, which nonetheless is more like a man than they are.'[16] As the comparison of animal faces drives home, mere similarity is not the aim of stylistic imitation, especially when this similarity undermines natural difference. Stressing these differences in natural talent or ingenium at the end of his letter, Poliziano returns to the liniamenta only to dismiss them as superficial.[17]

Immediately before he introduces into his conversation with Nosoponus the epistolary exchange between Poliziano and Cortesi, Bulephorus, like Poliziano himself, rejects the lineamenta Ciceronis on the grounds of their superficiality. Rehearsing the unflattering similarity between humans and apes, Bulephorus reminds Nosoponus that someone who looks nothing like Cicero may be much more attractive than someone whose features or lineamenta closely resemble Cicero's ('qui Ciceronis lineamenta propius exprimit'; CWE, vol. 28, p. 442, ASD I-2 705, l. 15; cf. CWE, vol. 28, p. 443, ASD I-2 706, l. 9). When Bulephorus finally offers Poliziano's letter as evidence of his own attitude towards stylistic imitation, he highlights his Italian predecessor's disapproval of those who merely reproduce 'Cicero's outward features' (lineamenta Ciceronis) (CWE, vol. 28, p. 444, ASD I-2 706, l. 22; cf. ASD I-2 706, l. 31). Even the facial resemblance between father and son — what Bulephorus calls the *oris lineamenta* (*CWE*, vol. 28, p. 448, *ASD* I-2, 609, l. 30) — is less important than the deeper affinities of character and talent. Sometimes, in other words, Erasmus enlists the metonym of the face, including its *lineaments*, to impress upon the reader that features of style, especially those acquired through imitation, may be skin-deep only; at other times, the face stands in for the deeper individuality that style penetrates and promotes. In both cases, the metonymy works on behalf of self-expression.

Without ever advertising his Erasmian credentials, as noted above, Montaigne ranks among the most influential apostles of Erasmus's stylistic theory, both endorsing individual difference, including stylistic difference, and doing so with the help of the human face. In the final chapter of his *Essais*, a well-known meditation on 'dissimilarity' among other things, Montaigne wraps up an Erasmian theme he has been developing throughout. 'As no event or forme doth wholly resemble another', he reckons in III.13, 'De l'experience',

> so doth it not altogether differ one from another. Oh ingenious mixture of Nature. If our faces were not alike, we could not discerne a man from a beast: If they were not unlike, we could not distinguish one man from another man. (Fl. 3.334)

> Comme nul evenement et nulle forme ressemble entierement à une autre, aussi ne differe nulle de l'autre entierement. Ingenieux meslange de nature. Si nos faces n'estoient semblables, on ne sçauroit discerner l'homme de la beste; si elles n'estoient dissemblables, on ne sçauroit discerner l'homme de l'homme. (V, p. 1070)

Like Erasmus, Montaigne fixes on sameness and difference — likeness and unlikeness — as our most basic cognitive markers. Without them, he reasons, we could not know anything, not even each other. And like Erasmus, Montaigne grants the human face a special status in marking out our individuality. Fully in keeping with this status, Montaigne introduces his collection of essays in 'Au lecteur' as a portrait. For it is principally the face that tells the tale, according to this 'unpremeditated philosopher' who prides himself on making distinctions.[18]

But Montaigne does much more than feature the human face as the index of difference in the final chapter and figure the *Essais* from its opening as his *auto-portrait*. He also ends the penultimate chapter, III.12, 'De la phisionomie' [Of Phisognomie], with two nearly catastrophic experiences that address what he calls 'the face and those lineaments' ('[le] visage et ces lineaments'; Fl. 3.321, V, p. 1058). In the first, Montaigne barely escapes the evil machinations of intruders into his own house; in the second, he is en route when a band of marauders seize all his property and threaten his life before changing their minds, restoring his belong-ings, and safeguarding his passage by warning him of other gangs along the way. In both cases, Montaigne concludes, his aggressors preserve him because of the corresponding openness of his face and his manner of speaking (Fl. 3.326, V, p. 1062).

Also like Erasmus, then, Montaigne strategically focuses attention on the human face in order to link it with style; and he does so by practising an Erasmian lexical variety, sometimes featuring *la face* and at others *le visage* as well as *la mine*.[19] And like Erasmus (and Poliziano), Montaigne notes the less-than-flattering similarity between the face of a man and that of an ape in the interest of identifying aping,[20] including his own, with the wrong kind of stylistic imitation:

> But I am of an Apish and imitating condition. When I medled with making verses (and I never made any but in Latine) they evidently accused the Poet I came last from reading: And of my first Essayes, some taste a little of the stranger [...]. Whom I behold with attention, doth easily convay and imprint something of his in me. What I heedily consider, the same I usurpe: a foolish countenance, a crabbed looke, a ridiculous manner of speach. (Fl. 3.103)

> Or j'ay une condition singeresse et imitatrice: quand je me meslois de faire des vers (et n'en fis jamais que des Latins), ils accusoient evidemment le poete que je venois dernierement de lire; et, de mes premiers essays, aucuns puent un peu à l'estranger [...]. Qui que je regarde avec attention m'imprime facilement quelque chose du sien. Ce que je considere, je l'usurpe: une sotte contenance, une desplaisante grimace, une forme de parler ridicule. (V, p. 875)

By his own admission, in other words, Montaigne has good reason to avoid reading when he writes, since his style, like his face, tends to take on the expression of others.[21]

As part of this admission of a 'condition imitatrice', Montaigne refers to his style as 'une forme de parler', a key phrase that recurs throughout the *Essais*. At the start of 'De la vanité' (III.9), for instance, he both attributes the increase of writers (himself included) to the corruption of the age and associates their scribbling [*l'escrivaillerie*] with various customs that similarly reflect social decay. Chief among these customs are ways of dressing [*les habillements*] and ways of speaking, 'les formes du parler' (V, p. 947). At the end of a much earlier chapter, I.26, 'De l'institution des enfans' [Of the Institution and Education of Children], Montaigne treats at some length this same alliance between sartorial and rhetorical style. Looking back at least as far as Cicero's *Brutus* (262, 274), this alliance figures prominently in the *Ciceronianus*, where Bulephorus draws the analogy between changes in dress and changes in style.[22] Exploiting this same analogy, Montaigne first describes the style that wins his approval as 'simple', 'naif', and 'desreglé' and then ties this stylistic disorderliness to the way the young men of his day wear their cloaks and stockings, hanging loose about them. While acknowledging that this nonchalance finds its clearest expression in clothing, Montaigne claims to prefer it in 'la forme du parler' (I.26, Fl. 1.183–84, V, pp. 171–72).[23]

Montaigne also considers 'les formes d'escrire', styles of writing, including those of such difficult authors as Anaxagoras, Democritus, and Parmenides:

> They have a manner of writing doubtfull both in substance and intent, rather enquiring than instructing: albeit here and there, they enterlace their stile with dogmaticall cadences. And is not that as well seene in *Seneca,* and in *Plutarke?* How much doe they speake sometimes of one face, and sometimes of another, for such as looke neere unto it? (II.12, Fl. 2.260)

> Ils ont une forme d'escrire douteuse en substance et un dessein enquerant plustost qu'instruisant, encore qu'ils entresement leur stile de cadances dogmatistes. Cela se voit il pas aussi bien et en Seneque et en Plutarque? Combien disent ils, tantost d'un visage, tantost d'un autre, pour ceux qui y regardent de prez! (V, p. 509)

Granting there is an element of dogmatism in the style of even the most committed philosophical doubters, Montaigne includes among these philosophers his two favourite stylists, Seneca and Plutarch. Again like Erasmus, Montaigne takes into account not only their *forme* from the Latin *forma* but their *stile* from the Latin *stilus*. And, like Erasmus, Montaigne figures an alteration in their styles metonymically as a change in their faces, here 'les visages'.[24]

When Montaigne returns to his two favourite authors later in Book II, he considers in turn his own style (II.17, Fl. 2.450, V, p. 637), questioning whether the term can be applied to 'un parler informe', a way of talking that is formless, without style. 'If I should undertake to follow this other smoothe, even and regular stile', he worries (Fl. 2. 452, V, p. 638), 'I should never attain unto it' ('Quand j'entreprendroy de suyvre cet autre stile aequable, uny et ordonné, je n'y sçaurois advenir'). On the other hand, he commends the legal procedure of ancient Rome in chapter III.11, 'Des boyteux' [Of the Lame or Crippel] precisely because its 'stile' underwrote a 'forme de parler' that preserved a salutary doubt.[25] In keeping with this commendation, Montaigne applauds Socrates for choosing the defence that the sceptical Plato wrote for his teacher's trial over the one composed by Lysias, even though the composition of the Greek orator was 'excellemment façonné au stile judiciare' [excellently fashioned in a judiciary stile] (Fl. 3.316, V, p. 1054). In his effort to judge Lysias as a stylist, Montaigne leverages a lexical variety that includes not only 'le stile' and 'la forme' — both, as we have seen, with Latin equivalents — but also 'la façon', used here as a verb, 'façonner'.

Throughout the *Essais*, in fact, Montaigne passes judgement on a number of stylists based on their 'façon', including their 'façon de parler', 'façon de dire', and 'façon d'escrire'. Cicero is roundly condemned for wordiness, 'for [...] his manner of writing semeth verie tedious unto me, as doth all such-like stuffe' ('car [...] sa façon d'escrire me semble ennuyeuse, et toute autre pareille façon, Fl. 2.118, V, p. 413). Both Terence and Caesar, on the other hand, have 'façons de dire' characterized by grace and beauty. Whereas the style of the military commander enriches his subject matter, that of the comic playwright displays such charm that it completely occludes his (II.34, 'Observations sur les moyens de faire la guerre de Julius Caesar' [Observations concerning the meanes to warre after the maner of Iulius Caesar], Fl. 2.581, V, p. 736; II.10, Fl. 2.115, V, p. 411). Tacitus, in contrast, writes 'after a sharpe and witty fashion: following affected and laboured stile of his age' ('d'une façon pointue et subtile, suyvant le stile affecté du siècle', Fl. 3.182, V, p. 941).[26]

Elsewhere Montaigne reinforces the traditional rhetorical dualism of *words* and *things* — style and subject matter — with the help of the same varied lexicon. His chapter II.10, 'Des livres', begins by warning his readers that they should attend in his writing not to 'the matters [aux matieres] but on the fashion [à la façon]' he gives them (Fl. 2.110, V, p. 408). In III.8, 'De l'art de conferer' [Of the Art of Conferring], he warns these same readers that 'we are upon the manner, and not upon the matter of speaking', assuring them that he himself has 'as great a regard to the forme, as to the substance [...] therein seeking [in the authors he reads] their manner [leur façon], not their subject' ('nous sommes sur la maniere, non sur la matiere du dire. Mon humeur est de regarder autant à la forme qu'à la substance [...]. Et tous les jours m'amuse à lire en des autheurs, sans soin de leur science, y cherchant leur façon, non leur subject', Fl. 3.166, V, p. 928). Just as he does with the human face, as we have seen, Montaigne varies his vocabulary for style. And sometimes, as we have also just seen with 'forme' and 'façon', he couples the terms that constitute his lexical field.[27]

This particular pair of terms, 'forme' and 'façon', figures prominently in Montaigne's discussions of style. In III.5, 'Sur des vers de Virgile', he uses it to make a point not about the relation between words and things but about the relation between words in French and in Latin. After insisting (like nearly every rhetorician before him) that 'full conceptions' must be the source of 'fine words', he turns to the difficulty of expressing himself in the vernacular, which offers both a sufficient supply of words and the potential for an even richer transfer of terms but still lacks Latin's strength and subtlety: 'I find sufficient store of stuffe in our language', Montaigne concedes,

> but some defect of fashion. For there is nothing but could be framed of our Hunters gibberish words or strange phrases, and of our Warriours peculiar tearmes; a fruitfull and rich soile to borrow of. And as hearbes and trees are bettered and fortified by being transplanted, so formes of speach are embellished and graced by variation. I finde it sufficiently plenteous, but not sufficiently plyable and vigorous. It commonly faileth and shrinketh under a pithy and powerfull conception. If your march therein be far extended, you often feele it droope and languish under you, unto whose default the Latine doth now and then present his helping hand. (III.5, Fl. 3.101)

> En nostre langage je trouve assez d'estoffe, mais un peu faute de façon: car il n'est rien qu'on ne fit du jargon de nos chasses et de nostre guerre, qui est un genereux terrein à emprunter; et les formes de parler, comme les herbes, s'amendent et fortifient en les transplantant. Je le trouve suffisamment abondant, mais non pas maniant et vigoureux suffisamment. Il succombe ordinairement à une puissante conception. Si vous allez tendu, vous sentez souvent qu'il languit soubs vous et fleschit, et qu'à son deffaut le Latin se presente au secours. (V, p. 874)[28]

Transplanting the language of horticulture to explain the linguistic transfers — the metaphors — that allow language itself to exfoliate, Montaigne acknowledges that some 'formes de parler', like some grasses, give way too easily under the pressure of frequent passage. This 'shrinking' and 'drooping' of the 'formes of speach' speak to their stylistic inadequacy, their lack of 'fashion' or *façon*.

In the closing address to Mme de Duras in the final chapter of the second book (II.37), which is not incidentally the closing chapter of the 1580 edition, Montaigne similarly couples these two terms in an effort to reinforce his claim that his style of writing throughout the first two books has corresponded to his style of speaking:

> And could I have assumed unto my selfe any other fashion, than mine owne accustomed, or more honourable and better forme, I would not have done it: For, al I seek to reape by my writings, is, they will naturally represent and to the life pourtray me to your remembrance.

> Quand j'eusse peu prendre quelque autre façon que la mienne ordinaire et quelque autre forme plus honorable et meilleure, je ne l'eusse pas faict; car je ne veux tirer de ces escrits sinon qu'ils me representent à vostre memoire au naturel. (Fl. 2.653, V, p. 783)

The first edition of the *Essais*, in other words, ends as it had begun in 'Au lecteur', not only by using this pair, 'forme' and 'façon', to introduce Montaigne's readers to his style, but by characterizing this personal style as 'ordinaire' and 'naturelle'. 'I desire therein to be delineated in mine owne genuine, simple and ordinairie fashion,' Montaigne explains for the first time in his Preface, 'without contention, art or study; for it is my selfe I pourtray. My imperfections shall therein be read to the life, and my natural forme discerned, so farre-forth as publike reverence hath permitted me' ('Je veus qu'on m'y voie en ma façon simple, naturelle et ordinaire, sans contention et artifice: car c'est moy que je peins. Mes defauts s'y liront au vif, et ma forme naïfve, autant que la reverence publique me l'a permis'; Fl. 1.12, V, p. 3). Clearly alert to Montaigne's recapitulation of the Preface in the last chapter of Book II, in other words, his early modern English translator John Florio both reiterates the opening language in the closing and overwrites this closing to echo the Introduction's attention to portraiture.[29] Florio's translation of the passage regarding Montaigne's style in the Preface, on the other hand, follows the original more closely (Fl. 1.12, V, p. 3).

Despite Florio's keeping close to the original prefatory pairing of 'forme' and 'fashion', however, he still cannot resist the opportunity to buttress the organizing figure of the portrait by translating Montaigne's desire to be *seen* ('Je veus qu'on m'y voie') as a desire to be *delineated*. This delineation echoes not only the stylistic *lineamenta* under scrutiny, as we have seen, in the *Ciceronianus*, but also the phrase that Florio himself uses even earlier in the Preface to translate Montaigne's concern with the 'traits de mes conditions et humeurs' that his literary portrait will preserve for his relatives and friends. In Florio's English rendering these 'traits' become 'the lineaments of my conditions and humours' (Fl. 1.12).[30]

But Florio's emphasis in the Preface on Montaigne's being 'delineated' in a simple and ordinary or customary 'fashion' bears witness to a more complex transplanting that Montaigne himself accomplishes with the 'helping hand' of Latin, the language not only of his childhood but his moments of crisis in adulthood.[31] For Florio's 'fashion' regularly translates Montaigne's 'façon', just as his English 'stile' and 'forme' throughout the *Essayes* render their French equivalents. As we have seen, both 'stile' and 'forme' in French look back not only to the Latin but to the leading roles of 'stilus' and 'forma' in Erasmus's stylistic theory. Unlike Montaigne's 'stile' and 'forme', on the other hand, his 'façon' seems to lack a clear Erasmian equivalent.

But this lack is only apparent, as Montaigne's frequent coupling of 'façon' with 'forme' suggests. For this pair renders into the vernacular a variation of the Erasmian pairing of *forma* and *facies*, a rendering that registers *facere* as the Latin verb from which not only Latin *facies* but French *façon* and *face* derive.[32] In keeping with this shared derivation, Montaigne's preoccupation with his face throughout the *Essais*, including as an object of portraiture, signals a preoccupation with his *façon*, his style. The one, like the other, reflects his individuality understood as personal difference communicated through self-expression.

By building on this shared derivation, Montaigne does more than simply recruit the metonym of the face used by Erasmus and others to talk about his peculiar style of communication. He embeds this metonym deeply into his vernacular treatment of style; and he does so, as Florio's translation helps to set in high relief, by exercising an Erasmian lexical variety that aligns *façon* — Florio's *fashion* — not only with *forme* but with *stile*, another metonym already deeply embedded in humanist discussions of style, including Montaigne's.[33] For Montaigne, as we have seen, considers his style, whether he calls it his 'forme', 'façon', or 'stile', the constant companion of his meandering thoughts, despite his many complaints against the art of rhetoric.[34] He also acknowledges that these thoughts give him pleasure only insofar as he can communicate them because 'no pleasure is fully delightsome without communication' ('Nul plaisir n'a goust pour moy sans communication', III.9, Fl. 3.237, V, p. 986). Often hailed nowadays as the poster boy of the early modern communication revolution, Montaigne leverages his Latin pedigree to compose a literary self-portrait in the vernacular that is indeed a facebook — one that exploits a traditional metonym to present its author as a communicator every bit as singular as his face.

Notes to Chapter 4

1. See the Introduction by Philip Ford, *Montaigne Studies*, 24 (2012), 3–6 (p. 6).
2. Although at first glance the figure under consideration here may seem more like synecdoche than metonymy, see the discussion below. For a reminder of the fine line between these two figures, see Quintilian, VIII. 6. 23.
3. On Montaigne's claim to literary innovation, see II.6 ('De l'exercitation' [Of Exercise or Practice]), Fl. 2.66, V, pp. 377–78, and II.8 ('De l'affectation des pères aux enfans' [Of the Affection of Fathers to their Children]), Fl. 2.75, V, p. 385. The abbreviation Fl. refers to *The Essays of Montaigne*, trans. John Florio (1603; London: David Nutt, 1892; New York: AMS, 1967), with volume and page number. On his fear of political innovation, see III.9 ('De la vanité' [Of Vanitie]), Fl. 3.200, V, p. 958. On the status of intellectual property in early modernity, see my *Friends Hold All Things in Common: Tradition, Intellectual Property, and the 'Adages' of Erasmus* (New Haven, CT: Yale University Press, 2001).
4. In III.2, 'Du repentir' [Of Repenting] (Fl. 3.27, V, p. 810), Montaigne famously imagines Erasmus speaking adages and apophthegms to his servants. On the Erasmian dimension of Montaigne's literary project, which goes well beyond the use of adages and apophthegms, see Margaret Mann Phillips, 'From the *Ciceronianus* to Montaigne', in *Classical Influences on European Culture AD 1500–1700*, ed. R. R. Bolgar (Cambridge: Cambridge University Press, 1974), pp. 191–97; Marc Fumaroli, 'Genèse de l'épistolographie classique: rhétorique humaniste de la lettre, de Pétrarque à Juste Lipse', *Revue d'histoire littéraire de la France*, 78 (1978), 886–905, who claims that '[l]a rhétorique des *Essais* est toute erasmienne' (p. 893, n. 25); and my *The Renaissance Rediscovery of Intimacy* (Chicago: University of Chicago Press, 2012), pp. 96–98. For the influence of Erasmian rhetoric everywhere in the curriculum of sixteenth-century Northern Europe, see T. W. Baldwin, *William Shakspere's Small Latine and Lesse Greeke*, 2 vols (Urbana, IL: University of Illinois Press, 1944), esp. pp. 75–133. For 'une prolifération de manuels dans le style érasmien', see Ian Maclean, 'Montaigne et le droit civil romain', in *Montaigne et la rhétorique*, ed. John O'Brien, Malcolm Quainton, and John Supple (Paris: Champion, 1995), pp. 163–76 (p. 167).
5. On this debate, see Remigio Sabbadini, *Storia del Ciceronianismo e di altre questioni letterarie nell' età della Rinascenza* (Turin: no pub., 1885); Izora Scott, *Controversies over the Imitation of Cicero* (1910; Davis, CA: Hermagoras, 1991); and Martin L. McLaughlin, *Literary Imitation in the Italian Renaissance: The Theory and Practice of Literary Imitation in Italy from Dante to Bembo* (Oxford: Clarendon Press, 1995).
6. *Collected Works of Erasmus* (Toronto: University of Toronto Press, 1974–), vol. 28, p. 383. Works from this collection will hereafter be cited as *CWE*. For the original Latin I have used *Opera*

omnia Desiderii Erasmi Roterodami (Amsterdam: North-Holland, 1969–), hereafter *ASD* and also cited in the text.

7. See Terence Cave, *The Cornucopian Text: Problems of Writing in the French Renaissance* (Oxford: Oxford University Press, 1979), pp. 39–49, and Jacques Chomarat, *Grammaire et rhétorique chez Erasme*, 2 vols (Paris: Les Belles Lettres, 1981), vol. 2, pp. 833–41.

8. On the difference between Erasmus and Montaigne regarding style as the mirror of the soul, see Cave, *Cornucopian Text*, p. 278: 'Although in the *Ciceronianus* and elsewhere the phrase *oratio speculum animi* had been attached to the constitution of a subject named "Erasmus", the singularity of this subject had on the whole remained subordinate to the topics of a representational discourse (the discourse of humanist theory). The personification of Erasmus is intermittent; but in the *Essais*, the production of a self, the writing of a "portrait" which will make good the absence of its subject, dominates all other activities.' In II.12, 'Apologie de Raimond Sebond' (Fl. 2.311, V, p. 543), Montaigne quotes Cicero (*Tusculan Disputations*, I. 28) on the face of the soul.

9. For Erasmus on metonymy, see *De copia*, *CWE*, vol. 24, pp. 339–40; *ASD* I-6, 68–70, especially 'those words that can be applied both to persons and to things' (p. 340). For Montaigne on metonymy, see I.51 ('De la vanité des paroles' [Of the Vanitie of Words]), Fl. 1.355, V, p. 307; and for Montaigne's use of Ceres and Bacchus, the handbook examples of metonymy, see II.12, Fl. 2.283, V, p. 525.

10. On the complex relation between these three Latin terms for the human face and what they disclose about ancient Roman culture, see Maurizio Bettini, *Le orecchie di Hermes: studi di antropologia e letterature classiche* (Turin: Einaudi, 2000), pp. 313–56, who confirms the virtual interchangeability of *forma* and *facies* (p. 347). For Erasmus on *forma*, *facies*, and *vultus* as roughly synonymous, see *De copia*, *CWE*, vol. 24, p. 481, *ASD* I-6, 56, and for *forma* and *facies*, see *CWE*, vol. 28, pp. 440–41; *ASD* I-2, 703, l. 32–704, l. 16. For Erasmus on lexical variety as one of the most important sources of *copia*, see *De copia*, *CWE*, vol. 24, pp. 307–09; and on the power of variety more generally, *CWE*, vol. 24, p. 302: 'Variety is so powerful in every sphere that there is absolutely nothing, however brilliant, which is not dimmed if not commended by variety. Nature above all delights in variety; in all this huge concourse of things, she has left nothing anywhere unpainted by her wonderful technique of variety.' For Erasmus on variety and synonymy, see Cave, *Cornucopian Text*, pp. 22–26. For Montaigne on variety as nature's style, see II.37 ('De la resemblance des enfans aux peres' [Of the Resemblance betweene Children and Fathers]), Fl. 2.657, V, p. 786; and on its impact on customs or conventions, see III.9, Fl. 3.236, V, p. 985. On the pleasure Montaigne takes in variety, see III.9, Fl. 3.236, V, p. 985 and Fl. 3.239, V, p. 988. For Petrarch on one's speech (*sermo*) as individual as one's face (*vultus*), see his letter to Boccaccio, *Rerum familiarium libri*, 22.2.17.

11. Before concluding that epistolary style has more than one *forma* and *facies*, Erasmus explains that 'variation and unevenness of style and subject-matter which would merit condemnation elsewhere here have a peculiar charm. In Gellius's *Noctes* and other miscellanies one can pardon constant changes of subject, but not a repeatedly shifting style, whereas in letters it is delightful to see how much a young man's language differs from that of an old man, and to note what age has added or taken away from the style' (*CWE*, vol. 25, p. 20). As we shall see below, Erasmus both returns to these variables and refers them to the face when discussing Jerome's epistolary style.

12. On Erasmus's *familiaritas* with Jerome, see Eden, *Renaissance Rediscovery of Intimacy*, pp. 86–88.

13. For the Latin I have used Erasmus's edition of *Hieronymi opera* (Basel: Froben, 1553), vol. 4, p. 8.

14. For Quintilian on the *vultus eloquentiae*, see IX. 1. 21. For Tacitus on the *vultus* and *facies eloquentiae*, see *Dialogus*, XVIII. 3 and XXXIV. 5 respectively. Amplifying Seneca, *Epistulae morales*, LXXXIV. 8, on the resemblance of son to father instead of image to original as a figure for stylistic imitation, Petrarch emphasizes this aspect of resemblance as seen especially in the face: 'In quibus cum magna sepe diversitas sit membrorum, umbra quedam et quem pictores nostri aerem vocant, qui in vultu inque oculis maxime cernitur, similitudinem illam facit, que statim viso filio, patris in memoriam nos reducat, cum tamen si res ad mensuram redeat, omnia sint diversa' [While often very different in their individual features, they have a certain something our painters call an 'air', especially noticeable about the face and eyes, that produces a resemblance; seeing the son's face,

we are reminded of the father's, although if it came to measurement, the features would all be different, but there is something subtle that creates this effect]; *Rerum familiarium libri*, XXIII. 19, *Le familiari*, ed. Vittorio Rossi, 4 vols (Florence: Sansoni, 1933–42), vol. 4, p. 206, and *Letters on Familiar Matters*, ed. and trans. Aldo S. Bernardo, 3 vols (New York: Italica, 2005), pp. 301–02. On the painter's 'air' as originally an aspect of the face, see Philip Sohm, *Style in the Art Theory of Early Modern Italy* (Cambridge: Cambridge University Press, 2001), pp. 12–13.

15. On the variability and individuality of the voice, compare Cicero, *Orator*, 60, 86, and *De oratore* III. 221. For Montaigne on Quintilian on the voice, see III.13 ('De l'experience' [Of Experience]), Fl. 3.357, V, p. 1088.

16. *Ciceronian Controversies*, ed. Joann DellaNeva, trans. Brian Duvick (Cambridge, MA: Harvard University Press, 2007), I.1, p. 2. For Seneca on the face and its lineaments in matters of style, see *Epistulae morales*, XXXIII. 5. For Seneca on the relation between *forma* and *facies*, see *Epistulae morales*, LVIII. 20–21.

17. *Ciceronian Controversies*, ed. DellaNeva, trans. Duvick, p. 4. On Poliziano's letter to Cortesi, which signals his commitment to *varietas*, see McLaughlin, *Literary Imitation in the Italian Renaissance*, pp. 191–209. Although McLaughlin addresses the images invoked as part of this debate, he does not consider the 'face' among them. On Montaigne as a reader of Poliziano, see Rowan Tomlinson's essay in this volume.

18. For Montaigne as the 'philosophe impremedité et fortuite', see II.12, Fl. 2. 316, V, p. 546; and for *distingo* as the keystone of his logic, see II.1 ('De l'inconstance de nos actions' [Of the Inconstancie of our Actions]), Fl. 2.7, V, p. 335. In keeping with this preference for distinctions, Montaigne ends the first edition of the *Essais* (1580) by drawing attention to the human face as the marker of difference: 'Et a l'aduanture ne fut il iamais au monde deus opinions entierement & exactement pareilles non plus que deux visages. Leur plus propre qualité c'est la diuersité & la discordance. FIN.' On this earlier ending, see François Rigolot, 'Les "visages" de Montaigne', *La Littérature de la Renaissance*, 13 (1984), 357–70 (p. 358, n. 13), who, singling out II.12 and II.17 ('De la praesumption' [Of Presumption]), notes that '[i]l reste que c'est au Livre II, c'est-à-dire au moment où s'esquisse l'autoportrait de l'écrivain que les "visages" se multiplient dans les *Essais*' (p. 361). On the actual portraits of Montaigne, see the first two articles in *Le Visage changeant de Montaigne*, ed. Keith Cameron and Laura Willett (Paris: Champion, 2003): George Hoffmann, 'Montaigne's Face? The Chantilly Portrait Revisited', pp. 15–32, and Laura Willett, 'Out of Nowhere? A New/Old Portrait of Montaigne', pp. 33–65. On Montaigne's acknowledgement of the relation between difference and similarity as the formulation of dialectic, see Maclean, 'Montaigne et le droit civil romain', pp. 163–76. On the extension of this relation to the early modern study of the human body, including the face, see Ian Maclean, 'The Logic of Physiognomy in the Late Renaissance', *Early Science and Medicine*, 16 (2011), 275–95.

19. For Montaigne's exploitation of an Erasmian variety, see Cave, *Cornucopian Text*, pp. 275–76. This lexical variety is especially well reflected in the passage noted above, even though Florio's translation fails to preserve it by rendering Montaigne's varied lexicon in each case with the English 'face': 'Yet me thinkes, that the same feature and manner of the face and those lineaments [*ce traict et façon de visage, et ces lineaments*], by which some argue certaine inward complexions, and our future fortunes, is a thing that doth not directly nor simply lodge under the Chapter of beauty and ill favourdnesse [...]. For, an ill favour and ill composed face [*face*], may sometimes harbour some aire of probity, and trust [...]. A mans looke or aire of his face [*mine*], is but a weake warrant; notwithstanding it is of some consideration.' 'Si me semble il que ce traict et façon de visage, et ces lineaments par lesquels on argumente aucunes complexions internes et nos fortunes à venir, est chose qui ne loge pas bien directement et simplement soubs le chapitre de beauté et de laideur [...]. Car en une face qui ne sera pas trop bien composée, il peut loger quelque air de probité et de fiancé [...]. C'est une foible garantie que la mine; toutesfois elle a quelque consideration'; Fl. 3.321, V, p. 1058. According to Rigolot ('Les "visages" de Montaigne', p. 360), Montaigne uses 'le visage' in either the singular or plural 193 times and 'la mine' 22 times. On the Latin roots of *visage* and *face*, see Georges Gougenheim, *Les Mots français dans l'histoire et dans la vie* (Paris: Picard, 1966), vol. 1, pp. 109–12.

20. On the importance of the face and on man's as closest to the ape's, see II.12, Fl. 2.221, V, p. 484: 'What beasts have not their face aloft and before, and looke not directly opposite, as we; and in

their natural posture descrie not as much of heaven and earth, as man doth? And what qualities of our corporall constitution, both in *Plato* and *Cicero* cannot fit and serve a thousand beasts? Such as most resemble man are the vilest and filthiest of all the rout: As for outward appearance and true shape of the visage, it is the Munkie or Ape.' 'Quels animaux n'ont la face au haut, et ne l'ont devant, et ne regardent vis à vis comme nous, et ne descouvrent en leur juste posture autant du ciel et de la terre, que l'homme? Et quelles qualités de nostre corporelle constitution en Platon et en Cicero ne peuvent servir à mille sortes de bestes? Celles qui nous retirent le plus, ce sont les plus laides et les plus abjectes de toute la bande: car, pour l'apparence exterieure et forme du visage, ce sont les magots.' As the quotations in this and the previous note make clear, the *visage* itself for Montaigne has both a *forme* and a *façon*.

21. In III.5 ('Sur des vers de Virgile' [Upon Some Verses of Virgil]), Montaigne similarly admits '[w]hen I write, I can well omit the company, and spare the remembrance of books; for feare they interrupt my forme'; '[q]uand j'escris, je me passe bien de la compaignie et souvenance des livres, de peur qu'ils n'interrompent ma forme' (Fl. 3. 102, V, p. 874).

22. For the impact of Cicero's *Brutus* on the *Ciceronianus*, see my 'Cicero *Redivivus* and the Historicizing of Renaissance Style', in *Inventing a Path: Studies in Medieval Rhetoric in Honour of Mary Carruthers*, ed. Laura Iseppi De Filippis (Turnhout: Brepols, 2012), pp. 143–69. In the *De copia*, Erasmus rehearses the same metaphor (*CWE*, vol. 24, p. 306; *ASD* I-6, 36–38): 'style [*elocutio*] is to thought as clothes are to the body. Just as dress and outward appearance can enhance or disfigure the beauty [*forma*] and dignity of the body, so words can enhance or disfigure thought. Accordingly a great mistake is made by those who consider that it makes no difference how anything is expressed, provided it can be understood somehow or other. The practice of giving variety to expression [*orationis variandae ratio*] is exactly like changing clothes.' On the garment of style, see also Rosemond Tuve, *Elizabethan and Metaphysical Imagery* (Chicago: University of Chicago Press, 1947), pp. 61–78. See also I.36 ('De l'usage de se vestir' [On the Use of Apparell]), Fl. 1.242–43, V, p. 226, and I.49 ('Des coustumes anciennes' [Of Ancient Customes]), Fl. 1.342–48, V, p. 296–300.

23. Compare I.49, Fl. 1.342, V, p. 296, and II.37, Fl. 644, V, p. 778. For Montaigne's use of *forme* elsewhere with 'une precision et une abstraction toutes scolastiques', see Ian Maclean, *Montaigne philosophe* (Paris: Presses universitaires de France, 1996), p. 37. See also Cave, *Cornucopian Text*, p. 277.

24. In the opening chapter of Book II, Montaigne similarly claims that he gives his soul 'tantost un visage, tantost un autre' by speaking of it 'diversement' (II.1, Fl. 2.7, V, p. 335). On the style or *façon* of Plutarch and Seneca, see also II.10 ('Des livres' [Of Bookes], Fl. 2.117, V, p. 413: 'Their instruction is the prime and creame of Philosophy, and presented with a plaine, unaffected, and pertinent fashion.' 'Leur instruction est de la cresme de la philosophie, et presentée d'une simple façon et pertinente.' In I.24 ('Divers evenemens de mesme conseil' [Divers Events from One Selfe Same Counsel]), Montaigne further leverages the alliance between style and the human face by claiming that 'un suffisant lecteur' (V, p. 127) will find in an author both more *sens* and more *visage* than the author himself intended.

25. For Montaigne on the judicial style in ancient Rome, see III.11, V, p. 1030: 'Le stile à Romme portait que cela mesme qu'un tesmoin deposoit pour l'avoir veu de ses yeux, et ce qu'un juge ordonnoit de sa plus certaine science, estoit conceu en cette forme de parler: Il me semble. On me faict hayr les choses vray-semblables quand on me les plante pour infaillibles. J'ayme ces mots, qui amollissent et moderent la temerité de nos propositions: A l'avanture, Aucunement, Quelque, On dict, Je pense, et semblables. Et si j'eusse eu à dresser des enfans, je leur eusse tant mis en la bouche cette façon de respondre, enquesteuse, non resolutive.' Here Montaigne aligns 'stile', 'forme', and 'façon'. On Montaigne's use of 'stile' as legal procedure, see Marc Fumaroli, *L'Âge de l'éloquence: rhétorique et 'res literaria' de la Renaissance au seuil de l'époque classique* (Geneva: Droz, 1980), pp. 427–622; André Tournon, *Montaigne: la glose et l'essai* (Lyon: Presses universitaires de Lyon, 1983), pp. 185–202; and my *Renaissance Rediscovery of Intimacy*, pp. 6–7. Rigolot notes that 'façon', 'forme', and 'lineamens' are all synonyms of the 'sens aspectuel du visage' but does not align these synonyms with 'la face'; 'Les "visages" de Montaigne', p. 359.

26. On the 'façon de parler' of the Pyrrhonians, see II.12, Fl. 2.253, V, p. 505. And on Leonardo Bruni's, see I.51 ('De la vanité des paroles'), Fl. 1.355, V, p. 307. On Montaigne's own *façon* or *stile*, see II.17, Fl. 2.450, V, p. 637.

27. On the doubling of words as Montaigne's signature stylistic technique, see R. A. Sayce, 'The Style of Montaigne: Word-Pairs and Word-Groups', in *Literary Style: A Symposium*, ed. Seymour Chatman (London: Oxford University Press, 1971), pp. 383–405.

28. See also I.23, Fl. 1.116, V, p. 118: 'These considerations do nevertheless distract a man of understanding from following the common guise. Rather, on the contrary, me semeth, that all severall, strange, and particular fashions proceed rather of follie, or ambitious affection, than of true reason: and that a wise man ought inwardly to retire his minde from the common presse, and hold the same liberty and power to judge freely of all things, but for outward matters, he ought absolutely to follow the fashions and forme customarily received.' 'Ces considerations ne destournent pourtant pas un homme d'entendement de suivre le stille commun; ains, au rebours, il me semble que toutes façons escartées et particulieres partent plustost de folie ou d'affectation ambitieuse, que de vraye raison; et que le sage doit au dedans retirer son ame de la presse, et la tenir en liberté et puissance de juger librement des choses; mais, quant au dehors, qu'il doit suivre entierement les façons et formes receues.' On this passage, see also Terence Cave's essay in the present volume. For the relationship between Latin and Montaigne's vernacular, see Carol Clark, *The Web of Metaphor: Studies in the Imagery of Montaigne's Essais* (Lexington, KY: French Forum, 1978), pp. 87–98, 156–63; Cave, *Cornucopian Text*, p. 288; and Hugo Friedrich, *Montaigne*, trans. Dawn Eng (Berkeley, CA: University of California Press, 1991), pp. 370–71.

29. As quoted above, n. 18, the end of the first edition compares the individuality of opinions to that of faces.

30. Montaigne himself uses *lineaments*, for instance, at III.12, 'De la phisionomie', Fl. 3.321, V, p. 1058.

31. On Latin as Montaigne's first language, see I.26, Fl. 1.185–86, V, pp. 173–74. On his reverting to it in times of crisis, see III.2, Fl. 3.28, V, p. 810. On Latin as the more durable language, see III.9, Fl. 3.232, V, p. 982, and as the more dignified and beguiling language, II.17, Fl. 2.445, V, p. 634.

32. At *De lingua latina* VI. 78, Varro derives *facere* from *facies*, not vice versa, and likens it to the derivation of *formare* from *forma*. Aulus Gellius, on the other hand, derives *facies* from *facere* and stresses that the word means more than the features of the face, including mouth, eyes, and cheeks, designating instead the 'forma omnis [...] corporis totius' (XIII. 30. 2). For both ancient historians of language, then, *facies* is aligned with *forma*. For the affiliation of *visage* with *vultus* see Rigolot, 'Les "visages" de Montaigne', p. 359, and Gougenheim, *Les Mots français*, pp. 109–10. Rigolot also mentions in passing *façon*, *forme*, *lineamens*, and *mine* as synonyms of *visage* (pp. 359–60).

33. On the metonym of *style* or *stile* from Latin *stilus* or pen, see Willibald Sauerländer, 'From Stilus to Style: Reflections on the Fate of a Notion', *Art History*, 6 (1983), 253–70.

34. Montaigne's contempt for rhetoric is well known. See, for instance, I.26, Fl. 1.179, V, p. 168: 'The world is nothing but babbling and words, and I never saw man, that doth not rather speake more than he ought, than lesse. Notwithstanding halfe our age is consumed that way. We are kept foure or five yeares learning to understand bare words, and to joine them into clauses; then as long in proportioning a great bodie extended into foure or five parts; and five more at least ere we can succinctly know how to mingle, joine, and interlace them handsomely into a subtil fashion, and into one coherent orbe. Let us leave it to those, whose profession is to doe nothing else.' 'Le monde n'est que babil, et ne vis jamais homme qui ne die plustost plus que moins qu'il ne doit; toutesfois la moictié de nostre aage s'en va là. On nous tient quatre ou cinq ans à entendre les mots et les coudre en clauses; encores autant à en proportionner un grand corps, estendu en quatre ou cinq parties, et autres cinq, pour le moins, à les sçavoir brefvement mesler et entrelasser de quelque subtile façon. Laissons le à ceux qui en font profession expresse.' See also I.51, Fl. 1.352–56, V, pp. 305–07, and III.4 ('De la diversion' [Of Diverting and Diversions]), Fl. 3.59, V, p. 838. On the ambivalence of Montaigne's attitude towards rhetoric, see Warren Boutcher's essay in the present volume.

CHAPTER 5

Uneasy States of Matrimony:
Marriage in Transit in Montaigne's *Essais*

Chimène Bateman

> [T]he influence on thought of the institution of marriage may be said to prevent fundamental changes in the notion of woman during the Renaissance. [...] Marriage is an immovable obstacle to any improvement in the theoretical or real status of woman in law, in theology, in moral and political philosophy.[1]

Describing marriage in the Renaissance as 'an immovable obstacle' to change, Ian Maclean underscores its status as orthodoxy. As a sacrament and as a contractual agreement, it is firmly enshrined in the discourses of theology and law; and in the early modern era, as Maclean observes, these are the discourses which tend to define gender in the most conservative terms. Even in the relatively more liberal disciplines of philosophy and medicine, marriage in the Renaissance is viewed as a 'natural' phenomenon, found among animals and humans alike. As Maclean further notes, early modern treatises on marriage also cohere remarkably well with the ancient texts on which they draw.[2] For the most part, the representations of marriage that recur throughout Montaigne's *Essais* seem to conform to this traditional paradigm: in many ways, the reader is confronted with a notion of marriage that seems quite consistent from chapter to chapter, and that illustrates Montaigne's thought at its most conservative. In the realm of marriage, as in that of politics, Montaigne is no advocate of revolution, and if the topic has received comparatively little critical attention to date, this is doubtless because marriage in Montaigne appears to function as a static concept: not subject to the kind of sceptical interrogation that he brings to so many other propositions.

Modern studies of gender in Montaigne have focused overwhelmingly on moments in the *Essais* where gender is, so to speak, 'in transit', and where Montaigne problematizes or reconceptualizes traditional gender norms: examples include the gender change of Marie Germain, and Montaigne's own predilection for describing himself and his writing style in terms typically associated with the feminine.[3] The tension between Montaigne's radical exploration of gender and his conventional depiction of marriage is in itself intriguing. Nevertheless, even when conceptualized in an orthodox way, marriage emerges as a highly complex phenomenon in the *Essais*, one in which (in a definition to which we will return) there are 'mille fusées estrangeres à desmeler parmy' [a thousand foreign tangles to unravel] (I.28, 'De l'amitié' [Of Friendship]; V, p. 186; F, p. 167). For of course in our day, as in his, it is an institution that brings together the personal and the political; the couple, the family and the state; the realms of sexuality, economics, religion, and law. For all its status in the Renaissance as 'immovable obstacle', it was also the source both of rhetorical debate and of social and political conflict. As Michael Screech remarks, '*An sit nubendum* [whether one should marry or not] was a favourite theme of rhetorical composition';[4] and it was not unusual for an author to present the pros and cons of matrimony in a single text. In political terms, from the twelfth century onward, the issue of whether young people could marry without parental consent made marriage a site of fierce controversy.[5] Clandestine marriages were valid in the eyes of the church, but were hotly contested by aristocratic families, and in 1556 Henri II issued an edict attempting to nullify such marriages and enable parents to disinherit the couples concerned.[6]

Given the many-sided nature of marriage as an institution, it is therefore unsurprising to discover, in a text as multi-layered as the *Essais*, that marriage turns out to be a notion 'in transit' after all, and in a number of different ways: Montaigne's treatment of the topic evolves from chapter to chapter, and from the 'A' to the 'B' and 'C' redactions of the text. It also varies from culture to culture, as the *Essais* reference not only marriage customs in early modern France, but also those in the ancient world and in the newly discovered Americas. My aim in this study is to examine four chapters in the centre of Book I, chapters 28 to 31, which approach the question of marriage from a series of different but complementary perspectives.[7] In none of these chapters is marriage itself the primary topic; rather, Montaigne uses the notion of marriage as a tool in order to tease out the ramifications of other complex phenomena, from ideal friendship (I.28, 'De l'amitié') and the textual legacy he has inherited from his deceased friend (I.29, 'Vingt et neuf sonnets d'Estienne de la Boétie'), to the virtue of moderation (I.30, 'De la moderation') and the customs of the so-called 'cannibals' of Brazil (I.31, 'Des cannibales'). However, as we follow the thread of matrimony from chapter to chapter, it becomes a compelling theme in its own right.

1. I.28, 'De l'amitié': marriage and intellectual unease

In 'De l'amitié', marriage appears as one of a series of different affective relationships that Montaigne compares negatively to friendship. The chapter moves from a discussion of paternal affection, to heterosexual erotic desire, to marriage, to homoerotic desire (this last category constituting a substantial C-addition to the text). Montaigne contrasts all of these relationships to the 'parfaicte amitié' [perfect friendship] (V, p. 186; F, p. 167) that he shared with the humanist scholar Étienne de La Boétie until his friend's death in 1563 at the age of 32. Yet there is a particular connection between Montaigne's recollections of his friend and the subject of marriage. In 1571, the same year Montaigne famously retired to his tower, he edited a collection of writings that La Boétie had left behind unpublished; Montaigne refers to this collection near the beginning of 'De l'amitié' as 'le livret de ses œuvres que j'ay fait mettre en lumiere' [the little volume of his works which

I have had published] (V, p. 184; F, p. 165). Along with a selection of La Boëtie's Latin and French verse, the 'little volume' consists of three ancient works on marriage translated by La Boëtie from Greek into French: Xenophon's *Oeconomicus* (*La Mesnagerie*) and Plutarch's *Conjugalia praecepta* (*Les Règles de mariage*), both treatises well known in the Renaissance; and Plutarch's *Consolatio ad uxorem* (*Lettre de consolation, de Plutarque à sa femme*), a letter that he wrote to his wife after their young daughter's death. Montaigne introduces Plutarch's letter with a dedication to his own wife, commenting on the recent loss of their own infant daughter. The volume's final text is Montaigne's letter to his father describing the death of La Boëtie (*Un discours sur la mort dudit Seigneur de la Boëtie, par M. de Montaigne*).[8] Thus, following his 1571 publication of La Boëtie's translations on the topic of marriage, accompanied by his own account of La Boëtie's death, Montaigne returns in 'De l'amitié' to theorize the subjects of marriage and friendship together.

The discussion of marriage in I.28 begins with a characteristically rich and complex Montaignian sentence:

> Quant aux mariages, outre ce que c'est un marché qui n'a que l'entrée libre (sa durée estant contrainte et forcée, dependant d'ailleurs que de nostre vouloir), et marché qui ordinairement se fait à autres fins, il y survient mille fusées estrangeres à desmeler parmy, suffisantes à rompre le fil et troubler le cours d'une vive affection; là où, en l'amitié, il n'y a affaire ny commerce, que d'elle mesme.

> [As for marriage, for one thing it is a bargain to which only the entrance is free — its continuance being constrained and forced, depending otherwise than on our will — and a bargain ordinarily made for other ends. For another, there supervene a thousand foreign tangles to unravel, enough to break the thread and trouble the course of a lively affection; whereas in friendship there are no dealings or business except with itself.] (V, p. 186; F, p. 167)

The institution of marriage is here depicted as falling short of the perfection of friendship for at least three reasons: matrimony is predicated largely upon lack of choice, it constitutes a kind of economic exchange (a 'marché'), and finally, a vast number of extraneous concerns are implicated within it. I will consider each of these aspects in turn. The first point, about lack of liberty, seizes upon a theme central to the whole of the chapter. Critics have fruitfully explored the links between the political freedom advocated by La Boëtie in *De la servitude volontaire* (the treatise that Montaigne originally intended to publish as the centrepiece of Book I of the *Essais*) and the freedom that is a defining feature of ideal friendship.[9] The concept of freedom in 'De l'amitié' is closely associated with that of selfhood, and of what is 'sien' [one's own]: contrasting friendship with familial bonds earlier in the essay, Montaigne states that 'nostre liberté volontaire n'a point de production qui soit plus proprement sienne que celle de l'affection et amitié' [our free will has no product more properly its own than affection and friendship] (V, p. 185; F, p. 166). The notion of a 'production [...] proprement sienne' is one Montaigne returns to in a later chapter when thinking about his own text: 'sa fin principale et perfection, c'est d'estre exactement mien' [its principal end and perfection is to be precisely my own] (III.5, 'Sur des vers de Virgile' [On Some Verses of Virgil]; V, p. 875; F, p. 809).

Marriage, then — unlike friendship and unlike the *Essais* themselves — is largely not a product of free choice and not an expression of the self. Montaigne reiterates and expands upon this idea in 'Sur des vers de Virgile': 'On ne se marie pas pour soy, quoi qu'on die; on se marie autant ou plus pour sa posterité, pour sa famille' [We do not marry for ourselves, whatever we say; we marry just as much or more for our posterity, for our family] (V, p. 850; F, p. 783). 'De l'amitié' specifies that at least the choice to enter into matrimony is free, but Montaigne states in the later chapter that he is quite willing for others to make the arrangements: 'Pourtant me plait cette façon, qu'on le conduise plustost par mains tierces que par les propres, et par le sens d'autruy que par le sien' [Therefore I like this fashion of arranging it rather by a third hand than by our own, and by the sense of others rather than by our own] (V, p. 850; F, p. 783). Montaigne's support for arranged marriage is shared by most other sixteenth-century humanists. Even Erasmus — who, in what Screech terms his 'philogamic propaganda', moves towards a companionate view of marriage, and undermines the notion that a man should marry 'vel gignendae proli vel refrenandae libidini' [only to beget children or curb his lust] — insists on the importance of parental consent.[10]

Once the marriage contract is made, 'De l'amitié' reminds us, as noted above, that 'sa durée [est] contrainte et forcée, dependant d'ailleurs que de nostre vouloir' [its continuance [is] constrained and forced, depending otherwise than on our will] (V, p. 186; F, p. 167). Montaigne does not question this feature of marriage; he only notes it. However, in a fascinating passage in II.15, 'Que nostre desir s'accroit par la malaisance' [That Our Desire Is Increased by Difficulty], he argues that the freedom to divorce in ancient Rome actually improved the quality of marriage, and deepened spousal affection: 'ce qui tint les mariages à Rome si long temps en honneur et en seurté, fut la liberté de les rompre, qui voudroit. Ils aymoient mieux leurs femmes d'autant qu'ils les pouvoient perdre' [what kept marriages in Rome so long in honor and security was everyone's freedom to break them off at will. They loved their wives the better because they might lose them] (V, p. 615; F, p. 566). Yet this glimpse of a culturally different form of marriage, one where 'liberté' and individual 'vouloir' could play a role, reinforces the fact that marriage in sixteenth-century France is *not* conceived by Montaigne as permitting the exercise of free choice and self-expression.

A second way in which 'De l'amitié' portrays contemporary marriage as falling short of the ideal friendship is that marriage is defined in economic terms ('marché'). The gay love of the Greeks is found lacking for this reason as well, since it is based upon an exchange: that of 'spirituelle beauté' for physical beauty (V, p. 187; F, p. 168). It is not only the inequality of such an exchange that Montaigne finds objectionable, but the very notion of exchange itself. In true friendship as he portrays it, there is no private property, for the distinction between self and other disappears. This merging of selves and consequent lack of private property are themes that the essay explores at length, and in order to illustrate his argument, Montaigne compares friendship with marriage a second time, saying of friends that

> ils ne se peuvent ny prester ny donner rien. Voilà pourquoi les faiseurs de loix, pour honorer le mariage de quelque imaginaire ressemblance de cette divine

liaison, defendent les donations entre le mary et la femme, voulant inferer par
là que tout doit estre à chacun d'eux, et qu'ils n'ont rien à diviser et partir
ensemble.

[they can neither lend nor give anything to each other. That is why the
lawmakers, to honor marriage with some imaginary resemblance to this divine
union, forbid gifts between husband and wife, wishing thus to imply that
everything should belong to each of them and that they have nothing to divide
or split up between them.] (V, p. 190; F, p. 171)

What is striking about this passage, and the discussion leading up to it, is that
Montaigne borrows the terms used in Plutarch's *Règles de mariage* to describe ideal
marriage, and transfers them instead into a representation of ideal friendship. He
audaciously dismisses marriage (itself a divine union according to the Church)
as bearing only 'some imaginary resemblance' to the 'divine union' of friends.
As George Hoffmann observes, Montaigne's portrait of perfect friendship 'seems
indebted to the sacramental language of matrimony':[11] the verbs 'confondre' [blend]
and 'mesler' [mingle], used in La Boëtie's translation of Plutarch to designate the
bond between man and wife, are redeployed in 'De l'amitié' in the context of
friendship. In fact, Montaigne's insistence on the impossibility of private property
between friends draws even more extensively upon a discussion in Plutarch's *Règles*
of the words 'mien' [mine] and 'tien' [yours]:

Platon dit que celle ville est heureuse et fortunee, en laquelle le moins qu'on
peult on oit dire: ceci est mien, cela n'est pas mien [...]. Mais encore fault il
bien plus oster du mariage ces mots de Mien et Tien [...]. Car la nature mesle
l'homme et la femme par l'union du corps, pour prendre de tous deux quelque
part, et puis apres, l'ayant meslee, rendre à tous deux en commun ce qui
en proviendra; mais de telle façon que l'un ny l'autre ne puisse discerner ne
recognoistre ce qui luy appartient en seul, ne ce qui est à l'autre. Donc, il faut
sur tout qu'entre les mariez il y aye une telle communion de biens, qu'ayant tout
assemblé et meslé, n'y aye celuy d'eux qui estime l'une chose particulierement
sienne, et l'autre non, mais tout sien et rien d'autruy.

[Plato calls that city happy and fortunate, in which people are least heard to
say, 'That is mine' or 'That is not mine' [...]. But it is all the more necessary
to remove the words 'mine' and 'yours' from marriage [...]. For nature blends
man and woman through a union of the body, taking something from them
both, and then blending it and giving what comes forth back to them to share
in common; but in such a way that neither of them can discern or recognize
what belongs to him or her alone, and what belongs to the other. Therefore,
it is necessary for a married couple above all to have such a communion of
goods, with everything amassed and blended, that neither person can consider
one thing to be particularly his or her own, and another thing not so: rather
everything is his or her own, and nothing is the other person's.][12]

Similarly, Montaigne says that in his relationship with La Boëtie, nothing was
'ou sien ou mien' [either his or mine] (V, p. 189; F, p. 170). Even more notably,
he takes up and expands upon Plutarch's comment that in marriage, the very
words 'mien' and 'tien' should be absent. In friendship, Montaigne would ban 'ces
mots de division et de difference: bien faict, obligation, reconnoissance, priere,
remerciement, et leurs pareils' [these words of separation and distinction: benefit,

obligation, gratitude, request, thanks, and the like] (V, p. 190; F, p. 171). Ironically, Plutarch seeks to establish in the *Règles* that marriage is more than an economic transaction between two parties, but Montaigne uses Plutarch's treatise to bolster his account of friendship, and relegate marriage to the prosaic status of 'marché'.

The third and arguably most intriguing characteristic of marriage in 'De l'amitié' is its plurality, characterized as the 'mille fusées estrangeres' cited above, which Montaigne opposes to the unity and self-containedness of ideal friendship (V, p. 186; F, p. 167). Marriage is problematic not just because of lack, but also because of excess. The fact that many different concerns intersect in the institution of matrimony is reflected in the genre of Renaissance treatises on marriage, which Maclean describes as particularly 'pluridisciplinary' in their subject matter. For instance, the influential text of the jurist André Tiraqueau, *De legibus connubialibus*, brings together 'commonplaces about women drawn from the whole range of scholarship', not unlike Montaigne's 'mille fusées'.[13] The word 'fusée', as defined by Cotgrave, literally means 'a spoole-full, or spindle-full, of thread', but can be used figuratively to mean 'matter', or in the plural, 'imployments, causes, occasions'.[14] In a powerful if rather convoluted metaphor, Montaigne states that the unsnarling of the 'thousand alien threads' found in marriage can sever the single thread of 'vive affection'.

The focus of the passage then shifts from the institution of marriage itself to women, who are deemed to be constitutionally incapable of friendship: 'la suffisance ordinaire des femmes n'est pas pour respondre à cette conference et communication, nourrisse de cette saincte couture; ny leur ame ne semble assez ferme pour soustenir l'estreinte d'un neud si pressé et si durable' [the ordinary capacity of women is inadequate for that communion and fellowship which is the nurse of this sacred bond; nor does their soul seem firm enough to endure the strain of so tight and durable a knot] (V, p. 186; F, p. 167). The metaphors here are in the same semantic field as that of thread: friendship is both a seam and a strong knot. In his use of the knot metaphor, Montaigne once again seizes upon a word that typically functions as a symbol of marriage, and makes it designate friendship instead; in Plutarch's *Règles de mariage*, the married couple are said to make each other stronger 'comme les neuds par l'entrelacement' [like knots through intertwining].[15] Other parts of 'De l'amitié' pick up the metaphorical theme of knots and seams in order to describe relationships, with terms like 'nouée[s]' [bound together, tied] (V, pp. 188, 190; F, pp. 169, 171), 'la couture' [seam] (V, p. 188; F, p. 169), and 'descoust' [dissolves] (V, p. 191; F, p. 172). The message that emerges overall is a consistent one: the bonds that characterize friendship are seamless and solid, but the bonds of marriage, as well as of other more contingent relationships, are knotted together in such a way that some or all of them risk being undone. 'Que nostre desir s'accroit par la malaisance', in its discussion of Roman divorce, enlarges eloquently on the paradoxical status of the contemporary marital knot:

> Nous avons pensé attacher plus ferme le neud de nos mariages pour avoir osté tout moyen de les dissoudre; mais d'autant s'est dépris et relaché le neud de la volonté et de l'affection, que celuy de la contrainte s'est estroicy.
>
> [We have thought to tie the knot of our marriages more firmly by taking away

all means of dissolving them; but the knot of will and affection has become loosened and undone as much as that of constraint has tightened.] (V, p. 615; F, p. 566)

In this quotation, the knot of marriage itself remains intact, but only through the rupture of other crucially important ties that can unite a married couple: those of free will and affection.

If 'De l'amitié' complicates our understanding of the 'immoveable object' of marriage, it does so most radically through its use of metaphor. As Elizabeth Guild has observed of Montaigne, '[o]ne of the processes by which his writing sustains tolerance and encourages plural interpretations is its exceptionally creative use of figuration'.[16] Whereas the chapter as a whole seeks to differentiate between ideal male friendship and other kinds of human relations, the imagery that recurs throughout — that of threads and knots being done and undone — tangles together the representations of male friendship and heterosexual marriage and suggests that the two alliances may on some level resemble each other. Furthermore, the famous extended metaphor that opens the chapter establishes a contrast between plurality and unity that bears an almost uncanny correspondence to the subsequent discussion of marriage and friendship. The 'tableau' that constitutes the missing centrepiece of the *Essais*, La Boëtie's treatise on tyranny, also evokes the 'parfaicte amytié' that is the essay's main topic, while the multitude of 'crotesques' [grotesques], remarkable for their 'varieté et estrangeté' [variety and strangeness] (V, p. 183; F, p. 164), could function as a figure not only for the *Essais* themselves but also and equally for the 'mille fusées estrangeres' that make up marriage.

Montaigne's repetition of the word 'suffisance' [ability] in this chapter (and which also appears in the title of the chapter preceding 'De l'amitié': I.27, 'C'est folie de rapporter le vray et le faux à nostre suffisance' [It Is Folly to Measure the True and False by Our Own Capacity]) forms another suggestive strand of meaning. If 'De l'amitié' presents women as unable to experience friendship due to their lack of 'suffisance', it is the theme of male 'suffisance' and the lack of it that provides the chapter with a frame. At its beginning, the 'suffisance' of the skilled painter (La Boëtie's figurative double) is contrasted with Montaigne's purportedly inferior powers ('ma suffisance ne va pas si avant que d'oser entreprendre un tableau riche, poly et formé selon l'art' [my ability does not go far enough for me to dare to undertake a rich, polished picture, formed according to art], V, p. 183; F, p. 164). The conclusion contrasts Montaigne and La Boëtie even more explicitly: La Boëtie is said to surpass Montaigne infinitely not only in friendship, but also 'en toute autre suffisance et vertu' [in every other ability and virtue] (V, p. 194; F, p. 175).

These echoes are not merely fortuitous. 'Parfaicte amytié' as theorized by Montaigne is an ideal, one so rare that it is extraordinary for it to come into being even once every three hundred years (V, p. 184; F, p. 165). It is a relationship that is utterly free and permits the full expression of the self, that eschews any notion of hierarchy or exchange, and that is completely unified, whole, and self-contained: an invisible seam to a tangle of threads. And while Montaigne declares himself to have lived this ideal, he also experienced its loss, and the *Essais* are presented as a mode of confronting that loss. In this movement from wholeness to loss, unity to plurality, the Imaginary to the Symbolic, love to desire, *suffisance* to inadequacy, La Boétie and ideal friendship remain on one side of the picture, with the messy diversity of the *Essais* and of an everyday relationship like marriage on the other. As Guild elegantly puts it, '[a]symmetry, lack and difference are for the living'.[17] In this sense, both the *Essais* and the institution of marriage belong very much to the realm of the living.

Whereas 'De l'amitié' explores the contiguity between marriage and intellectual or spiritual friendship-love, 'De la moderation' (I.30) turns to more corporeal concerns: the relationship between marriage and sex or erotic desire. The different directions that the *Essais* take when they address the topic of marriage illustrate the 'plural' nature of the institution, the way it sits awkwardly between different domains, with its borders proving surprisingly hard to chart. The transitional chapter between I.28 and I.30, 'Vingt et neuf sonnets d'Estienne de la Boétie' creates a link between the topic of male friendship and that of erotic passion in relation to marriage. Yet the aspect of this chapter that I will focus upon is its evocation of absence and silence, and the significance of these themes in relation to the *Essais*' treatment of matrimony.

2. I.29, 'Vingt et neuf sonnets d'Estienne de la Boétie': marriage and the unease of silence

I.29 is, of course, not so much a chapter in itself as the marker of a gap or absence; it consists only of a dedication to Diane, 'Madame de Grammont, Comtesse de Guissen', whose husband was a friend of Montaigne. The dedication is the result of a dizzying series of substitutions: we move from the proposed inclusion in the *Essais* of La Boétie's political text *De la servitude volontaire* (itself a tribute to its absent author), to the 29 love sonnets of La Boétie which Montaigne decides to substitute for the treatise, to Montaigne's omission of the sonnets in the *exemplaire de Bordeaux*, with the terse sentence 'Ces vers se voient ailleurs' [These verses may be seen elsewhere] (V, p. 196; F, p. 177). The potential literary and philosophical implications of these substitutions are many,[18] but the ultimate form of I.29 — an introductory dedication to a text which is 'somewhere else' — emphasizes the permanence of Montaigne's loss of his friend, and the unrepresentable nature of their 'parfaicte amytié'. However, yet another substitution or absence is also evoked within I.29: the 29 sonnets are described by Montaigne as 'le reste' [the remainder] (V, p. 196; F, p. 176) of a collection of other verses by La Boétie that Montaigne has already published and dedicated to Mme de Grammont's relative M. de Foix (these are the French verses that appear in the *livret* of 1571). The 29 love sonnets, according to Montaigne, compare favourably to those already published, for the latter were composed for La Boétie's wife-to-be, and 'sentent desjà je ne sçay quelle froideur maritale' [already smack of [I know not what] marital coolness] (V, p. 196; F, pp. 176–77). The 29 sonnets, in contrast, contain 'je ne sçay quoy de plus vif et de plus bouillant' [I know not what that is livelier and more ebullient], since they were composed in an earlier period, when his friend was 'eschauffé d'une belle et noble ardeur que je vous diray, Madame, un jour à l'oreille' [inflamed by a fine and noble ardour whose details, Madame, I will one of these days whisper in your ear] (V, p. 196; F, p. 176). The repetition of 'je ne sçay', while it tinges both descriptions with a hint of uncertainty, reinforces the opposition between the early verses and the later ones, between erotic heat and marital chill.[19]

Montaigne thus calls our attention to the 1571 volume on marriage, even as he distances himself from it. In keeping with the erotic theme of the sonnets, his address to Mme de Grammont is playfully sensual; he calls her 'Corisande d'Andoins', after the romance heroine of *Amadis de Gaule*, and promises to whisper in her ear the tale of La Boëtie's amorous adventures. In fact, the sensuality of the language aside, this dedication functions in a similar way to the other dedications scattered throughout the 1571 volume of La Boëtie's works: there, Montaigne heads each of La Boëtie's prose translations and collections of verse with a preface to an illustrious male figure, and lavishes praise simultaneously on La Boëtie's texts and on the dedicatee. In a similar vein, he praises Mme de Grammont for her ability to judge poetry, saying that this will enable her to appreciate the richness of La Boëtie's sonnets. Nevertheless, one dedication in the edition of La Boëtie's works is quite different from the rest: this is Montaigne's dedication to his own wife ('A Madamoiselle de Montaigne ma femme') which introduces the *Lettre de consolation de Plutarque à sa femme*.

Montaigne's short message to his wife is intriguing, especially given her relative absence from the *Essais*. But it reveals next to nothing about her to the reader. Unlike his other dedicatees, she is not praised for any individual qualities of her own. It is true that the letter opens on an unexpectedly erotic note: while the Montaigne of the *Essais* seeks to minimize the place of sensuality in marriage (as we will see in 'De la moderation'), the husband of the letter announces with jocularity that, although it is no longer the fashion to 'courtiser et caresser' [pay court and show affection to] one's wife, he prefers the ways of olden times: 'Vivons, ma femme, vous et moy, à la vieille Françoise' [You and me, my wife, let us live in the old French way] (F, p. 1300).[20] Nonetheless, despite the warmth of this direct address, the further comments in this brief letter (as in the *Essais*), rather than revealing the details of the life he shared with 'Madamoiselle de Montaigne', pertain to marriage as an institution. A C-addition to 'Sur des vers de Virgile' provides striking insight into his reticence on the topic:

> Les aigreurs comme les douceurs du mariage, se tiennent secretes par les sages. Et, parmy les autres importunes conditions qui se trouvent en iceluy, cette cy, à un homme langagier comme je suis, est des principales: que la coustume rende indecent et nuisible qu'on communique à personne tout ce qu'on en sçait et qu'on en sent.

> [The bitternesses of marriage, like the sweets, are kept secret by the wise. And among the other annoying conditions that are found in it, this, for a talkative man like myself, is one of the main ones: that custom makes it improper and prejudicial to communicate to anyone all that we know and feel about it.] (V, p. 870; F, p. 804)

Marriage in the *Essais* is thus associated with yet another limitation or constraint: that of silence. If the chatty narrator of the *Essais*, a self-described 'homme langagier', seeks to present himself in his 'forme naïfve' [natural form], marriage is one of those dark places where 'la reverence publique' [respect for the public] (V, p. 3; F, p. 2) prevents the torchlight of self-examination from shining. However, although Montaigne keeps the details of his own marital relationship to himself, he does complain of marriage and wives, not using 'je' but rather more general terms such as 'nous' or 'chacun'. In II.15 he remarks that 'Ce grand Caton se trouva, *aussi bien que nous*, desgousté de sa femme tant qu'elle fut siene' [That great man Cato found himself, *just like the rest of us*, weary of his wife as long as she was his] (V, p. 613; F, p. 564; italics mine); the chapter entitled 'De trois bonnes femmes' (II.35 [Of Three Good Women]) opens with the wry statement that 'Il n'en est pas à douzaines, *comme chacun sçait*, et notamment aux devoirs de mariage' [They don't come by the dozen, *as everyone knows*, and especially in the duties of marriage] (V, p. 744; F, p. 683; italics mine); and a phrase in III.5 is even more succinct: 'Ung bon mariage, s'il en est' [A good marriage, if such there be] (V, p. 851; F, p. 785). What revelations Montaigne does make about his own experience of marriage occur in III.5: he states that left to his own devices, he would have fled from marrying Wisdom herself, but that he has turned out to be rather more faithful to the 'laws of marriage' than he himself would have expected (V, p. 852; F, p. 786).

In brief, Montaigne's insistence on the institutional limitations of marriage — his conception of marriage as ultimately incompatible both with friendship and with erotic passion — may well reflect a more individual unhappiness, which he refrains from articulating in the first person. The story of his domestic life is further complicated by the fact that the message of consolation he addresses to his wife via La Boëtie's translation of Plutarch does not conclude the narrative of loss: all their children were to die 'en nourisse' [at nurse] apart from one daughter Léonor (II.8, 'De l'affection des peres aux enfans' [Of the Affection of Fathers for Their Children], V, p. 389; F, p. 341).[21] 'De la moderation' states of marriage that 'sa principale fin c'est la generation' [its principal end is generation] (V, p. 199; F, p. 179) — a view expressed by many authorities on marriage, including Xenophon in *La Mesnagerie* — and in this aspect of marriage, too, Montaigne is faced with disappointment.[22] He ultimately opts for the begetting of books rather than sons: 'Nous sommes pere et mere ensemble en cette generation' [We are father and mother both in this generation] (V, p. 400; F, p. 353), he writes, in a metaphor that, as Wes Williams notes, 'dispenses with the mother'.[23]

The unspecified 'froideur maritale' that Montaigne attributes to the later poems of La Boëtie corresponds more to the representation of marriage in the *Essais* than to that in the works of La Boëtie himself. In fact, there is plenty of passionate language in the 'Vers françois' that La Boëtie addresses to Marguerite de Carle. Yet these verses do contain fewer bitter complaints about the lover's loss of liberty and the inconstancy of the female beloved than appear in the 'Vingt et neuf sonnets'; the 29 sonnets could thus be said to be more compatible with 'De l'amitié', as they provide an unambiguous illustration of the deficiencies of heterosexual love in comparison to perfect friendship. Indeed, the image of marriage that emerges from the 1571 *livret* as a whole is in tension with the way it is portrayed in the *Essais*.[24] While the treatises translated by La Boëtie present a traditional view of matrimony in many respects, the choice of texts in itself reflects his interest in marriage; and in one of the Latin poems he wrote for Montaigne (also published in the *livret*), he encourages him to marry (Montaigne did marry in 1565, two years after La Boëtie died).[25] The final text of the *livret*, Montaigne's account of La Boëtie's death, paints a very positive picture of the relationship between La Boëtie and his wife: Montaigne notes La Boëtie's affectionate habit of calling her 'ma semblance' [my likeness], and records La Boëtie's praise of the 'sainct neud de mariage' [holy bond of marriage] (F, p. 1281).[26] However, in a scene that has been perceptively analysed by critics, La Boëtie sends her away from his bedside at the final moment, and dies with Montaigne's name on his lips.[27] In this way, Montaigne succeeds in terminating not only the story of his friend's death, but the entire volume of La Boëtie's works, with a vision of male friendship superseding marriage. And years later, in the *Essais*, when he refers once again to the subject of La Boëtie and marriage with the cryptic phrase 'je ne sçay quelle froideur maritale', he adheres to the policy of secrecy evoked in III.5: he is silent about both the 'douceurs' of his friend's marriage, and the 'aigreurs' of his own. Yet the discussion of 'froideur maritale' does not end there: in the next chapter, he turns 'froideur' into a veritable principle of matrimony.

3. I.30, 'De la moderation': marriage and erotic unease

In 'De la moderation', Montaigne argues that you can have too much of a good thing, and marital passion is the subject he takes up in order to prove his point. The chapter contains many B- and C-additions, but in the original 1580 version, the theme of marriage is particularly prominent: it is the first example used to illustrate the need for moderation. Marriage is here approached from the perspective of theology: 'L'amitié que nous portons à nos femmes, elle est très-legitime; la theologie ne laisse pas de la brider pourtant, et de la restraindre' [The affection we bear to our wives is very legitimate; yet theology does not fail to bridle and restrain it] (V, p. 198; F, p. 178). Montaigne goes on to speak approvingly of Aquinas's reason for forbidding marriage among close relatives, namely that 'il y a danger que l'amitié qu'on porte à une telle femme soit immoderée' [there is a danger that the affection a man bears to such a wife will be immoderate] (V, p. 198; F, p. 178). For if marital affection is already whole and perfect, Montaigne explains, overloading it with an additional type of affection will result in the husband being transported 'hors les barrieres de la raison' [beyond the barriers of reason] (V, p. 198; F, p. 178). Thus marriage is once again associated with a troubling excess; the terms 'surcharge' and 'surcroist' are used. But whereas the problem as described in 'De l'amitié' was an excess of externally imposed obligations, the 'danger' here is internal: that of too much affection within the couple itself.

The 'nous' here is unabashedly masculine ('the affection *we* bear to *our* wives'), and as the chapter continues, the male/male structure of address becomes even more striking: 'Je veux donc [...] apprendre cecy aux maris, [C] s'il s'en trouve encore qui y soient trop acharnez', says Montaigne [I want to teach husbands this — if there still are any who are too vehement] (V, p. 198; F, p. 178). The advice he dispenses to husbands is backed by the authoritative discourses of theology and philosophy: even the legitimate pleasures of the marriage bed can be wrong, unless moderation is observed. The C-additions to the passage put forward an even more pessimistic view of sex in marriage: Montaigne first intimates, in a wry addition, that the notion of a husband being 'too vehement' in the marriage bed is in itself an absurdity (presumably because the fact of being married kills desire), and then states, in a further insertion, that adventurous love-making is downright harmful for wives. The comment of the *exemplaire de Bordeaux* concludes: 'Qu'elles apprennent l'impudence au moins d'une autre main. Elles sont toujours assés esveillées pour nostre besoing. Je ne m'y suis servy que de l'instruction naturelle et simple' [Let them at least learn shamelessness from another hand. They are always aroused enough for our need. I have never [employed] in that any but the simple instruction of nature] (V, p. 198; F, p. 178). Here the structure of address, that of a husband advising other husbands, culminates in the undisguised objectification of women: '*they* are always aroused enough for *our* need' (italics mine). This declaration of masculine prerogative is particularly stark, but the passage as a whole conforms to a broader pattern evident in the *Essais*: when marriage is discussed, women are left out of the conversation. In this respect again, the *Essais* stand in contrast to the texts on matrimony translated by La Boétie: Plutarch's *Règles de mariage* are addressed to both bride and groom; and Xenophon's *Mesnagerie* contains a long speech by the husband Isomachus to his wife, though she remains unnamed, and the text also contains an illuminating discussion of how rarely most husbands converse with their wives, and why to do so would be a good idea.[28]

Montaigne's advice to husbands touches upon the troubled issue of women's sexual knowledge: on the one hand, he states that 'the simple instruction of nature' is enough for the marriage bed, but he leaves open the possibility of wives acquiring more knowledge 'from another hand'. An anxiety about women's erotic knowledge is expressed elsewhere in the *Essais*. In 'Que nostre desir s'accroit par la malaisance', for example, women are represented as feigning ignorance of sexual matters when in reality they know too much: Montaigne speaks of 'cette profession d'ignorance des choses qu'elles sçavent mieux que nous qui les en instruisons' [that profession of ignorance of things that they know better than we who instruct them in them] (V, p. 614; F, pp. 565–66). He takes up the topic again in 'Sur des vers de Virgile', declaring that 'nous ne sommes qu'enfans au pris d'elles en cette science' [we are but children compared with them in this knowledge] (V, p. 857; F, p. 790). Nor do women need to read erotic literature to acquire this expertise: 'c'est une discipline qui naist dans leurs veines' [it is a teaching that is born in their veins] (V, p. 857; F, p. 791).[29] The *Essais* thus vacillate between advising husbands not to teach their wives too much, and asserting that women are always already better informed than their husbands will ever be (just as they are always already 'aroused enough'). This unease surrounding female sexual knowledge, and the concomitant admissions of male inadequacy in the face of its mystical power, are a direct corollary of the essayist's casting of wives as other: they ('elles') are imagined not as participants in the famously dialogic mode of the *Essais*, but as an enigma for the masculine 'nous' to mull over.

However, when it comes to the difficulty of 'bridling' and 'restraining' desire in marriage, 'De la moderation' focuses not on lustful women but on lustful men: it is the husband, after all, who is initially said to risk being carried 'beyond the barriers of reason' (V, p. 198; F, p. 178). (In III.5, the wife is said to run this risk; V, p. 850, F, p. 783.) Again, it is the religious and sacramental status of marriage that is adduced as the reason for setting a limit on pleasure: 'C'est une religieuse liaison et devote que le mariage; voilà pourquoy le plaisir qu'on en tire, ce doit estre un plaisir retenu, serieux et meslé à quelque severité; ce doit estre une volupté aucunement prudente et conscientieuse' [Marriage is a religious and holy bond. That is why the pleasure we derive from it should be a restrained pleasure, serious, and mixed with some austerity; it should be a somewhat discreet and conscientious voluptuousness] (V, p. 198; F, p. 179). The qualifying words 'quelque' [some] and 'aucunement' [somewhat] reinforce the theme of moderation. Whereas marriage was portrayed in I.28 as an entirely different beast to 'parfaicte amytié', the distinction between marriage and extramarital erotic relationships is here conceptualized in a less definitive fashion: 'plaisir' and 'volupté' are not banished entirely from marriage, but the question is rather one of degree. Montaigne's remarks in 'Sur des vers de Virgile' on the verses of the title strike a similar note: he is critical of Virgil's depiction of Vulcan and Venus in bed because Virgil 'la peinct un peu bien esmeue pour une Venus maritale' [portrays her as a little too passionate for a marital Venus] (V, p. 849; F, p. 783). Again, it is that unspecified 'froideur maritale' that is lacking. Lucretius, on the other hand, is said to speak 'plus sortablement' [more appropriately] in his poetic account of the adultery of Venus and Mars, because he is describing 'une jouissance desrobée' [a stolen enjoyment] (V, p. 872; F, p. 806).

Although Montaigne's account of moderate sexual desire in marriage is clearly intended to be a plausible one — for 'moderation' itself is an appealingly plausible notion — the question of exactly how much desire marriage can safely accommodate is thorny. III.5 contains a comic anecdote about the queen of Aragon working out how many times a married couple should have sexual intercourse per day: 'cette bonne Royne, pour donner reigle et exemple à tout temps de la *moderation* et modestie requise en un juste mariage, ordonna pour bornes legitimes et necessaires le nombre de six par jour' [this good queen, to give for all time a rule and example of the *moderation* and modesty required in a just marriage, ordained as the legitimate and necessary limit the number of six a day] (V, p. 855; F, p. 788; italics mine). Beneath the jesting tone lies a more serious query: who will set the boundaries of marital desire, and how? The original 1580 version of 'De la moderation' gives two anecdotes (one taken from Plutarch's *Règles de mariage*) of men who resolve the dilemma by gratifying their 'appetits immoderez' (V, p. 199; F, p. 179) with women other than their wives; this is presented as a gesture of respect towards their spouses. The chapter thus suggests (moving smoothly away from theological doctrine towards ancient mores) that 'immoderate' sexual pleasure is not in itself reprehensible; it is only within the confines of marriage that moderation must be observed.

The 1588 version of the chapter, however, introduces a new twist with the exemplary story of Zenobia: she lets her husband get her pregnant, 'et cela fait, elle le laissoit courir tout le temps de sa conception, luy donnant lors seulement loy de recommencer: brave et genereux exemple de mariage' [and, that done, she let him run free all the time of her conception, allowing him only then to begin again: a fine and noble example of marriage] (V, p. 199; F, p. 179). Here a wife is represented as an active subject, and praised, but her role is to police male desire within marriage: to set down boundaries in order to ensure that marital sex is about procreation rather than passion. The C-version introduces a similar example, this time from an ecclesiastical source, of an unnamed woman 'qui repudia son mary pour ne vouloir seconder ses trop lascives et immoderées amours' [who repudiated her husband because she would not be a partner to his too lascivious and immoderate lovemaking] (V, p. 200; F, p. 180). The ideal wife is thus portrayed as able not only to curb her own desire, but also to impose a limit on that of her husband, redirecting him elsewhere if necessary: in short, she relieves him of the tricky task of working out how much 'affection' the marriage bed can bear.

The exemplary wives whose stories are told in II.35, 'De trois bonnes femmes', play an analogous role to that of Zenobia. Although the subject of this chapter is not restraining one's erotic desire, but rather finding the courage to commit suicide, two of the three 'bonnes femmes' prove strong where their husbands are weak, and shore up their spouses' lack of resolve. The three tales form a kind of crescendo: the first wife is 'de bas lieu' [of low estate] (V, p. 745; F, p. 684) and remains unnamed, the second is a Roman noblewoman called Arria, and the third is none other than the wife of Seneca himself, who unlike the first two husbands is eminently capable of engineering his own glorious death.[30] It is the first and nameless 'bonne femme', a neighbour of Pliny the Younger, whose case interests me here: having ascertained that her husband suffers from incurable and unbearably painful genital ulcers, she proposes the solution of a double suicide, which she says they will experience as 'plaisir' (V, p. 745; F, p. 684). In order to maintain the 'loyale et vehemente affection' that she has shown him throughout their marriage, she wants him to die in her arms, but she fears that as they jump from a window together, her grip on him will loosen. Therefore 'elle se fit lier et attacher bien estroittement avec luy par le faux du corps, et abandonna ainsi sa vie pour le repos de celle de son mary' [she had herself bound and attached very tightly to him around the waist, and thus abandoned her life for the repose of her husband's] (V, p. 745; F, p. 684). In this remarkable story, the knot of matrimony is literal and metaphorical at the same time: the 'vive affection' (V, p. 186; F, p. 167), which Montaigne envisioned in 'De l'amitié' as an easily severed thread, holds fast through the sheer determination of the wife. Not only is she willing to forego sexual pleasure (her husband's sexual organs having become a site of pain), but she refigures death itself as pleasure. As a counter-example to this model wife, one could cite 'Jeanne, Royne de Naples', whose story, related in a C-addition to III.5, also involves a window and a literal knot: she had her first husband strangled

> aux grilles de sa fenestre à tout un laz d'or et de soye tissu de sa main propre, sur ce qu'aux corvées matrimoniales elle ne luy trouvoit ny les parties, ny les efforts assez respondants à l'esperance qu'elle en avoit conceuë.

> [at the bars of her window with a gold and silk cord woven by her own hand, when in matrimonial duties she found that neither his parts nor his efforts

corresponded well enough with the expectations she had formed of them.] (V, p. 885; F, p. 820)

In the hands of this sexually frustrated queen, the matrimonial knot becomes her husband's death-noose.

One might protest that these examples are extreme, and indeed Montaigne himself states that the tales of II.35 are 'exemples un peu autres, et si pressans qu'ils tirent hardiment la vie en consequence' [slightly different examples, and so ardent that they entail a heroic sacrifice of life] (V, p. 745; F, p. 684). Yet these stories of women making different kinds of knots illustrate once again the difficulties inherent in Montaigne's formulation of 'moderate' marital affection. Like Pliny's neighbour with her 'vehement' love, Zenobia in laying down an inflexible sexual law for her husband seems more a model of heroic self-sacrifice than one of moderation. As Guild observes, 'the chapter entitled "De la moderation" is not, itself, moderate'.[31] With the essayist's tales of exemplary Stoic wives on the one hand, and the ruthless, sexually rapacious queen of Naples on the other, a practicable template for negotiating desire within marriage remains as elusive as ever.

Like 'De l'amitié', however, 'De la moderation' appears to contain its own implicit self-critique. In one of the powerful shifts of perspective so typical of the *Essais*, Montaigne turns to muse on the folly of those who believe that pain is somehow beneficial in itself, and that pleasure should be avoided. Man, states Montaigne, is such a miserable animal that as soon as he finds himself in a position to 'gouter un seul plaisir entier et pur' [taste a single pleasure pure and entire], he undertakes to 'le retrancher par discours' [curtail that pleasure by his [reasoning]] (V, p. 200; F, p. 180). The notion of curtailing pleasure brings us back full circle to the opening of the chapter, where theology is said to 'bridle and restrain' marital 'amitié'. Ironically, with his raft of anecdotes about how to keep lust out of marriage, the essayist himself demonstrates how to reduce pleasure 'par discours'.

What is clearly evident in 'De la moderation' is Montaigne's wish to present marriage as an immovable institution, as free as possible of the unpredictability that comes with sexual desire. To this end he adopts the discourse of didacticism, and seeks to institute a normative paradigm: a general rule for how married couples should behave in bed. Yet didacticism is not the usual mode of the *Essais*, and sits uncomfortably with the work's broader governing ethos of exploration by trial and error. 'De la moderation' ends with a 1588 addition that recounts how the King of Mexico's ambassadors approached Cortez to seek his 'amitié', and brought with them three different sets of gifts, to cover three possible eventualities: Cortez might prove to be a fierce god, a benign god, or simply a man (V, p. 201; F, p. 181). These ambassadors, as Terence Cave has put it, are practising a form of 'ethics as experimentation'.[32] When it comes to marriage, however, Montaigne is unwilling, or at best reluctant, to bring ethics as experimentation into play. Rather than acknowledging the infinite permutations that characterize marital affection, or representing erotic desire in marriage as a matter for mutual negotiation between spouses, 'De la moderation' proposes a one-size-fits-all model of matrimony. Even so, because of their colourful variety, the anecdotes of married life that are interspersed throughout the *Essais* serve at least as much to undercut the notion of a single normative model of marriage as they do to reinforce it.

In its concluding sentence, 'De la moderation' (giving a backward nod to I.28 through the reference to 'amitié') looks ahead to 'Des cannibales' through the telling of a story from the New World. The last of this series of chapters in Book I to thematize marriage, 'Des cannibales' gives the kaleidoscope a final twist, taking up and rearranging the ideas about matrimony that we encountered in Montaigne's three preceding chapters. 'Des cannibales' can be interpreted as offering a utopian image of marriage, in the sense that some of the elements of marriage that were represented as most problematic in the earlier essays prove to be happily absent from Brazilian culture. Nevertheless, even in Montaigne's picture of matrimonial utopia, tensions remain.

Conclusion. I.31, 'Des cannibales', marriage, and the unease of utopia

As David Quint has argued, the New World as portrayed in 'Des cannibales' is by no means an unqualified utopia. The Brazilians display traits of competitive cruelty and Stoic inflexibility that mirror the self-destructive behaviour of the nobles caught up in the French religious wars.[33] Yet as far as love and marriage are concerned, I would contend that the vision of New World society presented by Montaigne is in fact utopian. Twice in I.31 we are told that the moral code of the Brazilians consists of just two elements: 'la vaillance contre les ennemis et l'amitié à leurs femmes' [valour against the enemy and love for their wives], or as the second very similar formulation puts it, 'de la resolution à la guerre et affection à leurs femmes' [resoluteness in war and affection for their wives] (V, p. 208; F, p. 187). Each time these principles are articulated, the expression 'ne ... que' ('only') is used: 'Il ne leur recommande que deux choses' [He recommends to them only two things] and 'toute leur science ethique ne contient que ces deux articles' [their whole ethical science contains only these two articles] (V, p. 208; F, p. 187). The first factor, then, that distinguishes marriage in the New World from marriage in the Old is its simplicity. There are no longer 'a thousand foreign tangles to unravel', as described in I.28: 'amitié' or 'affection' is all that is required. A single, eminently practical reason is given to remind the husbands of why they should love their wives: it is the wives who warm their drink for them (V, p. 208; F, p. 187).

A second feature that is crucial to the ideal model of marriage among the Brazilians is that their desires are deemed to be naturally moderate. Although this statement is made in the context of military conquest rather than in relation to erotic desire, it is phrased as a general principle, and seems to respond directly to the concerns about excess that were explored in 'De la moderation': 'Ils sont encore en cet heureux point, de ne desirer qu'au tant que leurs necessitez naturelles leur ordonnent; tout ce qui est au delà, est superflu pour eux' [They are still in that happy state of desiring only as much as their natural needs demand; anything beyond that is superfluous to them] (V, p. 210; F, p. 189). The dilemma underlying the discussion of marriage in I.30 — the question of how to set boundaries on marital desire — here appears to be redundant. Indeed, in 'Que nostre desir s'accroit par la malaisance', not long after his discussion of how marriage jeopardizes the 'knot' of free will and affection, Montaigne makes a wistful reference to an unknown country where boundaries can be secured merely with 'un filet de coton' [a cotton thread] (V, p. 616; F, p. 567). Similarly, in the idealized space of the New World, no policing seems necessary, whether of physical borders or psychological ones.

Thirdly, in Brazilian society as described by Montaigne, emphasis is no longer on the couple. Husbands and wives are said to sleep apart (V, p. 207; F, p. 186), and polygamy is not only practised but is a sign of prestige: the more valiant the man, the more wives he has. This aspect of Brazilian life is uncannily close to the model for marriages that can be found in Plato's *Republic*, an intertext that Montaigne famously evokes in I.31, claiming that should Plato encounter the New World, he would acknowledge his own imagined republic to pale in comparison to 'cette perfection' (V, p. 207; F, p. 186). Where I.31 asserts that the New World has 'nul respect de parenté que commun' [no care for any but common kinship] (V, p. 206; F, p. 186), the *Republic* even more boldly proposes the abolition of the couple: when it comes to 'taking wives, marriage, and having children', it will be necessary for 'everything as nearly as possible [to be] "shared among friends"'.[34] But in a further formulation, the exact details of which are murky, the *Republic* describes a polygamous and eugenic model of marriage, in which the men who are best at war are rewarded by more marriages, so that the strongest members of the community will produce the most children.[35] As in the *Republic*, the system of sexual relations among the Brazilians is not quite clear. What is the status of the 'amie' evoked in a New World love song, for example: is she a mistress or a wife-to-be, or does this distinction not matter (V, p. 213; F, p. 192)? In any case, it is highly likely that Montaigne, when outlining marital relations in the New World, had Plato's utopia in mind.

I.31 thus gives us a glimpse of what ideal marriage might look like, however inaccessible such a model would be to the inhabitants of early modern Europe. Yet it is scarcely necessary to point out that the marital utopia envisioned here is a decidedly male one. The structure of male-to-male address found in Montaigne's preceding chapters is retained: first an old man and then a male prophet exhort an audience of men to love their wives. And as Quint has noted, the double injunction about wives and enemies derives from the fact that the two groups fulfil an analogous function: both wives and conquered enemies are symbols of male prestige.[36] The chapter's celebrated statement about cannibal ethics — that 'ils nomment les hommes moitié les uns des autres' [they [speak] of men as halves of one another] (V, p. 214; F, p. 193) — could be interpreted, a little perversely but quite accurately, as a statement about gender: it is men who are halves of one another in this utopia, not men and women.[37]

The longest statement about marriage in the New World, however, is an enthusiastic description of how, in the total absence of female jealousy, the wives vie with one another to procure additional wives for their husbands: 'c'est une beauté remerquable en leurs mariages, que la mesme jalousie que nos femmes ont pour nous empescher de l'amitié et bien-veuillance d'autres femmes, les leurs l'ont toute pareille pour la leur acquerir' [it is a remarkably beautiful thing about their marriages that the same jealousy our wives have to keep us from the affection and kindness of other women, theirs have to win this for them] (V, p. 212; F, p. 192). Brazilian wives are 'plus soigneuses de l'honneur de leurs maris que de toute autre chose' [more concerned for their husbands' honor than for anything else] (V, p. 212; F, p. 192), and are therefore keen for their husbands to accumulate more wives as a sign of prowess. With their self-effacing nature, and their concern for their husbands' honour, these wives resemble Zenobia in I.30, who lets her husband 'run free' with other women, and the 'trois bonnes femmes' ('three good wives') of II.35, who are willing to go to any length to protect the honour of their husbands. Yet in the New World, the exceptional wifely virtue of Zenobia has become an everyday occurrence: every single wife is exemplary. The Brazilian love song that Montaigne cites in I.31 paints a similarly harmonious picture of a woman helping a man forge a bond with another woman, although the women in the song are identified as sister and 'amie' rather than wives. A man addresses an adder: 'Couleuvre, arreste toy; arreste toy, couleuvre, afin que ma soeur tire sur le patron de ta peinture la façon et l'ouvrage d'un riche cordon que je puisse donner à m'amie' [Adder, stay; stay, adder, that from the pattern of your coloring my sister may draw the workmanship of a rich girdle that I may give to my love] (V, p. 213; F, p. 192). The details of the song also convey an image of trouble-free eroticism: the serpent, a Biblical symbol of sexual sin, is recuperated as a creature of symmetry and beauty; and the 'cordon', unlike the knots and nooses that appear elsewhere in the *Essais* as negative figures of matrimony, is here fashioned by a woman at a man's request, as a symbol of love.[38]

Yet Montaigne's utopian portrait of marital relations in the New World, with the women's eager embrace of polygamy, makes a stark distinction between 'our wives' and 'theirs'. This clash is foregrounded even more strongly with a C-addition to the chapter which inscribes a wifely voice of protest: 'Les nostres crieront au miracle; ce ne l'est pas: c'est une vertu proprement matrimoniale, mais du plus haut estage' [Our wives will cry 'Miracle!' but it is no miracle. It is a properly matrimonial virtue, but one of the highest order] (V, p. 213; F, p. 192). A list follows of Biblical and classical wives (stock examples according to Screech) who encouraged their husbands to sleep with female servants.[39] The tone of this inserted comment is colloquial, implying wry exasperation — French wives are designated only by the possessive pronoun 'les nostres' — and the effect of the statement is twofold. On the one hand, the imagined protest of European women is dismissed, and Brazilian wives are unambiguously declared to represent a matrimonial ideal. On the other hand, however, the late addition to the chapter suggests that Montaigne has himself become increasingly aware that his matrimonial utopia corresponds to masculine rather than feminine desire. He anticipates and acknowledges the discomfort of the female reader.

Ultimately, an investigation of marriage in the *Essais* upholds Ian Maclean's argument in *The Renaissance Notion of Woman*: if any early modern paradigm can be said to constitute a formidable stumbling block to the exploratory rethinking of gender in Montaigne's works, then marriage is it. At the same time, the pluridisciplinary mode in which Renaissance thinkers conceived of marriage — a mode Maclean also calls to our attention — renders the topic intriguingly complex: marriage is a 'miroüer' (I.26, 'De l'institution des enfans' [Of the Education of Children], V, p. 157; F, p. 141) that can reflect early modern society from numerous different angles. By theorizing marriage in a series of different contexts within the same sequence of essays, and by theorizing it as a set of tangled threads, Montaigne brings this complexity to the fore. Next to friendship, marriage is fragile. Next to extramarital love, it is chilly. Next to the frankness and loquacity that the essayist brings to a multitude of other topics, it requires a judicious silence. For it to work well, one needs to imagine an entirely different world. Montaigne does not untangle all the threads of early modern matrimony, or show his readers how to make the knot secure, but he does reveal how and where the threads might fray.

Notes to Chapter 5

1. Ian Maclean, *The Renaissance Notion of Woman: A Study in the Fortunes of Scholasticism and Medical Science in European Intellectual Life* (Cambridge: Cambridge University Press, 1980), pp. 84–85.
2. Maclean, *The Renaissance Notion of Woman*, pp. 20 and 57.
3. Excellent studies include Patricia Parker, 'Gender Ideology, Gender Change: The Case of Marie Germain', *Critical Inquiry*, 19.2 (1993), 337–64; Richard L. Regosin, *Montaigne's Unruly Brood: Textual Engendering and the Challenge to Paternal Authority* (Berkeley: University of California Press, 1996); and Todd W. Reeser, 'Theorizing Sex and Gender in Montaigne', in *Montaigne After Theory / Theory After Montaigne*, ed. Zahi Zalloua (Seattle: University of Washington Press, 2011), pp. 218–41. Reeser argues that gender in Montaigne oscillates between '*être*' and '*passage*', or 'being and becoming' (p. 233).
4. Michael Screech, *The Rabelaisian Marriage: Aspects of Rabelais's Religion, Ethics and Comic Philosophy* (London: Edward Arnold, 1958), pp. 5–13 and 37.
5. See Georges Duby, *Medieval Marriage: Two Models from Twelfth-Century France*, trans. Elborg Forster (Baltimore, MD: Johns Hopkins University Press, 1978).
6. See Barbara B. Diefendorf, *Paris City Councillors in the Sixteenth-Century: The Politics of Patrimony* (Princeton, NJ: Princeton University Press, 1983), especially pp. 156–91.
7. Elizabeth Guild, in *Unsettling Montaigne: Poetics, Ethics and Affect in the Essais and Other Writings* (Cambridge: D. S. Brewer, 2014), pp. 73–75, also sees this series of essays as thematically linked, but she focuses on the ethical concerns raised by metaphors of eating.
8. All these texts are found in *Œuvres complètes d'Estienne de La Boétie*, ed. Louis Desgraves (Bordeaux: Blake, 1991).
9. See François Rigolot, 'Montaigne et la "servitude volontaire": pour une interprétation platonicienne', in *Le Lecteur, l'auteur et l'écrivain: Montaigne 1492–1592–1992*, ed. Ilana Zinguer (Paris: Champion, 1993), pp. 85–103; Marc D. Schachter, *Voluntary Servitude and the Erotics of Friendship: From Classical Antiquity to Early Modern France* (Aldershot: Ashgate, 2008), pp. 73–105; and Richard Scholar, *Montaigne and the Art of Free-Thinking* (Oxford: Peter Lang, 2010), pp. 135–58.
10. Screech, *The Rabelaisian Marriage*, pp. 46–47. Erasmus, *Opera omnia Desiderii Erasmi Roterodami*, ed. F. Akkerman, G. J. M. Bartelink, J. Domanski, and others, vol. 5, tome 6: *Christiani matrimonii institutio*, ed. A. G. Weiler (Amsterdam: Elsevier, 2008), pp. 1–252 (p. 159); Erasmus, *The Institution of Marriage*, trans. Michael Heath, in *Erasmus on Women*, ed. Erika Rummel (Toronto: University of Toronto, 1996), pp. 79–130 (p. 88).
11. George Hoffmann, 'Was Montaigne a Good Friend?', in *Men and Women Making Friends in Early Modern France*, ed. Lewis C. Seifert and Rebecca M. Wilkin (Farnham: Ashgate, 2015), pp. 31–60 (p. 42).
12. *Œuvres complètes d'Estienne de La Boétie*, vol. 2, p. 16; my translation. See also Plato, *The Republic*, ed. G. R. F. Ferrari and trans. Tom Griffith (Cambridge: Cambridge University Press, 2000), V. 462c, p. 161.

13. Maclean, *The Renaissance Notion of Woman*, pp. 75 and 83.
14. Randle Cotgrave, *A Dictionarie of the French and English Tongues* (London: Printed by Adam Islip, 1611).
15. *Œuvres complètes d'Estienne de La Boétie*, vol. 2, p. 16; my translation.
16. Guild, *Unsettling Montaigne*, p. 14.
17. Guild, *Unsettling Montaigne*, p. 105.
18. See Leah Chang, *Into Print: The Production of Female Authorship in Early Modern France* (Newark: University of Delaware Press, 2009), p. 185; Guild, *Unsettling Montaigne*, pp. 75–81, 92–97; and François Rigolot, 'Montaigne's Purloined Letters', *Yale French Studies*, 64 (1983), 145–66 (pp. 154–56).
19. On 'je ne sçay' expressions in the *Essais*, see Richard Scholar, *The 'Je-Ne-Sais-Quoi' in Early Modern Europe: Encounters with a Certain Something* (Oxford: Oxford University Press, 2005), pp. 225–74.
20. *Œuvres complètes d'Estienne de La Boétie*, vol. 2, p. 35.
21. On the theme of fatherhood in the *Essais*, see Wes Williams, *Monsters and their Meanings in Early Modern Culture: Mighty Magic* (Oxford: Oxford University Press, 2011), pp. 141–50.
22. *Œuvres complètes d'Estienne de La Boétie*, vol. 1, p. 177.
23. Williams, *Monsters and their Meanings*, p. 147.
24. On differing views of matrimony in Montaigne, La Boétie, and Plutarch, see Gary Ferguson, *Queer (Re)Readings in the French Renaissance: Homosexuality, Gender, Culture* (Aldershot: Ashgate, 2008), pp. 224–25; Hoffmann, 'Was Montaigne a Good Friend?', p. 42; and Schachter, *Voluntary Servitude*, pp. 160–62.
25. 'Ad Michaëlem Montanum', in *Œuvres complètes d'Estienne de La Boétie*, vol. 2, pp. 71–79. For an English translation of the poem, see Étienne de La Boétie, *Poemata*, ed. James S. Hirstein and trans. Robert D. Cottrell, *Montaigne Studies*, 3.1 (1991), 27–47.
26. *Œuvres complètes d'Estienne de La Boétie*, vol. 2, p. 172.
27. See Chang, *Into Print*, pp. 182–83; and Anne-Marie Cocula, 'De la présence à l'absence: Marguerite de La Boétie dans l'œuvre de Montaigne', *Montaigne Studies*, 8 (1996), 35–46.
28. *Œuvres complètes d'Estienne de La Boétie*, vol. 1, p. 165.
29. On women's sexual knowledge in III.5, see Constance Jordan, 'Sexuality and Volition in "Sur des vers de Virgile"', *Montaigne Studies*, 8 (1996), 65–80 (pp. 68–71).
30. On how the women in II.35 embody masculine Stoic virtues, see Ann Moss, 'Montaigne et Shakespeare: rencontres au féminin', *Actes des congrès de la Société française Shakespeare*, 21 (2004), 209–19.
31. Guild, *Unsettling Montaigne*, p. 82.
32. Terence Cave, Montaigne reading group in Oxford, 22 March 2012.
33. David Quint, *Montaigne and the Quality of Mercy: Ethical and Political Themes in the Essais* (Princeton, NJ: Princeton University Press, 1998), pp. 75–101.
34. *Republic*, V. 424a, p. 116.
35. *Republic*, V. 460b, p. 158; 468c, p. 169.
36. Quint, *Montaigne and the Quality of Mercy*, p. 83.
37. La Boétie and Montaigne are also described as each other's 'moitié' (V, p. 193; F, p. 174): perfect friendship is another relationship of halves from which women are excluded.
38. For a different perspective on this song, see André Tournon, ' "Arrête-toi couleuvre...": l'alexandrinisme des Tupinambas', in *Rouen 1962: Montaigne et les cannibales*, ed. Jean-Claude Arnould and Emmanuel Faye, CÉRÉdI, *Actes de colloques et journées d'étude*, 8 (2013) <ceredi.labos.univ-rouen.fr/public/?arrete-toi-couleuvre-l.html> [accessed 27 October 2015].
39. Michel de Montaigne, *The Complete Essays*, ed. and trans. M. A. Screech (London: Penguin, 1987), p. 239. On wives in I.31, see also Susan K. Silver, 'Melancholy, Motherhood, and Writing Wrongs in "Des cannibales"', *Montaigne Studies*, 8 (1996), 81–95 (pp. 92–93).

CHAPTER 6

Montaigne's Vanity

Frank Lestringant

One of the richest, most digressive, and thematically mobile chapters of the *Essais*, III.9, 'De la vanité' [On Vanity], has been said to 'dominate the third book' (Pierre Villey, in V, p. 944). Among the complex connections this chapter establishes with other texts both within the *Essais* and beyond it are several points of contact with Montaigne's own *Journal de Voyage*, the record of his travels to and from Italy, which he left unpublished during his lifetime, but which clearly nourished his thoughts when he came to revise the *Essais* for the later (post-1580) editions. It is in 'De la vanité' that the clearest of these echoes of the travel journal in the *Essais* can be heard. They become especially clear towards the chapter's end, when Montaigne confesses to feeling a sense of pride in respect of the 'bulle authentique de bourgeoisie Romaine' [authentic bull of Roman citizenship] that had been accorded to him during his stay in the Eternal City (V, pp. 999–1001; F, p. 930).

The reference to the 'bulle authentique' is (of course) a joke: at once a papal bull and a vain bubble, it responds to the apparent joke with which 'De la vanité' begins. Indulging in more than simple word-play (as ever), Montaigne opens his chapter with the following claim: 'Il n'en est à l'avanture aucune plus expresse que d'en escrire si vainement' [There is perhaps no more obvious vanity than to write of it so vainly] (V, p. 945; F, p. 876). As if to prove his point, and following a brief allusion to Ecclesiastes 1. 2 ('Vanity of vanities, all is vanity'), words he seems to have taken no notice of himself, Montaigne proceeds, without any form of modulating transition, to spin out the two threads which he will then weave together throughout the chapter, and which will be my theme here: 'Qui ne voit que j'ay pris une route par laquelle, sans cesse et sans travail, j'iray autant qu'il y aura d'ancre et de papier au monde?' [Who does not see that I have taken a road along which I shall go, without stopping and without effort, as long as there is ink and paper in the world?] (ibid.). This single sentence brings together, by way of its singular movement, writing and travel, the writing of travel, and writing as travel — at once aimless and endless. Finally, as the argument both develops and turns back on itself, travel becomes a form of writing in itself: 'Ay-je laissé quelque chose à voir derriere moy? J'y retourne; c'est tousjours mon chemin. Je ne trace aucune ligne certaine, ny droicte ny courbe' [Have I left something unseen behind me? I go back; it is still on my road. I trace no fixed line, either straight or crooked] (V, p. 985; F, p. 916).

1. The excremental body

If 'De la vanité' reveals a Montaigne in transit and transition in a number of distinctive ways, among the most striking is the attention given in this chapter to the
physical experience of change. The body proves to be the primary locus for the
experience of vanity; of the many forms vanity takes on, the most revealingly
realistic and the most mundane is excrement. We are reminded of the saying
commonly (and falsely) attributed to St Augustine, and whose author could be
Porphyry of Tyre or Bernard of Clairvaux: 'Inter faeces et urinam nascimur' [We
are born between faeces and urine]. In excrement, as Montaigne reminds us, we
discover the human condition and its true nature. For it welcomes us at our birth
and accompanies us throughout life to the point of death. An essential feature of our
common destiny, it is also fundamental to good health: our physical natures need to
keep hold of excrement for a certain time and 'jusques à certaine mesure, comme le
vin a [besoin] de sa lie pour sa conservation' [to a certain extent, just as wine needs
its lees for its preservation] (II.37, 'De la ressemblance des enfans aux peres' [Of the
Resemblance of Children to Fathers]; V, p. 767; F, p. 705). Or so at least the experts
of the time believed, and, for once, Montaigne appears to agree with them. With La
Boëtie perhaps in mind, and with his friend's death from dysentery as if once again
before his eyes, Montaigne observes that: 'Vous voyez souvent des hommes sains
tomber en vomissemens ou flux de ventre par accident estranger, et faire un grand
vuidange d'excremens sans besoin aucun precedent et sans aucune utilité suivante,
voire avec empirement et dommage' [You often see healthy men having attacks
of vomiting or diarrhea from some accidental cause and evacuating vast quantities
of excrement without any preceding need or any following benefit, indeed rather
with impairment and damage] (ibid.). We can, then, die from not being able to
keep our excrement to ourselves, as if from losing hold of some essential part of our
substance, nature, and being.

In Christian terms, such mundane realism becomes the very expression of *miseria
hominis*, a specifically human form of transitional wretchedness, even as it also
evokes its opposite and complementary theme, that of *dignitas hominis*, precisely
insofar as humans are susceptible to divine grace. It is in this context and with this
interpretive tradition in mind that we should understand the strange comparison
whose incongruous appearance marks the beginning of Montaigne's account,
expanding on his opening remarks concerning the vanity of writing: 'Ce sont icy
[...] des excremens d'un vieil esprit' [Here you have [...] some excrements of an aged
mind] (III.9; V, p. 946; F, p. 876).

To compare the *Essais* with 'excrement', desiccated and shrivelled, is hardly
flattering, but we must take care to note that the word had a less restrictive sense in
the early modern period than it does today. Excrement, etymologically speaking,
is anything produced by the body, before being discharged: faeces, urine, nasal
mucus, sweat, and saliva; but also nails, hair, and teeth. What matters most about
the comparison, and what makes it no less brutal or shocking, is the notion of
Montaigne's thought being considered to be the excremental discharge of the body,
as of the mind. For, insofar as the *Essais* are rooted in living substance, they also

partake of death: writing is a human by-product, an effect of our at once animal and spiritual nature.

Once this has been understood, and once man and his lofty intellectual ambitions have been brought back to ground level — that of the body eating and excreting, growing and declining — the theme of vanity can be deployed across a range of contexts, in all its transitional dimensions. To start us on our journey, 'De la vanité' begins by introducing its readers to the evidence offered by an odd, yet exemplary case of anal fetishism: the collection of pungent relics offered 'en montre' [on display] to his visitors by one of Montaigne's acquaintances:

> Si ay je veu un Gentilhomme, qui ne communiquoit sa vie, que par les opera-tions de son ventre: Vous voyez chez luy, en montre, un ordre de bassins de sept ou huict jours: C'estoit son estude, ses discours: Tout autre propos, luy puoit.

> [I knew a gentleman who gave knowledge of his life only by the workings of his belly; you would see on display at his home a row of chamber-pots, seven or eight days' worth. That was his study, his conversation; all other talk stank in his nostrils.] (V, p. 946; F, p. 876)

Following this we find the comparison to Montaigne's own *Essais* already quoted in part above: 'Ce sont icy, un peu plus civilement, des excremens d'un vieil esprit, dur tantost, tantost lache et tousjours indigeste' [Here you have, a little more decently, some excrements of an aged mind, now hard, now loose, and always undigested] (ibid.).

Several temptations lie in wait for the critical reader hoping to engage with a passage such as this. The first is to see this coprophile gentleman as in truth Montaigne himself: off-loading, as it were, his own perversion at the expense of some anonymous, fictional third party. This hypothesis has little to recommend it, however, since the collected *Essais* already occupy exactly the same space, for Montaigne, as the malodorous chamber pots, whose existence then proves to be, strictly speaking, superfluous. A second, already more subtle temptation invites us to pursue the insistence of the scatological metaphor still further, and to set excretion alongside all those points in the *Essais* where flow, unleashing, and liquidity are in play. Following this course, Gisèle Mathieu-Castellani has rightly noted the recurrence of the 'paradigm of release' and the attendant ubiquity of images of emptying throughout the work: 'L'excrément dans ses deux états, dur tantost, tantost lache, alimente d'un côté la description critique du monde qui va à la vau-l'eau [sic], de l'autre la rêverie sur la roideur d'un style qui durcit sa matière' [Excrement, in its two different states, sometimes hard and sometimes loose, nourishes on the one hand Montaigne's critical account of the world as it heads down the drain [sic], and on the other his fantasy about a stylistic firmness which would lend a degree of solidity to its substance].[1] And yet we should not forget that, in the preamble to the chapter, the phrase 'dur tantost, tantost lache et toujours indigeste' [now hard, now loose, and always undigested] refers not to excrement itself, but to Montaigne's 'vieil esprit' [aged mind]. To skip over this detail is to err on the side of metonymic reductiveness — a detour which, of course, Montaigne's text maliciously invites us to make.

The third temptation is to infer from the opening of this chapter the workings of an anal-sadistic complex within Montaigne's psychological make-up. This is probably the most outlandish, but also the most challenging and stimulating of the three temptations on offer, particularly when it is set in the context of an era whose habits were neither bridled nor stifled by modern rules of decorum. Just think of Henri III giving audience from his commode on the morning when the monk Jacques Clément dealt him the fatal blow.

The anal-sadistic complex finds further extension in Montaigne in the symbolic equivalence he establishes between faeces and gold. One of the structuring axes of the libidinal economy, this equivalence is introduced in the prologue to 'De la vanité', before being developed by way of motifs of wealth and money, as part of Montaigne's sustained reflection on the ordering of his household and the proper management of expenditure, whether at home or on the road. The possibility of dying on the journey, far from home, serves as a yardstick to measure the vanity of all attachment, financial as well as physical. 'De notaire et de conseil, il m'en faut moins que de medecins' [Of notary and counsel I have less need than of physicians] he claims, bearing witness to the same indifference in respect of his purse as he affects towards his mortal remains (V, p. 982; F, p. 913). Yet there is of course a good deal of exaggeration in this pose, just as there is in the scorn he lavishes on those who micro-manage their own financial affairs: 'O le vilein et sot estude d'estudier son argent, se plaire à le manier, poiser et reconter. C'est par là que l'avarice faict ses aproches' [Oh, what a vile and stupid study it is to count one's money, to take pleasure in handling it, weighing it and counting it over and over! That is the way avarice makes its approach] (V, p. 953; F, p. 884).

Pure *sprezzatura*, this is a gesture as typical of the gentleman busily caring little for how much he spends as it is of the moralist exaggeratedly condemning all attachment to the material world. In truth, such avowed abhorrence of greed, like an insistence on cleanliness, may well reveal the opposite of what it represses: '*Ni ordonné, ni entêté, ni économe*: le portrait que construit l'analyse consciente semble *fait pour* récuser le diagnostic' [*Ni ordonné, ni entêté, ni économe*: [*Neither well ordered, nor stubborn, nor yet thrifty*]: the portrait which Montaigne's conscious analysis offers of itself here appears to have been *specifically designed* to resist any workable diagnosis].[2] We know that Montaigne's relation to money was difficult and complicated, but never indifferent.[3] A literary portrait is one thing; a public persona is another; yet another is the eldest son of a large family, and one clearly given preferential treatment by the father's will. The protracted legal settlement of Pierre de Montaigne's estate makes things plain: the supposedly negligent householder portrayed in the third book of the *Essais* was also capable of engaging in bitter and hard-fought negotiations with his mother over the estate; and she proved far from accommodating to his (or his father's) wishes.[4]

2. The vanity of movement

Even the literary portrait is itself changeable and subject to contradiction. The stigmatization of greed in 'De la vanité' is complemented by — and contrasts with — a late addition to an earlier chapter: I.14, 'Que le goust des biens et des maux depend en bonne partie de l'opinion que nous en avons' [That the Taste of Good and Evil Depends in Large Part on the Opinion We Have of Them]. At about the time of his retirement to the tower, Montaigne seems to have suffered a particularly strong bout of avarice, the symptoms of which he describes in this chapter in vivid terms:

> Ma seconde forme, ç'a esté d'avoir de l'argent [...]. Cela ne se passoit pas sans penible sollicitude. [...] Allois-je en voyage, il ne me sembloit estre jamais suffisamment prouveu [...]. Laissoy-je ma boyte chez moy, combien de soubçons et pensements espineux, et, qui pis est, incommunicables. J'avois tousjours l'esprit de ce costé.

> [My second situation [or form of life] was to have money. [...] This did not go on without painful worry. [...] Was I going on a journey, I never thought I was sufficiently provided [...]. Did I leave my strongbox at home, how many suspicions, how many thorny, and what is worse, incommunicable thoughts! My mind was always turned in that direction.] (V, p. 64; F, p. 53 [with one modification])

Just like the old man in *Aulularia* [*The Pot of Gold*], a comedy by the Roman playwright Plautus, Montaigne feared for his gold. Would he go so far as to bury his casket at the bottom of his garden? Perhaps not, but he clearly suffered a similar anguish to that of Molière's at once miserable and miserly Harpagon. His only thought was for his 'boyte' [strongbox], the same box that masked riders would take from him at a turning in the forest, as he made his way to Paris in the winter of 1588. Restriction, confinement, a form of melancholic prostration, and an obsession with death: all these symptoms converge in the serious depressive crisis he suffered in the late 1560s.

So Montaigne set himself to the task of writing the *Essais* and invested his gold. He opened himself up to the world and to expense; but only in order to accumulate still more goods. He engaged in a series of land acquisitions, extended the estate, and expanded his home.[5] Throughout all this, he was still concerned with what he called his 'seconde forme'; in a less morbid fashion than before, perhaps, but no less vain for all that. This lasted 'several years'. Until, that is, he began his long journey across Europe, a 'voyage de grande despence' [a journey of great expense], which in one and the same move suddenly turned his 'sotte imagination' [foolish fantasies] concerning avarice upside down and significantly reduced the value of his accumulated wealth (V, p. 65; F, p. 54). Montaigne renounced hoarding and sacrificed himself to the pleasure principle. Then, lastly and most significantly, there was the shock of 1586: the devastation of his home by soldiers loyal to the king, the visitation of the Plague, and the several months of enforced wandering that followed. Ruined, Montaigne finally acquired economic wisdom. He was cured of his avarice. And so began a 'third way of life', one more pleasant, with no cares either for the future or for the present: living, as he puts it, 'du jour à la journée' [from day to every day] (V, p. 65; F, p. 54; translation altered).

Cured of his errors and returned home from wanderings, Montaigne now found himself in a position to abhor greed and to reduce it, along with his own textual production, to the level of excrement. The trials of his final years doubtless contributed to his growing sense of detachment, but so, too, did his reading of St Augustine and the phrase cited above: 'Inter faeces et urinam nascimur.' Illness also had its part to play in this re-evaluation of his life's work — an illness, furthermore, which reminded him each day of the claims that the lower organs of the body made on his attention: stomach, bladder, and penis. Such reminders were undoubtedly painful, with the expulsion of his stones sometimes leading Montaigne to the point of losing consciousness; but they were joyous, too, in that they allowed him, like Socrates before him, to discover in the proofs of daily experience the truth of the 'l'estroitte alliance de la douleur à la volupté' [the close alliance between pain and pleasure]:

> Mais est-il rien doux au pris de cette soudaine mutation: quand d'une douleur extreme, je viens par le vuidange de ma pierre à recouvrer, comme d'un esclair, la belle lumiere de la santé, si libre et si pleine: Comme il advient en nos soudaines et plus aspres choliques: y a il rien en cette douleur soufferte, qu'on puisse contrepoiser au plaisir d'un si prompt amandement.

> [But is there anything so sweet as that sudden change, when from extreme pain, by the voiding of my stone, I come to recover, as if by lightning, the beautiful light of health, so free and so full, as happens in our sudden and sharpest attacks of colic? Is there anything in this pain that we suffer can be said to counterbalance the pleasure of such improvement?][6]

Once Socrates had been freed from his prison chains, shortly before drinking the hemlock, he suddenly felt 'la friandise de cette demangeson, que leur pesanteur avoit causé en ses jambes' [the relish of the itching that their weight had caused in his legs] (ibid.).[7] The same was true of Montaigne; except that it was not the legs, but rather higher up his body, in his lower abdomen, that he felt that same strange 'alliance', or combination, of pain and pleasure. The dis-ease to which his stone subjected him also taught him the very essence of his human condition. For Nature, scornful as she is, mocks all our dreams of grandeur by lodging 'peslemesle nos delices et nos ordures ensemble' [our delights and our excrements together pell-mell] (V, p. 877; F, p. 811).

Montaigne eventually confesses to being unable either truly to enjoy the pleasures of the mind or wholly to despise those of the body: 'Quel monstrueux animal qui se fait horreur à soy mesme, à qui ses plaisirs poisent; qui se tient à mal-heur' [What a monstrous animal to be a horror to himself, to be burdened by his pleasures, to regard himself as a misfortune!] (III.5, 'Sur des vers de Virgile' [On Some Verses of Virgil]; V, p. 879; F, p. 813). The avaricious hoarder of turds is as deserving of blame as is his counterpart, the man whose madness is such that he cannot abide 'de voir manger ny qu'on le voye, et fuyt toute assistance, plus quand il s'emplit que s'il se vuide' [to see anyone eat or to be seen eating, and avoids any company even more when he is filling than when he is emptying himself] (ibid.).

The closing moves of III.13, 'De l'experience' [Of Experience], the final chapter of the *Essais*, and the recapitulation of the various themes orchestrated throughout the book, dwells insistently on the peculiarly 'mixed' condition of mankind. This insistence appears all the more striking since it arises out of Montaigne's painstaking attention to the detailed changes in his own health:

Mais moy, d'une condition *mixte*, grossier, ne puis mordre si à faict à ce seul object [*sc.* de l'imagination la plus éthérée]; si simple que je ne me laisse tout lourdement aller aux plaisirs presents de la loy humaine et generale, *intellectuellement sensibles, sensiblement intellectuels.*

[But I, being of a *mixed* constitution, and coarse, am unable to cling so completely to this single object [imagination at its most ethereal]; and too simple to keep myself from grossly pursuing the present pleasures of the general human law — *intellectually sensual, sensually intellectual.*] (V, p. 1107; F, p. 1035; emphasis added).[8]

Such a mixed man was Socrates, and Montaigne presents himself in similar terms. Nature, who made man both corporeal and carnal, and not only intellectual or spiritual, 'est un doux guide, mais non pas plus doux que prudent et juste' [is a gentle guide, but no more gentle than wise and just] (V, p. 1113; F, p. 1042). It is in the acceptance of this intermediate condition somewhere between the angel and the beast that true wisdom lies. Philosophers who despise our physical nature fool themselves and fall prey to the sin of pride: 'Ils veulent se mettre hors d'eux et eschapper à l'homme. C'est folie: au lieu de se transformer en anges, ils se transforment en bestes; au lieu de se hausser, ils s'abattent' [They want to get out of themselves and escape from the man. That is madness: instead of changing into angels, they change into beasts; instead of raising themselves up, they lower themselves] (V, p. 1115; F, p. 1044) — an observation to which Pascal will, of course, return when he comes to write his *Pensées.*[9]

This degree of humility, appropriate to man, and especially to the Christian, is, however, expressed by Montaigne (in this respect distinctly *unlike* Pascal after him) in deliberately inappropriate terms. The language he uses is that of the body; astonishingly physical in their nature, his words draw their readers' attention to the lowest and basest of material realities. In part, the scatological register is ventriloquized, attributed to the fabulist Aesop about whom Montaigne writes: 'Esope, ce grand homme, vid son maistre qui pissoit en se promenant: Quoy donq, fit-il, nous faudra-il chier en courant?' [Aesop, that great man, saw his master pissing while walking, 'What next?' he said. 'Shall we have to shit while running?'] (V, p. 1115; F, p. 1043; translation altered). 'While flying', reads the Greek original of Planudes' *Life of Aesop*; but 'while running' is more likely than 'flying', and above all, the better suited to human capabilities and actions.

But then there is the later thought, slipped into the margin of the Bordeaux Copy of the *Essais*: two sentences, two pithy comparisons that serve to bring human ambition back down to its proper level: 'Si avons-nous beau monter sur des eschasses, car sur des eschasses encore faut-il marcher de nos jambes. Et au plus eslevé throne du monde si ne sommes assis que sur nostre cul' [There is no use our mounting on stilts, for even on stilts we must still walk with our own legs. And on the loftiest throne in the world we are still sitting on our arses] (V, p. 1115; F, p. 1044; translation altered).[10] A doubly determined fall that leads back down to earth and the ground, and, within the body, down its lower parts, its legs, its 'arse'. This final word, placed in a position of prominence by the scribe, occupies by itself the bottom line of the handwritten addition to the page, one of the very last of the *Essais*.

In returning one last time to the chapter 'De la vanité', we ask, once again, why does Montaigne travel? It seems clear that we should not take all his answers seriously; some even border on bad faith. As Jean Céard has pointed out, a distaste for household management coupled with an inability to remain untroubled by domestic duties and difficulties offer reason enough for Montaigne's leaving home for a time. But Céard is also surely right to suggest that a wry smile accompanies the assertion that he travels so that his wife can better acquire for herself 'la science du menage' [the science of housekeeping], and so that his absence might rekindle 'l'amitié maritale' [marital love].[11] Other reasons Montaigne gives are clearly more serious: an apprenticeship in mourning, and a means to the possession, through the power of the imagination, of the lost, absent, loved one (V, pp. 976–77; F, pp. 906–08). Talk of friendship and of mourning opens up new a sense of transition in this chapter, echoing once again those resonant passages from the *Journal de Voyage* which prove that La Boëtie, although he was by then 20 years in the grave, was nonetheless still felt to be powerfully present/absent throughout Montaigne's Italian journey in 1581. Recall for instance the notes made at the Bains della Villa, on a Thursday morning in May of that year: 'Et ce même matin, écrivant à M. d'Ossat, je tombai en un pensement si pénible de M. de La Boétie, et y fus si longtemps sans me raviser, que cela me fit grand mal' [This same morning, writing to Monsieur d'Ossat, I was overcome by such painful thoughts about Monsieur de la Boétie, and I was in this mood so long, without recovering, that it did me much harm].[12]

When Montaigne writes of La Boëtie: 'Nous remplissions mieux et estandions la possession de la vie en nous separant: il vivoit, il jouissoit, il voyoit pour moy, et moy pour luy, autant plainement que s'il y eust esté [...]. La separation du lieu rendoit la conjonction de nos volontez plus riche' [We filled and extended our possession of life better by separating; he lived, he enjoyed, he saw for me, and I for him, as fully as if he had been there [...]. Separation in space made the conjunction of our wills richer] (V, p. 977; F, p. 907), he gives voice to the desire to extend, by means of travel, the virtual presence of the lost friend, whose imagined presence has become co-extensive with the world. But when he follows this by adding: 'Cette faim insatiable de la presence corporelle accuse un peu la foiblesse en la jouyssance des ames' [This insatiable hunger for bodily presence betrays a certain weakness in the enjoyment of souls] (V, p. 977; F, pp. 907–08), he both exposes himself to the charge of self-contradiction, and reveals, all too easily, the weakness of his own soul. The exclamation which follows, just a few pages later: 'O un amy!' [Oh, a friend!], suddenly takes on an almost pathetic tone (V, p. 981; F, p. 912). The absent centre no longer holds; only the bodily presence of the beloved has any real purchase: 'Si à si bonnes enseignes je sçavois quelqu'un qui me fut propre, certes je l'irois trouver bien loing' [If by such good signs I knew of a man who was suited to me, truly I would go very far to find him] (V, p. 981; F, pp. 911–12). In this world, travel is an exercise in mourning and in death, an ample demonstration of the vanity of human attachment.

But travel and transition as understood by Montaigne are rarely ever reducible to the exercise in melancholy just described. The dominant tone of this chapter is one of alacrity: 'Je ne l'entreprens ny pour en revenir, ny pour le parfaire; j'entreprens seulement de me branler, pendant que le branle me plaist. Et me proumeine pour me proumener' [I am not undertaking this journey either to return from it, nor complete it; I undertake only to move about while I like moving. And I walk for the sake of walking] (V, p. 977; F, p. 908). The real reason for a journey is the journey itself. To echo Céard once again, 'il ne s'agit que de se livrer au plaisir du mouvement et du changement, nullement d'embrasser la diversité' [all that matters [to Montaigne] is giving himself over to the pleasure of movement and change; it is not about embracing diversity]: to summarize and reduce the world, cosmographically, as it were, into a single book.[13] Or, to listen again to Montaigne: 'Ouy, je le confesse, je ne vois rien, seulement en songe et par souhait, où je me puisse tenir; la seule varieté me paye, et la possession de la diversité, au moins si aucune chose me paye' [Yes, I confess, I see nothing, even in a dream, or a wish, that I could hold myself to; variety alone satisfies me, and the enjoyment of diversity, at least if anything satisfies me] (V, p. 988; F, p. 919). Travel is, then, a way to set oneself in tune with the movement and the variety of the world, and, as Montaigne himself put it, to 'servir la vie selon elle' [serving it in its own way]; to travel is to act in service to life, itself defined as 'un mouvement materiel et corporel, action imparfaicte de sa propre essence, et desreglée' [a material and corporeal movement, an action which by its very essence is imperfect and irregular] (ibid.).

Conclusion

Whether travel is defined as escape, flux, or physical release, or whether it is allegorically legitimized under the twinned signs of wandering and error, it is shadowed by the theme of vanity throughout a chapter that develops and shifts focus in all manner of ways. For vanity has infinite forms and many faces. By turns, the vanity in question might be that of: a writer or of travel; life at home in the chateau at Saint-Michel de Montaigne or human life in general, as conveyed by the grand and ancient metaphor: *homo viator*. As the Old Testament teaches us, we are all travellers and exiles here on earth, and at times Montaigne seems to want to match his own personal practice of travel with this ancient allegorical account of the human condition: 'Et le voyage de ma vie se conduict de mesme' [And the journey of my life is conducted in the same way] (V, p. 978; F, p. 908). For of course the general truth of this metaphor is grounded in particulars; it has no 'proof' other than that found in the co-ordinates of commonly shared experience. Vanity in this chapter also encompasses the contemporary political situation in France, those interminable wars of religion, which Montaigne tries to escape by traveling abroad. And, throughout, there is the excremental vanity of the *Essais* themselves.

By putting the body so determinedly on the road, this chapter offers, then, a complete and peculiarly eloquent account of the transitional poetics of Montaigne's writing. There is no better example of 'l'alleure poetique, à sauts et à gambades' [the poetic gait, with leaps and gambols] (V, p. 994; F, p. 925), which he so cherishes, than this digressive chapter, constantly on the move, perpetually in transit from one theme to the next; nor is there any more probing illustration of 'cette art legere, volage, demoniacle' [that light, flighty, demonic art] which Montaigne so appreciated in Plutarch's work. The turns of phrase mark the movement of Montaigne's thought: 'Je m'esgare, mais plustot par licence que par mesgarde. Mes fantasies se suyvent, mais par fois c'est de loing, et se regardent, mais d'une veuë oblique [...]. J'entends que la matiere se distingue soy-mesmes' [I go out of my way, but rather by license than carelessness. My ideas follow one another, but sometimes it is from a distance, and look at each other, but with a sidelong glance [...]. I want the matter to make its own divisions] (V, pp. 994–95; F, pp. 925–26).

In respect of the *bulle* marking the gift of Roman citizenship which Montaigne displays by way of conclusion to the chapter, and with which we began this discussion, we might note how this play on words effects one final transition: from words to images, and from textual to painterly vanity. For of course the *bulle*/bubble also calls to mind those visually striking emblems of emptiness and human frailty that can be found in the images — still lives for the most part — who share their generic name with this chapter: 'vanités'. Vanity's *bulle* has, then, a marked pictorial sense, too. All the more so since Montaigne's time is also the golden age of 'vanities' in painting: meditations on objects drawn from the familiar and intimate world, these works mark the transitory nature of human life and, at the same time, serve as an invitation to serene contemplation, preparing oneself for death. The same is true of this chapter as it moves through its paces: now ambling, now with alacrity, but always by way of as many detours as possible, marking out a series of moves towards cheerful old age and inevitable death.

Translated by Wes Williams

Notes to Chapter 6

1. Gisèle Mathieu-Castellani, 'Des excréments d'un vieil esprit: Montaigne coprographe', *Littérature*, 62 (1986), 14–24 (pp. 17–18).
2. Mathieu-Castellani, 'Des excréments d'un vieil esprit', p. 19.
3. See Roger Trinquet, 'Montaigne et l'argent', in *O un amy! Essays on Montaigne in Honor of Donald M. Frame*, ed. Raymond C. La Charité (Lexington, KY: French Forum, 1977), pp. 290–313. See also Jonathan Patterson, *Representing Avarice in Late Renaissance France* (Oxford: Oxford University Press, 2015), Chapter 5.
4. Trinquet, 'Montaigne et l'argent', p. 296.
5. Trinquet, 'Montaigne et l'argent', p. 299.
6. III.13. V, p. 1093 (text amended on the basis of the Bordeaux Copy, fol. 485r–v); F, p. 1021.
7. Montaigne follows Plato here: *Phaedo*, 60b.
8. Translator's note: the concluding chiasmus here is notoriously difficult to translate and Frame's 'sensual[ly]' is not right. Florio makes a separate sentence of the phrase and plumps for 'Intellectually sensible and sensibly-intellectuall'; Montaigne, *Essays or Morall, Politike and Millitarie Discourses*, trans. John Florio (London: by Val. Sims for Edward Blount, 1603), fol. 659; for his part, Screech (who adds his own long explanatory note) paraphrases as follows: 'things are sensed through the understanding, understood through the senses'; Montaigne, *The Complete Essays*, trans. M. A. Screech (London: Allen Lane Penguin, 1991), p. 1257.
9. See Wes Williams, *Mighty Magic: Monsters and their Meanings in Early Modern Culture* (Oxford: Oxford University Press, 2011), Chapter 5.
10. Text amended with reference to the Bordeaux Copy, fol. 496r.
11. Jean Céard, *La Nature et les prodiges: l'insolite au XVIᵉ siècle, en France* (Geneva: Droz, 1977), p. 400; the reference is to V, p. 974–75, F, p. 905. For more on Montaigne and marriage, see Chimène Bateman's essay in this volume.
12. Montaigne, *Journal de voyage en Italie*, ed. Fausta Garavini (Paris: Gallimard, 1983), p. 277; ed. François Rigolot (Paris: Presses universitaires de France, 1992), p. 162. The translation is that of Frame, p. 1207.
13. Céard, *La Nature et les prodiges*, p. 401.

CHAPTER 7

Butchering the Cannibals: *Essais* I.31 Dismembered for Florio's Modern Readers

Warren Boutcher

Introduction

Ian Maclean is one of a rare breed of scholars to have made groundbreaking contributions across the range from the genesis and composition to the production and diffusion of texts. He has written on both the pure history of ideas and the history of the publishing business. On the one hand, his analyses of the *Essais'* critique of university philosophy have shown that Montaigne inhabits 'the building which he is bent on destroying'.[1] In the name of a natural logic and rhetoric, the essayist repeatedly declares the arts of discourse to be superfluous. But the principles of those arts nevertheless shape his thought, which develops analogous principles of its own.[2] His text, 'a principle of movement on the static page', is designed as a contrast to 'scholasticism's orderly, logical, impersonal discourse'.[3] To grasp the nature of the principle and the contrast one needs to be able to perceive — within Montaigne's discourse — the traces of the very building he purports to be dismantling. Most modern readers do not have this ability.

Maclean has not, on the other hand, written so directly on the *Essais'* relationship to the business and practices of publishing. But his studies of the learned book in the marketplace invite us to consider texts in the material formats and commercial fields in which and for which they were produced. The producer of Montaigne's first Parisian quarto and folio editions, Abel L'Angelier, was no humanist printer-publisher in the mould of Aldus Manutius. According to the preface to his 1509 Horace, Manutius inserted *distinctiones* (probably colons and periods) and *subdistinctiones* (probably semi-colons and commas) in classical texts himself, believing that when well placed they could do the job of a commentary. He also corrected them frequently in *errata*.[4] L'Angelier was an entrepreneurial publisher, marketer, and seller of learned works in the vernacular who contracted out his printing and correcting.[5] As we shall hear below, he has been accused of presiding over the neglect, even the censoring, of punctuation marks in Montaigne's case.

Maclean's work on the marketplace for learning invites us to consider other agents, beyond the publisher and primary author, whose actions shaped the forms in which texts were produced. In Montaigne's case these included secretaries who took his dictation, scribes who prepared copies, compositors, 'promoters' such as Lipsius, 'retrievers' such as Mme de Montaigne and Pierre de Brach, and 'editors', including Marie de Gournay.[6] In the case of Bordeaux 1580, Montaigne acted as his own corrector in the printshop. Some of his corrections were effected during printing, some appeared in Millanges's printed *errata*. The latter pay more attention to punctuation than those included in any other work of Millanges's. They take the trouble, for example, to substitute a 'coma' (our colon) for a 'virgule' (our comma) on vol. 1, p. 270 (actually p. 278) of Bordeaux 1580. After publication, he continued his corrections using copies such as the *exemplaire Lalanne*.[7] Later, he began the same process after the printing of Paris 1588.

However, the instructions Montaigne wrote on the verso of the title-page of one copy of Paris 1588, the *exemplaire de Bordeaux* (*EB*), show him communicating not, as is often said, with a printer, but with a scribe who will make a fair copy of the revised text. He gives his scribe responsibility for correcting orthography, the headline text, capitalization, lineation of the citations. Having set aside a large number of corrections (perhaps of straightforward typographical errors?) that he says the printer will take care of himself, he tells the scribe to focus on punctuation, on 'pouints', because they are of great importance 'en ce [sti]le': the *style coupé*.[8] If we want to understand the nature of Montaigne's rhetorical style, we need to pay particular attention to the way it is 'pointed'.

Everyone who reads the *Essais* attempts mentally or orally to 'point' the text for rhythm or sense, to divide it up by changes of topic or trains of thought; in this, they are guided more directly by the printed punctuation and paragraph breaks included by their editor than by any separate commentary or annotation. The use of *distinctiones* and *subdistinctiones*, or marks of separation, as a form of — in lieu of — commentary is the subject of this chapter. In scholastic Latin (recalled in Montaigne's usage of 'distinguer' and 'distinction') 'distinctio' also had meanings in the field of logic; it referred, among other things, to the dividing up of a subject matter or *res* according to logical distinctions or classifications. Such divisions could be marked typographically in texts in various ways, including paragraphing.[9]

I shall add translators and producers of translations to the normal list of agents — from authors to correctors — who might introduce *distinctiones* of various kinds into a text. This is for two reasons. The first is the simple fact that they too have to decide which text to use, and how to punctuate and divide it. Recently, for example, an important modern Italian translation of the *Essais* has been re-edited in line with André Tournon's approach to the text of the *EB*, especially with respect to its punctuation.[10] The second, related reason is that I am engaged in the process of editing a translation of Montaigne's work.

There is no better way to comprehend the movements of the *Essais* in transit — in constantly changing and evolving forms — to new publishers and markets and readers, than to edit it oneself. I am preparing a selected edition of John Florio's translation of Montaigne for the Oxford World's Classics series, which produces editions of classic texts for the general and student reader. An editor of an original composition has to balance respect for the work, the text, and the reader. An editor of a past translation has further to balance respect for the original author's work and text with respect for the translator's. This is especially the case when the readership (as in the case of the Oxford World's Classics series) primarily requires not a critical edition of the translator's text, but a readable English text of the source author's work.

In particular, I have to make decisions about how to divide and punctuate the text for a reader trained to expect modern sentences and paragraphs, where an early modern reader such as Florio was trained to look for rhetorical 'members', *sententiae*, periods, and *partes*. What should I do when the punctuation dictates a pause for breath or a periodic form that conflicts with the articulation of the syntactical sense? Or when it is simply wrong and misleading? What paragraph breaks should be introduced, given that they are barely present in Montaigne's and Florio's early editions? The decisions should be based on rational principles derived from an understanding of the composition and production of the copytext (the London 1603 edition of Florio's translation) and its relationship to its own source text.[11]

This involves simultaneous engagement with Montaigne's and Florio's places both in the sets of relations that produced their printed texts, and in the history of rhetorical composition, of which *distinctio* is a part. In 1934, Frances Yates wrote that Florio 'is rhetorical and Montaigne is not'. The latter was one of the first great writers in a modern tongue 'to write in a modern manner'. Florio brought 'sound-similarity [...] sound-repetition', 'balanced phrases' built into rhetorical periods that advanced in a 'balanced, musically adorned manner', with 'colour, harmony, majesty'.[12] However, Yates's notion that Florio profoundly modified Montaigne's style by turning modern sentences into rhetorical periods is shaped in part by the editions she was using.[13] Whereas she used a critical edition of Florio's text, with original orthography and punctuation, she used a modernized edition of the French *Essais*, with syntactical punctuation. Even now, because of long reliance on the Villey–Saulnier edition, Montaigne scholars regularly refer to 'sentences' and 'paragraphs' in the *Essais*.

In reality Florio, though not Latin-literate, saw what any Renaissance reader with some rhetorical training would have seen in the *Essais*: the traces of the rhetorical building — or building-works — Montaigne disowns. Far from turning modern prose into rhetorical periods, Florio sees periodic organization at work in his source text and reproduces it — along with much of its punctuation — in accentuated forms. He knows that Montaigne, in pursuit of the effects of a natural ethos (itself a rhetorical construct), all at once deployed, hid, and subverted the rhetorical resources and compositional techniques with which he and his readers had been provided during their education. Like the orators Crassus and Antonius in Cicero's *De oratore*, Montaigne sought — for reputational reasons — to hide the traces of his literary training, by not citing or naming the authors whose borrowed words compose his text.[14] The one major intervention Florio and his publisher Edward Blount make in this respect is to have the scholar Matthew Gwinne not only translate but source (in marginal notes) all the borrowings.[15]

Furthermore, Florio explicitly states that the 'Essayes', despite the strange title, are exercises in rhetorical composition: each chapter consists of 'mens school-themes pieced together [...] several texts'; all is in the 'choise & handling', *inventio* and *dispositio*. He sees instinctively what it now takes a scholar to uncover.[16] Themes (essays on moral topics), along with letters, were the principal forms of Latin prose composition practised in the Elizabethan grammar schools. As described by Hermogenes or Aphthonius (who use the term *thesis*) they were structured exercises on doubtful questions, designed to prepare for full oratorical *inventio*, but without specifying persons and circumstances (as in *hypothesis*). So although Montaigne had clearly been educated by means of such exercises, they had not led on to more fully developed declamations or treatises — at least not in the case of the *Essais*. Montaigne has just pieced together series of themes written in a 'disioynted, broken and gadding stile'; many times, they do not correspond to the titles of the chapters and have 'no coherence together'. This does not mean, of course, that one cannot tell where one theme ends and another begins.[17]

Is it possible or advisable for an editor of the *Essais/Essayes* to find rational principles upon which to divide and punctuate the text so that its 'sentences' and 'paragraphs' provide the modern reader with — please excuse the pun — a stronger 'period lens' through which to see the traces of the rhetorical house still there in deconstructed form? Bernard Croquette has forcefully argued that it is not. Any experiment that introduces paragraphing on apparently satisfying principles will end up butchering the text.[18] This is certainly true in the case of a critical edition of the French text intended for scholarly and expert readers. But if our goal is to produce an edition for the general Anglophone reader, or, more specifically still, for the eighteen-year-old undergraduate not majoring in literature, then some help must be given if we want the text to continue on its journey.

For such a reader lacks the rhetorical eye that Florio and other educated early modern readers had. These latter readers could discern the switches in style and theme, the patterns and figures that — however abrupt or disordered — shape Montaigne's writing; they could see at a glance what it now takes a specialist to lay out in a monograph. Just as Maclean argued that Montaigne's anti-philosophical discourse was parasitical on school philosophy's procedures, so I shall argue in what follows, with other scholars' help, that Montaigne's anti-rhetorical style is parasitical on the classical rules of rhetorical composition. He did not consistently write in Ciceronian *periodi* and divide his discourses into *partes orationis* (*exordium*, *narratio*, *confirmatio*, *confutatio*, *peroratio*). But nor did he write in sentences and paragraphs. His prose is loosely written in unmarked segments that he creates on his own principles, but that are analogous to rhetorical 'periods' and 'parts' or 'themes'. It can be analysed in detail in these terms.

Readers who wish to know immediately what an analysis of this type might look like can go straight to the Appendix at the end of this chapter, where I.31, 'Des cannibales' [Of Cannibals], is butchered for their consumption. I propose in the new Oxford World's Classics selected edition of Florio's Montaigne to mark each rhetorical period with an indented paragraph, and each new part or theme with a double linespace (without indentation).

1. Montaigne *rhétoricien*

At many points Montaigne claims to eschew the rules of *inventio, dispositio, elocutio* altogether, and to compose his text in a free style, as chance occasions and his own pleasure and imagination move him — 'rappiecez de divers membres, sans certaine figure, n'ayants ordre, suite ny proportion que fortuite' [pieced together of diverse members, without definite shape, having no order, sequence, or proportion other than accidental]. If the reader does perceive elements of compositional *ordo, iunctura, numerus* in the text, he or she should see them as accidental, not deliberate.[19] At other points, he hints that his disordered style is itself the result of deliberate rhetorical choices.[20] We know that early in his literary career he was inclined to write in rounded, regular, and balanced rhetorical periods; his translation of the *Theologia naturalis* turns the *style coupé* of Sebond's Latin into quasi-Ciceronian eloquence of the kind advocated by Jacques Amyot. Joseph Coppin found a similar style at work in his dedications to the works of La Boétie and in a few passages of the early *Essais*.[21]

In 1949, Hugo Friedrich produced what is still one of the more sophisticated analyses of the rhetorical form and style of the *Essais*.[22] The *Essais* combine the 'pointed' style with the 'extended rhetorical period', the laconic style of Seneca with the narrative, broad style of Cicero and Livy. The relationship between these two types changes over the years — the long rhetorical periods decrease in favour of the 'maxim' style. Friedrich was a highly trained romance philologist, steeped in the classical tradition. He remains one of the few critics to see that Montaigne's laconic style can 'swell to an undulating breadth and accumulation of rhetorical periods' when he is retelling stories from history and myth.[23] Should not an editor help a modern reader to see something of what he saw?

More recently, the essayist has been caught out disingenuously using and experimenting with the very arts of rhetorical composition and persuasion he disowns *en masse*. Edwin Duval, for example, shows how many of the early chapters encourage the reader to see classical *dispositio* at work — the arrangement of the discourse into *partes* with distinct functions — only so that their expectations may be confounded in the end.[24] The 'Ciceronian' element that Friedrich found in the *Essais* has been further explored. Kathy Eden has recently found the Ciceronian figure of *epiphonema* alive and well in Montaigne's work. We shall see below that this can act as a form of rhetorical punctuation.[25]

There has developed, meanwhile, a wide range of views concerning the nature of Montaigne's oppositional relationship to the rules of rhetorical composition. At one end, the conservative end, it has been equated with anti-Ciceronianism, and with a European trend towards the imitation of Silver Age writers such as Seneca and Tacitus. Morris Croll saw Montaigne as one of the architects of the 'quaternary' *période coupée* — four, asymmetrical *cola* on the same thought, but with no or minimal conjunctions (*asyndeton*). The *période coupée* is typical of the Senecan stylistic 'movement', and distinct from the 'loose' period.[26] Marc Fumaroli made greater cultural and historical sense of Montaigne's resistance to a 'finished' rhetorical form by showing how several generations of professionals in Renaissance

France adjusted their style to the *forme idéale* of the Ciceronian orator. But he retained the sense of an anti-Ciceronian trio — Lipsius, Muret, Montaigne — who were reinventing the orator through the *style coupé*, intended for less public, less oratorical interventions.[27]

At the other end of the range are the trenchant and original views of André Tournon, which developed in relation to his preparation of a new edition of the *EB* for the Imprimerie nationale. Tournon rooted his views on Montaigne's relationship to rhetoric in an account of the composition and revision of his text, especially with respect to punctuation. Montaigne's repunctuation of his copy of Paris 1588, Tournon showed, had never been scrupulously reproduced in any edition of that copy. This was a very serious omission because the new punctuation revealed the essayist's desire to enact a conception of discourse that was completely different ('tout autre') from traditional rhetoric. Instead of the Ciceronian period or the *sententia* brought to a satisfying close with a striking expression, Montaigne deployed a novel form of punctuation (including the *majuscule de scansion*, a capital letter used not to start a new sentence, but abruptly to start a new thought mid-sentence, after a colon) to deny his readers any rests or rhythmically emphasized conclusions. Readers are constantly moved forward by 'starts' or *élans du langage*, which mimic the style of thought of the *esprit généreux* whose *inquisitions* in this world never stop: the Pyrrhonist.[28] In short, the style of punctuation found in the *EB* is textually constitutive of Montaigne's whole philosophy of *mouvement*. Ever since the publication of Paris 1595 editors have unconsciously censored Montaigne's radical new form of punctuation because they have internalized norms of rhetoric and dialectic.[29]

Others have adapted Tournon's important *aperçus* about Montaigne's punctuation to more rounded accounts of the variety of rhetorical styles and forms he uses across the work — accounts more compatible with Friedrich and Croll. Marie-Luce Demonet shows how classical rhetoricians, in classifying styles of speech, used as one of their criteria the range from *oratio soluta* to *oratio vincta*, from phrases or *membra* ('membres' in French) strung together more loosely in dialogues and letters to those more tightly and hierarchically bound together in oratorical *periodi*. Quintilian (IX. iv. 19–20) specifies, however, that even *oratio soluta* has its own peculiar rhythms (*pedes*), rhythms that are very difficult to analyse. The structural cohesion of dialogues and letters is loose rather than non-existent ('potius laxiora in his vincula quam nulla sint'). On the most general level, then, Montaigne's style is characterizable as *oratio soluta*, in which each *lopin* can stand on its own as a *corps*. But Demonet shows how the text is nevertheless composed of different, semi-hidden forms that more or less tightly bind units of discourse together. These include instances of the oratorical *periodus* and of the brief style or *style coupé*.[30] Once again, these are forms that a general reader in the contemporary world will not be able to discern without editorial help.

In a compatible treatment, Jean Lecointe has argued that rhetorical modes of composition are apparent in Montaigne's style. The repunctuation evident in the *EB* and Paris 1595 does not always act to dismember the text in the manner shown by Tournon.[31] Indeed, it represents a 'periodic organization' ('organisation périodique') of the *style coupé* — re-membering the *lopins* into quasi-periodic units of discourse comprised of *commata* and *cola*. The result is effects of protasis/apodosis and *balancement* different but derived from those found in more classic *periodi*. There are also supra-periodic units of discourse, formed by groups of periods that balance or contrast and counterpoint one another. Lecointe goes so far as to say that this more 'integrated' ('intégrée') image of the *style coupé*, though difficult to recover, must make the cultivated appearance of natural disorder look somewhat specious — which is what many of Montaigne's early readers thought.[32]

But how might an editor of an actual chapter of the text — the text, furthermore, of a translation of Paris 1595 into English — assist the modern, non-specialist reader in seeing these elements of periodic and supra-periodic organization? No one, to my knowledge, has produced an analysis of both the *organisation périodique* and thematic partitions of a whole chapter. The partial exception to this lies in the history of editorial introduction of paragraphs, which on some occasions can correspond to periods, on others to thematic partitions. For nearly three centuries editors of the text for general readers have agreed that divisions need to be introduced to make it more intelligible. But they have not undertaken this division on analytical foundations. Bernard Croquette has revealed their history — from Pierre Coste in 1724 to Pierre Villey in 1923 — and the confusing, unclear principles upon which division by paragraph has largely been based. Twentieth-century readers inherited the irregular paragraphing introduced by Villey, which was partly based on the 'archaeological' layers of the text, partly based on an unarticulated sense of its logic.[33]

Croquette's analysis does not extend to translations, and translators' choices. So he misses the important early attempt by Girolamo Canini (1633) to divide the text of each chapter into numbered parts.[34] He might have analysed the paragraphing in Hazlitt's 1842 English edition of the *Works*, which does not follow Coste. He might have pointed out that Donald Frame takes Villey's divisions, but adds further subdivisions. Later, Screech would take Villey/Frame's breaks and adapt or ignore them as he saw fit. With some minor exceptions the recent selected edition of Florio's Montaigne, prepared and published in the United States, uses Frame's paragraphing and lightly modernized punctuation.[35]

So, with occasional exceptions such as Garavini's and Tournon's edition, translators and their editors have been no more explicitly rational in their approach to paragraphing and punctuation than producers of French texts. Meanwhile, questions about punctuation remain unasked in the recent spate of studies at the interface between book history and translation studies. Along with the usual questions about style and meaning, much attention is paid to the ways in which material features of the source edition — *mise en page*, paratexts — are translated and adapted in the target edition.[36] But a potentially more fundamental question has not been asked: are punctuation choices in the source edition — whether made by author or scribe, corrector or compositor — reproduced or adapted in the target edition, and by whom?

2. Punctuation in Paris 1595 and London 1603

So let us pause for a moment to ask that question, if in a very preliminary fashion. In many places London 1603 translates not just the text but the punctuation of Paris 1595, which must mean that Florio paid close attention to it when preparing his English copy. It also means that the *organisation périodique* of Montaigne's style — as idiosyncratic and variable as it may be — is more apparent in Florio's than in modern translations. Unlike almost all modern editions, London 1603 uses the same four-part scheme of punctuation for dividing up periods into *commata* and *cola* as Paris 1595 and the *EB* (comma, semi-colon, colon-with-lowercase, colon-with-uppercase). Take this example from I.47, 'De l'incertitude de nostre jugement' [Of the Uncertainty of our Judgement]:[37]

> D'autres ont reglé ce/ doubte en leur armée de cette maniere : Si les ennemis vous courent fus,atten-/dez les de pied coy : s'ils vous attendent de pied coy, courez leur fus.
> Au paffage que l'Empereur Charles cinquiefme fit en Prouence[.][38]

> Others have ordered this doubt in their army after this maner:If/ your enemies headlong runne vpon you, ftay for them aud bouge not : If they without ftir-/ring ftay for you,runne with fury vpon them.
> In the paffage which the Emperour *Charles* the fift made into *Provence*[.][39]

Here is a rhetorically rich *tricolon*, including a double *polyptoton* (which Florio cannot ape), punctuated by colons followed in the first instance by an uppercase, and in the second by a lowercase letter. There follows an indented paragraph to give greater emphasis to the military aphorism. London 1603 reproduces the punctuation exactly, with only two exceptions: the compositor does not have room at the end of the line to set the first colon with spaces either side; the second colon is followed by an uppercase rather than a lowercase letter. London 1603 also uses italics to emphasize proper names, as it does throughout.

But this reproduction or adaptation of the source text's punctuation is neither systematic nor, when it does occur, consistent in its principles. In the period before this one, on the same folio, Paris 1595 divides a narrative *tetracolon* using three colons followed by lowercase letters. London 1603 divides the period into four members at exactly the same points, but uses three semi-colons (followed by lowercase letters). Elsewhere, however, colons are not translated into semi-colons in this consistent fashion. In the rhetorical set-piece that follows the quoted passage (sigs Q1v.–2r.), Montaigne builds two lengthy periods of examples on either side of the deliberative question as to whether François Ier should have met Charles V in battle on his own territory or in Italy — before typically declaring that it all (including our very discourse) depends on 'fortune' or 'hazard' anyway. These are mostly divided by commas and colons-and-lowercase in Paris 1595. London 1603 (sigs O5v.–6r.) does not, like modern editions and translations, break the two periods down into more manageable sentences, with full stops and semi-colons. But neither does it consistently reproduce or adapt the use of colons — sometimes commas are used, sometimes colons-and-uppercase. There is no apparent rationale to the changes.

More strikingly still, London 1603 reproduces none of the other five paragraph breaks exceptionally included in I.47 from Bordeaux 1580 onwards, while elsewhere paragraph breaks are occasionally introduced where they are not present in the source text.[40] Was the unsystematic, inconsistent nature of this attention to Paris 1595's punctuation in London 1603 down to the translator or to one or other scribe, corrector, or compositor? It is difficult to say. But what we can say is that attention was paid. The punctuation used in the first posthumous edition and its derivatives, especially insofar as it builds long rhetorical periods, often without full stops, does shape to a significant degree — though not in a consistent or regular manner — the form taken by the text of London 1603.

3. *Essais* I.31 divided into periods

It is now time to substantiate my earlier claim that a whole chapter might be analysed in a way that, while not turning it into a systematic treatise, will help the modern reader see the text with a stronger 'period lens'. I.31 'Des cannibales' [Of Cannibals] was chosen for the experiment because the selected edition of Florio's Montaigne I am preparing will certainly include that chapter. As it happens, it also constitutes a good choice when it comes to assessing the broader applicability of arguments about rhetoric and punctuation (Tournon's) based heavily on reflective passages first composed after 1588. The fundamental outline of I.31 was already in place in Bordeaux 1580 and includes much natural-historical and ethnographic description, along with narrative. But there are enough revisions and additions both in Paris 1588, and on the *EB* and in Paris 1595, to make it revelatory of the evolution of the text and its punctuation.

The results of this analysis support Lecointe's contention that, in many cases, the revising and repunctuating of the text in the French editions tends not to dis-member but to re-member the text into periods. The best example is period no. 2 (see Appendix).[41] In Bordeaux 1580, it appeared in this very loose, six-*cola* form:[42]

> I'ay eu long temps auec moy vn hõme/ qui auoit demeuré dix ou douze ans en/ cet autre monde , qui a efté defcouuert/ en noftre fiecle en l'endroit ou Vilegai-/ gnon print terre , qu'il furnomma la/ France Antartique. Céte defcouuerte/ d'vn païs infini de terre ferme , femble/ de grande confideration. Ie ne fçay fi ie/ me puis refpondre que céte cy foit en-/core la derniere qui fe fera,[43] tant de grãds/ perfõnages ayãs efté trompez en l'autre[44]/p. 301/ I'ay peur que nous auons les yeus plus/ grands que le ventre, comme on dict,/ & le dit on de ceus, aufquels l'appetit &/ la faim font plus defirer de viande,qu'ils/ n'en peuuent empocher . Ie[45] crains auffi/ q̃ nous auõs beaucoup plus de curiofité/ q̃ nous n'auõs de capacité.nous embraf-/fons tout : mais[46] ie crains que nous n'ef-/treignons rien que du vent.

By 1595, it had been licked into shape as follows:

> I'ay eu long temps auec/ p. 118/ moy vn homme qui auoit demeuré dix ou douze ans en cet autre monde, qui/ a efté defcouuert en noftre fiecle,en l'endroit ou Vilegaignon print terre,qu'il/ furnomma la France Antartique. Cette defcouuerte d'vn païs infiny , femble/ de grande confideration.[47] Ie ne fçay fi ie me puis refpondre,qu'il ne s'en face à/ l'aduenir quelqu'autre, tant de

> perſonnages plus grands que nous ayans eſté/ trompez en cette-cy.I'ay peur que
> nous ayons les yeux plus grands que le ven-/tre,& plus de curioſité,que nous
> n'auons de capacité : Nous embraſſons tout,/ mais nous n'eſtreignons que du
> vent.[48]

In Bordeaux 1580 the passage is an instance of the loosest *oratio soluta*, and is so
segmented and hesitant that it could hardly be described as a 'period', even in
the broader sense we are using here. It is barely held together by the idea of the
découverte, and by the repeating *Je*: 'I'ay eu [...] Ie ne ſçay [...] I'ay peur [...] Ie crains'.
It is also poorly composed for the press (missing full stop at 'l'autre I'ay peur',
lack of capital letter and spacing at 'capacité.nous'). It has the erratic rhythms and
awkward repetitions of actual speech, and might plausibly be the result of dictation
to a secretary ('comme on dict, & le dit on ce ceus [...] Ie crains aussi [...] mais ie
crains que').

It is not that Paris 1595 contains any more *vincula*, that is, conjunctions or connections to bind the period together. But we do now have the rhythmically more
assured and measured outline of a *période coupée* contained within a larger five-*cola*
period. The first *colon* is little changed, except that the punctuation now gives
us four *commata*. The removal of 'de terre ferme' makes the second *colon* more
balanced. The same is true for the removal of 'mais ie crains que' from the last
colon, the *clausula* or fitting 'close' to the period, which balances the two *commata*
and completes the thought in the second *colon* (this discovery *seems* worthy of great
consideration, but we are incapable of properly grasping it). The sententious *clausula*
is, furthermore, given greater emphasis by the introduction of a *majuscule de scansion*
('capacité : Nous embrassons'), and by more compact sound-effects of rhyme
('Nous [...] tous [...] nous nous [...] du'; 'embrassons [...] n'estreignons'), alliteration,
and assonance ('vent' is now closer to 'ventre'). The third and fourth *cola* have
three *commata* each, with 'cette-cy' placed more effectively at the end of the third
colon to recall the first 'Cette'. The grammatical correction of indicative 'auons' to
subjunctive 'ayons' in the fourth *colon* creates an assonance with 'ayans'. In short,
after the first *colon*, the rest is tidied up as an asymmetrical *tetracolon* with a closing
sententia emphasized by the punctuation.

In my view, the shape of this period can only be brought out for a modern reader
of an edition of Florio's text by indenting it — along with all other periods in the
text — as a paragraph. And what about the punctuation? In this case London 1603
approximately reproduces all the *commata* (as divided by commas), although it adds
one (my underlining), and uses a full-stop-and-capital in place of the colon-and-
capital:

> I have had long time dwelling with mee/ a man, who for the ſpace of tenne
> or twelve yeares had dwelt in that other world, which in/ our age was lately
> diſcovered in thoſe partes where *Villegaignon* firſt landed, and ſurnamed/
> *Antartike France*. This diſcoverie of ſo infinite and vaſt a countrie , ſeemeth
> worthie great/ conſideration. I wot not whether I can warrant my ſelfe, that
> ſome other be not diſcovered/ hereafter, ſithence ſo many worthie men, <u>and
> better learned then we are</u>, have ſo many ages/ béene deceived in this. I feare
> me our eyes be greater then our bellies,and that we have more/ curioſitie then
> capacitie. We embrace all, but we faſten nothing but winde.[49]

It would clearly be going too far to re-introduce the colon-and-full-stop from Paris 1595 ('capacity: We embrace'). The principle should be that London 1603's punctuation is left as it is unless it actively misleads or confuses the modern reader trying to follow the sense syntactically. Here, there might be an argument for removing the comma after 'my selfe' (as the New York Review Books selected edition of Florio does) but I would argue that, in this instance, the sense remains comprehensible if it is left in. So the edited text of this period/paragraph, with lightly modernized orthography, would look like this:

> [...] not by the common report.
>
> I have had long time dwelling with me a man, who for the space of ten or twelve years had dwelt in that other world, which in our age was lately discovered in those parts where Villegagnon first landed, and surnamed Antarctic France. This discovery of so infinite and vast a country, seemeth worthy great consideration. I wot not whether I can warrant myself, that some other be not discovered hereafter, sithence so many worthy men, and better learned than we are, have so many ages been deceived in this. I fear me our eyes be greater than our bellies, and that we have more curiosity than capacity. We embrace all, but we fasten nothing but wind.
>
> Plato maketh Solon to report [...]

The reader who wishes to follow the analysis of the whole chapter in detail can consult the Appendix. The right-hand Notes column offers comments on the textual evolution and shapes of some of the 68 periods into which this editor has divided the chapter.

Here, some general observations will suffice. The first and most important is that this is indeed *oratio soluta* — the prevailing trend is for loose periods which contain elements of periodic form and balance, but whose *membres* are not bound together in any kind of truly regular, Ciceronian pattern. Having said that, one often finds four-*cola* patterns — it is particularly interesting that this is the case with the Amerindian prisoner's song (no. 55). Period no. 1 has a similar structure, although it is narrative rather than reflective, more elaborate, and is 'punctuated' — divided from the next period — by a sententious *epiphonema*. In other cases it is more difficult to decide whether or not a larger unit should be divided into two smaller ones, on the basis of rhythm or emphasis. Such divisions are all to a greater or lesser extent debatable; different editors could make different decisions based on the same principle.

For example, one could argue that nos. 11 and 12 should be run together as a single loose period exploring the same thought, as the beginning of no. 12 clearly picks up the *propos* again from the beginning of no. 11. But the rhetorical repetition of 'parfait' sounds a minor close to a compact, quaternary period, while no. 12 — also a *tetracolon* in its final form — offers a more unsettling close. The same is true of nos. 59 and 60, which V and F unite as a single paragraph. But one can also see no. 59 as a discrete *période coupée* and no. 60 as an anaphoric *tricolon*.

So although the table in the Appendix shows that periods with four *cola* are the most frequent, *tetracola* are not regular enough to be considered the normal form of Montaignian periodic organization: the patterns used vary too widely, and the switches from more to less regular forms of periodic organization are too frequent.

Some periods are quite balanced and even pleasingly circuitous, such as the one tracing the movement of the natives over the mountains to war and back again (no. 37). Others are more irregular. There are also three-*cola* apophthegms (no. 14) and five-*cola* periods (no. 56). And there are many other shapes and sizes of period, including the four-*commata*, one-*colon* variety (no. 63). The shortest and simplest of them all (no. 28), and the one closest to what we would wish to call a sentence, occurs in part VII (as it is designated in the analysis offered in the Appendix), which describes the New World people's country, villages, manners, diet, and religion. This is how it appeared in Paris 1595 and London 1603:

> Toute la iournée se passe à dancer.

> They fpend the whole day in dancing.[50]

The lengthiest examples are either designated (in the Appendix) 'loose' periods, often running to eight or nine disarticulated *cola* on the same thought, or as instances of the more circuitous *periodus*, with more syntactic articulation, usually involving some kind of protasis and apodosis (suspension then completion of the main thought). One of the simplest of the latter (no. 20), one *colon* with five *commata* reproduced exactly in London 1603, tells the story of the first man who rode a horse into the Amerindians' village (they killed him, even though they knew him). Somewhere in between is no. 6, which mimics the unpredictable movements of the river, and ends with *anaphora*. The tightest style of *periodus* is usually reserved for high events in history, such as the deliberations of Ischolas at Thermopylae (no. 52) or the decision of the cannibals to leave their ancient manner of taking vengeance in favour of the crueller forms of death imposed by the Portuguese (no. 39). These effects of suspension and completion can also be used ironically, as when a complex narrative *periodus* ends with Montaigne losing his memory (no. 64). A looser period can also incorporate a *periodus*, alongside more independent *cola* (no. 50).

Of course, the variation in the complexity and height of the periodic style, the irregularity of its movements and rhythms, is closely related to the subject of the chapter. This is the tension between the natural, simple way of life of the Amerindians and the artificially corrupted way of life in Europe, between the simple testimony of Montaigne's servant and the heavily mediated accounts of more expert and articulate witnesses, including Plato and Aristotle in classical antiquity. The interplay between nature, art, and chance is apparent at the level of periodic organization. 'Art' is to be found in the simplest periods describing the 'natural' people's manners and songs. Nature and chance disrupt and divert the more artificial circuits of rational thought — as in no. 12 (a *tricolon* from Bordeaux 1580 to Paris 1588), where a balanced antithesis between wild, natural fruits and our taste for grafted, corrupted fruits is disrupted by a chance thought added to the *EB* that, actually, we like both!

4. *Essais* I.31 divided into parts

The rhetorical occasion and form of the chapter sets itself against a more conventional classical oration in praise of a city and its people, such as Pericles' oration in praise of the Athenians who died in the Peloponnesian war. The classical contest in virtue between nations such as the Athenians and the Spartans is, indeed, the setting for Montaigne's praise of the martial valour and marital ethos of the cannibals. But they are cannibals. His discourse is paradoxical: an epideictic speech in praise of the honour of a 'barbarous' people. Furthermore, as Edwin Duval has shown, the grounds on which he offers praise shift throughout the chapter, forming a deliberate pattern of contradictions as the terms central to the *propos* — 'barbare', 'sauvage', 'art', 'nature' — are repeatedly re-semanticized.[51] Hardly surprising, then, that we cannot divide the chapter into a four- or five-part discourse with *exordium*, *narratio*, and so on. In 1633 Girolamo Canini divides it into six sections with separate summary titles. The first might in his mind have made an *exordium*, the second and third a *narratio*, and the fourth a *probatio* or *confirmatio*, but the project of a precise division in these terms is doomed.[52]

Montaigne gives a clear indication, however, of what his approach to the 'division' of his subject matter is:

> J'entends que la matiere se distingue soy-mesmes. Elle montre assez <u>où elle se change, où elle conclud, où elle commence, où elle se reprend</u>, sans l'entrelasser de paroles, de liaison et de cousture introduictes pour le service des oreilles foibles ou nonchallantes, et sans me gloser moymesme.

> I want the matter to make its own divisions. It shows well enough <u>where it changes, where it concludes, where it begins, where it resumes</u>, without my interlacing it with words, with links and seams introduced for the benefit of weak or heedless ears, and without writing glosses on myself.[53]

If not *partes* in the strict rhetorical sense there are parts formed by the *res* or subject-matter itself, which shows where it changes, concludes, begins, resumes — self-evident *distinctiones* in lieu of an authorial gloss. If, then, we can identify these points of change, conclusion, commencement, recommencement, we have the basis for a division of the text into parts. Each part, furthermore, should be identifiable by a particular 'theme' (Florio's term), expressible in an editorial title. The left-hand column in the table in the Appendix shows the results of just such a division of the chapter.

But how apparent are such points of change? Montaigne says the points where a distinct 'matter' begins or ends are not explicitly marked or glossed as changes of direction, but a few are ('Table', part VI, no. 11; part VII, no. 17; part X, no. 54). Other commencements of new matter are not much more difficult to discern (parts II, IV, VII, VIII, XIII). There is then what might be called rhetorical punctuation. Kathy Eden has, as noted above, identified Montaigne's use of the Ciceronian and Erasmian figure *epiphonema*. This can be specifically defined as a shrewd or pungent exclamation in the *clausula* or close of an utterance or discursive section, or more broadly defined (by Edmund Spenser) as the 'morall of the whole tale' in the final verses of a poem.[54]

The *matière* in Montaigne's text does frequently show, by means of shrewd, pungent, or sententiously emphatic remarks, where 'it concludes'. This is clearly the case at the end of parts I and V. Parts II and IV close with instances of more straightforward *conclusio*, while part X has a more elaborate three-*cola conclusio* directly relevant to the main *propos*. Part III ends with no more than a vivid picture of moving sands, but it is a B–C addition before what is clearly a new departure at the beginning of part IV. In Bordeaux 1580, part VI ended with a pungent *interrogatio* concerning Plato's republic, after the rhetorical set-piece outlining what he would say to the Greek about the cannibals' nation (period no. 16). In Paris 1595 one quotation, and in the *EB* two Latin quotations, are added to mark the *clausula* still more decisively.

Period no. 16 is the one that caught Shakespeare's attention in Florio's translation. It is interesting, however, that in Gonzalo's mouth (*The Tempest*, II. 2. 142–64) it becomes a more conventional *periodus*, with a conditional protasis and a lengthy apodosis ('Had I plantation of this isle, my lord [...]/ I'th'commonwealth I would by contraries/ Execute all things. For no kind of traffic/ Would I admit'). This is a very good example of a contemporary reader of Florio's seeing his text with a rhetorical eye, both as reader and rewriter.

Perhaps the most striking example of all is the end of part VII. In Bordeaux 1580 this ends with a pungent narrative *epiphonema* (no. 35) concerning the mistaken prophet who is never seen again (because he knows if he is caught he will be cut into a thousand pieces). But the *EB* and Paris 1595 add a *periodus* (no. 36) that can only be described as a mini-peroration. It circles from the statement that abuse of the divine gift of divination should be 'punished as imposture' back to an emphatic final repetition of the word ('imposture') at the end of another rhetorical question.

On only one occasion is a whole new part created by B–C additions. In Bordeaux 1580 and 1582 period no. 46 still incorporates what then becomes in the *EB* and Paris 1595 the first *colon* of part IX, which 'distinguishes' itself from part VIII (on the cannibals' wars) by gathering comment and examples on the theme of true victories and triumphant defeats.

The final part comprises just one short period (no. 68), and the best example of *epiphonema* in the whole chapter. It consists of an exclamation that could almost be construed as a *subiectio* (mock question-and-answer with a fictitious interlocutor who is generally the refuted opposing party): 'Tout cela ne va pas trop mal: mais quoy, ils ne portent point de haut de chasses' ('All this is not too bad — but what's the use? They don't wear breeches'). For in these closing words we directly hear, for the first time in the chapter, the tones of the 'voix commune' ('popular say' or voice) whose pronouncements on barbaric races like the cannibals are implicitly being refuted throughout.[55]

Only when I was about halfway through the division of the chapter into themed parts did I realize that one editor had got there before me. One of the unsung merits of André Tournon's edition of the *EB* is that he has completely revised the paragraphing that has been handed down from Villey. The principle he used must be similar to the one espoused here, for it produced, in the case of I.31, identical results. The difference is that I propose to use indented paragraphs to mark rhetorical periods, and a double linespace followed by no indentation to mark transitions between themes (the editorial titles will perhaps be included in notes at the back).

There are drawbacks to these editorial proposals — drawbacks that may result in their modification prior to final publication of the Oxford World's Classics selected edition. To apply the principle consistently, one has to create a lot of paragraphs when Montaigne writes in short, independent, one-*colon* periods for long passages (see part VII in the Appendix) — even if one could argue that doing so makes the simplifying of his periodic organization at that point graphically clear on the page in a way that it would not be if the whole chapter was presented as one undivided block of text. Before they are finalized, the proposals need to be tested more extensively against chapters other than I.31. On the one hand, it is certainly more difficult in some chapters in Book III to differentiate one 'loose period' from the next, even if changes in theme can still be discerned. On the other hand, falling back on Tournon's principle of using *alinéas* only for changes in the theme would mean the reader surviving seven pages and more on multiple occasions without a paragraph break. The degree of form/formlessness in Montaigne's prose varies radically according to subject matter and argument; carefully handled paragraph breaks might serve to reveal this variation.

I am proposing these choices for two principal reasons. Firstly, because I believe that if the work is to continue in transit to new readers and markets, it has to be packaged and edited accordingly, as editors have realized for three centuries. If a language teacher and rhetorician of the early seventeenth century (Florio) could find the text disjointed and incoherent, then the early twenty-first-century general reader lacking a period lens must need fairly drastic help. But such help should be offered on the basis of a rationale that does not simply apply modern expectations anachronistically to an early modern text: in this case, that means a rhetorical analysis of the text into Montaigne's idiosyncratic periods and parts.

My second reason is that it is now possible to direct readers to publicly accessible, high-quality, online facsimiles of London 1603 and Paris 1595.[56] They will be encouraged to compare and contrast these early editions' presentation with that of the modernized edition (a table of corresponding pages will be provided) — an excellent exercise for undergraduates who can get some assistance in following Montaigne's rhythms and trains of thought, before considering the material forms in which early readers encountered the text. The Introduction to the Oxford World's Classics edition will emphasize how important the original punctuation and lack of paragraphing were to Montaigne's design for a natural form of discourse that would contrast with the divisions and subdivisions of scholastic philosophy and humanist declamations.

Of course, you may still not like your Florio butchered in this way. So contact the editor and tell him why![57]

Appendix: Table of Rhetorical Periods and Parts in Montaigne, *Essais*, I.31 'Des cannibales'

Editions are abbreviated in the following fashion: Bordeaux 1580 is '80; Paris 1595 is '95; London 1603 is '03, etc.

Parts/themes	References	Periods	Notes
I. On judging so-called 'barbarous' peoples rationally, against common opinion.	1. V, p. 202, l. 29; F, p. 182, l. 1.	1. [A] Quand le Roy [...] par la voix commune./ ᴬWhen King Pyrrhus [...] not by popular say.	1. Four *cola* in *EB*/'95. Paragraph in V and F. *Clausula* to part I is an argumentative *epiphonema*.
II. On whether the recently discovered New World, described by Montaigne's servant, is the island of Atlantis, described by Solon in Plato.	2. V, p. 203, l. 1; F, p. 182, l. 11.	2. J'ay eu long temps [...] que du vent./ I had with me for a long time [...] only wind.	2. Loose six-*cola* period '80–'88, ending with *sententia*. Tighter, more balanced five-*cola* period in *EB*/'95. '03 adds a *comma*. Paragraph in V and F.
	3. V, p. 203, l. 9; F, p. 182, l. 21.	3. Platon introduit Solon [...] engloutis par le deluge./ Plato brings in Solon [...] swallowed up by the Flood.	3. Indirect narrative *periodus*. Paragraph in F.
	4. V, p. 203, l. 21; F, p. 182, l. 34.	4. Il est bien vray-semblable [...] *sentit aratrum*./ It is quite likely [...] feels the heavy plow.	4. Three *cola* in *EB*, with citations as *commata* (punctuated by commas). Punctuation in '95 and '03 less clear.
	5. V, p. 204, l. 1; F, p. 183, l. 9.	5. Mais il n'y a pas [...] isle pour cela./ But there is no great [...] an island on that account.	5. Argumentative *periodus* circling back to 'isle'. *Clausula* to part II is a *conclusio* to the argument. '03 punctuation faulty, making a different conclusion.
III. On natural and extreme movements of rivers and seas, and how they change topography.	6. V, p. 204, l. 10/ F, p. 183, l. 19.	6. [B] Il semble qu'il y aye [...] tantost elles se contiennent./ ᴮIt seems that there are [...] now they keep to their course.	6. Begins with one-*colon* definitional statement with three *commata* in *EB*/'95. Then descriptive *periodus* in four *cola* in '95, six in *EB*, ending with *anaphora* (or *epanaphora*). '03 broadly reproduces.
	7. V, p. 204, l. 18; F, p. 183, l. 28.	7. Je ne parle pas [...] et gaignent païs./ I am not speaking [...] keep conquering land.	7. Again, begins with definitional statement, then descriptive *periodus*, with *clausula* reinforced in *EB*/'95 by *evidentia*.

Section	Citation	Quotation	Analysis
IV. Whether Aristotle's narration of the Carthaginians' discovery of an island in the Atlantic fits the New World.	8. V, p. 204, l. 27/ F, p. 184, l. 1.	8. [A] L'autre tesmoignage [...] avec nos terres neufves./ ^AThe other testimony [...] any better than the other.	8. Contains an indirect narrative *periodus*, with protasis and apodosis, in three *cola* '80-'95. '03 integrates the first *colon* more into the period. Paragraph in V and F. Concise *conclusio* to the period and to part IV.
V. Why the character of Montaigne's servant makes his information more reliable than that of clever, expert people.	9. V, p. 205, l. 1; F, p. 184, l. 16.	9. Cet homme que j'avoy [...] ce que les cosmographes en disent./ This man I had [...] what the cosmographers say about it.	9. Loose argumentative period with nine *cola* '80-'95. Paragraph in V and F.
	10. V, p. 205, l. 15; F, p. 184, l. 30.	10. Il nous faudroit des topographes [...] plusieurs grandes incommoditez./ We ought to have topographers [...] many great abuses.	10. Loose argumentative period with seven *cola* '88-'95. Paragraph in V and F. Part V ends with moral *conclusio*.
VI. These people are only barbarous and savage in the sense that they are closer than we are to an original naturalness which not even classical antiquity could imagine.	11. V, p. 205, l. 25; F, p. 185, l. 3.	11. Or, je trouve, pour revenir à mon propos [...] usage de toutes choses./ Now, to return to my subject [...] manners in all things.	11. Four-*cola* period ('88-'95) returns to *propos*, and ends with repetition of 'parfaict'.
	12. V, p. 205, l. 31; F, p. 185, l. 9.	12. Ils sont sauvages [...] sans culture./ Those people are wild [...] as that of our own.	12. Three-*cola* period from '80 to '88, with *colon* added in EB/'95.
	13. V, p. 205, l. 40; F, p. 185, l. 19.	13. Ce n'est pas raison [...] la tissure de la chetive araignée./ It is not reasonable [...] the web of the puny spider.	13. Five-*cola* period in '80, expanded with verse citation in '88-'95. Mispunctuated between nos. 12 and 13 in '95 (followed by '03).
	14. V, p. 206, l. 11; F, p. 185, l. 30.	14. [C] Toutes choses, dict Platon [...] par la derniere./ ^CAll things, says Plato [...] by the last.	14. Three-*cola* apophthegm. '03 italicizes and punctuates as *bicolon*.
	15. V, p. 206, l. 15; F, p. 185, l. 34.	15. [A] Ces nations me semblent donq ainsi barbares [...] de soudeure humaine./ ^AThese nations, then, seem to me barbarous [...] human solder.	15. Eight-*cola*, loose argumentative period.
	16. V, p. 206, l. 28; F, p. 186, l. 8.	16. C'est une nation, diroy je à Platon [...] *primum dedit*./ This is a nation, I should say to Plato [...] first ordained.	16. Three-*cola* period in '80 with *interrogatio*. Four-*cola* period in '88-'95 ends part VI with Latin citation (two citations on *EB*).

VII. On the New World people's country, villages, manners, diet, and religion.			
	17. V, p. 207, l. 4; F, p. 186, l. 20.	17. [A] Au demeurant, ils vivent [...] courbé de vieillesse./ ^AFor the rest, they live [...] bent with age.	17. Three-*cola* period '80–'95. '03 removes colons.
	18. V, p. 207, l. 7; F, p. 186, l. 23.	18. Ils sont assis [...] d'estendue en large./ They are settled [...] wide in between.	
	19. V, p. 207, l. 10; F, p. 186, l. 25.	19. Ils ont grande abondance [...] que de les cuire./ They have a great abundance [...] than cooking.	
	20. V, p. 207, l. 12; F, p. 186, l. 27.	20. Le premier qui y mena un cheval [...] le pouvoir recoignoistre./ The first man who rode a horse [...] they could recognize him.	20. Five-*commata* period with protasis and apodosis. Reproduced in '03 with main clause at the close.
	21. V, p. 207, l. 14; F, p. 186, l. 31.	21. Leurs bastimens sont fort longs [...] et sert de flanq./ Their buildings are very long [...] and acts as a side.	21. Five *commata* in '80 become eight *commata* in '88–'95. Reproduced in '03 (with one change to a semi-colon).
	22. V, p. 207, l. 18; F, p. 186, l. 35.	22. Ils ont du bois si dur [...] à cuire leur viande./ They have wood so hard [...] to cook their food.	
	23. V, p. 207, l. 20; F, p. 186, l. 37.	23. Leurs lits sont [...] à part des maris./ Their beds are [...] apart from their husbands.	
	24. V, p. 207, l. 22; F, p. 187, l. 1.	24. Ils se levent [...] autre repas que celuy là./ They get up [...] no other meal than that one.	
	25. V, p. 207, l. 24; F, p. 187, l. 3.	25. Ils ne boyvent pas lors [...] plusieurs fois sur jour, et d'autant./ Like some other Eastern peoples [...] several times a day, and to capacity.	
	26. V, p. 207, l. 26; F, p. 187, l. 5.	26. Leur breuvage est faict [...] tres-agreable à qui y est duit./ Their drink is made [...] who is accustomed to it.	

Reference	Text	Commentary
27. V, p. 207, l. 31; F, p. 187, l. 10.	27. Au lieu du pain [...] un peu fade. / In place of bread [...] a little flat.	
28. V, p. 207, l. 33; F, p. 187, l. 13.	28. Toute la journée se passe à dancer. / The whole day is spent in dancing.	
29. V, p. 207, l. 33; F, p. 187, l. 13.	29. Les plus jeunes [...] leur principal office. / The younger men [...] their chief duty.	
30. V, p. 207, l. 35; F, p. 187, l. 15.	30. Il y a quelqu'un des vieillars [...] qui leur mantiennent leur boisson tiede et assaisonée. / Some one of the old men [...] their drink warm and seasoned.	30. Narrative *periodus* '80–'95.
31. V, p. 208, l. 7; F, p. 187, l. 24.	31. Il se void en plusieurs lieux [...] la cadance en leur dancer. / There may be seen in several places [...] time in their dances.	
32. V, p. 208, l. 11; F, p. 187, l. 28.	32. Ils sont ras par tout [...] de bois ou de pierre. / They are close shaven all over [...] a wooden or stone razor.	
33. V, p. 208, l. 12; F, p. 187, l. 30.	33. Ils croyent les ames eternelles [...] du costé de l'Occident. / They believe that souls are immortal [...] in the west.	
34. V, p. 208, l. 15; F, p. 187, l. 33.	34. Ils ont je ne sçay quels prestres [...] affection à leurs femmes. / They have some sort of priests [...] affection for their wives.	34. Four-*cola* period '80–'95.
35. V, p. 208, l. 22; F, p. 187, l. 40.	35. Cettuy-cy leur prognostique [...] on ne le void plus. / He prophesies to them [...] is never seen again.	35. Four-*cola* period '80–'95. Part VII ends here in '80 with narrative *epiphonema*.
36. V, p. 208, l. 28; F, p. 188, l. 7.	36. [C] C'est don de Dieu [...] la temerité de leur imposture? / Divination is a gift of God [...] the temerity of their imposture?	36. Complex, six-*cola periodus* in *EB/*'95 ends part VII with a rhetorical question, and with emphatic repetition of 'imposture' from the second *colon* as the closing word of the period.

VIII. On their wars with the nations beyond the mountains, and their treatment and cannibalization of prisoners.	37. V, p. 208, l. 38; F, p. 188, l. 16.	37. [A] Ils ont leurs guerres [...] à l'entrée de son logis./ ^AThey have their wars [...] the entrance to their dwelling.	37. Four-*cola* narrative period tracing movement beyond mountains and back. First *colon* divided into seven *commata* in '95 and eight in '03, which follows '95's punctuation closely. F divides across two paragraphs.
	38. V, p. 209, l. 5; F, p. 188, l. 23.	38. Apres avoir long temps [...] representer une extreme vengeance./ After they have [...] to betoken an extreme revenge.	38. Four-*cola* period in '95, divided by full stops, with a strong concluding thought.
	39. V, p. 209, l. 15; F, p. 188, l. 33.	39. Et qu'il soit ainsi [...] pour suivre cette-cy./ And the proof of this came [...] to follow this one.	39. *Periodus* '80–'95 with colon marking transition from protasis to apodosis. Semi-colons in '03.
	40. V, p. 209, l. 24; F, p. 189, l. 3.	40. Je ne suis pas marry [...] que de le rostir et manger apres qu'il est trespassé./ I am not sorry [...] than in roasting and eating him after he is dead.	
	41. V, p. 209, l. 35; F, p. 189, l. 12.	41. Chrysippus et Zenon [...] en toute sorte de barbarie./ Indeed, Chrysippus and Zeno [...] in every kind of barbarity.	41. Six-*cola* period in '80, with verse citation incorporated in '88, with balanced concluding four-*commata colon* in '88–EB/'95 (divided by one colon in '80, one colon and a comma in '82).
	42. V, p. 210, l. 9; F, p. 189, l. 27.	42. Leur guerre est toute noble [...] superflu pour eux./ Their warfare is wholly noble [...] superfluous to them.	42. Seven-*cola* period comprising opening *tricolon* then *tetracolon* divided at mid-point by a full-stop '80–'95. Paragraph in F. '03 punctuation very close.
	43. V, p. 210, l. 17; F, p. 189, l. 35.	43. Ils s'entr'appellent [...] les produisant au monde./ They generally call those [...] bringing them into the world.	
	44. V, p. 210, l. 22; F, p. 190, l. 1.	44. Si leurs voisins passent [...] et s'en contenter./ If their neighbours cross [...] and be content with it.	44. Re-pointed as a two-*cola periodus* in '88. '03 mirrors pivotal central colon.

Reference	Text	Commentary
45. V, p. 210, l. 28; F, p. 190, l. 7.	45. Autant en font ceux-cy [...] requerir seulement de ne l'estre pas./ These men of ours do the same [...] so much as ask not to be.	45. Four-*cola* period (with variants in punctuation) '80–'95. '03 error in punctuation runs together nos. 45/46.
46. V, p. 210, l. 34; F, p. 190, l. 13.	46. Ils les traictent en toute liberté [...] faict force à leur constance./ They treat them very freely [...] broken down their firmness.	46. In '80–'82 a four-*cola* period still incorporates ('constance: car aussi a le bien prendre [...]') what in '88, then *EB* and '95, becomes the first *colon* of no. 47, in part IX.

IX. On true victories and triumphant defeats.

Reference	Text	Commentary
47. V, p. 211, l. 2; F, p. 190, l. 20.	47. Car aussi, à le bien prendre [...] s'armer des lors en avant contre eux./ For indeed, if you take it the right way [...] to take up arms against them.	47. In '88, changes in punctuation make 'Car aussi' the beginning of a new period, but an addition in *EB*/'95 extends it, so that 'Assez' now begins no. 48.
48. V, p. 211, l. 10; F, p. 190, l. 30.	48. [A] Assez d'avantages [...] suffisant à l'escrime./ ᴬWe win enough advantages [...] to be an able fencer.	48. Five-*cola* period of independent clauses in *EB* and '95, incorporating four parallel *cola* (with *anaphora*) beginning with a *majuscule de scansion*: 'nostres: C'est [...]'.'03 uses capital letters to begin all four *cola*.
49. V, p. 211, l. 16; F, p. 190, l. 35.	49. L'estimation et le pris d'un homme [...] mais en la nostre./ The worth and value of a man [...] but in our own.	49. Four-*cola* period divided by full stops in '80–'82, and by colons-and-lowercase in '88–*EB*/'95. '03 reproduces '95 punctuation almost exactly, adding a *majuscule de scansion* at the midpoint.
50. V, p. 211, l. 20; F, p. 190, l. 39.	50. Celuy qui tombe obstiné [...] les plus infortunez./ He who falls obstinate [...] the most unfortunate.	50. In '80–'82, a period which beautifully balances an opening *periodus* containing subordinate relative clause and main clause, with two independent *cola*. In '88 another *colon* is added; in *EB*/'95 a citation and other changes bring imbalance. Closing *sententia* split off by V as a separate paragraph, because a 'B' addition.
51. V, p. 211, l. 27; F, p. 191, l. 5.	51. [C] Aussi y a il des pertes triomphantes [...] que luy de sa ruine?/ ᶜThus there are triumphant defeats [...] than he did his destruction?	51. Four-*cola* period added in *EB*/'95, incorporating a *periodus* in second *colon*, and culminating in two rhetorical questions.

Section	Reference	Text	Commentary
	52. V, p. 211, l. 34; F, p. 191, l. 14.	52. Il estoit commis à deffendre [...] comme il advint./ He was charged to defend [...] And so it turned out.	52. *Periodus* added in *EB*/'95, tracing deliberations of Ischolas at Thermopylae. In *EB*/'95 ends ': comme il advint.'
	53. V, p. 212, l. 9; F, p. 191, l. 26.	53. Car estant tantost environné [...] non à battre./ For he was presently surrounded [...] not in beating.	53. Four-*cola* period in '95, ending with a balanced, sententious *epiphonema*.
X. On the condemned prisoners' defiance, in life and art.	54. V, p. 212, l. 15; F, p. 191, l. 32.	54. [A] Pour revenir à nostre histoire [...] perdües contre les leurs./ ᴬTo return to our story [...] lost to the prisoners' own people.	54. *Periodus* with protasis and apodosis, in *commata* only.
	55. V, p. 212, l. 20; F, p. 191, l. 38.	55. J'ay une chanson faicte [...] qui ne sent aucunement la barbarie./ I have a song composed [...] does not smack of barbarity.	55. Four-*cola* paraphrase of the Amerindian prisoner's song, contained within larger period. Repunctuation with colons-and-lowercase after '82.
	56. V, p. 212, l. 27; F, p. 192, l. 5.	56. Ceux qui les peignent mourans [...] et de contenance./ Those that paint these people dying [...] by word and look.	56. Five-*cola* period.
	57. V, p. 212, l. 31; F, p. 192, l. 9.	57. Sans mentir [...] entre leur forme et la nostre./ Truly here [...] between their character and ours.	57. Three-*cola conclusio* in relation to main *propos* to end part X.
XI. On the wives' care for their husbands' valour.	58. V, p. 212, l. 35; F, p. 192, l. 12.	58. Les hommes y ont plusieurs femmes [...] tesmoignage de la vertu du mary./ The men there have several wives [...] sign of their husbands' valour.	58. Three-*cola* period. Paragraph in V and F.
	59. V, p. 213, l. 3; F, p. 192, l. 19.	59. [C] Les nostres crieront un miracle [...] plus haut estage./ ᶜOur wives will cry 'Miracle!' [...] of the highest order.	59. Four-*cola* period.
	60. V, p. 213, l. 4; F, p. 192, l. 20.	60. Et, en la Bible [...] aux estats de leur pere./ In the Bible [...] to their father's estates.	60. Three-*cola* paratactic period, with anaphoric 'et'. Nos. 59/60 make a paragraph in V and F, corresponding to a single C addition.

Section	Reference	Text	Commentary
XII. On their abilities and language.	61. V, p. 213, l. 11; F, p. 192, l. 27.	61. [A] Et, afin qu'on ne pense point [...] traits de leur suffisance./ ^A And lest it be thought [...] examples of their capacity.	
	62. V, p. 213, l. 15; F, p. 192, l. 31.	62. Outre celuy que [...] tout à fait Anacreontique./ Besides the warlike song [...] altogether Anacreontic.	62. Five-*cola* loose period containing the Anacreontic song.
	63. V, p. 213, l. 23; F, p. 192, l. 39.	63. Leur language, au demeurant [...] aux terminaisons Grecques./ Their language, moreover [...] Greek in its endings.	63. Brief return to one-*colon* (four-*commata*) period, repunctuated in *EB*/'95, to conclude the ethnographic description begun at period no. 17 (with repetition of 'au demeurant').
XIII. On the visit of three of their people to Rouen, and what they said.	64. V, p. 213, l. 26; F, p. 193, l. 1.	64. Trois d'entre eux [...] j'en ay encore deux en memoire./ Three of these men [...] I still remember two of them.	64. Complex narrative *periodus* ironically ending with loss of memory.
	65. V, p. 213, l. 36; F, p. 193, l. 14.	65. Ils dirent qu'ils trouvoient [...] missent le feu à leurs maisons./ They said that in the first place they thought it [...] set fire to their houses.	65. *Periodus* divided into two long *cola* with multiple *commata*.
	66. V, p. 214, l. 8; F, p. 193, l. 26.	66. Je parlay à l'un d'eux [...] je n'en peus tirer guiere de plaisir./ I had a very long talk with one of them [...] I could get hardly any satisfaction.	66. Short period divided into four *commata* (colon in '80 removed for a comma).
	67. V, p. 214, l. 10; F, p. 193, l. 29.	67. Sur ce que je luy demanday [...] passer bien à l'aise./ When I asked him [...] I pass quite comfortably.	67. Loose period of reported speech.
XIV. A concluding remark.	68. V, p. 214, l. 20; F, p. 183, l. 38.	68. Tout cela ne va pas trop mal: mais quoy, ils ne portent point de haut de chasses./ All this is not too bad — but what's the use? They don't wear breeches.	68. A final, bathetic, three-*colon* (*EB* two-*colon*) *epiphonema*.

Notes to Chapter 7

1. Ian Maclean, '"Le païs au delà": Montaigne and Philosophical Speculation', in *Montaigne: Essays in Memory of Richard Sayce*, ed. I. D. McFarlane and Ian Maclean (Oxford: Clarendon Press, 1982), pp. 101–32 (p. 105).
2. See Ian Maclean, *Montaigne philosophe* (Paris: Presses universitaires de France, 1996), p. 52.
3. Maclean, 'Le païs au delà', pp. 128–29.
4. See *Aldo Manuzio editore*, ed. Giovanni Orlandi, 2 vols (Milan: Il Polifilo, 1975), vol. 1, p. 102 ('distinctiones subdistinctionesque, ut quisque locus exigebat, apposui, quae, cum bene collocatae sunt, commentariorum vice funguntur'); vol. 2, p. 361. My thanks to Carlo Caruso for this reference.
5. See Jean Balsamo and Michel Simonin, *Abel L'Angelier & Françoise de Louvain (1574–1620): suivi du catalogue des ouvrages publiés par Abel L'Angelier (1574–1610) et la veuve L'Angelier (1610–1620)* (Geneva: Droz, 2002).
6. See George Hoffmann, *Montaigne's Career* (Oxford: Clarendon Press, 1998), pp. 40, 45–46, and Ian Maclean, *Scholarship, Commerce, Religion: The Learned Book in the Age of Confessions, 1560–1630* (Cambridge, MA: Harvard University Press, 2012), p. 53 (quoting Conrad Rittershausen).
7. See Alain Legros, 'Petit "dB" deviendra grand...: Montaigne correcteur de l'exemplaire "Lalanne" (Bordeaux, S. Millanges, 1580, premier état)', *Montaigne Studies*, 14 (2002), pp. 179–93, 183, 200; and Hoffmann, *Montaigne's Career*, p. 94 and n. 31. I shall refer to early editions of the *Essais* in the main text by place of publication and date, e.g. 'Bordeaux 1580'.
8. Michel de Montaigne, *Essais*, ed. André Tournon, 3 vols (Paris: Imprimerie nationale, 1998), vol. 1, pp. 663–64. Some of the imperatives are expressed in the second person ('escriuez', 'mettez') directly to the scribe. Others, towards the end, are expressed in the third person ('Qu'il serre les mots'), which may indicate instructions intended to be referred on to the printer by the scribe or another party.
9. See Maclean, *Montaigne philosophe*, pp. 35–37.
10. See Michel de Montaigne, *Saggi*, ed. Fausta Garavini and André Tournon (Milan: Bompiani, 2014).
11. My thanks to Judith Luna, Commissioning Editor for Oxford World's Classics until mid 2015, whose sharp and focused interventions helped me think through all these issues.
12. Frances A. Yates, *John Florio: The Life of an Italian in Shakespeare's England* (Cambridge: Cambridge University Press, 1934), pp. 227–28.
13. Yates, *John Florio*, p. 234.
14. Michel de Montaigne, *The Essayes or Morall, Politike and Millitarie Discourses*, trans. John Florio (London: Valentine Simmes for Edward Blount, 1603), sig. A5v.
15. *Essayes*, trans. Florio, sig. A3r.
16. *Essayes*, trans. Florio, sig. A5v; Peter Mack, 'Rhetoric and the Essay', *Rhetoric Society Quarterly*, 23.2 (1993), 41–49.
17. *Essayes*, trans. Florio, sig. A5v.; Peter Mack, *Elizabethan Rhetoric: Theory and Practice* (Cambridge: Cambridge University Press, 2002), pp. 24–31.
18. Bernard Croquette, 'Faut-il (re)découper les *Essais*?', in *Éditer les 'Essais' de Montaigne: actes du colloque tenu à l'Université Paris IV-Sorbonne les 27 et 28 janvier 1995*, ed. Claude Blum and André Tournon (Paris: Champion, 1997), pp. 197–201 (pp. 198–99).
19. I.28, 'De l'amitié' [Of Friendship], V, p. 183; F, p. 164. See also I.26, 'De l'institution des enfans' [Of the Education of Children], V, pp. 168–72; F, pp. 150–56.
20. For example, I.26, V, p. 172; F, p. 155: 'J'ay volontiers imité cette desbauche qui se voit en nostre jeunesse, au port de leurs vestemens: [...] Mais je la trouve encore mieus employée en la forme du parler'; 'I have been prone to imitate that disorder in dress [...] it is even better employed in our form of speech.'
21. Joseph Coppin, *Montaigne: traducteur de Raymond Sebon* (Lille: Imprimerie H. Morel, 1925), pp. 227–35. My thanks to Kathy Eden for this reference.
22. Hugo Friedrich, *Montaigne*, ed. Philippe Desan, trans. Dawn Eng (Berkeley: University of California Press, 1991), pp. 351–76.
23. Friedrich, *Montaigne*, pp. 351, 365, 375–76.

24. Edwin M. Duval, 'Rhetorical Composition and "Open Form" in Montaigne's Early *Essais*', *Bibliothèque d'Humanisme et Renaissance*, 43 (1981), 269–87.

25. Kathy Eden, 'Montaigne's Portion of Cicero's Acclaim', in *Brill's Companion to the Reception of Cicero*, ed. William H. F. Altman (Leiden: Brill, 2015), pp. 39–55. I am very grateful to Professor Eden for sharing her paper with me at draft stage. See also her contribution to this volume.

26. Morris W. Croll, 'The Baroque Style in Prose', in *Style, Rhetoric, and Rhythm: Essays*, ed. J. Max Patrick and Robert O. Evans (Princeton, NJ: Princeton University Press, 1966), pp. 207–33. Here and in the Appendix I shall use 'loose period' for longer, disconnected groups of *cola* developing the same thought in different ways and directions; *période coupée* or *tetracolon* for asymmetrical (and symmetrical) quaternary periods in the Senecan, aphoristic style; *periodus* for more circuitous and regular periods in the strict sense. See Janel Mueller, 'Periodos: Squaring the Circle', in *Renaissance Figures of Speech*, ed. Sylvia Adamson, Gavin Alexander, and Katrin Ettenhuber (Cambridge: Cambridge University Press, 2007), pp. 60–77, on the way in which, in seventeenth-century English prose, the combination of 'aphoristic effect with an enlarged, relaxed periodicity' (p. 75) consolidated itself in the four-membered period that did not trace a circuit in the manner of a period *sensu stricto*.

27. Marc Fumaroli, *L'Âge de l'éloquence: rhétorique et 'res literaria' de la Renaissance au seuil de l'époque classique* (Geneva: Droz, 2002), pp. 30, 152–54.

28. André Tournon, 'L'Énergie du "langage coupé" et la censure éditoriale', in *Montaigne et la rhétorique: actes du colloque de St Andrews (28–31 mars 1992)*, ed. John O'Brien, Malcolm Quainton, and James J. Supple (Paris: Champion, 1995), pp. 117–33 (pp. 121–23, with 'tout autre' on p. 121).

29. Tournon, 'L'Énergie du "langage coupé"', p. 130.

30. Marie-Luce Demonet, *'À plaisir': sémiotique et scepticisme chez Montaigne* (Orléans: Paradigme, 2002), pp. 183, 188–98.

31. For Tournon's acknowledgement of this, see André Tournon and Vân Dung Le Flanchec, *'Essais' de Montaigne: 'livre III'* (Paris: Atlande, 2002), pp. 259–67.

32. Jean Lecointe, 'L'Organisation périodique du "style coupé" dans le livre III des *Essais*', in *Styles, genres, auteurs*, vol. 2: *Montaigne, Bossuet, Lesage, Baudelaire, Giraudoux*, ed. Anne-Marie Garagnon (Paris: Presses de l'Université de Paris-Sorbonne, 2002), pp. 9–24 (p. 22).

33. Bernard Croquette, 'Les *Essais* mis en pièces', in *Montaigne: les derniers 'Essais': actes de la Journée d'étude Montaigne, samedi 30 novembre 1985*, ed. Françoise Charpentier ([Paris]: UER 'Sciences des textes et documents', 1986), pp. 9–18.

34. Michel de Montaigne, *Saggi [...] ouero Discorsi, naturali, politici, e morali*, trans. Girolamo Canini (Venice: Marco Ginammi, 1633).

35. Michel de Montaigne, *The Complete Works of Montaigne*, trans. Donald M. Frame (Stanford, CA: Stanford University Press, 1957; references are to the London, Everyman's Library 2003 edition); Michel de Montaigne, *The Complete Essays*, trans. M. A. Screech (London: Penguin, 2003); Michel de Montaigne, *Shakespeare's Montaigne: The Florio Translation of the Essays*, ed. Stephen Greenblatt and Peter G. Platt, trans. John Florio (New York: New York Review Books, 2014).

36. See 'Translation and Print Culture in Early Modern Europe', special issue of *Renaissance Studies*, ed. Brenda Hosington, 29.1 (2015); and *Translation and the Book Trade in Early Modern Europe*, ed. José María Pérez Fernández and Edward Wilson-Lee (Cambridge: Cambridge University Press, 2014).

37. Paris 1595, sig. Q1v.; V, pp. 284–85; F, p. 252.

38. *EB*: manie-/re:si les ennemis [...] de pied coy, s'ils vous attendent. Textual variants are given in footnotes in this form, without inverted commas. All apparent errors of spacing, punctuation, and spelling in these and subsequent quotations from early editions in the main text and footnotes are transcriptions of errors made in those editions. Italics and other regular typographical features are likewise transcribed as accurately as possible.

39. London 1603, sig. O5v.

40. Some of these paragraph breaks do occur after noteworthy *sententiae* or turns in the argument, but not all of them.

41. My thanks to Tim Chesters for focusing my attention on this example.

42. Bordeaux 1580, sig. T6r.–v. All page references to passages in V and F in I.31 'Des cannibales' [Of Cannibals] can be found in the Appendix in the second column.

43. Bordeaux 1582, Paris 1588: que il ne s'en face a l'aduenir quelqu'autre.
44. Bordeaux 1582, 1588: en ceste-ci.
45. Bordeaux 1588: empocher: Ie crains.
46. Bordeaux 1582: capacité. Nous/ Bordeaux 1588: capacité: nous embrassons tout, mais.
47. *EB*: semble estre de confideration.
48. Paris 1595, sig. K5r.–v.
49. London 1603, sig. K2v.
50. Paris 1595, sig. L1v.; London 1603, sig. K4r.
51. Edwin M. Duval, 'Lessons of the New World: Design and Meaning in Montaigne's "Des cannibales" (I:31) and "Des coches" (III:6)', *Yale French Studies*, 64 (1983), 95–112.
52. *Saggi*, trans. Canini, sig. K2r.
53. III.9, 'De la vanité' [On Vanity], V, p. 995; F, p. 926 (my underlining).
54. Kathy Eden, 'Cicero's Portion of Montaigne's Acclaim'; Edmund Spenser, *The Shepheardes Calender* (London: Hugh Singleton, 1579), sig. F2r.
55. V, p. 214, F, p. 193; V, p. 202, F, p. 182.
56. The Schoenberg Center for Electronic Text and Image at the University of Pennsylvania hosts the best facsimile of London 1603: <http://sceti.library.upenn.edu/sceti/printedbooksNew/index.cfm?textID=montaigne&PagePosition=1> [accessed 15 October 2015]. Michael Wyatt is currently preparing a proposal for a scholarly edition of Florio's Montaigne. For Paris 1595 see: <http://www.bvh.univ-tours.fr/Consult/index.asp?numfiche=862>, in the 'MONtaigne à L'Œuvre' (MONLOE) collection, hosted online by the Université de Tours [accessed 15 October 2015].
57. At the time of writing in June 2015, the edition was due for submission to Oxford University Press in 2019. Readers are invited to contact the editor by email (warrenboutcher@me.com) with their views, whether in advance of or after publication in the Oxford World's Classics series.

PART III

Diffusion and Reception

CHAPTER 8

Montaigne and Juvenal:
Intertextual Recognition and the
Readership of the *Essais*

Emma Herdman

Si quid igitur vel a Comico non satis argumento pudico processerit: aut a Satyro vitium aliquod apertius exprobatur. ut ne legat hec mulier ne ve inspitiat volo.[1]

[Since a comic poet's argument may be immodest and a satirist's condemnation may reveal a vice too openly, I do not want a woman to read or even look at them.]

Women in the Renaissance were not supposed to read the Latin satirists.[2] Yet while women may not (in theory) have been reading Juvenal, they certainly were reading Montaigne — and through him, Juvenal, who is the fifth most frequently quoted Latin poet in the *Essais*, after Horace, Lucretius, Virgil, and Ovid.[3] What happens, then, when women are exposed to Juvenal via Montaigne? And to what extent might their supposed unfamiliarity with the *Satires* impinge upon their reading and reception of the *Essais*? How might the deferred reception of Juvenal among Montaigne's earliest readers — held by the presence of the *Essais* at one remove from the *Satires* — compare with Montaigne's own reception of Juvenal, or to the readings of and responses to the *Satires* that initially constituted one of the many points of genesis in the *Essais*? And to what extent might Montaigne have allowed awareness of his readership's responses to both the *Essais* and the *Satires* to influence the production of his work?

By focusing on Montaigne's quotations of Juvenal, this essay acts as a point of transition within this volume: the incorporation of a quotation from a classical author into the *Essais* represents a moment of delicate fluctuation in their transit between genesis and reception, between production and diffusion, as Montaigne simultaneously looks backwards to his source and forwards to the anticipated responses to that source amongst his readers. Responses to an author as feisty as Juvenal are seldom muted. Where Renaissance humanists worried about Juvenal's obscenity and modern commentators worry about his misogyny, this essay focuses more on a different aspect in the reception of Juvenal and of Montaigne: it considers the value of contextual recognition in Montaigne's quotations from Juvenal, and suggests that it is often in such contextualization that Montaigne's satire lies.

1. Contextual recognition

One of the many challenges that Montaigne poses to the would-be 'suffisant lecteur' of his *Essais* is the confident assumption in II.10, 'Des livres' [Of Books], that his many quotations are sufficiently familiar for their original authors to need no further identification: [C] 'Ils sont tous, ou peu s'en faut, de noms si fameux et anciens qu'ils me semblent se nommer assez sans moi' [They are all, or virtually all, from such famous and ancient names that they seem to identify themselves sufficiently quite independently of me] (V, p. 408). This confidence in the literary culture of his readers is not always shared by his publishers: Marie de Gournay and the first editors of the *Essais* agreed (reluctantly) to their publishers' request to identify and translate the quotations, although some seventeenth-century editions still chose to omit them entirely.[4] Yet Montaigne's assertion that his quotations speak for themselves is not merely a question of recognition; it also reflects the status (and survival) of the quotations he has appropriated in the genesis of the *Essais* once they have been adapted and incorporated into their new context, a process he describes both in III.12, 'De la phisionimie' [Of Physiognomy] (V, p. 1034) and in I.26, 'De l'institution des enfans' [On Educating Children]: [C] 'Je tors bien plus volontiers une bonne sentence pour la coudre sur moy, que je ne tors mon fil pour l'aller quérir' [I am much more willing to twist a fine phrase in order to stitch it into my cloth than I am to twist the thread of my argument in order to go and find one] (V, p. 171).[5] Thus, while Montaigne's literary allusiveness relies upon his readers' intellectual recognition and sensitive reception of his sources for full appreciation of their relevance to his theme, that same recognition also reveals the distortions through which Montaigne makes the quotations his own.[6] The reader who recognizes the quotations is thereby faced with the further challenge of establishing how much such contextual recognition matters: Montaigne's quotations retain an ambiguous status, belonging somewhere between their original contexts and their new contexts in the *Essais*.

Moreover, it is not necessarily the case that each quotation will be equally familiar to each reader — and this depends as much upon the texts Montaigne quotes as upon his readers themselves. Juvenal is a case in point: while Lucretius, Horace, Ovid, and most obviously Virgil all feature visibly in the *Essais*, and while Montaigne freely evokes his reading of less commonly quoted authors — specifically Catullus, Lucan, Martial, and Gallus — in 'Des livres' (V, pp. 410–12), Juvenal is the most frequently quoted author in the *Essais* never to be referred to by name.[7] Yet Juvenal's presence in the *Essais* is discreetly evident not only in Montaigne's quotations from the *Satires*, but also in his many satirical themes, echoes, and techniques. Montaigne's assessment of his *Essais* in II.17, 'De la praesumption' [Of Presumption] is illustrated by frequent quotations from Lucilius, Horace, Juvenal, and Martial: his *Essais* share the rich subject matter but rough style of satire in a literary medley described through culinary images that reflect the self-deprecation and the assembly method of the Roman satirists.[8] Montaigne's self-examination qualifies him, like the satirists, to judge the world with indignation or laughter, and to include both Juvenalian invective and the *obscaena* that led Estienne Pasquier to interpret III.5, 'Sur des vers de Virgile' [On Some Lines from Virgil], as a sign of Montaigne's senility.[9] With his considerable but unacknowledged presence in the *Essais*, Juvenal is thus the author whose familiarity to Montaigne's readers is most frequently put to the test.

If Juvenal may have been unfamiliar to Montaigne's readers, it was not for want of trying. New editions of the *Satires* were printed in France almost every year throughout the sixteenth century, and this widespread diffusion places Juvenal immediately behind the most commonly read poets: Terence, Horace, and Virgil.[10] Yet his popularity was ambiguous: humanist reception of Juvenal was torn between anxiety over his obscenity and defence of his moral utility. While Juvenal's denunciation of political corruption was appreciated during the religious wars, with Justus Lipsius defending his moral value in a corrupt age and Agrippa d'Aubigné imitating his vituperative and tragic invective, many preferred the satirical urbanity of Horace as a comforting antidote to hatred and violence.[11]

Despite his moral ambiguity, Juvenal was generally considered to be suitable material for the final year of a liberal humanist education (although Calvin banned him from the curriculum in Geneva), and he is not short of Renaissance commentators, most notably Jodocus Badius Ascensius and Celio Secundo Curio.[12] Furthermore, the rediscovery of Aristotle's *Poetics* permitted a new, and not exclusively Horatian, assessment of satire: Julius Caesar Scaliger, who advises against exposing young boys to Juvenal's obscenity, nevertheless prefers his satire to Horace's and suggests that laughter — which is appropriate for minor faults, but not for major crimes — is not always obligatory in satire.[13] Perhaps because of his obscurity — Marc-Antoine Muret speculates in his *Variarum Lectionum* that line 175 of Satire XI has been interpreted more variously than any other in all classical poetry[14] — Juvenal is the first of the Latin satirists to be translated, albeit partially, into French, with the first complete translation, by André Du Chesne, published in 1607.[15] Montaigne's quotations of Juvenal date largely from between 1582 and 1588: his interest in Juvenal thus coincides with a wider renewed interest in the *Satires*, marked by significant increases in first their diffusion, following Pierre Pithou's new, superior edition of 1585 (although this is not the edition used by Montaigne), and, later, in their reception, following Isaac Casaubon's essay of 1607 defining the name and nature of satire.[16]

If Juvenal's obscenity was treated with caution in boys' education, it was certainly not recommended even for the classically highly literate noblewomen who were reading Montaigne.[17] Yet Marie de Gournay, whose self-perception as an exceptional reader of the *Essais* depends on her combination of erudition and friendship with Montaigne, claims in 1595 that the *Essais* are appreciated more by their female readers than by men, and critics have increasingly questioned whether Montaigne's ideal reader — the ghost of his father or of Étienne de La Boëtie — is male.[18] Montaigne's willingness to write to and for women, suggesting a concern for and interest in his readership and, by extension, the reception of the *Essais*, is often taken as a mark of his desire for intimacy with his readers: the intimacy of friendship with his dedicatees, who are able to testify to the likeness of his self-portrait, and a potentially more erotic intimacy in Book III.[19] Yet this focus on friendship and intimacy is not entirely at the expense of his readers' intellect. While Montaigne argues in III.3, 'De trois commerces' [Of Three Kinds of Associations], against women being over-educated, he still allows them to be well read: when he suggests that women should confine themselves to reading poetry, history, and moral philosophy (V, p. 823), he lists precisely the genres quoted most frequently in the *Essais*.[20] Three of the chapters originally addressed to women include, albeit mostly as later additions, quotations from Juvenal.[21]

Yet while Juvenal's peculiar combination of obscurity and obscenity is reserved only for readers robust enough to handle the colour and difficulty of his Latin, many of his epigrams would have been well known to Renaissance readers as commonplaces, even if the *Satires* may otherwise have remained largely murky. Erasmus, who objected to Juvenal's bad taste, nevertheless contributed to his diffusion and reception by including over 50 of Juvenal's epigrams in the *Adages*, and Rabelais's three quotations of Juvenal all come via Erasmus.[22] As an exclusive author of moral epigrams that prove curiously detachable from their original, sullying context, Juvenal is thus a doubly useful test case for questioning the value of contextual recognition in Montaigne.

2. Juvenal in Montaigne

Critical discussion of Montaigne's satire has tended to focus more on parallels with Horace, whose satire prefers self-criticism to castigation of others and suggests that the satirist and reader might themselves share the faults they benignly mock, than with Juvenal, whose sharp and emotional invective, aimed more at indignation than laughter, can seem hard to reconcile with Montaigne's dispassionate curiosity about the world.[23] Bénédicte Boudou tries to resolve the dissonance between Juvenal and Montaigne by focusing on the illustrative nature of the Juvenalian images that Montaigne cites, effectively detaching them, in the style of Erasmus, from their original contexts.[24] Ruth Calder nevertheless describes these illustrative quotations as 'wittily vituperative', and Jean Balsamo highlights how fitting Juvenal is for Montaigne's condemnation, during the religious wars, of the vices of his age.[25]

Certainly, Montaigne's readings of and reactions to Juvenal contribute significantly to the genesis of the *Essais*. There are numerous thematic resonances between the *Satires* and the *Essais*, even before 1580, when Montaigne's quotations from Juvenal become more frequent. Some of these later quotations simply identify the source of an existing satirical theme. Thus the quotation from Satire xv that Montaigne adds to his extended comparison between human and animal rationality in II.12, 'Apologie de Raimond Sebond':

> [B] *quando leoni*
> *Fortior eripuit vitam Leo? quo nemore unquam*
> *Expiravit aper majoris dentibus apri?* (V, p. 473; Juvenal, xv. 160–62)
>
> [When has a stronger lion ever taken a weaker lion's life? In which woods has a boar ever died at the teeth of a bigger boar?]

echoes Montaigne's original comment a few pages earlier: [A] 'Et si elles ont cela de plus genereux, que jamais Lyon ne s'asservit à un autre Lyon, ny un cheval à un autre cheval, par faute de cœur' (V, p. 462) [And indeed they are nobler in this respect, that no lion has ever become enslaved to another lion, nor any horse to another horse, out of faintness of heart]. The textual parallel is slightly displaced and not quite exact, but it is still close enough to suggest that Montaigne may originally have had Juvenal's lines in mind. Similarly, Montaigne's later addition of a quotation from Satire x in I.50, 'De Democritus et Heraclitus', seems textually redundant:[26]

> [A] Democritus et Heraclytus ont esté deux philosophes, desquels le premier, trouvant vaine et ridicule l'humaine condition, ne sortoit en public qu'avec un visage moqueur et riant; Heraclitus, ayant pitié et compassion de cette mesme condition nostre, en portoit le visage continuellement atristé, et les yeux chargez de larmes,
>> [B] *alter*
>> *Ridebat, quoties a limine moverat unum*
>> *Protuleratque pedem; flebat contrarius alter.* (V, p. 303)

> [Democritus and Heraclitus were two philosophers, the first of whom, finding the human condition vain and ridiculous, only ever went out in public with mockery and laughter on his face; Heraclitus, feeling pity and compassion for this same condition of ours, wore a perpetually sad expression, his eyes brimming with tears:
>> One laughed, whenever he set foot out of doors; the other, in contrast, wept.]

The quotation itself adds little to the existing text, suggesting that Montaigne included it primarily to acknowledge Juvenal's influence over the genesis of the *Essais* and to highlight their thematic parallels with the *Satires*.

These parallels are found primarily in the satires quoted most frequently by Montaigne.[27] Juvenal's theme in Satire xiv is the importance of a good education and the corresponding dangers of bad parental example; it finds obvious parallels particularly in Montaigne's 'De l'institution des enfans' and in I.25, 'Du pedantisme' (V, p. 140; Juvenal, xiv. 34–35). The satire culminates in an extended attack upon the Roman lust for money, a favourite topic for Juvenal, though not for Montaigne. In III.8, 'De l'art de conferer' [Of the Art of Discussion], Montaigne nevertheless quotes Juvenal's condemnation of the nouveaux riches for their lack of 'sensus communis' — common sense, but also sensitivity, a social conscience, and feeling for others — but applies it to his own bugbears: the would-be *sçavans*, who not only show inhumanity to their students, but lack even ordinary, common sense (V, p. 931; Juvenal, viii. 73–74). Similarly, in the 'Apologie', Montaigne quotes Juvenal's moral that money cannot buy either health or happiness, but applies it to his own attack on human reason, stating that knowledge has less value than health or sexual pleasure, and adding, in an ironic echo of Juvenal's original context, that it is also insufficient consolation for poverty (V, p. 487; Juvenal, xiv. 156–58).

There is a strong thematic link in Juvenal between Satire xiv, on the value of a good education, and Satire viii, on the value of character rather than ancestry. The theme finds particular resonances in Montaigne: in 'Du pedantisme', he emphasizes the value of intellectual self-reliance over borrowed knowledge (V, p. 138; Juvenal, viii. 14–15); in 'De l'institution des enfans', he satirically suggests that a duke's son might as well be a pastry-cook if that is what his character befits him for (V, pp. 162–63); most particularly, in I.46, 'Des noms' [Of Names], he reflects on the folly of trusting in a grand name (V, p. 280; Juvenal, x. 137–41). The main theme of this chapter — the thirst for fame rather than for virtue — is retrospectively explained by Montaigne's concluding quotation from Satire x; the context of Juvenal's satire, advocating Democritus's worldly detachment from the folly of human ambition, anticipates the theme of Montaigne's 'De Democritus et Heraclitus'. Montaigne, like Juvenal, prefers Democritus's satirical criticism of the world to Heraclitus's sorrowful withdrawal from it, but, unlike Juvenal, he rejects Heraclitus's tears not as insufficient for the tragedy of the world, but as a sign of emotional attachment to it.

Philosophical detachment from the world becomes actual in Satire III, in which Umbricius lists his reasons for leaving a corrupt Rome. Juvenal's theme finds echoes both in Montaigne's defence of the private rather than the public life in I.39, 'De la solitude' [Of Solitude] (V, p. 238; Juvenal, XIII. 26–27), and in his increasingly bitter reflections on the corruption wrought on France by the civil wars. In 'De la praesumption', Montaigne, like Umbricius, finds his moderate virtues to be out of place in a corrupt world (V, p. 642; Juvenal, XIII. 54–55), yet where Juvenal claims in Satire XIII — a mock *consolatio* that satirizes the genre on the grounds that there can be no consolation amid such corruption — that mere honesty is now treated as an extraordinary virtue, Montaigne goes further, portraying parricide and sacrilege as among the crimes made acceptable by the civil war (V, p. 646; Juvenal, XIII. 60–63). This in turn prompts him in III.9, 'De la vanité' [Of Vanity], to justify his desire to travel abroad and escape the cruelty of the civil wars,[28] withdrawing, like Umbricius, from a world in which honesty itself is a marvellous portent:

> [B] Qui a ses meurs establies en reglement au dessus de son siecle, ou qu'il torde et émousse ses regles, ou, ce que je luy conseille plustost, qu'il se retire à quartier et ne se mesle point de nous. Qu'y gagneroit-il?
>> *Egregium sanctumque virum si cerno, bimembri*
>> *Hoc monstrum puero, et miranti jam sub aratro*
>> *Piscibus inventis, et foetae comparo mulae.* (V, p. 993; Juvenal, XIII. 64–66)

> [Anyone who sets his moral standards higher than those of his time must either twist or relax his standards or — as I would rather advise him — draw apart and have nothing to do with us. What would he gain by it?
>> If I see a singularly moral man, I compare this unnatural portent
>> to a boy with a double member, or to the fish suddenly dug up by
>> an astonished plough, or to a pregnant mule.]

As Pithou's commentary notes, the comparably marvellous prodigies satirically imagined by Juvenal in Satire XIII are those which supposedly appeared before the civil war between Caesar and Pompey; they are sadly apt for Montaigne's reflections on the religious wars.[29]

Juvenal's famous description of Egyptian cannibalism in Satire xv finds echoes in Montaigne's I.31, 'Des cannibales' [Of Cannibals] (V, p. 210; Juvenal, xv. 93–94), and II.11, 'De la cruauté' [Of Cruelty] (V, p. 434; Juvenal, xv. 2–4, 7–8). Montaigne and Juvenal both cite cannibalism as an extreme example of what may be morally justifiable in order to condemn something far worse: the Egyptians' gratuitous cannibalism in Juvenal, and in Montaigne, the cruelty of the *conquistadores*, comparable to the cruelties of the religious wars.[30] The contrast, towards the end of 'De la cruauté' (V, pp. 434–35), between man's cruelty to man and his sympathy for animals, worshipped by Juvenal's Egyptians as gods, heralds the prolonged attack, sustained largely through comparison with the wisdom of animals, on human reason in the 'Apologie', in which Montaigne again quotes Satire XV, asserting that one of the marks of animals' superiority over humans is that they do not kill their own kind (V, p. 473; Juvenal, XV. 160–62) and citing cannibalism as an example of the diversity of human customs (V, p. 582; Juvenal, XV. 36–38). Juvenal's insistence that the Egyptians' cannibalism is the culmination of an animosity inspired by religious difference may have darkly appealed to Montaigne during the religious wars.[31]

Montaigne's quotations from Juvenal hint not only at thematic similarities between the *Essais* and the *Satires*, but also at Montaigne's range of satirical techniques. When Montaigne quotes Satire III in III.6, 'Des coches' [Of Coaches], it is as much for the irony of the quotation as for its thematic appropriateness to his ambivalent praise of Roman amphitheatres (V, p. 906; Juvenal, III. 153–55).[32] One of the finest examples of Montaigne putting a Juvenalian technique into practice occurs at the end of 'Du pedantisme'. Just as Juvenal, at the end of Satire II, reconciles himself to the moral corruption of Rome, filled with homosexuals and foreigners, by reflecting that the foreigners corrupted by Rome's homosexuals will be reduced to effeminate impotence just as effectively as they used to be by Rome's formerly virile military strength, so Montaigne reconciles himself to pedantry at the end of the chapter by contrasting effete scholarship with military valour, only to demonstrate the cultural superiority of those whose libraries have strategically been preserved by enemy barbarians for their effeminizing effect (V, pp. 143–44; cf. Juvenal, II. 166–70). The virtues of libraries and of homosexuals emerge from the supposedly scathing contrast with military valour paradoxically enhanced.

Montaigne's quotations from Juvenal are often technically easy to detach from their contexts: he tends to quote the illustrative side of an analogy, retaining an epic simile (II.31, 'De la colere' [Of Anger], V, p. 714; Juvenal, VI. 648–50) or the 'si' clause of a conditional sentence (I.25, 'Du pedantisme', V, p. 138; Juvenal, VIII. 14–15), but changing the point of comparison to fit his context. Yet equally often Montaigne disguises his satire precisely by burying it within the contexts from which his Juvenalian images are taken. A prime example of this occurs towards the beginning of II.31, 'De la colere', in a vignette condemning the disproportionate fury that can be aroused in parents by their children:

> [A] Entre autres choses, combien de fois m'a-il prins envie, passant par nos rües, de dresser une farce, pour venger des garçonnetz que je voyoy escorcher, assommer et meurtrir à quelque pere ou mere furieux et forcenez de colere! Vous leur voyez sortir le feu et la rage des yeux,
>
> > [B] *rabie jecur incendente, feruntur*
> > *Praecipites, ut saxa iugis abrupta, quibus mons*
> > *Subtrahitur, clivoque latus pendente recedit,*
>
> (et, selon Hippocrates, les plus dangereuses maladies sont celles qui desfigurent le visage), [A] à tout une voix tranchante et esclatante, souvent contre qui ne faict que sortir de nourrisse. (V, p. 714; Juvenal, VI. 648–50)

[Amongst other things, how often have I felt the urge, passing through our streets, to stage some jest to avenge the small boys I saw being flayed alive, knocked senseless or beaten black and blue by some furious father or mother raging with anger! You see them flash fire and fury from their eyes,

> Burning with anger, they are carried headlong, just like boulders torn from a high ridge when the ground gives way and the steep slope of the mountainside vanishes from under it

(and according to Hippocrates, the most dangerous ailments are those that disfigure the face), as they thunder with cutting voices often against a child that has barely left its wet-nurse.]

The quotation from Satire VI, Juvenal's diatribe against women, is in itself disproportionate, illustrating Montaigne's theme: in context, it applies to the anger of Medea and Procne, driven by justifiable anger with their husbands to slay their own children.[33] Yet for all the violence of the parents' 'rage' and of its imagery in Montaigne, infanticide (with, in Procne's case, induced cannibalism) is hardly in question here. Montaigne's sympathy with the young boys whom he wishes to avenge has not prevented him from enjoying himself as he proceeds to 'dresser une farce' at their hapless parents' expense.

The interpolated quotation from Juvenal — a literal piece of stuffing, like the parenthesis that follows, in an already convoluted sentence, reflecting the theme of disproportion and excess — is thus central to the satirical intention in Montaigne's farce.[34] The very act of quoting Juvenal is in fact Juvenalian, for Montaigne's stuffing is itself stuffed: Juvenal's epic simile is closely modelled on a Virgilian image, from Book 12 of the *Aeneid*, describing the heroic rage of Turnus as he hears of the suicide of Amata, Queen of the Latins, and anticipates defeat at Aeneas's hands.[35] The textual echo that equates Turnus's noble rage with the murderous fury of Medea and Procne is part of Juvenal's satirical technique — a technique shared by Montaigne as he bathetically reduces Turnus's heroic anger to the level of ordinary infuriation in parents. Montaigne clearly recognized Juvenal's allusion to Virgil: a couple of chapters later, in II.34, 'Observations sur les moyens de faire la guerre de Julius Caesar' [Observations on Julius Caesar's Methods of Warfare], he cites Virgil's image to describe the celerity of Julius Caesar's expeditious military conquests (V, p. 739).[36]

Virgil's description of Turnus's self-propulsion under the influence of anger is fully applicable to the self-determination behind Caesar's swift actions. In Juvenal's image, in contrast, it is the withdrawal of the mountain — 'quibus mons subtrahitur' — rather than any autonomous impetus that causes the boulder's fall.[37] This is because it is in Juvenal's satirical interests, if not fully to exonerate Medea and Procne, at least to mitigate their crimes by presenting them as irrational victims of legitimate passion. As such, Juvenal may cite them as superlative examples of monstrous women, 'grandia monstra' (Juvenal, VI. 645), driven to criminal wickedness by anger — superlative examples which, in a typically satirical move, have nevertheless been surpassed by the cold-blooded depravity of the Roman women driven by financial greed to crime. At the end of 'De la colere', Montaigne applies the same sense of passive helplessness before anger that may be disproportionate and the same falling image to himself:

[B] Mes valets en ont meilleur marché aux grandes occasions qu'aux petites: les petites me surprennent; et le mal'heur veut que, depuis que vous estes dans le precipice, il n'importe qui vous ayt donné le branle, vous allez tousjours jusques au fons: la cheute se presse, s'esmeut et se haste d'elle mesme. (V, p. 720)

[My servants fare better on big occasions than on little ones: the little ones take me by surprise, and as bad luck will have it, once you have started to fall it does not matter what tipped you over the edge, you still go right to the bottom: the fall finds its own impetus as it rushes and urges itself on.]

Just as the image of the falling rock has shifted satirically in Juvenal from Turnus to Medea and Procne, satirically again in Montaigne from Medea and Procne to the enraged parents, and then more benignly to Montaigne himself, so the sense of whether such anger is culpable has also shifted. While the comic exaggeration of the analogy with Medea and Procne discreetly satirizes Montaigne's angry parents, the condemnation is paradoxically tempered both by the comparison with them as victims of passion and by the further comparison with Montaigne himself, who, like them, can be viciously indiscriminate with his tongue when he falls into anger: Montaigne's Horatian self-inclusion in his satire adds an essential lightness of touch to his *farce*.[38] Recognition of the benign parallel between the image of the falling rock and Montaigne's own anger depends upon a reading knowledge of Latin, but recognition of the more satirical analogy with Medea and Procne depends upon familiarity with Juvenal. Without this context, Medea and Procne remain invisible in 'De la colere', even though, as murderously angry mothers, they are highly pertinent to the chapter's theme.

The folly of entrusting children's upbringing to their parents is a recurrent theme in Montaigne: at the beginning of 'De la colere', he compares it unflatteringly with the practice of the Cyclopes, calling it a 'grande simplesse': [A] 'Qui ne voit qu'en un estat tout dépend de son education et nourriture? et cependant, sans aucune discretion, on la laisse à la mercy des parens, tant fols et meschans qu'ils soient' (V, p. 714) [Who cannot see that everything in a State depends on their education and upbringing? And yet they are left without a second thought to the mercy of the parents, however foolish or wicked they may be]. The theme and comparison both echo Satire XIV, on the parental corruption, illustrated through analogy with the cruelty of Polyphemus (Juvenal, XIV. 20), that is automatically inherited by younger generations. Whereas the chief threat here to children's education is that their parents will be cruel, in 'Du pedantisme', it is that their teachers will be corrupt. Montaigne praises Adrien Turnèbe as a rare counter-example to the pedants he derides, a scholar who has survived the influence of his pedantic environment, and who perhaps spares his pupils from it in turn:

[A] Ce sont natures belles et fortes,
        [B] *queis arte benigna*
   Et meliore luto finxit praecordia Titan,
[A] qui se maintiennent au travers d'une mauvaise institution. (V, pp. 139–40; Juvenal, XIV. 34–35)

[They have fine, strong natures,
        whose hearts skilful Prometheus generously fashioned from finer clay,
who emerge intact from a bad education.]

Montaigne's quotation of Juvenal is particularly apposite to his praise of Turnèbe, whose *Adversariorum libri triginta* draw frequently on the *Satires* both to exemplify grammatical and historical points in other writers and as subjects of critical interest in themselves.[39] Juvenal's pessimistic lines from Satire XIV on the inevitability of generational decline complement his attitude in Satire VIII, quoted shortly beforehand by Montaigne (V, p. 138; Juvenal, VIII. 14–15), in which parental nobility and virtue are not necessarily inherited by their descendants: it is only vice which is passed on automatically. The rare exceptions to this degeneration — as in those who are forged, according to Ovid's myth (*Metamorphoses*, I. 82–83), by Prometheus out of clay — depend upon the absence of parental influence. It is only in 'De l'institution des enfans', presumably out of deference to his addressee, the expectant mother Diane de Foix, that Montaigne portrays parents as jeopardizing their children's upbringing by being not cruel or corrupt, but too kind (V, p. 153).

3. Juvenal and Montaigne's female readers

This last example shows Montaigne modifying the virulence of his satirical source out of respect for one specific female reader, allowing his recognition of one reader's potential reception of Juvenal to influence the production of the *Essais*. It is not necessarily the case, however, that Montaigne's awareness of the women among his readership generally tempers his quotations from Juvenal. Whereas the comically exaggerated analogy with murderous mothers in 'De la colere' is both thematically and satirically legitimate, the contextual satire latent in some of Montaigne's quotations of Juvenal can seem to be less than sensitive, as in the anecdote that opens III.4, 'De la diversion' [Of Diversion]:

> [B] J'ay autresfois esté emploié à consoler une dame vraiement affligée: car la
> plus part de leurs deuils sont artificiels et ceremonieux:
>> *Uberibus semper lachrimis, semperque paratis*
>> *In statione sua, atque expectantibus illam,*
>> *Quo jubeat manare modo.* (V, p. 830; Juvenal, VI. 273–75)

> [I was once required to console a woman who was genuinely distraught — for
> their grief is mostly feigned and superficial:
>> she always has a wealth of ready tears on stand-by, awaiting her
>> orders to flow as she commands.]

Beyond the casual misogyny of the general rule that women can rely on crocodile tears in any eventuality, the context of the quotation from Satire VI is starkly inappropriate, even in contrast, to the truly grieving woman whom Montaigne had failed to console. The ready tears Juvenal describes are those of the faithless wife who manipulatively responds to her husband's accusations of adultery by weeping over his sexual failings and defending her infidelity as an imitation of his own. Perhaps the image of feigned grief over marital infidelity, contrasted with the genuine grief of a woman mourning presumably for a husband or possibly a child, is intended to act again as a light-hearted distraction, in keeping with the theme of the chapter, from the grief it initially describes.[40]

This background reference to adultery demonstrates that while Montaigne keeps his quotations from Juvenal largely clean, the contexts they bring with them are less so. In 'De l'institution des enfans', Montaigne illustrates his claim that the joy of philosophy should be reflected on the face with a quotation from Satire IX:

> [A] Mais quant aux discours de la philosophie, ils ont accoustumé d'esgayer et resjouïr ceux qui les traictent, non les renfroigner et contrister.
>> [B] *Deprendas animi tormenta latentis in aegro*
>> *Corpore, deprendas et gaudia: sumit utrumque*
>> *Inde habitum facies.*
> [A] L'ame qui loge la philosophie, doit par sa santé rendre sain encores le corps. (V, p. 161; Juvenal, IX. 18–20)

> ['But as for philosophical reflection, it tends to make those who engage in it feel happy and joyful, not sullen or sad.'
>> You will see the soul's hidden torments in a sick body, and you will see its joys: it causes the face to assume either expression.
> The soul that houses philosophy should through its own health make the body healthy as well.]

Where Juvenal claims simply that the face, like the body, offers a true reflection of a psychological state, Montaigne argues that both health and happiness are actively influenced by the philosophically sound soul.[41] Taken on its own terms, Juvenal's epigram may seem like little more than a platitude; in context, however, it is graphically illustrated by the bisexual prostitute Naevolus, whose miserable face reflects the thanklessness of his sexual labours to gratify Virro — and Virro's wife — in exchange for meagre financial reward. While Naevolus condemns Virro's avaricious ingratitude, the satirist does not explicitly condemn Naevolus, either for his methods of failing to make money, or — more culpably, perhaps — for the extremity of his desire to do so; his face is its own condemnation. Montaigne may have thoroughly detached the quotation from its context, but he seems to be enjoying himself here, nonetheless: how many of the young scholars whose ideal education he envisages in this chapter would have been reminded, in the midst of this paean to philosophy, of Naevolus's sorry state?

Naevolus discreetly reappears in 'Sur des vers de Virgile' as Montaigne quotes his complaint that a well-proportioned member is of scant use if fortune does not also play its part. Montaigne's argument is that sexual infidelity need not pose a threat to marriage, which is based on something more serious and less arbitrary than the sexual attraction on which adultery depends:

> [B] La beauté, l'oportunité, la destinée (car la destinée y met aussi la main),
>> *fatum est in partibus illis*
>> *Quas sinus abscondit: nam, si tibi sidera cessent,*
>> *Nil faciet longi mensura incognita nervi,*
> l'ont attachée à un estranger, non pas si entiere peut estre, qu'il ne luy puisse rester quelque liaison par où elle tient encore à son mary. (V, p. 853; Juvenal, IX. 32–34)

> [Beauty, opportunity and destiny (for destiny has a hand in it as well),
>> Fate governs those parts we keep cloaked: for if your star falls then even a long member of unparalleled size will be good for nothing,
> have attached her to another, but perhaps not so completely as to leave her without any tie still holding her to her husband.]

The idea of *fatum* or fortune seems to have a double meaning in Satire IX. For Montaigne, the fate that governs sexual arousal is necessary to ensure that sexual relations will be physically successful; for Naevolus, who has not been paid by Virro, the fortunes of sexuality also govern whether sexual prowess will be lucrative even for the well-endowed. As in the earlier example from the 'Apologie' (V, p. 487; Juvenal, XIV. 156–58), the desire for money in Juvenal has once again been adapted by Montaigne to apply to the more pressing concern of health, including sexual pleasure, instead.

If Naevolus is cited as a titillating but warning counter-example to those tempted to prefer sex to philosophy, other Juvenalian counter-examples in Montaigne rely less on obscenity than on unflattering gender switches for their effect. In 'De l'experience', Montaigne illustrates the superiority of flexibility over dogmatic stubbornness with a quotation from Satire VI:

> [B] Un jeune homme doit troubler ses regles pour esveiller sa vigueur, la garder de moisir et s'apoltronir. Et n'est train de vie si sot et si debile que celuy qui se conduict par ordonnance et discipline.
>> *Ad primum lapidem vectari cum placet, hora*
>> *Sumitur ex libro; si prurit frictus ocelli*
>> *Angulus, inspecta genesi collyria quaerit.* (V, p. 1083; Juvenal, VI. 577–79)

> [A young man must shake off his habits to keep his youth alert and prevent it from seizing up and losing its strength. And there is no way of life led so foolishly and feebly as that which follows rules and regulations.
>> When she wishes to be taken on a very short journey, she refers to a book to decide when to go; if she has a rubbing itch in the corner of her eye, she fetches a salve only when she has consulted her horoscope.]

Montaigne's advice is clearly addressed to young men. Nothing in the Latin indicates that the quotation originally describes a woman: Juvenal's list of the many ways in which a wife may bankrupt her husband includes superstitious dependency on astrological consultation regarding the propitiousness of even the most trivial of activities. Juvenal's attack on superstitious women should surely have been recognized by the sort of young man whom Montaigne imagines himself addressing here, even if not necessarily by the more casual reader; Montaigne may have disguised Juvenal's misogyny by pushing it into the background, but its recognition nevertheless adds weight to his argument by intensifying the disincentive to behave in the manner Juvenal derides.

There is a similarly unflattering gender switch in Montaigne's quotation from Satire VI at the beginning of II.28, 'Toutes choses ont leur saison' [All Things Have their Season]:

> [A] Toutes choses ont leur saison, les bonnes et tout; et je puis dire mon paternostre hors de propos, [C] comme on desfera à T. Quintius Flaminius de ce qu'estant general d'armée, on l'avoit veu à quartier, sur l'heure du conflict, s'amusant à prier Dieu en une bataille qu'il gaigna.
>> [B] *Imponit finem sapiens et rebus honestis.* (V, p. 702; Juvenal, VI. 444)

> [All things have their season, even the good ones, and I can say my Lord's Prayer at an inappropriate moment, just as T. Quintus Flaminius was taken

to court for having been seen, as the general of the army, to stand aside at the moment of engagement and spend his time praying to God during a battle that he won.

The philosopher puts a limit even on virtue.]

The reflection is inspired by the example of Cato the Elder learning Greek in his old age, condemned by Montaigne both as a detraction from true virtue, which should lack ambition, and as inappropriate in the elderly, who should be concerned with preparing to leave life, rather than coveting new things from it. Montaigne's version of Juvenal's *sapiens* thus places limits on education as well as on prayer. In Juvenal, the *sapiens'* restraint is contrasted with the incessant chatter of the blue-stocking who attempts thereby to show off her erudition: he concludes that the good wife — that *rara avis* — should ideally be ignorant. In Montaigne's context, the mocked blue-stocking who Juvenal suggests ought to dress as a man truly is in male attire, recast as the virtuous Elder Cato with one foolish ambition: learning Greek.

Montaigne's dismissal of inappropriate Greek is a displacement of Juvenal's complaint in Satire VI (Juvenal, VI. 191–99) about women — supposed to be erotic rather than learned — who affect to speak Greek even in bed: while the eroticism of speaking Greek is acknowledged, its affectation cannot compensate for a salacious old woman's unenticing appearance.[42] Montaigne adapts Juvenal's lines in 'De trois commerces', replacing 'graece' with 'docte' in order to fit his theme, which is a renewed attack on the pedants who have tried to make women *sçavantes* rather than *sages*:

> [B] A toute sorte de propos et matiere, pour basse et populaire qu'elle soit, elles se servent d'une façon de parler et d'escrire nouvelle et sçavante,
>> *Hoc sermone pavent, hoc iram, gaudia, curas,*
>> *Hoc cuncta effundunt animi secreta; quid ultra?*
>> *Concumbunt docte;*
> et alleguent Platon et Sainct Thomas aux choses ausquelles le premier rencontré serviroit aussi bien de tesmoing. (V, p. 822; Juvenal, VI. 189–91)

> [On every sort of subject and topic, however humble or commonplace it may be, they employ a new and learned style of speech and writing,
>> They express their fears in this language and pour out their anger, their joy, their anxieties and all the secrets of their souls; what else?
>> Even their pillow-talk is learned;
> and they invoke Plato and St Thomas as evidence of things to which the man in the street could have testified just as well.]

The women's inappropriate references to Plato and St Thomas recall the limits to be placed on education and on prayer in 'Toutes choses ont leur saison', as does Livy's praise of Cato the Elder, cited at the very beginning of 'De trois commerces' (V, p. 818). Cato is thus doubly punished for his misplaced ambitions as a Hellenist: he is unflatteringly compared both directly with Juvenal's blue-stocking, mocked for her exaggerated display of false knowledge, and more indirectly with Juvenal's salacious old woman, whose seductively Greek voice, erotically undermined by her elderly face, is of as little advantage to her as Greek is to Cato in his old age. Yet as in 'De la colere', the condemnation is then tempered by a further analogy with Montaigne himself. While Juvenal mocks eroticism in old age, Montaigne relies on his own age to license his frank discussion of sex, in which he incidentally reveals himself to be just as salacious as Juvenal's lascivious old woman.[43] Once again, Montaigne includes himself in what he mocks, employing the themes of Juvenalian satire to Horatian ends.

Conclusion

What, then, happens when women who are not supposed to read Juvenal do so in Montaigne? The danger of exposing women to obscenity through Juvenal is hardly a concern in the *Essais*: with one notable exception, in 'Sur des vers de Virgile' (V, p. 854; Juvenal, VI. 129–30), Montaigne's quotations from Juvenal are not themselves obscene, and certainly not in comparison with some of his quotations from Horace or Martial; any obscenity lies in the context from which they are taken. Moreover, far from compromising out of deference to his readers, Montaigne clearly expects the educated noblewomen among his readers to be able to cope, with sublimely aristocratic nonchalance, with a bit of dirty Latin. He parenthetically acknowledges the smuttiness of his Latin to the female addressee of the 'Apologie': [A] '(J'use en liberté de conscience de mon Latin, avecq le congé que vous m'en avez donné.)' (V, p. 475) [(I make free and easy use of my Latin, as you have given me permission to do so.)] In context, the acknowledgement draws explicit attention to the obscenity of the epigram by Martial that Montaigne has just quoted.[44] While Montaigne may hide some of his more controversial subjects behind Latin quotations, suggesting that he is relying on his reader finding his Latin less immediately penetrable than French, this is perhaps less out of delicacy than out of a desire to enhance the *Essais*' eroticism through a teasing game of veiling and revelation: [B] 'Que Martial retrousse Venus à sa poste, il n'arrive pas à la faire paroistre si entiere. Celuy qui dict tout, il nous saoule et nous desgouste' (III.5, V, p. 880) [Let Martial hitch Venus's skirt up as far as he likes: he will not manage to reveal her so entirely. He who tells all overfills us and destroys our appetite].[45] The indelicacy of Montaigne's discreet quotations from Juvenal lies precisely in their reliance upon contextual recognition: none is needed to appreciate Martial's frank obscenity, preserving supposedly delicate readers from admitting whether or not they regularly read Martial. In contrast, the satire and occasional obscenity of some of Montaigne's quotations of Juvenal depend entirely upon allusive, and thus perhaps more titillating, recognition of their original contexts.

While Juvenal's obscenity may have troubled some of his Renaissance critics, his attitude to women did not: in his *Variarum Lectionum*, Marc-Antoine Muret simply acknowledges Juvenal's antipathy especially to educated, talkative women.[46] As the *Querelle des femmes* shows, exposing women to misogyny is hardly a Renaissance concern. In contrast, modern critics have tried to reconcile Satire VI with more contemporary attitudes by suggesting that the misogyny of its narrative persona is itself mocked as a sign of impotent rage and inadequacy faced with the uncontrollable opposite sex.[47] Equally, Montaigne's attitude to women is a lively modern concern: Marc-André Wiesmann and Floyd Gray both argue that, in

'Sur des vers de Virgile', Montaigne tempers the misogyny of his quotations from Juvenal through his willingness to blame men, themselves excessive, for women's sexual misbehaviour as for their own.[48] Wiesmann suggests that this moderation reflects Montaigne's awareness of the women among his readers, but he adds that Montaigne is mischievously also writing for a readership that was fully familiar with Juvenal's satire.[49] This implies that Montaigne is conscious of writing for at least two audiences, and that he is willing to tailor the *Essais* to suit them both, as he delicately avoids treating his frank subject matter with obscene vocabulary for the sake of some while alluding more titillatingly and learnedly to Juvenal's eroticism and misogyny for others.

Certainly, Montaigne is capable of moderating Juvenal's misogyny. In II.23, 'Des mauvais moyens employez à bonne fin' [Of Bad Means Employed to a Good End], he reflects both on the dangers of idleness and on the immorality of preventing it by engaging arbitrarily in war:

> [A] Par fois aussi ils [les Romains] ont à escient nourry des guerres avec aucuns, leurs ennemis, non seulement pour tenir leurs hommes en haleine, de peur que l'oysiveté, mere de corruption, ne leur apportast quelque pire inconvenient,
>> [B] *Et patimur longae pacis mala; saevior armis,*
>> *Luxuria incumbit;*
> [A] mais aussi pour servir de saignée à leur Republique et esvanter un peu la chaleur trop vehemente de leur jeunesse. (V, p. 683; Juvenal, VI. 292–93)

> [Sometimes as well the Romans deliberately fostered wars with their enemies, not only to keep their men occupied, out of fear that idleness, the mother of corruption, might bring them worse misfortune,
>> And we suffer the evils of a long peace; luxury, more ferocious than war, weighs down upon us;
> but also as a means of letting some of their Republic's blood and of cooling slightly the excessively violent heat of their young men.]

The quotation comes from Juvenal's reflection in Satire VI on the moral corruption wrought by idleness, luxury, and excess in a time free from poverty, labour, and fear: women remained chaste when they lived humbly, spinning wool and fearing Hannibal's attack on Rome. Montaigne's Romans are more afraid of the unspent energies of idle fighting men than of women, suggesting that violence and civil disobedience rather than licentious sexuality are their chief concerns: where Juvenal attacks women's excessive lust when it is not distracted by work, Montaigne attacks the excess of fighting spirit or vigour that is left unoccupied in men.

Yet Juvenal's misogyny is not entirely absent from Montaigne, as the quotation from 'De la diversion' shows, although it is largely heavily disguised: it is not apparent in either 'Toutes choses ont leur saison' or in 'De l'experience' that the quotations from Satire VI — which simply sound like classic moral epigrams — have anything to do with women. Like the obscenity in the background to Montaigne's references to Naevolus in 'De l'institution des enfans' and 'Sur des vers de Virgile', the misogyny lies in the context from which the quotations are drawn. Yet in each case, this is also where the satire lies: rather than tempering Juvenal for the sake of his female readers, Montaigne seems to be echoing Juvenal, whose satire (as in the allusion to Virgil's Turnus in Satire VI) often involves the juxtaposition of various incongruous sources. If Montaigne shows any deference to his female readers, it is more to their unfamiliarity with Juvenal than to their sensitivity to misogyny or obscenity: in 'De la colere', Medea and Procne may remain invisible to those who do not know the *Satires*, but their absence is partly compensated for by the later analogy with another mitigating figure — Montaigne himself. This modest concession towards one element of his readership does not come at the cost of the other: Juvenal's misogyny, obscenity, and vituperation still remain implicitly present in the *Essais* to be appreciated by those who can.

Coda

The status in the *Essais* of the Latin quotations that Montaigne takes as a point of genesis and cavalierly makes his own remains ambiguous: Pierre Villey sees them as foreign bodies, while Daniel Russell draws a parallel between Montaigne's superficially disjointed mode of compilation and the construction of emblems, whose overall interpretation depends not on the production of individually detachable elements but on the diffusion and reception of the symbiosis between them.[50] A parallel could equally be drawn with the related genre of satire: Adrien Turnèbe, acknowledging the disjointed variety of certain chapters in his *Adversariorum libri triginta*, compares them firstly with emblems and secondly with satire.[51] Gournay remains sceptical about the value of quotation-spotting in understanding Montaigne: 'Un Lecteur qui cognoist ces passages-là, n'est pas plus prest de demesler ce Livre à point, que celuy qui ne les cognoist pas, s'il n'est d'ailleurs ferré à glace' [The reader who understands these passages is no nearer to getting a firm grip on this book than the reader who doesn't, unless he is also wearing crampons].[52] Gournay suggests that the intelligibility of the *Essais* does not depend on being able to read at a literal level the Latin quotations; readers who wish to grapple with this slippery text require a further foot-hold if they are to grasp Montaigne's meaning. The foot-hold remains undefined, although the context and Gournay's own erudition suggest that it lies in the humanist appreciation, expected in Montaigne's male readers, of the contexts from which his quotations are, often wittily, taken. Yet for all the security that such a scholarly reading might offer, the coldness and rigidity of Gournay's imagery are at odds with the intimate warmth of Montaigne's writing and the elusive mobility of his thought. The connotations of Gournay's image thus subtly undermine its meaning, implicitly promoting the more flexible, emotional and intuitive response to Montaigne that she herself also felt, and such as might more readily have been expected from his female readers. Her comment suggests that, having identified and translated Montaigne's many quotations, she did not think that this was where the chief pleasure of the *Essais* lay. On the evidence of Montaigne's quotations from Juvenal, perhaps the chief satirical pleasure in the *Essais* lies neither in Montaigne's words nor in Juvenal's, but — emblematically, satirically — somewhere between the two.

Notes to Chapter 8

1. Leonardo Aretini, *De studiis et litteras ad illustrem dominam Baptistam de Malatesta tractatulus* (Leipzig: Wolfgang de Monaco, 1496), fol. [Avi]r. All translations are my own.

2. See Eva Matthews Sanford, 'Renaissance Commentaries on Juvenal', *Transactions and Proceedings of the American Philological Association*, 79 (1948), 92–112 (p. 98).

3. See Pierre Villey, *Les Sources et l'évolution des 'Essais' de Montaigne*, 2 vols (Osnabrück: Otto Zeller, 1976), vol. 1, pp. 165 (Horace), 188 (Lucretius), 266 (Virgil), 205 (Ovid), 170 (Juvenal). Villey's figures are not always quite consistent: I have counted 49 quotations of Juvenal.

4. See Valerie Worth-Stylianou's essay in this volume.

5. Montaigne emphasizes the importance of this process in I.25, 'Du pedantisme' [Of Pedantry] (V, pp. 136–37): see Cathleen M. Bauschatz, 'Montaigne's Conception of Reading in the Context of Renaissance Poetics and Modern Criticism', in *The Reader in the Text: Essays on Audience and Interpretation*, ed. Susan R. Suleiman and Inge Crosman (Princeton, NJ: Princeton University Press, 1980), pp. 264–72.

6. On Montaigne's literary allusiveness, see in particular Mary McKinley, *Words in a Corner: Studies in Montaigne's Latin Quotations* (Lexington, KY: French Forum, 1981) and Dorothy Gabe Coleman, *The Gallo-Roman Muse: Aspects of Roman Literary Tradition in Sixteenth-Century France* (Cambridge: Cambridge University Press, 1979), pp. 108–79. On Montaigne's citations of various classical authors, see 'Montaigne et les Anciens', special issue ed. Catherine Magnien, *Montaigne Studies*, 17 (2005).

7. Satirists are not a category in Montaigne's list of his preferred authors in 'Des livres': it is as poets that Martial and Horace are praised.

8. See Ruth Calder, '"Une marqueterie mal jointe": Montaigne and Lucilian Satire', *Bibliothèque d'Humanisme et Renaissance*, 54 (1992), 385–93 (pp. 385–88).

9. See Jean Balsamo, 'Montaigne "admirable", les libertins et l'esprit "satyrique"', *Montaigne Studies*, 19 (2007), 57–66 (pp. 59–61); see also Balsamo, 'Satire', in *Dictionnaire de Michel de Montaigne*, ed. Philippe Desan (Paris: Champion, 2007), pp. 1040–41.

10. See David J. Shaw, 'La Publication des *Satires* de Juvénal en Europe avant 1601', in *Le Livre dans l'Europe de la Renaissance*, ed. Pierre Aquilon and Henri-Jean Martin (Nantes: Promodis, 1988), pp. 297–304 (p. 299); and Pascal Debailly, 'Juvénal en France au XVIᵉ et au XVIIᵉ siècle', *Littératures classiques*, 24 (1995), 29–47 (pp. 29–30).

11. See Sanford, 'Renaissance Commentaries on Juvenal', pp. 111–12, and Debailly, 'Juvénal en France', pp. 32, 37–38.

12. See Sanford, 'Renaissance Commentaries on Juvenal', pp. 108–10, and Debailly, 'Juvénal en France', pp. 31–32.

13. Julius Caesar Scaliger, *Poetices libri septem* ([n.p.]: Antoine Vincent, 1561), pp. 323 and 149. See also Stuart Gillespie, 'Imperial Satire in the English Renaissance', in *A Companion to Persius and Juvenal*, ed. Susannah Braund and Josiah Osgood (Oxford: Wiley-Blackwell, 2012), pp. 386–408 (p. 388); Pascal Debailly, 'Le Rire satirique', *Bibliothèque d'Humanisme et Renaissance*, 56 (1994), 695–717 (pp. 705–06); and Debailly, 'Juvénal en France', p. 32.

14. 'Vix ullam reperiri posse versum in omnibus antiquorum poematis puto, quem tam multi tam variae interpretati sint'; Marc-Antoine Muret, *Variarum lectionum libri XV* (Antwerp: Christophe Plantin, 1586), 10.6, p. 262.

15. See Debailly, 'Juvénal en France', p. 32.

16. See Gilbert Highet, 'Juvenal in and after the Renaissance', in *Juvenal the Satirist* (Oxford: Clarendon Press, 1954), pp. 206–18 (p. 207); Sanford, 'Renaissance Commentaries on Juvenal', p. 112; and Debailly, 'Juvénal en France', pp. 31, 36. Only five of the 49 quotations appear in 1580, and no more are added after 1588: Villey, *Les Sources*, vol. 1, p. 170 and V, pp. xxxv–xxxviii.

17. See Neil M. Larkin, 'The *Essais*' Dedications', *Romanic Review*, 73 (1982), 401–10 (p. 401). On the literary erudition of Montaigne's dedicatees, see for example Éliane Viennot, 'Écriture et culture chez Marguerite de Valois', in *Femmes savantes, savoirs des femmes: du crépuscule de la Renaissance à l'ombre des Lumières*, ed. Colette Nativel (Geneva: Droz, 1999), pp. 167–75 (pp. 167–68), and Cathleen M. Bauschatz, '"Leur plus universelle qualité, c'est la diversité": Women

as Ideal Readers in Montaigne's *Essais*', *Journal of Medieval and Renaissance Studies*, 19 (1989), 83–101 (p. 95).

18. See the *Dictionnaire de Montaigne*, ed. Desan, p. 454; Bauschatz, 'Leur plus universelle qualité'; Floyd Gray, *Gender, Rhetoric and Print Culture in French Renaissance Writing* (Cambridge: Cambridge University Press, 2000), pp. 107–11, 127–31; and Richard L. Regosin, *Montaigne's Unruly Brood: Textual Engendering and the Challenge to Paternal Authority* (Berkeley: University of California Press, 1996), pp. 8–9.

19. See Bauschatz, 'Leur plus universelle qualité', pp. 96–97; Steven Rendall, *Distinguo: Reading Montaigne Differently* (Oxford: Clarendon Press, 1992), p. 93; and *Dictionnaire de Montaigne*, ed. Desan, p. 452. See also Marc-André Wiesmann on the *cabinet* Montaigne imagines his female readers having for a vital, erotic, and nourishing intimacy with books: 'Verses Have Fingers: Montaigne Reads Juvenal', *Journal of Medieval and Renaissance Studies*, 23 (1993), 43–67 (pp. 49–50).

20. Villey, *Les Sources*, vol. 2, pp. 470–71. Aubigné praises educated noblewomen but fears that an over-educated woman of lower rank may become proudly unfit for her humble station, filled with 'le mépris du ménage et de la pauvreté, celuy d'un mari qui n'en sait pas tant, et la dissension' [contempt for household work and for poverty, contempt for a husband who is not as well educated, and dissension]; Agrippa d'Aubigné, *Œuvres*, ed. Henri Weber, Jacques Bailbé, and Marguerite Soulié (Paris: Gallimard, 1969), p. 854.

21. I.26, 'De l'institution des enfans', V, p. 161 (Juvenal, IX. 18–20); II.12, 'Apologie de Raimond Sebond', V, p. 462 (Juvenal, XIV. 74–75, 81–82), V, p. 466 (Juvenal, XII. 107–10), V, p. 473 (Juvenal, XV. 160–62), V, p. 487 (Juvenal, XIV. 156–58), V, p. 576 (Juvenal, X. 4–6), V, p. 577 (Juvenal, X. 346–48, 350), V, p. 582 (Juvenal, XV. 36–38); II.37, 'De la ressemblance des enfans aux peres' [Of the Resemblance of Children to their Fathers], V, p. 768 (Juvenal, III. 236–37).

22. See Debailly, 'Le Rire satirique', p. 704, and Highet, *Juvenal the Satirist*, pp. 211–12. Juvenal's moral epigrams are often picked out by bucolic diaeresis: Juvenal, *The Satires*, ed. John Ferguson (London: Bristol Classical Press, 1999), p. xxx. This poetic emphasis perhaps facilitates Renaissance moralists' tendency to detach them from their original contexts.

23. See Bénédicte Boudou, 'La Présence de Juvénal dans les *Essais*', *Montaigne Studies*, 17 (2005), 119–33 (p. 119). On Montaigne's reception of Horace, see particularly Anna Holland, 'Montaigne et Horace', *Montaigne Studies*, 18 (2006), 67–77 (p. 69); Coleman, *The Gallo-Roman Muse*, pp. 116–30; McKinley, *Words in a Corner*, pp. 39–61; and Ruth Calder, 'Montaigne as Satirist', *The Sixteenth Century Journal*, 17 (1986), 225–35. See also Calder, 'Une marqueterie mal jointe', pp. 385–93.

24. Boudou, 'La Présence de Juvénal', pp. 124–29, 133.

25. Calder, 'Montaigne as Satirist', p. 231; Balsamo, 'Satire', p. 1041.

26. The same is true of Montaigne's quotation from Satire VIII in I.42, 'De l'inequalité qui est entre nous' [Of the Inequality that Exists Between Us] (V, p. 259; Juvenal, VIII. 57–59).

27. Montaigne quotes Satires VI and XIII nine times, Satire VIII six times, Satires III, X, XIV, and XV five times, Satire IX twice, and Satires V, VII, and XII once.

28. See Frank Lestringant's essay in this volume.

29. Pierre Pithou, *A. Persii Satyrarum liber I. D. Iunii Iuvenalis Satyrarum lib. V. Sulpiciae Satyra I.* (Paris: Mamert Patisson for Robert Estienne, 1585), p. 251.

30. Voltaire, employing similar arguments, cites Juvenal's satire in his entry 'Anthropophages' in the *Dictionnaire philosophique*, ed. Alain Pons (Paris: Gallimard, 1964), pp. 41–43.

31. For examples of cannibalism under torture during the religious wars, see Richard Verstegan, *Le Théâtre des cruautés*, ed. Frank Lestringant (Paris: Chandeigne, 1995), pp. 91, 105.

32. Juvenal's ironic application of *pudor* to the shame of being poor rather than to the moral indecency of evicting the poor from the best seats underlines the irony in Montaigne's admiration for the excessive opulence on display. Montaigne's rejection of the cruelty of gladiatorial shows is reflected in his quotation of Satire III in II.26, 'Des pouces' [Of Thumbs], on the fickle public favour that can mean life or death to gladiators (V, p. 691; Juvenal, III. 36–37). See also Terence Cave's essay in this volume.

33. The disproportion of Montaigne's quotation is noted by Floyd Gray, *Montaigne bilingue: le latin des 'Essais'* (Paris: Champion, 1991), pp. 71–72.

34. *Satyra* was commonly thought to share with *farce* an etymological association with stuffing: see

Debailly, 'Le Rire satirique', p. 708. The moralizing intention, as found here in Montaigne, is common to both genres.

35. Virgil, *Aeneid*, XII. 684–88.

36. Pithou's commentary points towards Virgil, though without a precise reference (*A. Persii Satyrarum liber I*, p. 205); see also Juvenal, *Satires*, ed. Ferguson, p. 214.

37. See Juvenal, *Satires*, ed. Ferguson, p. 214.

38. Whereas for Juvenal, both the cause of anger and its irrational effects are relevant in exonerating Medea and Procne, for Montaigne it is the passion itself — the cause being immaterial — that is its own excuse. Montaigne's acknowledgement of the danger of denying anger an outlet (II.31, V, pp. 717–18) develops the theme of I.4, 'Comment l'ame se descharge ses passions sur des objects faux, quand les vrais luy defaillent' [How the Soul Vents its Passions upon False Objects in the Absence of Real Ones] (V, pp. 22–24); in each case, his source is Plutarch's 'Comment il fault refrener la cholere': *Les Œuvres morales & meslees de Plutarque translatees du Grec en François par Jacques Amyot*, ed. M. A. Screech, 2 vols (Wakefield: S. R. Publishers, 1971), vol. 1, fols 56r–63r.

39. Adrien Turnèbe, *Adversariorum libri triginta*, 3 vols (Paris: Martin Le Jeune, 1580), especially 10.27 on Satire III (vol. 1, pp. 340–41), 15.7 on Satire II (vol. 2, pp. 91–94), 20.8 and 28.24 on Satire I (vol. 2, pp. 179–80; vol. 3, pp. 146–47).

40. Montaigne dedicated La Boëtie's translation of the *Lettre de consolation de Plutarque à sa femme* to his own wife following the death of their first child; see Larkin, 'The *Essais*' Dedications', p. 402. Might Montaigne be referring to her here?

41. Montaigne's claims about facial expression often echo Juvenal: see for example III.13, 'De l'experience' [Of Experience] (V, p. 1098; Juvenal, XIII. 162), 'De la colere' (V, p. 714; Juvenal, VI. 648–50) and II.5, 'De la conscience' [Of Conscience] (V, p. 367; Juvenal, XIII. 195). See Kathy Eden's essay in this volume.

42. See Wiesmann, 'Verses Have Fingers', p. 48. See also Cave's essay in this volume.

43. Wiesmann, 'Verses Have Fingers', pp. 58–59.

44. In Martial's epigram (XI. 20. 3–8), Augustus dismisses Fulvia's threat to fight him unless he sleeps with her on the grounds that he values his life less than his penis: Martial cites the emperor's frank vocabulary to legitimize his own.

45. On Montaigne's preference for allusiveness, see Coleman, *The Gallo-Roman Muse*, pp. 133, 171–73, and Weismann, 'Verses Have Fingers', p. 63. On the respective values of Latin and French as virile and effeminate languages, see Gray, *Gender, Rhetoric and Print Culture*, p. 117; on Latin and French as 'foreign' languages, see Philip Ford, *The Judgment of Palaemon: The Contest between Neo-Latin and Vernacular Poetry in Renaissance France* (Leiden: Brill, 2013), pp. xiii–22.

46. 'Iuvenalis, in ea satyra, qua mulierum improbitatem detexit, non obscure significavit, displicere sibi mulieres eruditas, & disertas'; Muret, *Variarum Lectionum*, 8.21, p. 221.

47. See W. R. Johnson, 'Male Victimology in Juvenal 6', *Ramus*, 25 (1996), 170–86. The satire involves copious and casual abuse of women, nonetheless.

48. Wiesmann, 'Verses Have Fingers', p. 54; Gray, *Gender, Rhetoric and Print Culture*, p. 116.

49. Wiesmann, 'Verses Have Fingers', pp. 54, 58.

50. Villey, *Les Sources*, vol. 2, p. 133; Daniel Russell, 'The Term "Emblème" in Sixteenth-Century France', *Neophilologus*, 59 (1975), 337–51 (pp. 341–43); Russell, 'Montaigne's Emblems', *French Forum*, 9 (1984), 261–75 (pp. 261–62). The transition from detachability to symbiosis reflects the change in meaning of the term 'embleme', referring originally to a detachable ornament's individual components, and later to the sense that emerges from their combination, thus focusing less upon the emblem's construction than on its effect; Russell, 'The Term "Emblème"', pp. 337–38; see also Calder, 'Une marqueterie mal jointe', p. 388.

51. Turnèbe, 1.17 (vol. 1, p. 18) and 22.22 (vol. 2, p. 293, citing Juvenal, XI. 20).

52. In *Les Essais de Michel de Montaigne* (Paris: Claude Rigaud, 1617), p. 989; see Philip Ford, 'Montaigne in England', *Montaigne Studies*, 24 (2012), 3–6 (p. 4). For more on the Latin quotations, see Valerie Worth-Stylianou's essay: the next in the present volume.

CHAPTER 9

'Bugge-beares' or 'Bouquets'? Translations of the Latin Quotations in Florio's and Gournay's Versions of the *Essais*

Valerie Worth-Stylianou

In his *Deffence et illustration de la langue françoyse* (1549), Joachim Du Bellay used a metaphor foregrounding the binary opposition between birth and sterility to deplore the time writers must expend on learning classical languages: 'Car ci le Tens que nous consumons à aprendre les dites Langues, estoit employé à l'etude des Sciences, la Nature certes n'est point devenue si Brehaigne, qu'elle n'enfantast de nostre Tens des Platons, et des Aristoteles.'[1] He equates creative composition to birth, whereas learning and deploying a foreign language are implicitly associated with sterility. As debates over the merits and demerits of translation continued to exercise writers across early modern Europe,[2] John Florio, the first to publish a complete English translation of Montaigne's *Essais*, looked to similar metaphorical oppositions to articulate these tensions.[3] His preface of 1603, addressed to his patronesses Lucy, Countess of Bedford, and her mother Lady Anne Harrington, combines jocular wit with serious literary insights: indulging his taste for dramatic impersonation, Florio adopts the identity of the 'fondling foster-father' of a work downgraded to the category of 'this defective edition (since all translations are reputed femalls, delivered at second hand)'.[4] His oppositions, more complex than simply birth/sterility, revolve around birth-/foster-fatherhood, male/female offspring, but also male/female performative roles in birthing.[5]

This was an age when daughters might still be considered to result from nature's failure to produce a male. In 1625, the French physician Louis de Serres, a champion of women, entitled one chapter of his *Discours de la nature, causes, signes, et curation des empeschemens de la conception, et de la sterilité des femmes*: 'Si les femmes qui ne font que de filles doivent ester appellées steriles?'[6] Yet Florio's apparent denigration of his female 'offspring' needs to be read against his respect and admiration for his patronesses. These are women capable of reading Montaigne 'in fine French', generously encouraging Florio's English version. Florio delights in acting the part of the birthing woman who delivers the translation only after a hard labour, accomplished in the Countess of Bedford's house: 'your Honor having dayned to read it, without pitty of my failing, my fainting, my labouring, my langishing, my gasping for some breath (O could so Honorable, be so pitty-lesse?).'[7] Florio plays the stereotypically weak woman, while Lucy, forbidding him to renounce his task, is the stronger presence. She might be thought to play a masculine role, except that Florio also teases her with the language of a Petrarchan suitor: 'Madame, now doe I flatter you?',[8] before adding a further twist by likening her to 'the Spartan imperious Mother' who equips her son with a shield to fight on.[9]

Whether adopting the persona of son, male admirer, or labouring woman, Florio convinces the reader of the herculean nature of his undertaking. Such, indeed, that the countess must provide him with several companions, so that the version becomes a collaborative effort.[10] Theodore Diodati, tutor to John Harrington (heir of the Harrington-Russell household), is credited with guiding Florio through the labyrinth of Montaigne's prose 'like Ariadne's thread', while Doctor Matthew Guinne (or Gwinne), a former student and then perpetual Fellow of St John's College, Oxford, and first Professor of Physic (1597) at Gresham College, London, was the 'scholler' who translated Montaigne's quotations.[11] Florio uses a combination of popular legend and heroic male figures to conjure Gwinne's part:

> So Scholler-like did he undertake what Latine prose; Greeke, Latine, Italian or French Poesie should crosse my way (which as Bugge-beares affrighted my unacquaintance with them) to ridde them all afore mee, and for the most part drawne them from their dennes [...]. So was hee to mee in this bundle of riddles an understanding *Oedipus*, in this perilous-crook't passage a monster-quelling *Theseus* or *Hercules*.[12]

Like Florio, Gwinne displays protean qualities, as virtuosic monster-tamer; Shake-spearean tableaux unfold before our eyes. Yet these metaphors also indicate the way in which Florio viewed the quotations' relationship with his translation, at once frightening, unwelcome monsters to be 'drawn' from their lair, and crooked riddles that only a male 'scholar' can unravel.[13] Gwinne had already acquired an impressive literary reputation, alongside his medical practice. He collaborated in 1590 with Fulke Greville on the edition of Sidney's *New Arcadia*; composed a neo-Latin tragedy of some 5000 lines, *Nero*, published in 1603; and in 1605 his poem *Tres Sibyllae*, in dactylic hexameters, was performed in both Latin and English — the latter being for the royal family.

This is in striking contrast to the approach of Marie de Gournay, Montaigne's *fille d'alliance*, editor of the 1595 posthumous edition of the *Essais* and of subsequent revised editions until 1635.[14] Until 1617 — well after the first edition of Florio's translation had circulated widely in England — the French *Essais* offered no translations of the quotations. The only concession was the identification of the sources in the margins of the 1611 edition.[15] According to Gournay, the references were compiled by 'un incogneu', but she herself had corrected and augmented them in 1617.[16] I would hypothesize, however, that printers in Paris used the 1603 English edition as their basis in 1611, in which case the 'incogneu' would be Gwinne.[17]

However, as McKinley has shown,[18] it was only with apparent reluctance that Gournay acceded, in 1617, to the printer's desire:

L'Imprimeur m'a encore pressée de tourner les passages Latins des Essais, sur le desir qu'il pretend, que plusieurs ignorans de leur langage, ont de les entendre [...]. Neantmoins pour servir à l'utilité du mesme Imprimeur, je me suis flechie à les tourner.[19]

I have argued elsewhere that the time that elapsed between the first edition of the *Essais* in 1580 and the 1617 edition witnessed a significant transformation in the French linguistic and cultural landscape, so that Gournay was left defending a stylistic position that came to appear anachronistic.[20] As Blum has observed, increasingly the taste of court circles for *honnêteté* displaced previous generations' respect for humanist learning, with the result that French readers were unwilling or ill-equipped to appreciate the subtleties of a bilingual text.[21]

We might have expected Gournay, who had taught herself Latin, to be sympathetic at least to women readers, most of whom would have received little or no education in the classics. Yet her attitude echoes Montaigne's comment in III.5, 'Sur des vers de Virgile' [On Some Lines from Virgil]: 'Je m'ennuie que mes essais servent les dames de meuble commun seulement, et de meuble de sale. Ce chapitre me fera du cabinet.'[22] On the surface, her preface does not engage with the gender of readers. Rather, she focuses on their competence to appreciate Montaigne, a quality she explicitly distinguishes from mere classical scholarship. Her choice of metaphor nonetheless evokes masculine rather than feminine spheres of activity: 'un Lecteur qui cognoist ces passages-là [les citations], n'est pas plus prest de demesler ce Livre à point, que celuy qui ne les cognoist pas, s'il n'est d'ailleurs ferré à glace'.[23] Implicitly portraying herself as an ideal reader of Montaigne, she can ride across the ice, barely stumbling, because she appreciates the true value of 'ceste masse ou plustost nuée et moisson d'autheurs Latins [...] la cresme et la fleur choisie à dessein, comme on void, de l'ouvrage des plus excellents Autheurs'.[24] Hence, she feels equipped to meet the double challenge posed by translating these quotations, respecting both Montaigne's use of them and their original source.[25] Her discussion is couched in abstract terms, the only use of a metaphor of birthing being reserved for Montaigne's 'excellente application' of these authors that is sometimes 'opposite de leur intention natale'.[26] But is there any indication in the preface that she presents her translation as a gendered performance? Her use of the marked form 'traductrice' invites attention, since, when theorizing about translation in general, she uses the masculine form, 'un pertinent traducteur'. In contrast, she applies to herself adjectives that suggest female domestic virtues: 'fidelle traductrice', 'une austere traductrice'. In addition, the closing sentence of the preface acknowledges that her status as a self-educated woman could expose her to criticism from 'un Lecteur habile homme'. Her lexis, especially 'me quereller' evokes stereotypical disputes between husband and wife:

Enfin s'il se trouve quelque faute en mon ouvrage, j'espere qu'elle sera faute, non de prevoyance, ains de Grammaire, en laquelle je suis peu versée: et que partant un Lecteur habile homme; prendra la peine de m'advertir, plustost que de me quereller.[27]

In short, where Florio had delighted in playfully feigning feminine weakness, deferring to another to translate the quotations, Gournay parries criticism of her work by shielding herself behind her identity as a female without formal education;

to translate may be a 'female' act of delivery at second hand, but it is not necessarily a skill expected of a Renaissance woman.[28]

★   ★   ★   ★   ★

When we turn from the prefaces to the 1603 English and 1617 French texts, the different status Florio and Gournay accorded the quotations is apparent from the typographic presentation. Florio had argued that 'every language hath its Genius and inseparable forme', selecting examples such as '[t]he Tuscan altiloquence, the Venus of the French, the sharpe state of the Spanish, the strong significancy of the Dutch'.[29] Hence, to translate the Latin and Greek quotations within the *Essais* was a similar challenge to translating Montaigne's French.[30] It is his own English version for which Florio apologizes: 'Why then belike I have done by Montaigne, as Terence by Menander, made of good French no good English [...]. His horse I set before you; perhaps without his trappings; and his meate without sause'.[31] Indeed, he compares it unfavourably with the rendering of the quotations by Gwinne, his 'peerelesse deere-deerest and never sufficiently commended friend', underlining the ease with which his version accommodated the translation of the quotations.

The layout adopted by the printer, Valentine Sims, would have pleased Montaigne, for it distinguishes the poetic borrowings: prose quotations run on, but verse is carefully inset. For the prose, Sims uses italics for both the Latin and English. The Latin verses are also set in italics, but the printer reverts to Roman type for the English translation, which is also indented. Because they share the same font, the reader's eye runs effortlessly from the English version of the verse quotations to Florio's translation; only the Latin verse obtrudes, in italics. On the one hand, Florio's reader is thus initially still conscious of the foreign bugbears. Yet for the verse passages, all but the most scholarly readers might adopt a pattern of reading only the text in roman font, so that the bilingual character is at once present yet domesticated. This pattern would be interrupted, producing a sudden visual and conceptual jolt, only when a quotation is not translated, notably in the case of some racy or erotic verses. It was an approach which also set the template for Charles Cotton's new English translation of the *Essais* in the late seventeenth century (1685–86).[32]

In contrast, Gournay did not make it easy for her readers to avoid the mental encounter with Montaigne's Latin quotations. Although the title page of the 1617 edition advertised the new features (*Edition Nouvelle. Enrichie d'annotations en marge, du nom des Auteurs citez, et de la version du Latin d'iceux*), the translations are placed at the end of the *Essais*, in an appendix — paradoxically making of them a florilegium for the desultory reader. This format was maintained in the 1625 edition, but in 1635, the final edition overseen by Gournay, the translations of the quotations moved one stage nearer to integration within the French text, being placed at the end of each chapter. In moving from one chapter to another, particularly the short chapters of Book I, French readers could no longer ignore their presence.

While the typographic presentation of the 1617 edition suggests that Gournay was reluctant to disturb the bilingualism of the *Essais*, her preface emphasizes the difficulties inherent in her task. She was not an inexperienced translator: she had produced a polished version of Book 2 of the *Aeneid* (published in 1594) and a draft translation of one of Ovid's *Heroides*, and had probably completed substantial extracts from Tacitus and Sallust. However, she was acutely aware that the quotations posed a particular challenge. The adjectives she chooses to characterize the classical writers are telling: 'autheurs outreplus figurez et pressez' (1617) or 'figurez et succincts' (1625–35).[33] In her extensive writings on poetic theory, Gournay defended the Renaissance love of daring metaphors and tropes against the restrictions the Malherbian camp sought to impose upon poetic language, and her treatise 'Sur la Version des Poetes antiques' (1626) is subtitled 'ou des Metaphores'. To translate the idiom of Montaigne's favourite poets was to grant an unfashionable licence for a rich metaphorical style. The other adjective, 'pressez'/'succincts', signals her awareness of the challenges of translating without excessive paraphrase. While claiming to have respected 'les loix d'une austere traductrice',[34] she concedes that in a few places she has incorporated an explanatory gloss within her translation; yet she cannot overlook the competing demands of the quotations as independent Latin or Greek texts, remodelled or even distorted by the writing in which they are embedded.

Editors of the *Essais* in the 1650s and 1660s continued to reproduce Gournay's 1635 version, word for word, with Christophe Journel including a French translation of Montaigne's Italian quotations in 1659. This apart, Gournay dictated the reception of the quotations in French for approximately half a century, from 1617 to 1669.[35] However, there was one notable advance in the 1652 edition by Henri Estienne: the translations of the Latin and Greek quotations were finally printed in the margins of the text.[36] It was a sure sign that at the mid-point of the century Montaigne had passed from the hands of readers numbering many humanist scholars to those of the 'honnêtes gens'. Estienne, a scion of the famous humanist printing dynasty, recommended his modern layout as serving the need of 'ceux qui n'ont pas cét advantage d'entendre lesdites Langues [Grecque et Latine]', and in particular of the female reading public: 'J'espere qu'un chascun, et les Dames mesmes, y prendront tres-bonne part, puisqu'en cette Edition il n'y a plus rien de l'estranger, qu'elle est toute Françoise, et toute intelligible par le moyen de ladicte traduction.'[37] Gournay would hardly have been flattered by this estimation of women's intellectual capacities, nor, one suspects, would she or Montaigne have approved of the way in which the verse translations were crammed into the margin without regard for the start of lines.

★   ★   ★   ★   ★

The discipline of translation studies requires a dual approach in the appraisal of literary translations: on the one hand, paratextual materials and typographic choices, of the type discussed above, illuminate the cultural contexts in which target texts circulate; on the other hand, a philological analysis of the practices of the individual translator is essential to defining a target text's literary identity. Despite the significant, long-standing interest in Florio and the modest recent interest in Gournay, there is as yet no comparison of the translation of Montaigne's Latin and Greek quotations in their two versions.[38] Yet the manner in which the quotations are translated, as much as their physical presence within the published text, contributed to how Montaigne was read in England or France. We have established that readers of Florio's Montaigne never had to tussle with the original Latin or Greek quotations unless they chose to, and that the presentation of the English editions assimilated the translations within the body of the text, whereas French readers of the earlier seventeenth century had no translation of the quotations, and later the translations were still confined to an appendix. Does this contrast between the principles of assimilation/distancing also hold true when we compare the translation styles of Florio–Gwinne[39] and of Gournay? Hamlin, for example, has shown that handwritten marginal annotations commented on Gwinne's versions of the quotations, proposing improvements;[40] however, Gournay's translations, separated — until 1652 — from Montaigne's text, by contrast avoided claiming a literary life of their own.

One striking difference between the versions is that whereas Gwinne has a proclivity for turning both short and longer quotations into English verse, Gournay generally prefers prose. Her partial translation of the *Aeneid* attested her competence in using alexandrine rhyming couplets,[41] but most of her writings throughout her life were in prose. Furthermore, keenly aware of the stylistic value Montaigne attributed to his quotations from Latin poets, she is almost abruptly defensive of her position:

> Si j'ay rendu la Poësie comme l'oraison, sous le seul genre de la prose, pour estre plus fidelle, à l'exemple d'autres versions authorisées de nostre siecle; on m'en doibt reputer soulagée de temps, non de solicitude ayguë: la moins espineuse et scabreuse circonstance de telle traduction estant de la bastir en vers.[42]

Her appeal to precedent is flimsy, for by this date few French translations of Latin poets used prose; even partial translations of poetry were usually in verse.[43] Rather, the key point is her desire, as self-appointed custodian of the integrity of the transmission of the *Essais*, to be a 'fidelle traductrice', avoiding imposing her own style upon them. Nevertheless, she allows several concessions. Firstly, some 'breves sentences' are rendered by one or two lines of verse, to makes them 'plus faciles à retenir'.[44] Secondly, several more substantial passages are rendered in verse, 'tant par esbat, que pour piquer, si je puis quelqu'un par exemple à faire le mesme du reste' (ibid.). The first reason reinforces the idea that translation stimulates a creative impulse that is hard to resist. Yet the second seems to contradict Gournay's general approach: nowhere else does she invite others to collaborate in defining the transmission of the *Essais*. The statement is probably better read as a literary trope, the challenge intended to indicate the adequacy of the present version,[45] while ensuring the reader appreciates the scale of her labours.

I have offered a detailed appraisal of Gournay's translations in the Introduction to her *Œuvres complètes*,[46] so propose here to concentrate on the Florio–Gwinne version. However, it is important first to highlight one aspect of her mediation of Montaigne's quotations, to set up a contrast. Many critics have explored how Montaigne played with the bilingual texture of the *Essais*,[47] exploiting readers' close familiarity with his sources by making subtle changes within quotations, conflating quotations from several sources into a *cento*, and — especially in 'Sur des vers de Virgile' — opposing intricate Latin poetry with earthy French prose. It is precisely the distance between Latin and French which achieves these effects. When

Gournay accepts the obligation in 1617, to make the *Essais* speak in a single voice, she follows as far as possible Montaigne's tactics, keeping the playful distortions of original sources, retaining *centones*. However, monolingualism imposes choices between echoing the Latin source or Montaigne's French: there is a perceptible movement of gravity away from calques derived from the Latin, and towards a lexis inspired by Montaigne's own French.[48] For example, in II.18, 'Du dementir' [Of Giving the Lie], where Montaigne cites humorous lines from Perseus to define the essence of the *Essais*:

> Je ne dresse pas icy une statue à planter au carrefour d'une ville, ou dans une Eglise, ou place publique:
>> *Non equidem hoc studeo, bullatis ut mihi nugis*
>> *Pagina turgescat.*
>> *Secreti loquimur.*[49]

Gournay offers the following translation, many of the words (my italics) recalling other comments by Montaigne in the course of the *Essais*: 'Ce n'est pas *mon dessein*, de *bouffir* ce Livre, du vent seigneurial de ces magnifiques *frivoles*. Je parle *bassement* en *particulier*.'[50] When translating into the same language as that used by her adoptive father, she was subject to his influence in a way that Gwinne was not.

Beyond Florio's acknowledgement in the preface of Gwinne's role as translator of the 'bugbear' quotations, we are given no insights into his method of translation. Yet we may assume the versions were intended to stand up to close scrutiny by the elite English readership of the early seventeenth century, since they are printed with the Latin or Greek in parallel. Overall, his versions are those of a proficient classical scholar: he looks to translate neatly, conveying the sense clearly but also pleasingly. His style is necessarily constrained by the brevity of the sources. In the prose quotations, he generally avoids expansion; in verse, however, he allows some padding in order to produce a rhyming couplet, even for a single line of Latin. For example, at the end of I.37, 'Du jeune Caton' [Of Cato the Younger] Gwinne substitutes a couplet where Montaigne concluded his appraisal of Cato with a part-line of Virgil:

>> — His dantem jura Catonem
>> Chiefe justice *Cato* doe decree
>> Lawes that for righteous soules should be.[51]

In contrast, longer verse quotations are usually rendered by the same number of lines in English, demonstrating that Gwinne is not unnecessarily verbose by habit. Indeed, some of his translations have a distinctively snappy quality, reminiscent of Montaigne's taste for 'un parler succulent et nerveux'.[52] For example, in 'Sur des vers de Virgile', arguing the need for limiting sexual relations in marriage, Montaigne cites a line form the *Georgics* in which Virgil depicts a cow kept hungry for its encounter with the bull:

> [les medecins] disent d'autre-part, qu'à une congression languissante, comme celle là est de sa nature, pour la remplir d'une juste et fertile chaleur, il s'y faut presenter rarement et à notables intervalles,
>> *Quo rapiat sitiens venerem interiusque recondat.*[53]

Where Florio's prose translation of Montaigne's French is exact, but unadventurous, Gwinne's couplet adds a brisk, playful note:

> Some other [Phisicions] say, besides, that to a languishing congression (as naturallie that is) to store it with a convenient and fertile heate, one must but seldome, and by moderate intermissions present himselfe unto it;
>> Thirsting to snatch a fit,
>> And inly harbor it.[54]

Gwinne's confidence as a translator is also clear in his readiness to adapt syntax to suit his metre, particularly reordering clauses on occasions. It is notable that he tends to eschew enjambments,[55] even when present in the source text, preferring a tidier translation, as in the rendering of the two lines from Terence, cited by Montaigne towards the close of I.28, 'De l'amitié' [On Friendship], to express his grief for the loss of La Boëtie:

> je ne fay que trainer languissant; et les plaisirs mesmes qui s'offrent à moy, au lieu de me consoler, me redoublent le regret de sa perte. Nous estions à moitié de tout; il me semble que je luy desrobe sa part,
>> *Nec fas esse ulla me voluptate hic frui*
>> *Decrevi, tantisper dum ille abest meus particeps.*[56]

Gwinne's translation of 'Decrevi' is set at the start of the couplet, simplifying the structure, but carefully preserving the first person ('frui'/'I may') at the end of the first line, contrasted with the double reference in the following line to the absent La Boëtie ('ille [...] particpes'/'he my partner'):

> I doe but languish, I doe but sorrow: and even those pleasures, all things present me with, in stead of yeelding me comfort, doe but redouble the griefe of his losse. Wee were copartners in all things. All things were with us at halfe; mee thinkes I have stolne his part from him.
>> I have set downe, no joy enjoy I may,
>> As long as he my partner is away.[57]

The way that Gwinne's lexis echoes Florio's (my partner/co-partners), provides intralingual imitation of Montaigne's bilingual echo of the last word of Terence ('sa part'/'particeps'), the careful crafting perhaps paying testimony to the position of 'De l'amitié' as the emotional summit of Book I.[58]

In addition, there are some features of the translations in which we may distinguish Gwinne's voice. Like Florio, he is charmed by novel compound forms, on occasion experimenting with several in close succession. In II.37, 'De la ressemblance des enfans aux peres' [Of the Resemblance of Children to their Fathers] this is prompted by the source text, where Montaigne borrows Cicero's periphrasis describing a tortoise, to conclude his caustic comments on physicians' use of unintelligible language:

> quoy qu'en sente la philosophie, que c'est follie de conseiller un homme pour son profit par maniere non intelligible: *Ut si quis medicus imperet ut sumat: Terrigenam, herbigradam, domiportam, sanguine cassam.*[59]

> Howbeit Philosophie supposeth it to be folly to perswade a man to his profit, by wayes not understood: 'As if a physitian should bid a man take.
> One, earth-borne, goe-by-grasse, house-bearing, slimilie, bloodlesse.'[60]

However, on other occasions Gwinne introduces compounds independently, particularly in 'Sur des vers de Virgile' where the rich poetic texture stems in large part from the accumulation of allusive quotations. For example, Montaigne cited Ovid's *Amores* to criticize the overly strict chaperoning of Italian women:

> Il leur faut un peu lacher les resnes:
> *Vidi ego nuper equum, contra sua frena tenacem,*
> *Ore reluctanti fulminis ire modo.*[61]

Gwinne's version is calculated to catch the reader's attention:

> They must have the reynes given them a little.
> I saw, spite of his bit, a resty colte,
> Runne head-strong headlong like a thunder-bolt.[62]

His attention to sound patterns both responds to the poetic qualities of the source text, but also pushes the boundaries of translation towards independent writing; in addition, the couplet provides a striking illustration of his mastery of the decasyllabic rhyming couplet — a fresh, modern metre.[63] A quotation from Virgil earlier in the same chapter displays Gwinne's ability to imitate the sound-patterning and alliteration that in Latin derived partly from the inflected forms (my italics):

> Omne adeo genus in terris homin*um*que ferar*um*que,
> Et genus aequore*um*, pecudes, *p*ictaeque volucres,
> In furias ignémque *ruunt.*[64]

Swirling streams of echoes (again, my italics) compensate for the absence of inflections:

> All *k*indes of things on earth, wilde beasts, man-*k*inde,
> Field-beasts, *f*aire-*f*ethered *fowle*, and *fish* (we *finde*)
> Into loves *fire* and *furie runne* by *kinde.*[65]

In the Introduction to her translation of Gwinne's neo-Latin tragedy *Nero*, Dana Sutton defends Gwinne's Latin style from earlier detractors, arguing that he was 'attempting to develop a novel poetics by importing Euphuism into Latin'.[66] We might counter that euphuism was scarcely novel in England in 1603; critics have also located various features of it in Florio's translation.[67] Nonetheless, Gwinne's translations of the quotations show various euphuistic qualities: a fondness for couplets expressing antitheses, the use of protracted word repetition ('kinde' in the above example), and extreme use of alliteration. He is not, in short, a translator seeking to hide his light under Florio's or Montaigne's bushel. Only in the case of the most directly erotic quotations does he pass up the challenge. Hamlin has analysed in detail the omission of 22 such passages, which he suggests matches Florio's limited but delicate censorship of some of the most forthright passages of Montaigne's French text.[68] Whether the choice not to translate these quotations was made singly or collaboratively by Gwinne, Florio, or even the printer, we cannot know, but it is testimony to the resistance of one trait of Montaigne's bilingual text. It is paralleled by Gournay's declaration that she is content to 'avoir laissé dormir les libertins, souz le voile de leur langue estrangere, ny d'avoir tors le nez à quelque mot joyeux de l'un d'entr'eux'.[69] She omits to translate some 20 quotations in 1617, and excises several more in 1635, a sign of the growing distaste for coarseness as *préciosité* gained ground.[70]

One other aspect of Gwinne's translation reinforces a novel feature of Florio's translation, identified by Hamlin: the foregrounding of dialogic qualities inherent Montaigne's text.[71] Hamlin argues that its unusual sensitivity — by comparison with contemporary prose treatises — to many of the strategies routinely drawn upon by dramatists rendered it all the more readily assimilable to the literary projects of dramatists such as Shakespeare, Marston, and Daniel. Gwinne's translation of the quotations lends momentum to the tendency for Montaigne's text to be read almost as a theatrical series of conversations. It is notable that Gwinne's own Latin orations were peppered with classical quotations, and Sutton shows that his *Nero* is replete with the rhetorical devices of stichomythia and antilabe.[72] I would surmise that he was at ease with an antiphonal style in which dialogue moved rapidly between speakers. Gwinne sometimes adds personal pronouns or adjectives in his translation of the quotations, implicitly drawing the reader into the text. For example, in 'De l'institution des enfans', a quotation from Perseus's satire upon education elaborates upon what Montaigne considers a child should be taught. The source text uses only impersonal constructions until the introduction of 'te' at the end of the third line:

> Aux exemples se pourront proprement assortir tous les plus profitables discours de la philosophie, à laquelle se doivent toucher les actions humaines comme à leur reigle. On luy dira,
>> *quid fas optare, quid asper*
>> *Utile nummus habet; patriae charisque propinquis*
>> *Quantum elargiri deceat: quem te Deus esse*
>> *Jussit, et humana qua parte locatus es in re;*
>> *Quid sumus, aut quidnam victuri gignimur.*[73]

We can assume that Gwinne was quite familiar with the original context, and thus aware of Perseus's deliberate oscillation between universal (impersonal) forms and direct address to the reader,[74] but it suits his dramatic purpose better to use the second-person singular from the outset:

> Unto examples may all the most profitable Discourses of Philosophie bee sorted, which ought to be the touch-stone of humane actions, and a rule to square them by, to whom may be saide,
>> What *thou* maiest wish, what profit may come cleare,
>> From new-stampt coyne, to friends and countrie deare
>> What *thou* oughtst give: whom God would have thee bee,
>> And in what parte mongst men he placed thee.
>> What we are, and wherefore,
>> To live here we were bore.[75]

Or, to take another example, from 'Sur des vers de Virgile', Montaigne cites Virgil's simple half-line concluding Venus's appeal for Vulcan to forge her son's armour:

> Voire elle luy faict requeste pour un sien bastard,
>> *Arma rogo genitrix nato,*
> qui luy est liberalement accordée.[76]

Gwinne renders this by a couplet in English, and — in the absence of inflections

— employs personal pronouns to carry the emotive force of the appeal, thereby conjuring up a scene of two actors on stage, talking of an absent third character:

> And which is more, she becomes a suter to him in the behalfe of a bastard of hirs,
> A mother for a sonne, *I* crave,
> An armor *he of you* may have.
> Which is freely granted hir.[77]

In such ways, I would argue that his translations of the quotations contributed a further modern edge to Florio's work through their jauntiness, the self-confident play with sound patterns and neologistic compounds, and the theatrical thrust of the personalizations.

★   ★   ★   ★   ★

Both the English professional male scholar and the French female autodidact of limited social means had produced from Montaigne's classical quotations 'femalls, delivered at second hand', but the two infants looked rather different, the cultural influences of nurture having refashioned the original products of nature. To use Lawrence Venuti's terminology, we might contrast the domesticating, assertive translation into English with the foreignizing, more restrained translation into French. Yet both translators essentially accomplished the same end: what Hamlin has defined, in respect of Florio–Gwinne's work, as 'the immense extension of audience, across class and gender boundaries'.[78] Translating Montaigne's quotation was not a sterile occupation; the physician Serres might well have included them as testimony to the fertility of bearing daughters. The undertaking caused both Gwinne and Gournay — two highly skilled readers of Montaigne — to reflect substantially upon the bilingual texture of the *Essais*, but also upon the capacity of their respective and rapidly evolving vernaculars to ensure a transit across national, cultural, and linguistic frontiers.

Successive translators would continue to wrestle with the bugbears or bouquets, particularly the erotic quotations, but whereas Gournay in 1617–35 seems to have worked without any reference to Gwinne's English translations, Coste, a century later, clearly had Cotton's new version before him, and found in it at least one novel solution. Latin was not the only language in which a Frenchman of the Enlightenment could entertain salacious thoughts. In place of a translation, Coste provides the following footnote on the quotation:

> 'Et nudam pressi corpus adusque meum' (from Ovid):
> ce que le Traducteur Anglois a rendu par ces deux vers,
> > And in the naked Arms of mine
> > Her naked Body I did twine.
> On ne sauroit dire la même chose si ouvertement en François: et plus enve-loppée, elle feroit un contraste ridicule avec ce que Montaigne ajoute immediatement après.[79]

Veiled by the cloak of translation into another vernacular, Montaigne's bilingualism is recreated for Enlightenment Anglophiles!

Notes to Chapter 9

I am grateful to Colin Burrow and Will Hamlin for reading drafts of this chapter and generously sharing their insights with me. All remaining errors of fact or judgement are my own alone.

1. [For if the time we expend learning these languages were spent on studying knowledge, Nature has certainly not become so sterile that she could not today produce Platos and Aristotles]; Joachim Du Bellay, *La Deffence, et Illustration de la langue francoyse* (1549) in *Œuvres complètes*, ed. Francis Goyet and Olivier Millet (Paris: Champion, 2003), I.10, vol. 1, p. 39. All translations from French are my own unless otherwise indicated.

2. See Theo Hermans, 'The Task of the Translator in the European Renaissance', in *Translating Literature*, ed. Susan Bassnett (Cambridge: D.S. Brewer, 1997), pp. 14–40, and Peter Burke, 'Cultures of Translation in Early Modern Europe', in *Cultural Translation in Early Modern Europe*, ed. Peter Burke and Ronnie Po-chia Hsia (Cambridge: Cambridge University Press, 2007), pp. 7–38. Translation studies have recently prompted a succession of revisionist accounts pertaining to early modern England, including: Massimiliano Morini, *Tudor Translation in Theory and Practice* (Aldershot: Ashgate, 2006); *The Oxford History of Literary Translation in English*, vol. 2: *1550–1660*, ed. Gordon Braden, Robert Cummings, and Stuart Gillespie (Oxford: Oxford University Press, 2010); *Tudor Translation*, ed. Fred Schurink (New York: Palgrave Macmillan, 2011); Sara Barker and Brenda Hosington, *Renaissance Cultural Crossroads: Translation, Print and Culture in Britain, 1473–1640* (Boston, MA: Brill, 2013); and *The Culture of Translation in Early Modern England and France, 1500–1660*, ed. Tania Demetriou and Rowan Tomlinson (Palgrave Macmillan, 2015).

3. Two recent major studies are key to this chapter: William Hamlin examines annotations by early readers of Florio's translation in *Montaigne's English Journey: Reading the Essays in Shakespeare's Day* (Oxford: Oxford University Press, 2013); Warren Boutcher considers Florio's translation in *The School of Montaigne in Early Modern Europe*, vol. 2: *The Reader-Writer* (Oxford: Oxford University Press, 2016).

4. *The Essayes or Morall, Politike and Millitarie Discourses of Lo: Michaell de Montaigne* (London: by Val. Sims for Edward Blount, 1603), fol. A2ʳ.

5. Critics discussing the imagery of the foundling father and of birth include: Jonathan Goldberg, *Desiring Women Writing: English Renaissance Examples* (Stanford, CA: Stanford University Press, 1977), pp. 75–82; Georgianna Ziegler, 'En-gendering the Subject: Florio's Feminization of Montaigne's Moy-mesme', *Montaigne Studies*, 8 (1996), 125–44 (pp. 131–32); Christopher Johnson, 'Florio's Conversion of Montaigne, Sidney and Six Patronesses', *Cahiers élisabéthains*, 64 (2003), 9–18 (pp. 8–10); Massimiliano Morini, *Tudor Translation in Theory and Practice*, p. 84; Neil Rhodes, 'Status Anxiety and English Renaissance Translation', in *Renaissance Paratexts*, ed. Helen Smith and Louise Wilson (Cambridge: Cambridge University Press, 2011), pp. 107–20 (pp. 112–19); and Oana-Alis Zaharia, '*Translata Proficit*: Revisiting John Florio's Translation of Michel de Montaigne's *Les Essais*', *Sederi*, 22 (2012), 115–36 (pp. 124–26). My interest lies in the intertwining of performative and gendered aspects of the metaphor. For a wider analysis of appropriations of metaphors of female fertility by early modern male authors, see Katharine Eisaman Maus, 'A Womb of His Own: Male Renaissance Poets in the Female Body', in *Sexuality and Gender in Early Modern Europe: Institutions, Texts, Images*, ed. James Grantham Turner (Cambridge: Cambridge University Press, 1993), pp. 266–88.

6. [Treatise on the Nature, Causes, Signs and Remedies Concerning Failures to Conceive, and Sterility among Women, Chapter 3: 'Whether Women Who Bear Only Daughters Should Be Called Sterile?']. See my translation of the text in François Rousset, Jean Liebault, Jacques Guillemeau, Jacques Duval, and Louis de Serres, *Pregnancy and Birth in Early Modern France: Treatises by Caring Physicians and Surgeons (1581–1625)*, ed. and trans. Valerie Worth-Stylianou (Toronto: Center for Reformation and Renaissance Studies, 2013), pp. 318–33.

7. *The Essayes*, 1603, fol. A2ᵛ.

8. See Johnson, 'Florio's Conversion of Montaigne', p. 12.

9. On the interplay between friendship and textual production in the prefatory materials, see Andrew Keener, 'Prefatory Friendships: Florio's Montaigne and Material Technologies of the

Self', in *Renaissance Papers 2013*, ed. Jim Pearce and Joanna Kucinski (Rochester, NY: Camden House, 2014), pp. 83–100.

10. For the growing scholarship on collaborative translation, see Belén Bistué, *Collaborative Translation and Multi-Version Texts in Early Modern Europe* (Farnham: Ashgate, 2013).

11. Francis Matthiessen's *Translation: An Elizabethan Art* (Cambridge, MA: Harvard University Press, 1931), and Frances Yates's *John Florio, the Life of an Italian in Shakespeare's England* (Cambridge: Cambridge University Press, 1934), have been substantially augmented by the work of Warren Boutcher: 'Marginal Commentaries: The Cultural Transmission of Montaigne's *Essais* in Shakespeare's England', in *Montaigne et Shakespeare: vers un nouvel humanisme*, ed. Jean-Marie Maguin and Pierre Kapitanak (Montpellier: Société française Shakespeare, 2004), pp. 13–27, and 'The Origins of Florio's Montaigne: "Of the institution and Education of Children, to Madame Lucy Russell, Countess of Bedford"', *Montaigne Studies*, 24 (2012), 7–32. See also Michael Wyatt, *The Italian Encounter with Tudor England: A Cultural Politics of Translation* (Cambridge: Cambridge University Press, 2005).

12. *The Essayes*, 1603, fol. A3^r.

13. Gwinne had travelled to France attending the ambassador Sir Henry Unton, and displayed familiarity with the *Essais* as early as his 1598–99 Gresham College orations (published in 1605); see Boutcher: 'Marginal Commentaries', p. 19.

14. On the editorial history of French editions of the *Essais*, see Richard Sayce and David Maskell, *A Descriptive Bibliography of Montaigne's Essais 1580–1700* (London: Bibliographic Society, 1983); and Philippe Desan, 'Éditer et publier les *Essais* au XVIIe siècle', *Cahiers de l'Association internationale des études françaises*, 51 (1999), 205–23. On Gournay's editorship, see Claude Blum's essay, 'L'Éditrice des *Essais*', in the critical edition of her works: Marie de Gournay, *Œuvres complètes*, ed. Jean-Claude Arnould, Evelyne Berriot, Claude Blum, Anna Lia Franchetti, Marie-Claire Thomine, and Valérie Worth-Stylianou (Paris: Champion, 2002), vol. I, pp. 27–43.

15. See Maskell and Sayce, *A Descriptive Bibliography*, p. 66, n. 1.

16. Gournay, *Œuvres complètes*, p. 335.

17. I am assuming that one or more copies of the 1603 translation reached Paris before 1611: even though Gournay and most printers did not know English, the references would still have been intelligible. In the 1617 edition overseen by Gournay, however, she substantially revises the *loci*, as she points out in her preface; *Les Essais de Michel seigneur de Montaigne* (Paris: chez Michel Nivelle, 1617), fol. 12^v.

18. Mary McKinley, ' "Fleurs estrangeres": Gournay's Translation of Montaigne's Quotations in the 1617 *Essais*', *Montaigne Studies*, 7 (1995), 19–30. Based on the paratexts (rather than the translations of the quotations), she argues that this edition represented a new stage in Gournay's editorial relationship with the *Essais*.

19. [The printer also urged me to translate the Latin passages in the *Essais* because he claimed that some people that do not know this language wish to understand them. [...] Nevertheless, to satisfy the printer's requirements, I reluctantly translated them]; *Essais*, 1617, p. 989. In the 1635 edition, Gournay pluralizes the reference to '[l]es imprimeurs [...] à l'utilité des mesmes Imprimeurs ou Libraires'; Gournay, *Œuvres complètes*, p. 338.

20. Valérie Worth-Stylianou, 'Marie de Gournay et la traduction: défense et illustration d'un style', *Bulletin de la Société des Amis de Montaigne*, 7 (1996), 193–206. By 1617, even Gournay accepted that the vocabulary of the *Essais* needed some modernization, an editorial task she herself undertook; Blum, 'L'Éditrice des *Essais*', in Gournay, *Œuvres complètes*, p. 43.

21. Gournay, *Œuvres complètes*, p. 285. On the early reception of the *Essais* in France, see also Jules Brody, 'La Première Réception des *Essais* de Montaigne: fortunes d'une forme', in *L'Automne de la Renaissance*, ed. Jean Lafond and André Stegmann (Paris: Vrin, 1981), pp. 19–30, and Olivier Millet, *La Première Réception des 'Essais' de Montaigne (1580–1640)* (Paris: Champion, 1995).

22. [I am annoyed that my essays serve the ladies only as a public article of furniture, an article for the parlor. This chapter will put me in the boudoir]; V, p. 847; F, p. 781.

23. [A reader who knows those passages is no nearer to making good sense of this book than someone that does not know them, unless he wears hobnailed boots]; *Essais*, 1617, p. 989.

24. [This mass or rather swarm and wealth of Latin writers [...] the cream and the flower carefully chosen, as we see, among the work of such excellent writers]; *Essais*, 1617, p. 990.

25. 'Ç'a esté certes une de mes peines, me trouvant sur quelque passage contourné ou frelaté, de l'exprimer en telle sorte, qu'il quadrast sortablement s'il estoit possible, à la composition originaire et à l'application' [It was one of the challenges when I came upon a passage which had been adapted or doctored, to express it so that, as far as possible, it fitted both the original text and the new use of it]; *Essais*, 1617, p. 991.

26. [Excellent borrowing [...] different from their original conception]; *Essais*, 1617, p. 991.

27. [Finally, if any error is found in my work, I trust it will be not of interpretation but only of syntax, in which I am not expert. And an expert reader would do well to draw my attention to it rather than upbraiding me]; *Essais*, 1617, p. 991.

28. When publishing translations of extracts from Tacitus and Sallust in 1619, Gournay emphasized that she had worked from the Latin text, rather than from existing French translations for 'quelques-uns croyent qu'une femme ne peut entendre le Latin, et que je traduis sur les Traducteurs' [some people believe that a woman cannot understand Latin, and that I work from other translations]; Gournay, *Œuvres complètes*, p. 1436.

29. Since Richard Jones's foundational study of the cultural nationalism of translation in the Renaissance (*The Triumph of the English Language* (Stanford, CA: Stanford University Press, 1953)), critics reappraising the issue include, notably, Sean Keilen, *Vulgar Eloquence: On the Renaissance Invention of English Literature* (New Haven, CT: Yale University Press, 2006), pp. 21–27, and Catherine Nicholson, *Uncommon Tongues: Eloquence and Eccentricity in the English Renaissance* (Philadelphia: University of Pennsylvania Press, 2013), pp. 2–11. Florio's list of national linguistic traits may be compared with Thomas Dekker's a few years later: *Lantern and Candlelight*, ed. Viviana Comensoli (Toronto: Center for Reformation and Renaissance Studies, 2007), p. 83.

30. In contrast, Girolamo Naselli's early partial translation of the *Essais* into Italian (*Discorsi morali, politici, et militari* (Ferrara: Mamarello, 1590)) — which probably inspired Florio's choice of title for his English translation — left the quotations in the original languages, and did not identify any of the sources. See Marcel Tetel, 'Idéologie et traductions de Girolamo Naselli à John Florio', *Montaigne Studies*, 7.1–2 (1995), 169–82.

31. 'To the curteous Reader', *The Essayes*, 1603, fol. A5^{v}.

32. A comparison with the versions of Florio–Gwinne shows Cotton to be a competent if less adventurous translator: his assimilation of the quotations fits his pragmatic approach to Englishing the entire text. See Philip Ford's comparison of sections of the translations by Florio and by Cotton, 'Charles Cotton's Montaigne', *Montaigne Studies*, 24 (2012), 105–20.

33. [Most figurative and concise authors; figurative and succinct]; *Essais*, 1617, p. 989; Gournay, *Œuvres complètes* (1635 text), p. 349.

34. [The rules of a strict translator]; *Essais*, 1617, p. 990.

35. The late seventeenth century saw two radical abridgements of the *Essais*, one by Charles de Sercy (*L'Esprit des Essais de Michel, seigneur de Montaigne* (Paris: chez Charles de Sercy, 1677)), retaining fewer than 50 of the quotations, of which hardly any are translated or glossed; and the other (attributed to Artaud), entitled *Pensées de Montaigne, propres à former l'esprit et les mœurs* (Paris: chez Anisson, 1700), in which all the quotations are excised, without comment from the editor. In addition, Guillaume Bérenger's polemical defence of Montaigne in 1667 presented short passages from Montaigne's text, together with some of his quotations: see Philippe Desan, 'Les Essais en cinq cents pensées ou la réponse de Guillaume Bérenger aux "injures et railleries" d'Arnaud et Nicole contre Montaigne (1667)', *Renaissance Journal*, 2.4 (2005), 6–13. However, it was not until the complete edition of the *Essais* published by Pierre Coste (*Les Essais de Michel seigneur de Montaigne* (London: J. Tonson and J. Watts, 1724)), that a new French translation of the quotations replaced Gournay's. Coste's approach and typography are resolutely scientific, anticipating modern editions: Montaigne's quotations are set in italics in the text; they are translated in numbered footnotes at the bottom of the page, in much smaller type, indicating the source. They have the status of apparatus for the reader to judge Montaigne, including measuring his shortcomings with a critical eye (as Coste does in his running commentary on the unclear allusions and errors in the *Essais*).

36. See Maskell and Sayce, *A Descriptive Bibliography*, p. 145, n. 2.

37. [Those who do not possess the advantage of understanding the Greek and Latin languages [...]

I hope that everyone, even the ladies, will benefit from it, since this edition has left nothing foreign; it is entirely in French, and completely comprehensible thanks to the translation]; *Les Essais de Michel, Seigneur de Montaigne* (Paris: Henri Estienne, 1652), fol. aiii^r.

38. Gwinne's role is rarely accorded more than a cursory nod by critics. Even in the *The Oxford History of Literary Translation in English*, vol. 2: *1550–1660*, Cummings writes off Gwinne's contribution in half a sentence (p. 400). Keener explores the prefatory acknowledgement of the friendship ('Prefatory Friendships', pp. 87–89), while Hamlin's more detailed appraisal is a notable and welcome exception; *Montaigne's English Journey*, pp. 54–55.

39. Hereafter, for simplicity, I shall speak of the translation of the quotations as the work of Gwinne, although it is possible that Florio (or Diodati) had some hand in polishing the English draft. Nonetheless, Florio's preface clearly acknowledges this work was accomplished by Gwinne.

40. Hamlin, *Montaigne's English Journey*, pp. 19–20.

41. See my analysis in Gournay, *Œuvres complètes*, pp. 63–64.

42. [I have translated the poetry, like the prose passages, simply into prose to be a more faithful translator, following the practice of some other translations that have won approval in our age. It may be said that I spared myself some time, but not painful effort, for versifying a translation is the least delicate and tricky part of the task]; *Essais*, 1617, p. 989.

43. See, for example, Book 5 of the second volume of *Les Meslanges* (1583) of Jean de La Jessée, a Gascon contemporary of Montaigne, consisting of fragmentary and partial translations into French verse from a host of Latin and Greek poets.

44. *Essais*, 1617, p. 990.

45. Compare her apparent admiration for two earlier translators of Virgil, Du Perron and Bertaut, when she published her own version of parts of the *Aeneid*; yet setting extracts from these two translations alongside her own in fact drew attention to the shorter, more modern style of her own versions. See Worth-Stylianou, 'Marie de Gournay et la traduction', pp. 199–202.

46. Worth-Stylianou, 'Marie de Gournay traductrice', in Gournay, *Œuvres complètes*, pp. 56–79.

47. Notably the detailed studies of Mary McKinley, *Words in a Corner: Studies in Montaigne's Latin Quotations* (Lexington, KY: French Forum, 1981), and Floyd Gray, *Montaigne bilingue: le latin des 'Essais'* (Paris: Champion, 1991).

48. See my discussion in Gournay, *Œuvres complètes*, pp. 76–79.

49. [I am not building here a statue to erect at the town crossroads, or in a church or a public square: "I do no aim to swell my page full-blown/ With windy trifles .../ We two talk alone."]; V, p. 664; F, p. 611; Perseus, v. 19.

50. *Essais*, 1617, p. 1055.

51. *The Essayes*, 1603, p. 115; *Aeneid*, VIII. 670. Compare Gournay's brief prose version: 'Caton est là, qui donne à tous la loy'.

52. I.26, 'De l'institution des enfans' [On Educating Children]; V, p. 171.

53. V, p. 850 (*Georgics*, III. 137 — Virgil's line started with 'Sed', which Montaigne changed to 'Quo'). By contrast, Gournay did not translate this spicy quotation.

54. *The Essayes*, 1603, p. 510.

55. In this respect, his style departs from euphuistic emulation of the fluid syntax of classical inflected languages, discussed by Nicholson, *Uncommon Tongues*, pp. 77–78.

56. V, p. 193 (Terence, *Heautontimoroumenos*, I. i. 97).

57. *The Essayes*, 1603, p. 95.

58. Gournay, translating into prose, reworks this quotation significantly in 1625 and 1635, adding a concluding paraphrastic clause (my italics) for similar effect: 'Et j'ay donné cét arrest contre moy-mesme; que je ne pourrois pas loisiblement jouyr d'aucun plaisir, tandis qu'il est separé de moy: luy qui estoit mon personnier *et mon adjoint en toutes choses*'; Gournay, *Œuvres complètes* (1635 text), p. 376.

59. V, p. 770 (Cicero, *De divinatione*, II).

60. *The Essayes*, 1603, p. 441. Gournay's French version also imitates the ridiculous compounds: 'Comme si quelque Medecin luy commande de prendre, la terre nee, l'herbe marche, la porte maison, la vide de sang'; *Essais*, 1617, p. 1061.

61. V, p. 883 (Ovid, *Amores*, III. 4. 13: Montaigne substituted 'frena' for 'vincla').

62. *The Essayes*, 1603, p. 530.

63. In contrast, Gournay's prose translation departs little from the Latin: 'je vis nagueres un cheval cabré contre son frein; le luttant d'une bouche revesche, s'envoler comme un foudre'; *Essais*, 1617, p. 1061.

64. V, p. 859 (Virgil, *Georgics*, III. 242–44).

65. *The Essayes*, 1603, p. 516.

66. A hypertext critical edition by Dana Sutton (posted 1997, revised 2012) <http://www. philological.bham.ac.uk/Nero/intro.html>, section 32ff [accessed 20 October 2015].

67. For an analysis of this 'wayward style', and notably of the influence of John Lyly, see Nicholson, *Uncommon Tongues*, pp. 72–99.

68. Hamlin, *Montaigne's English Journey*, pp. 55–66.

69. *Essais*, 1617, p. 990.

70. The translation of 'Omne adeo' (rendered in prose in 1617) is one of those excised in 1625/1635. McKinley's points to this quotation's 'levelling force, putting the women's passion on the same plane with the mare's frenzy'; *Words in a Corner*, pp. 88–89.

71. Hamlin, *Montaigne's English Journey*, pp. 35–49.

72. <http://www.philological.bham.ac.uk/Nero/intro.html>, section 43.

73. V, p. 158 (Perseus, *Satire*, III. 69–72, 67 — i.e. Montaigne has rearranged the order of the lines).

74. Gournay's prose translation preserves this opposition, but replaces 'te' with the first-person plural: 'Ce qu'il est licite de souhaitter; quelle utilité git en la pecune gravée: ce qu'il est seant de faire pour les proches cheris, et pour la patrie: quels Dieu nous commande d'estre: quels nous sommes en effect: quelle est nostre charge au monde, et pourquoy nous naissons'; *Essais*, 1617, p. 1001.

75. *The Essayes*, 1603, p. 75.

76. V, p. 864 (*Aeneid*, VIII. 383).

77. *The Essayes*, 1603, p. 519. In contrast, Gournay's prose translation ('Mere je te requires des armes pour mon fils') echoes the poetic simplicity of the Latin.

78. Hamlin, *Montaigne's English Journey*, p. 66.

79. [Which the English translator rendered by these two lines [...]. We could not say the same thing so openly in French; and if it were dressed up more delicately, it would make a ridiculous contrast with what Montaigne adds immediately afterwards]; Ovid, *Amores*, I. 5. 24.

CHAPTER 10

Montaigne beyond the Rhine: The *Essais* in the Work of Christoph Besold

John O'Brien

Seven times rector of the University of Tübingen, the city in which he was born, Christoph Besold (1577–1638) belongs to an important subset of readers of the *Essais* in early modern Europe: the legal profession.[1] In his large number of works of juridical, political, and theological learning, he quotes from or refers to the essayist over 100 times, always in French even though his own writings are in Latin. From the page numbers that he scrupulously includes on most occasions in his quotations and references, it is clear that he owned one of the early seventeenth-century editions of the *Essais*. The pattern of his publications suggest that the likeliest is either the 1608 or the 1611 French edition of the *Essais*.[2]

The purpose of this chapter will be to discuss the distinctive contribution Montaigne makes to Besold's work by examining key instances of his occurrence. As we shall see, such occurrences not only provide an insight into a crucial moment in the history of reading, but also have a larger philosophical rationale. In the process, the transit of the *Essais* will emerge not just as a passing through, nor even a transmission of conceptual positions or materials for study and writing, important though these are, but as a momentum which involves their reframing. Besold offers a particularly significant example of this notion of transit, precisely because he has a strong sense of belonging to an intellectual tradition reaching back to Montaigne, while nonetheless remodelling his author for his own specific context and needs. His attempt to combine these two aspects results in tensions that are indicative of historical change.

Besold's high regard for the French writer comes through constantly in his writings. The essayist is 'magnus Montanus' [the great Montaigne] or 'Magnus Michaël Montanus' [the great Michel de Montaigne],[3] 'Gallorum Socrates' [the French Socrates],[4] 'seculi nostri inter Philosophos Phœnix' [the philosophical phoenix of our age].[5] There is more than personal admiration at stake here. Two of the descriptors also adumbrate a view of him as a philosopher of a particular kind. Montaigne as a French Socrates is a special variant on Montaigne as Thales, Lipsius's sobriquet which a number of early modern writers quote.[6] Some understanding of what this idea means to Besold is provided by his comment in the *Specimen locorum communium philosophiæ* of 1626, where an entry entitled 'Philosophia. Eruditio' (Philosophy. Learning) runs as follows:

> Cùm philosophia studium sapientiæ sit; necesse est, ut continuus labor existat: Et nec eam Socrates habebat pro arte, sed tantùm pro exercitio quodam; omnia refutans, nihil probans. Aliud est studium Theologiæ, quod Socrates certum statuebat; & de eo, à communi antiquâ persuasione, ratiocinabatur. vide omninò Lactantium, *lib.3.cap.2.* quod & ubivis intendere videtur Michaël Montanus: *in Gallicis exercitationib. suis.*[7]

> [Since philosophy is the love of wisdom, it necessarily involves a continuous activity. And nor did Socrates hold it to be an art, but only a sort of exercise; refuting everything, proving nothing. Quite different is the study of Theology, which Socrates considered certain; and he used to argue about it from long-established common opinion. See in general Lactantius book 3, chapter 2. Michel de Montaigne also seems to aim for this everywhere in his *Essais*.][8]

Recalling Cicero's definition of philosophy as the love of wisdom, but departing from him by disassociating human things from divine things,[9] Besold no less rejects Lactantius's condemnation of philosophy as idle conjecture by turning philosophy into a Socratic enquiry which is an exercise or an activity, not an art or a craft. Montaigne would agree. In what seems a precursor of Besold's 'omnia refutans, nihil probans', his essay II.12, 'Apologie de Raimond Sebond' [Apology for Raymond Sebond] similarly pictures Socrates as 'tousjours demandant et esmouvant la dispute, jamais l'arrestant, jamais satisfaisant' [always asking questions and stirring up discussion, never concluding, never satisfying] (V, p. 509; F, p. 458), while in I.30, 'De la moderation' [Of Moderation], Montaigne remarks that, in respect of human behaviour, philosophy and theology 'se meslent de tout' [enter in everywhere] (V, p. 198; F, p. 178), in the same way that Besold juxtaposes in this passage a theologian and a philosopher. A twofold picture thus emerges of Montaigne's project in Besold's thinking. It is conceived of as a Socratic practice of flexible scope, an 'exercitium' or 'exercitatio' echoed in the very Latin title he gives the *Essais*: *exercitationes*. Yet, secondly, Montaigne's discussion of theological topics is no less Socratic, in that it respects theology as certain and deploys 'communis antiqua persuasio'; his well-known theological conservatism now becomes an intelligible feature of his overall Socratic outlook. At the same time, however, Besold's use of the modal 'videtur' [seems] — 'intendere videtur' [seems to aim at this] — introduces a note of grammatical caution into the description; putting into practice the earlier 'nihil probans' [proving nothing], it refuses to resolve, preferring refutation to assertion as part of the exercise, *exercitium*, of which it is itself a linguistic illustration.

As a counterpart to this extract, the preface to *Principium et finis politicæ doctrinæ*, published in 1625, a year before the *Specimen*, is less reserved in its approach. Here Besold speaks in his own name and of his own task:

> Adhuc dum versor in novorum Academicorum Schola: Quæro omnia, dubitans plerunque & mihi diffidens. Sæpè non tàm id sensi, quod dictum à me est: quàm exercere ingenium volui, materiæ difficultate. vide Montaig. lib.2.cap.12.fol.m.467.&c.&.fol.480. Pherecides morti appropinquans, Thaleti sua scripta commendavit: de iis ita sensit, nullam ea certitudinem continere,

quâ sibimetipsi satisfacere possint. Idem ego censeo de meis. Acquiesco solùm in perpetuo Ecclesiæ vetustioris consensu: sed eum adhuc indago.[10]

[While I am still at the school of the New Academics: I search into everything, doubting most things and mistrusting myself. Often, it is not so much that I have believed what I have said as that I wanted to exercise my wits on the difficulty of the material. See Montaigne book 2, chapter 12, page 467 in my copy etc. and page 480. Pherecydes drawing close to death entrusted his writings to Thales: his opinion of them was they contained no certainty with which he might be satisfied. I think the same about my writings. I assent only to the unbroken agreement of the older Church: but I still enquire into it.]

With its dense textual echoes and patterning, this passage is altogether a much more complex exercise than its neighbour, not least because it also constitutes one of the rare episodes in self-reflection in Besold's entire corpus. The references to Montaigne provide a way into his thinking. Both are to the 'Apologie de Raymond Sebond', but Besold reverses the order in which they appear in the 'Apologie', opening his statement with the later passage:

Cicero mesme, qui deuoit au sçavoir tout son vaillant, Valerius dit que sur sa vieillesse il commença à desestimer les lettres. Et pendant qu'il les traictoit, c'estoit sans obligation d'aucun party: suiuant ce qui luy sembloit probable, tantost en l'vne secte, tantost en l'autre: se tenant tousiours sous la dubitation de l'Academie. *Dicendum est, sed ita vt nihil affirmem: quaeram omnia, dubitans plerumque & mihi diffidens.* (1608/1611, 468; V, p. 501)

[As for Cicero himself, who owed all his worth to learning, Valerius says that in his old age he began to lose his esteem for letters. And while he practised them, it was without obligation to any party, following what seemed probable to him now in one sect, now in another, keeping himself always in Academic doubt. *I must speak, but in such a way as to affirm nothing; I shall search into all things, doubting most things and mistrusting myself.*] (F, pp. 370–71)

The Latin quotation is from Cicero's *De divinatione* II. 8, where Cicero is replying to his brother Quintus, but Besold detaches it from its original context, which is suppressed or at best summarily represented by the phrase '[a]dhuc dum versor in novorum Academicorum Schola' [while I am still at the School of the New Academics]. He then re-attaches it to a quite different quotation from a different author embedded in another, later part of the 'Apologie', where Montaigne complains that with philosophical sects such as the 'nouuelle Academique',

n'ayans rien trouué de si caché dequoy ils n'ayent voulu parler, il leur est souuent force de forger des conjectures foibles & folles, non qu'ils les prinssent eux mesmes pour fondement, ne pour establir quelque verité, mais pour l'exercice de leur estude: *Non tam id sensisse, quod dicerent, quàm exercere ingenia materiæ difficultate videntur voluisse.* (1608/1611, 480; V, p. 512)

[having found nothing so occult that they did not want to talk about it, they often had to forge weak and foolish conjectures; not that they took themselves for a foundation, or to establish any truth, but for the exercise of their study. *They seemed not so much to believe what they said as to want to exercise their wits on the difficulty of the matter.*] (F, p. 461)

Quintilian II. 17. 4 is the source of the Latin quotation here.

The next phase of the Besold extract, involving an anecdote about Pherecydes, paraphrases a slightly longer passage in Montaigne, as follows:

> Pherecydes, l'vn des sept sages, escrivant à Thales, comme il expiroit, I'ay, dit il, ordonné aux miens, apres qu'ils m'auront enterré de t'apporter mes escrits. S'ils contentent & toy & les autres Sages, publie les: sinon, supprime les. Ils ne contiennent nulle certitude qui me satisface à moy-mesme. Aussi ne fay-ie pas profession de sçauoir la verité, ny d'y atteindre (1608/1611, 467–68; V, p. 501).
>
> [Pherecydes, one of the Seven Sages, writing to Thales as he was dying, said: 'I have ordered my friends, after they have buried me, to bring you my writings. If they satisfy you and the other sages, publish them; if not, suppress them they contain no certainty that satisfies myself. Nor do I profess to know the truth and to attain it.'] (F, p. 370)

When this passage re-appears in Besold, the German jurist adds a closing comment about enquiring into the unbroken consensus of the Church. This takes Montaigne's text in an unforeseen direction; but it will herald a specific recontextualization of the essayist — in the theological sphere — whose importance will be considered later.

This whole passage in the *Principium et finis* is of typical Besoldian complexity and displays a set of clearly defined technical features. In the first place, it composes a mosaic or marquetry which brings together passages not previously immediately connected in Montaigne in such a way as to forge them into a new coherent whole with a revised purpose. This technique was common to legal writing in the early seventeenth century and in respect of Montaigne, the dominant model was Pierre Charron. When, for example, the Toulouse *parlementaire* La Roche Flavin composed his own marquetry of Montaigne passages in his *Treze Livres des Parlemens de France* of 1617, a number had already appeared in Charron, and he not infrequently quotes Charron rather than directly citing Montaigne.[11] In following that model, Besold implicitly thinks of his purpose as that of the philosopher-jurist, according to a tradition of which Montaigne was considered to be a significant modern predecessor. Secondly, starting with the initial 'versor', the first-person pronoun now co-ordinates all the diverse quotations, whose syntax is reworked as necessary to foreground the singular voice of the lawyer-philosopher. It is no longer Cicero or Quintilian or Montaigne who predominates, even though they are plainly visible, but Besold, and the composite passages of which this extract is composed are marshalled into activity by the constantly repeated 'ego' of the writer ('versor', 'quæro', 'sensi', 'censeo', 'acquiesco', 'indago'). Thirdly, the highly allusive quality of this extract develops the same technique that Montaigne himself employs. While Besold sends his readers back to the original contexts by specifying pages in a particular edition, his intricate surface manipulations of these underlying texts clearly rely on the reader's intimate knowledge and understanding of the *Essais*. In a sense, Besold seeks to out-Montaigne Montaigne; but he is not the only one of the essayist's readers to do so.

The technical versatility of this passage points, in turn, to its intellectual purpose. It represents a conceptualization of Besold's role as a writer and thinker, but also equips him for his task as a particular type of investigator. Of prime importance here is the role played by the New Academy. In declaring himself a student at their School, Besold seems to make no clear distinction between Academic and Pyrrhonian scepticism; but, as Schmitt has shown, this was by no means uncommon in early modern writing.[12] The pairing of Cicero and Pherecydes, under the umbrella of New Academy, may seem equally disconcerting, as only Cicero could be considered, strictly speaking, the classical representative of this sect.[13] However, the inclusion of Pherecydes widens its ambit to embrace one of the Seven Sages who regards his own writings as not attaining certainty and truth. The context of the quotation from *De divinatione* also shows Cicero himself practising Academic doubt by switching to and fro between tenets held by different philosophical schools. The passage from Besold's *Specimen*, quoted at the beginning of this chapter, can also be brought in at this point. Socrates, pictured there as proving nothing and refuting everything, was reclaimed by Arcesilaus, the founder of the New Academy, as a Sceptic with the mission to refute: 'the outcome of philosophical enquiry is the elimination of poorly founded beliefs. This is accomplished by arguing against anything anyone is willing to defend'.[14] Cicero likewise traces that New Academy practice of refutation back to Socrates and has Varro say of him in the *Academica*, 'ita disputat ut nihil affirmet ipse refellat alios' [he argues in such a way that he himself affirms nothing but refutes others] (I. 16).[15] Echoing that description from the *Academica*, a work familiar to his readers, Besold attaches himself to that same tradition, in which, for him, Montaigne is the key figure adumbrating in his work a history of Sceptical philosophy, a method of enquiry and a manner of writing: all three are compacted together in these two passages. In Besold's reworking of the classical philosophical traditions, it is Montaigne who, as the French Socrates, is the modern embodiment of all these characteristics.

Nothing like a full philosophical programme is set out in Besold; these quoted passages are the closest to a broader conceptualization of his outlook that he provides. Like other lawyers who read the French essayist, such as Bernard Automne and Claude Expilly in France,[16] he prefers to engage pragmatically with his author, using him as a source of quotations and allusions in order to substantiate or refute particular points of view. Nevertheless, in the light of the two passages we have studied already, a number of other statements in Besold's *œuvre* now become intelligible. In the *Politica* of 1620, for example, he sketches a one-sentence alignment of classical philosophers in whom he clearly discerns an affinity: 'Undè Socrates nihil se scire professus est, Phyrro [sic] de omnibus dubitavit: Democritus in puteo veritatem submersam esse dixit' [Whence Socrates declared that he knew nothing and Pyrrho doubted about all matters; Democritus said that truth was at the bottom of a well].[17] What connects these thinkers is the rather loose association of ignorance, doubt, and a truth that is out of reach, in the same way that the earlier anecdote about Pherecydes highlights the question of uncertainty. Montaigne is credited with that same Socratic ignorance in *De verae philosophiae fundamento* of 1630. In that work, Besold complains about those who deny knowledge either as necessary or even possible and who impose limits on knowing. 'Exemplum si petis,' he continues, 'profero Magni Michaëlis Montani: qui ipse fatetur, in omnibus se versatum, in nullo aliquid scire. Sed malim viri tanti inscitiâ fruisci, quàm imaginariam eruditionem sciolorum possidere' [If you want an example, I mention the great Michel de Montaigne, who himself admits that he was schooled in every discipline, but knows nothing about any. But I would prefer to enjoy the ignorance of such a great man than to possess the imaginary learning of those with only a smattering of knowledge].[18] A printed note in the margin of *De verae philosophiae fundamento* at that point refers the reader to I.26, 'De l'institution des enfans' [Of the Education of Children], at the beginning of which Montaigne does indeed admit that the cursory knowledge he gained as a child left him with 'un peu de chaque chose et rien du tout' [a little of everything and nothing thoroughly] (V, p. 145; F, p. 129). Yet, notice how the passage displays a shift in Besold's attitude. At the outset, Montaigne is cited as an instance of the trend of which Besold disapproves, with a specific allusion to the *Essais* to support his claim; but then, as the tell-tale epithet 'magni' (great) hints, the perspective switches and the extract ends with praise of Montaigne's ignorance. A few pages earlier in the same work comes a quotation from III.13, 'De l'experience' [Of Experience], with the comment: '*De l'experience que j'ay de moy, je trouve assez, dequoy me faire sage, si j'estois bon escholier*, inquit Gallorum Socrates, Michaël Montanus' ['Of the experience I have of myself, I find enough with which to make myself wise, if I were a good student', says the French Socrates, Michel de Montaigne].[19] 'Sagesse', 'sapientia', 'wisdom' is the philosopher's traditional goal and by joining together Socrates and Montaigne with education and experience, Besold's praise of ignorance which follows is drawn into the same ambit, transforming Montaigne's personal admission into a philosophical avowal.

How does this philosophical sense of Montaigne as a Socratic enquirer affect Besold's use of him in the course of his writings as a whole? Two principal areas will be examined: theology and politics.[20] In the case of the first of these, the need to reconcile a philosophical mission with a confessional identity was paramount. In the passage from *Principium et finis* quoted earlier, we saw that Besold closes with the statement that he assents to the unbroken consensus of the older Church, but nonetheless enquires into it: that closing rider gains in significance in the light of Besold's understanding of Montaigne's philosophical project, for the theological implications, or the potential theological implications, of the *Essais* are sometimes uppermost in Besold's mind. The *Specimen*, for example, is remarkable for including two of Montaigne's most famous pronouncements: 'Certes, c'est un subject merveilleusement vain, divers, et ondoyant, que l'homme. Il est malaisé d'y fonder jugement constant et uniforme' [Truly man is a marvellously vain, diverse and undulating subject. It is hard to found any constant and uniform judgement on him] (V, p. 9; F, p. 5); and: 'Chacun regarde devant soy; moy je regarde dedans moy' [Everyone looks in front of him; as for me, I look inside of me] (V, p. 657; F, p. 606). Neither has theological implications in its original context, but Besold repositions them within a framework of *imitatio Christi* combined with the Lutheran principle of justification, classifying the first under the heading 'Judicare proximum, et cuncta, ut debemus' [To judge our neighbour and all things as we ought] and the second under 'Interna conversatio' [Inward conversation].[21] In *De consilio politico*, he uses the French writer as a weapon against the dangers of atheism, adducing him on two occasions in a short sequence of axioms on this topic. Francesco Guicciardini is the target in one: 'Species Atheismi est, omnia facta, omnesque eventus, rationi alicui politicæ assignare: eoque nomine peccare Guicciardinum, prudentissimum aliàs, civilisque disciplinæ callentissimum scriptorem; notat Montanus. *lib.2.des essais. cap.10.*' [It is a kind of atheism to attribute all deeds and all events to some political reason; and on that account Montaigne notes in book 2 of the *Essais*, chapter 10, that Guicciardini goes astray, although in other respects a very learned writer and a great expert in political thought].[22] Montaigne's criticism of Guicciardini comes after he has recognized that the Italian conceals nothing out of hatred, favour, or vanity. He then expresses reservations:

> J'ay aussi remerqué cecy, que de tant d'ames et effects qu'il juge, de tant de mouvemens et conseils, il n'en rapporte jamais un seul à la vertu, religion et conscience, comme si ces parties là estoyent du tout esteintes au monde. (1608/1611, 386; V, p. 419)

> [I have also noted this, that of so many souls and actions that he judges, so many motives and plans, he never refers a single one to virtue, religion, and conscience, as if these qualities were wholly extinct in the world.] (F, p. 370)

Montaigne does not specifically ascribe Guicciardini's characteristics to atheism and the trio he lists includes virtue and conscience along with religion; he also adds — which Besold omits — that Guicciardini's penchant in this regard may indicate that he judged everyone according to his own tastes and preferences. Elsewhere, Besold draws on I.27, 'C'est folie de rapporter le vray et le faux à nostre suffisance' [It Is Folly to Measure the True and False by our Own Capacity] for evidence that to believe in nothing other than what conforms to reason is the way closest to atheism ('proxima est ad Atheismum via').[23] On this occasion, Besold does not specify a page number, but he may have in mind Montaigne's attack on those who disbelieve miracles in comments such as the following: 'C'est une hardiesse dangereuse et de consequence, outre l'absurde temerité qu'elle traine quant et soy, de mespriser ce que nous ne concevons pas' [It is a dangerous and fateful presumption, besides the absurd temerity that it implies, to disdain what we do not comprehend] (V, p. 181; F, p. 163). There is no mention of atheism in this Montaignian context, except perhaps by implication; the point is the obedience we owe the laws of ecclesiastical polity. In both instances, Besold reads the essayist according to concerns about ecclesiastical orthodoxy and confessional identity.

Such theological concerns could affect Besold's view of Montaigne himself. In the theological perspective, he reflects in a different way on the French writer's Sceptical outlook:

> Atheorum etiam proprium est, statuere omnia esse incerta: ut Pyrrhonici faciunt; cuncta defendere, omnia evertere [...]. Tales etiam sunt auctores, qui quæque certissima convellere, & in dubium vocare nituntur, quemadmodum Sanchez. *in tr. Quod nil scitur.* Certè quod invitus dico, multa habet ad Atheismum declinantia Michael Montanus, *in libro des essais.* Gallorum Socrates, & quem summis laudibus evehit Lipsius, *in Epistol. ad eum scriptis.* Hic certè perpetuò dubitat, jus naturæ rationale negat, gentes solo naturæ ductu viventes, quales fuêre olim Amiricani [*sic*], aliis præfert: sensibus certitudinem adimit, brutis rationem adscribit; sed tandem tentatio Atheismi est felicitas impiorum, *Psalm.73.vers.10.&c.*[24]

[It is also the characteristic of atheists to decree that all things are uncertain, as the Pyrrhonians do; to defend everything and to overturn all things [...]. Such are the writers who strive to tear up certainty and call it into doubt, like Sanchez in the treatise *That Nothing is Known*. Certainly, though I say so unwillingly, Michel de Montaigne, the French Socrates, so very highly extolled by Lipsius in his letters to him, has much in his *Essais* that tends towards atheism. He certainly constantly doubts, he denies the rational law of nature and prefers peoples living under the sole guidance of nature, such as the Americans once did, to others; he deprives the senses of certainty and attributes reason to animals; but in the end the temptation of atheism is the happiness of the impious, Psalm 73 v. 10 etc.]

The key term here is 'doubt'. *Aporetike* is one of the terms, along with *skeptike* and *ephektike*, that is used in Sextus Empiricus to describe the philosophical activity of Ancient Sceptics. In Henri Estienne's Latin 1562 translation of Sextus (which is in fact a reprint of Traversari's of 1433), this term and its associated verb, *aporein*, are translated as 'dubitatoria' (doubtful) and 'dubitare' (to doubt): Scepticism is 'doubtful' in the sense that it enquires into everything without final resolution.[25] Yet the origin of this Latin translation stretches further back. It is Cicero who, in the *Academica*, introduces the term 'dubitatio' (doubt) (e.g. *Academica*, I. 17, 'Socraticam dubitationem' [Socratic doubt]) and the verb 'dubito' (to doubt) (e.g. *Academica*, II. 8, 106 and II. 11) into his discussion of Scepticism. Perhaps under his influence, the idea caught on, and doubt is certainly the hallmark of Pyrrhonian Scepticism for Montaigne. One of the most famous passages in the 'Apologie' characterizes Pyrrhonism in just that way (V, p. 503), but Montaigne makes it clear in context that doubt is related to Sceptical contradiction-as-refutation and to the preference for non-assertion. Modern critics such as Tournon have also emphasized that doubt for Montaigne has to be understood strictly in the context of Pyrrhonian *zetesis* and not outside of that framework.[26] In historical terms, however, even before the time Besold comes to publish in the early seventeenth century, Academic and Pyrrhonian doubt has become associated with an active destruction of certainty in the religious sense and writers such as Francisco Sanchez and, earlier, Sebastian Castellio are taken as evidence of that tendency.[27] Indeed, in writing elsewhere about education and literature, Besold also connects Sanchez's name with atheism, insofar as, Besold argues, he seeks to destroy knowledge and to claim that nothing can be known, although he also notes that Montaigne defends Pyrrhonism.[28] In the present context, Montaigne's name is added to that of Sanchez regretfully, almost as an afterthought, and Besold rounds off his reflections with a closing gloss from Scripture.

The list of dubious opinions Besold discerned here in the essayist was nonetheless to be broadly echoed in some other writers of any religious persuasion, in the context of the essayist's alleged libertinism.[29] By way of comparison with Besold, it is worth instancing occasions when the 'Apologie' features in that respect. For example, in 1651, the Lutheran legal scholar, Kaspar Klock, could be found maintaining as follows:

Providentiam Divinam si quis removeat, & Naturæ omnia tribuere velit, istum Atheum esse omninò; quo & illa Lucretii intendunt:

Corpoream naturam animi esse necesse est,
Corpor[e]is quoniam telis, ictúque laborat.
Idemque suggerit Iul. Cæsar Vanninus [...] ut & Michael Montanus *libr. 2. des Essais. cap. 12. fol. 519.* quorum hic atheismi subtilioris suspectus.

[If anyone removes divine providence and wishes to attribute everything to Nature, he is an utter atheist. These lines of Lucretius move in that direction: 'The nature of the mind is necessarily corporeal, since it labours under physical cuts and blows.' Giulio Cesare Vanini suggests the same [...], as does also Michel de Montaigne in book 2 of the *Essais*, chapter 12, p. 519. The second of these is suspected of a subtler atheism.]³⁰

These lines of Lucretius are quoted in the 'Apologie' by Montaigne (V, p. 550) as a way of highlighting the troubled, uncertain nature of the human mind ('animus'), but the page reference given by Klock — to an edition identical to or with the same pagination as 1608 — carries a printed marginal summary that refers not to the mind, but to the soul ('âme', 'anima' in Latin rather than 'animus'). Klock may thus have thought that Montaigne was citing Lucretius in support of a material view of the soul, a clearly heterodox opinion. Interestingly, he also claims shortly before this passage that he is merely quoting Besold's *De majestate*, but in fact in that work Besold attributes to Giulio Cesare Vanini the heterodox views summarized by Klock without once mentioning Montaigne.³¹ Klock thus provides a composite account, partly drawn from Besold and partly from his own reading. Evoking Vanini alongside Montaigne steers the essayist into dangerous waters, but it is not without precedent at that point in the seventeenth century: in a letter of 1647, Guez de Balzac makes the same connection, more expressly than François Garasse, for example, who had associated Vanini with Charron, but not Montaigne.³² On the Catholic side of the confessional divide, the Franciscan Jean Boucher (? — 1631) was no less forthright. In *Les Triomphes de la religion chrestienne* of 1628, he referred to one of the same pages of the 'Apologie' as Besold in *Principium et finis* and in the same or a similar edition, but with the opposite opinion. Objecting to Montaigne's description of God as 'recevant et prenant en bonne part l'honneur et la reverence que les humains luy rendoient soubs quelque visage, sous quelque nom et en quelque maniere que ce fut' [accepting and taking in good part the honour and reverence that human beings rendered him, under whatever aspect, under whatever name, in whatever manner] (1608/1611, 480; V, p. 513; F, p. 462), he counters that this statement encourages heretics, schismatics, and pagans to persist in the error of their ways.³³ He then attempts to turn Montaigne's reasoning against him when he quotes the later argument from the 'Apologie' that it is a strange fancy to pay for divine goodness with our afflictions (1608/1611, 489; V, p. 522; F, p. 471).³⁴ Contextually, it is clear that these are two quite separate points, but for Boucher they are proof of the way in which Montaigne 'a mal mené la Religion' [has mistreated religion] (ibid.). Klock and Boucher were not the only early modern readers who found the 'Apologie' of theological interest,³⁵ but by comparison Besold's criticisms, while clearly reflecting his disquiet, seem mild and are restricted to one part of one work.

If theology holds an important place in Besold's dealings with Montaigne, a much larger group of quotations from and references to the *Essais* relates to the political sphere. While the overarching context in Besold is that of the debate between absolutism and constitutionalism, politics also covers a broad spectrum whose sub-areas include military science and civic life as well as statecraft.[36] It may well be that Besold, without expressly stating it, saw a parallel between Montaigne's experience of the Wars of Religion and his own during the Thirty Years War and certainly many of his references to Montaigne here occur in the framework of war and warfare. For example, he derives from the *Essais* a sharp sense of the fickleness of Fortune. At one level, fortified by his reading of I.34, 'La Fortune se rencontre souvent au train de la raison' [Fortune Is Often Met in the Path of Reason], he resists submission to Fortune as incompatible with the Christian's obedience to God.[37] His more general view, however, acknowledges the ubiquity of the very force he opposes. Thus in the *Dissertatio de arte iureque belli* of 1624, two quotations from I.48, 'Des destriers' [Of War Horses], both along the same lines, emphasize the uncertainty of technology. The pistol, for instance:

> Il est bien plus apparent de s'asseurer d'une espée que nous tenons au poing, que du boulet qui eschappe de nostre pistole, en laquelle il y a plusieurs pieces, (la poudre, la pierre, le rouet,) desquelles la moindre qui viendra à faillir, vous fera faillir vostre fortune. (V, p. 290)

> [It is much more sensible to rely on a sword that we hold in our hand than on the bullet that escapes out of our pistol, in which there are many parts (— the powder, the flint, the lock —) the least of which, by failing, will make your fortune fail.] (F, p. 256)[38]

Even the horse can seem a unnecessary complication: 'vous engagez (quoy que die Chrysantez en Xenophon) vostre valeur et vostre fortune à celle de vostre cheval: ses playes & sa mort, tirent la vostre en consequence; son effroy ou sa fougue vous rendent ou temeraire ou lâche' [(No matter what Chrysanthas says in Xenophon) you stake your valor and your fortune on that of your horse; his wounds and his death bring on yours as a consequence; his fright or his impetuosity makes you either rash or cowardly] (V, p. 289; F, p. 211).[39] And from this 'elegant formulation', Besold draws his conclusion: 'Ac certa & secura multò magis est stataria peditum pugna' [Fighting on foot is much more certain and secure] (ibid.).[40] 'More certain and secure' might seem just a sensible reaction, but Besold's point here is also Montaigne's: the horse, like the pistol, is to be seen as the embodiment of fortune, not a taken-for-granted necessity of modern warfare. It is that basic uncertainty and fickleness which colours the German writer's approach, as it does his French source.

Unsurprisingly in this context, I.47, 'De l'incertitude de nostre jugement' [Of the Uncertainty of our Judgement], attracts Besold's attention and it informs his attitude towards a specific question of military tactics:

> Sed pro eo an hostis sit domi expectandus, Rationes sunt ex utraque parte, quas adducit Michaël Montanus, *lib. 1. des essais, cap. 47.fol.m.261.&c.* qui tandem concludit: nil hîc certi statui posse, cùm in bello præsertim, etiam optimè deliberata, sortiantur tristem eventum. *Nous avons bien accoustume* [sic] *de dire, avec raison, que les evenemens & yssues dependent notamment en la guerre pour la plus part de la fortune: la quelle ne se veut pas renger & assujettir à nostre discours & prudence.* (= V, p. 286)

[But on the issue of whether the enemy is to be awaited on home ground, there are arguments on both sides, as set out by Michel de Montaigne in book 1 of the *Essais*, chapter 47, p. 261 etc in my copy, and his eventual conclusion is that there is no possible certain resolution on this question since, in war especially, even the most carefully laid plans may turn out badly. 'Thus we are quite wont to say, with reason, that events and outcomes depend for the most part, especially in war, on Fortune, who will not fall into line and subject herself to our reason and foresight.'] (F, p. 253)[41]

The crucial features that Besold identifies in his reading of 'De l'incertitude' are its deployment of arguments *in utramque partem* (on both sides of the question: 'ex utraque parte' is Besold's expression) and the ultimate impossibility of any secure solution to the problems the chapter raises. Both features tally not only with the concept of fortune, but with those of equipollence and uncertainty that characterize Montaigne's thinking in Sceptical mode as well as Besold's. The terminology the German jurist uses in this passage does not need to be specified as Sceptical, for its very choice combined with the presence of Montaigne disposes his reader in that direction. In other places, Besold can make greater assumptions still. When discussing how to deal with particularly baffling situations, he simply advises: 'Attamen in rebus planè dubiis, licet ἐπεχεῖν' [Nevertheless, in matters that are completely doubtful, one may suspend one's judgement].[42] The Sceptical lexicon of this whole sentence and the choice of ἐπεχεῖν (to suspend one's judgement), one of the key Pyrrhonist notions, confirm the intertextual reminiscence. Nothing in the original context prepares for the sudden introduction of such terminology, which is assumed to be part of the intellectual *koine* of the educated reader. At the level of conceptual approach as well as compositional technique, the influence of the *Essais* can be felt, even when, as in the last example, there is no express reference to Montaigne's work.

With its Montaignian colouring, Besold's thinking about uncertainty similarly affects his view of statecraft, especially the issues of counsel, forethought, and planning ahead. These too are thought to be susceptible to Fortune. In *De consilio politico*, this point is phrased as a general one, through a series of aphorisms spread over successive pages: it is impossible to set down a rule to which Fortune does not present an exception; human forethought is futile, as Fortune maintains her grip over events; anyone wishing to make provision for his plans must allow room for Fortune. In each case, the aphorism is accompanied by precise quotations from Montaigne illustrating the same principles.[43] It is against this background that we should situate Besold's preference for continuity over change in matters of government. One of many statements of his views on this matter is likewise to be found in *De consilio politico*, quoting from II.17, 'De la praesumption' [Of Presumption]:

Et magis conservando, quàm immutando statui studere debemus. [...] *Et pourtant, selon mon humeur, és affaires publiques, il n'est aucun si mauvais train, pourveu, qu'il aye de l'aage, & de la constance, qui ne vaille mieux, que le changement, & le remuement, &c.* Quæ est sententia magni Montani.*2.des essais.c.17.f.m.629.*

[And we must strive more to preserve than to change the state. [...] 'And, therefore, to my mind, in public affairs there is no course so bad, provided that it is old and stable, that is not better than change and commotion' etc. (F, p.

604). Which is the opinion of the great Montaigne, book 2 of the *Essais*, chapter 17, p. 629 in my copy.] (= V, p. 655)[44]

In general political terms, Besold advocates a mixed sovereignty, especially in his *De statu reipublicae mixto* of 1614 and 1625,[45] yet he acknowledges, for example, that to live under a monarchy is considered the highest form of freedom in France ('in Galliis, summam esse Libertatem, vivere sub Rege, Michel de Montaigne, *lib.1.des Essais, cap.42.f.mihi.244*').[46] The specific page reference he makes here, to I.42, 'De l'inequalité qui est entre nous' [Of the Inequality That Is Between Us], misreads Montaigne's point, however. The essayist is arguing that the French gentleman living far from court, in Brittany for instance, can live in freedom because he hears of the king hardly twice in his life; if he leads a retired existence of this kind, 'il est aussi libre que le Duc de Venise' [he is a free as the Doge of Venice] (V, p. 266; F, p. 236). What is a qualified statement in Montaigne becomes an absolute statement in Besold. This is not the only such occasion. In the same work, *De reipublicæ* [...] *comparatione*, Besold recognizes that Montaigne prefers Epaminondas to other princes and leaders and then exclaims: 'Quot quæso, viros virtute præstantes, similes alios, laudare possunt Democratiæ?' [How many men pre-eminent in virtue and others similar can democracies praise, prithee?].[47] Democracy for Besold is an unmixed, absolute constitution, little more than the rule of the mob, devoid of virtue, and he now recruits Montaigne to the cause of a specific political idea, turning the essayist's own political conservatism into a deeper hostility to particular forms of government. By extension, some of Besold's models for civic life and princely government are to be found overseas. He uses Montaigne's Brazilians to exemplify how some think the rule of the many is preferable to the rule of one, even though the latter is, in his opinion, clearly the better option,[48] how the Golden Age was to be found among the 'Americani' before the coming of the Spanish and exists among the 'Meridionales' even today,[49] and how kings used to lead their troops into battle, a custom still observed 'apud Canibales' (among the Cannibals).[50] This last point exercised Besold on more than one occasion: should the king fight at the head of his troops? It was a well-known 'indeterminate' question, with arguments *pro et contra*. On this point, the German writer referred his reader to II.21, 'Contre la faineantise' [Against Do-nothingness], where a post-1588 addition debates precisely this issue, maintaining that it is inconsistent with a prince's office and standing to delegate the fighting to another (V, pp. 676–77).[51] As in Montaigne himself, changing perspective — moving abroad, seeing things from elsewhere — allows Besold to comment in general terms on the practices of contemporary German society, though with a more limited degree of critique than is usual in his French model.

This brief survey of Besold's debt to Montaigne has necessarily omitted a number of spheres where the essayist's influence can be distinctly traced; marriage, medicine, embassies, and parleys are among them. Taken all together, they indicate the German jurist's absorption of the *Essais* at the levels of intellectual approach and of technique and composition. The Montaigne who emerges from his work presents not so much an integrated portrait as a series of snapshots adjusted to the needs of any particular context. The *Essais* are at once fragmented and dispersed among Besold's large corpus and yet re-organized and systematized in order to feed a new set of ideas. Besold's Montaigne is both prismatic and polymorphic; he is adapted to particular perspectives and angles of vision, but also sponsors a large variety of uses and forms. Some underlying connecting themes are nonetheless apparent, notably the Sceptical strain of thinking Besold adopts or highlights on particular occasions (but is never a key to unlock all of his work). Yet more is at stake in Besold's use of Montaigne than personal devotion to a favourite author. Ian Hunter provides the larger backcloth against which to view the German jurist's activity here. He argues that, far from demonstrating the independence of early modern German philosophy from confessional or political identities, the competing programmes for philosophical training derived intrinsically from such identities.[52] Philosophy was, he claims, a set of cognitive exercises aligned with 'practices of the self whose outcome is the special and prestigious *persona* of the philosopher'.[53] Besold's incorporation of the *Essais* into his array of works can be viewed from the same standpoint. First and foremost, his emphasis on Montaigne as the embodiment of Socrates now takes on its full meaning: in the same way that Socrates offered Montaigne a philosophical persona, so now the French essayist performs the same function for Besold. Equally, in the telling passage from the preface of *Principium et finis*, he articulates his own self-perception of his role and purpose in the light of Montaigne's ideas, while quotations from the *Essais* among the philosophico-theological aphorisms of the *Specimen* or in the political doctrine of *De consilio politico* or *De reipublicae* [...] *comparatione* are essential, not incidental, features in 'the cultivation of an intellectual deportment required to accede to the truth',[54] of which *De verae philosophiae fundamento*, also informed by reading Montaigne, is one summative expression. Such a framework is a distinctive expression of Montaigne's transit through German juridical thought and Besold was not alone in seeing the French essayist in this way. Later in the seventeenth century, Samuel von Pufendorf made extensive reference to the *Essais* in his *De jure naturae et gentium*;[55] this has still to receive proper study, as indeed has the full story of the lawyers' understanding and use of Montaigne in early modern Europe. Besold's special contribution to this story nonetheless allows us to glimpse some of the avenues that await further investigation.

Notes to Chapter 10

1. On Besold, see Barbara Zeller-Lorenz and Wolfang Zeller, 'Christoph Besold, 1577–1638. Polyhistor, gefragter Consiliator und umstrittener Konvertit', in *Lebensbilder zur Geschichte der Tübinger Juristenfakultät*, ed. Ferdinand Elsner (Tübingen: Mohr, 1977), pp. 9–18; Barbara Zeller-Lorenz, 'Christoph Besold (1577–1638) und die Klosterfrage', doctoral thesis, University of Tübingen, 1986; Horst Dreitzel, *Absolutismus und ständische Verfassung in Deutschland: Ein Beitrag zur Kontinuität und Diskontinuität des politischen Theorie in der frühen Neuzeit* (Mainz: Zabern, 1992); Bernhard Pahlmann, 'Christoph Besold', in *Deutsche und Europäische Juristen aus neun Jahrhunderten. Eine biographische Einführung in die Geschichte der Rechtswissenschaft*, ed. Jan Schröder und Gerd Kleinheyer (Heidelberg: Müller, 1996), pp. 56–59; and Christoph Strohm, 'Recht und Jurisprudenz im reformierten Protestantismus, 1550–1650', *Zeitschrift der Savigny-Stiftung für Rechtsgeschichte*, 123 (2006), 453–93.
2. The 1611 edition of the *Essais* was set from that of 1608: see R. A. Sayce and David Maskell, *A Descriptive Bibliography of Montaigne's 'Essais', 1580–1700* (London: Bibliographical Society,

1983), pp. 54–59 (1608) and 62–67 (1611). Besold must have purchased his copy of Montaigne before 1615, for he referred to his copy by page number in the first edition of *De aerario publico* in that year. The editions of 1608 and 1611 are the only two before 1615 which would fit the page numbers he gives. The catalogue of Besold's library in Harvard lists two editions of the *Essais*, but gives no indication of the publication year. I am grateful to William Stoneman of the Houghton Library, Harvard, for this information and for a photograph of the entries in question in MS Riant 5.

3. Christoph Besold, *De consilio politico axiomata aliquámmulta* (Tübingen: Wild, 1622), p. 107; *De verae philosophiae fundamento* (Tübingen: Brunnius, 1630), p. 24.

4. Besold, *De verae philosophiae fundamento*, p. 19.

5. Christoph Besold, *De nuptiis iuridico-politicus discursus* (Tübingen: Cellius, 1621), p. 6.

6. Dominique Baudier [Dominicus Baudius], *Epistolarum centuriæ tres* (Leiden: Van der Marse, 1636), p. 15, letter to Adriaan van Blijenburgh, undated [1588]: 'Michaël Montanus (quem Thaletem Gallicum appellat Thales noster Belgicus)'; Theodore van Tulden [Diodorus Tuldenus], *Dissertationum Socraticarum libri duo* (Leuven: Dormal, 1622), pp. 71–72: 'Michael Montanus ille [...] quem Thaletem Gallicum appellare Lipsius solebat'; François Langlois Francan, *Le Tombeau des romans* (Paris: Morlot, 1626), pp. 31–32: 'le sieur de Montagne, le Thales de nostre siecle, comme le nomme Lipsius'; Matthias Bernegger, *Diatribae in C. Suetonii Tranquilli C. Jul. Caesarem...* (Strasbourg: Typis Berneggerianis, 1654), p. 22: 'Michaël Montanus (Thaletem Gallicum hunc vocat Lips. miscellan. centur. 1. epist. 43)'.

7. Besold, *Specimen locorum communium philosophiæ*, in *Axiomata philosophico-theologica* (Strasbourg: Heirs of Zetzner, 1626), p. 347. Both here and elsewhere in this chapter, italics are original.

8. Unless otherwise stated, translations are my own.

9. Cicero, *De officiis*, II. 2: 'nec quidquam aliud est philosophia, si interpretari velis, praeter studium sapientiae. Sapientia autem est (ut a veteribus philosophis definitum est) rerum divinarum et humanarum causarumque quibus eae res continentur scientia' [philosophy, if you wish to translate it, is nothing other than the love of wisdom. Moreover, wisdom is — according to the old philosophical definition — the knowledge of matters human and divine and of the causes by which these things are controlled].

10. Christoph Besold, *Principium et finis politicæ doctrinæ* (Strasbourg: Heirs of Zetzner, 1625), preface, sig. A 2v.

11. See John O'Brien, 'Le Magistrat comme philosophe: La Roche Flavin, lecteur de Montaigne et de Charron', *Bulletin de la Société internationale des Amis de Montaigne*, 55.1 (2012), 221–34.

12. Charles Schmitt, *Cicero Scepticus. A Study of the Influence of the 'Academica' in the Renaissance* (The Hague: Nijhoff, 1972), pp. 7 and 74.

13. In addition to Schmitt's classic study and the article by J. R. Maia Neto, 'Academic Skepticism in Early Modern Philosophy', *Journal of the History of Ideas*, 58 (1997), 199–220, see Carlos Lévy, *Cicero academicus: recherches sur les 'Académiques' et sur la philosophie cicéronienne* (Rome: École française de Rome, 1992).

14. Harald Thorsrud, *Ancient Scepticism* (Berkeley: University of California Press, 2009), p. 43.

15. Similarly, in *Academica*, I. 46, Plato's work is described in the following terms: 'nihil affirmatur et in utramque partem multa disseruntur, de omnibus quaeritur, nihil certi dicitur' [nothing is affirmed, many arguments are advanced on either side, everything is under investigation and nothing is considered certain].

16. On both of these, see the articles by Michel Simonin, 'Bernard Automne (1564 — après 1628), témoin et lecteur de Montaigne', and Alessandra Preda, ' "Les siècles à venir te loueront à bon droit": Montaigne et Claude Expilly', both in 'La *Familia* de Montaigne', special issue ed. John O'Brien, *Montaigne Studies*, 13 (2001), 316–60 and 187–206.

17. Christoph Besold, *Politica* (Frankfurt: Cell, 1620), p. 6.

18. Besold, *De verae philosophiae fundamento*, p. 24.

19. Besold, *De verae philosophiae fundamento*, p. 19.

20. For the theological background in Besold, see Robert von Friedeburg, 'Church and State in Lutheran Lands, 1550–1675', in *Lutheran Ecclesiastical Culture 1550–1675*, ed. Robert Kolb (Leiden: Brill, 2008), pp. 387–409, especially 395–98.

21. Besold, *Specimen*, pp. 125 and 185; for the framework, see Stefania Salvadori, 'From Spiritual

Regeneration to Collective Reformation in the Writings of Christoph Besold and Johann Valentin Andreae', *Aries*, 14 (2014), 1–19 (p. 6).

22. Besold, *De consilio politico*, p. 135, no. 50.

23. Besold, *De consilio politico*, p. 138, no. 55.

24. Besold, *Dissertatio iuridico-politica de majestate* (Tübingen: Cell, 1625), sectio secunda 'De ecclesiastico majestatis jure', p. 104.

25. This feature can most easily be seen in the parallel Greek and Latin folio reprint of Sextus in the early seventeenth century: *Sexti Empirici opera quae exstant* (Geneva: Chouet, 1621), p. 2 D.

26. André Tournon, 'Doute', in *Dictionnaire de Michel de Montaigne*, ed. Philippe Desan (Paris: Champion, 2007), pp. 329–31; compare also Gianni Paganini, *Skepsis: le débat des modernes sur le scepticisme* (Paris: Vrin, 2008).

27. See Schmitt, *Cicero Scepticus*, pp. 64–65 on Théodore de Bèze's refutation of what Bèze perceives as Castellio's New Academic use of incomprehensibility (*akatalepsia*) in the sphere of religion.

28. Besold, 'De educatione', in *Discursi politici singulares de informatione et coactione subditorum* (Strasbourg: Heirs of Zetzner, 1626), pp. 3–107 (p. 28). Besold gives precise page references, once again in the 'Apologie': 1608/1611, 473 and 522 = V, pp. 505 and 553.

29. See Mathurin Dréano, *La Pensée religieuse de Montaigne* (Paris: Beauchesne, 1937), pp. 447–70.

30. Kaspar Klock, *Tractatus de aerario* (Nuremberg: Endter, 1651), p. 521.

31. Besold, *De majestate*, p. 103.

32. Balzac: Marcella Leopizzi, *Les Sources documentaires du courant libertin français: Giulio Cesare Vanini* (Fasano: Schena, 2004), p. 572. Garasse: Alan Boase, *The Fortunes of Montaigne: A History of the 'Essais' in France, 1580–1669* (London: Methuen, 1935), pp. 166, 168.

33. Jean Boucher, *Les Triomphes de la religion chrestienne* (Paris: Rouillard, 1628), p. 128. Boucher has an entry in Olivier Millet, *La Première Réception des 'Essais' de Montaigne (1580–1640)* (Paris: Champion, 1995), pp. 219–20, and in Boase, *The Fortunes of Montaigne*, pp. 176–78.

34. Boucher, *Triomphes*, p. 129.

35. A more positive reaction to the 'Apologie' is evident in William Corker, Major Fellow of Trinity College Cambridge in 1660 and Prebendary of Sarum, who left his copy of the Doreau 1602 edition of the *Essais* to his college library (shelfmark G 4 42). The first 20 pages of the 'Apologie' bear extensive enthusiastic underlinings in his hand.

36. For the background, see Robert von Frideburg, '*Cuius regio, eius religio*: The Ambivalent Meanings of State Building in Protestant Germany, 1555–1655', in *Diversity and Dissent: Negotiating Religious Difference in Central Europe, 1500–1800*, ed. Howard Louthan, Gary B. Cohen, and Franz A. J. Szabo (New York: Berghahn, 2011), pp. 73–91, especially pp. 83–86.

37. Besold, *Dissertatio de arte iureque belli* (Strasbourg: Heirs of Zetzner, 1624), p. 102.

38. Besold, *De arte iureque belli*, p. 44. The words in parentheses are omitted by Besold.

39. Besold, *De arte iureque belli*, p. 38. The words in parentheses are omitted by Besold.

40. 'Elegant formulation' ['eleganter loquitur'] is Besold's description of Montaigne's phraseology.

41. Besold, *De arte iureque belli*, p. 109.

42. Besold, *De consilio politico*, p. 241, axiom 110.

43. Besold, *De consilio politico*, pp. 226, 227, and 239, axioms 53, 54, and 102, quoting (in order) *Essais* II.4 (V, p. 365) and I.24 twice (V, pp. 127 and 128).

44. Besold, *De consilio politico*, p. 228, axiom 60.

45. See Kinch Hoekstra, 'Early Modern Absolutism and Constitutionalism', *Cardozo Law Review*, 34 (2013), 1079–98.

46. Besold, *De reipublicæ formarum inter sese comparatione* (Strasbourg: Heirs of Zetzner, 1641), p. 199.

47. Besold, *De reipublicae [...] comparatione*, p. 186.

48. Besold, *Principium et finis*, p. 225.

49. Besold, *Principium et finis*, p. 68.

50. Besold, *De majestate*, p. 83.

51. Besold, *De arte iureque belli*, p. 182.

52. Ian Hunter, 'The University Philosopher in Early Modern Germany', in *The Philosopher in Early Modern Europe: The Nature of a Contested Identity*, ed. Conal Condren, Stephen Gaukroger, and Ian Hunter (Cambridge: Cambridge University Press, 2006), pp. 35–65.

53. Hunter, 'The University Philosopher', p. 42.

54. Hunter, 'The University Philosopher', p. 64.
55. Samuel von Pufendorf, *De jure naturæ et gentium* (Lund: Haberegger for Junghans, 1672).

CHAPTER 11

Isaac D'Israeli, Reader of Montaigne

Ingrid A. R. De Smet

[A] vital spirit in his page,
kindred with the souls of a Bayle and a Montaigne.
— Benjamin Disraeli about his father Isaac[1]

The Bodleian Library at Oxford is home to a copy of the 1588 edition of Montaigne's *Essais*. As its class-mark 'Douce M.101' indicates, the volume belonged to the private book collection that the nineteenth-century antiquarian Francis Douce bequeathed to the Bodleian.[2] Although the book bears the hallmarks of a collector's item, it clearly served as a working copy too. The text of the *Essais* itself shows slight annotations in a late sixteenth-century or early seventeenth-century hand, but the volume appears to have been thoroughly cleaned at the time of its restoration in the early nineteenth century.[3] Douce, however, pencilled in some brief notes of his own in the course of his perusal of the text. The book also has copies of various portraits of Montaigne and a title-page of the 1641 Rouen edition glued into it. Above all, it contains on yet another piece of paper pasted inside some additional manuscript notes by Douce. The first of these, most notably, replicates Montaigne's French signature, based on 'Montaigne's autograph in a copy of De Guise *Illustrations de la Gaule Belgique* in the possession of I. D'Israeli Esqre'. Douce, in other words, apparently observed this signature in a copy of the *Premier [-tiers] volume des illustrations de la Gaulle Belgique, antiquitez du pays de Haynnau et de la grand cité de Belges*, published in Paris in 1531–32 by François Regnault and Galliot Dupré. This voluminous text, which until recently was not known to have belonged to Montaigne's library, is the abbreviated French translation by Jean Wauquelin — but often erroneously attributed to Jean Lessabé (or de Leussauch) — of the *Annales Hannoniae* by the fourteenth-century chronicler Jacques de Guyse.[4]

The owner of this signed copy, then, was the writer Isaac D'Israeli (or Disraeli),[5] a close friend of Douce's and father to the famous British Prime Minister Benjamin Disraeli. So far our quest for this lost volume has not unearthed Montaigne's copy — assuming it still exists — but it has thrown light on the fortunes of this chronicle by a contemporary of Jean Froissart, an author who was demonstrably present on Montaigne's bookshelves. It has also highlighted the intrinsic interest of the reception of Montaigne in the late eighteenth and early nineteenth centuries, among writers and bibliophiles such as D'Israeli and Douce, who had links to

France, and of the influence of Montaigne, across languages and across periods, on the practice of essay writing.[6] It is this particular, British aspect of Montaigne's reception that this chapter intends to deepen, with specific reference to D'Israeli's essay-craft. Two titles in D'Israeli's *œuvre* will be of notable importance here, *viz.* the *Curiosities of Literature* and *Miscellanies; or, Literary Recreations*. Taking inspiration from the French fashion of the *ana*, the *Curiosities* first appeared, anonymously, in 1791. It purported to consist of 'anecdotes, characters, sketches, and observations, literary, critical, and historical'. Somewhat like Montaigne's *Essais*, the popular and variegated collection not only accrued several more volumes over time; its individual pieces also went through varying degrees of revision and re-ordering in the course of at least 14 subsequent editions (including a French translation in 1810), until the collection found its definitive form in Isaac D'Israeli's *Complete Works*, posthumously published by his son Benjamin in 1849.[7] Not dissimilarly, the slightly longer pieces of the *Miscellanies* of 1796 went through a second edition in 1801 and were revised again in 1840.[8]

1. Montaigne, English Romantic book-collectors, and the taste for French writers

In some respects, both D'Israeli and his friend Douce's attention to Montaigne relates to the so-called bibliomania that swept through England in the Romantic period between the mid-eighteenth and mid-nineteenth century. The fashion for book collecting signalled a thorough shift in literary taste and kindled a new appreciation of printed books and manuscripts as physical objects — which in turn triggered scornful observations in some parts that hoarding books is not equivalent to reading them.[9] D'Israeli himself devoted a short chapter to the trend in his initial *Curiosities* of 1791. After considering the dangers (such as a vulnerability to hoaxes) that lurk within 'this luxury of literature', the author ends, from 1794 onwards, on a positive note that no doubt reflected the hope that he might pass on his own love of books and his actual library to his son: 'This passion, when hereditary in illustrious families, ceases to be a *mania*; it then claims our admiration and our love.'[10] In the 1807 edition of *Curiosities of Literature*, however, 'Libraries' became the opening piece, giving D'Israeli cause to rewrite the ensuing article on 'The Bibliomania' in a much more negative light and to redefine the concept as 'the collecting an enormous heap of Books, without intelligent curiosity'.[11] Nonetheless, 'Libraries' likewise starts from the idea of a general 'passion' (the word is repeated four times in the essay) for books, a passion which can arguably lead to an 'intemperance of studies' and 'curious collectors' seeking out rare bindings such as de Thou's or Grolier's, but which may also be of inordinate national benefit when significant private collections become the nuclei of great national libraries such as the British Museum.[12] It is entirely in keeping with this bibliophilic movement — to use a later and less loaded term — that D'Israeli should have owned a copy of Wauquelin's *Illustrations de la Gaulle belgique* with Montaigne's autograph in it, or that in his essay 'On Reading', published in 1796, he should pick up on Montaigne's habit, famously described in II.10, 'Des livres' [Of Books], of annotating the books he had read with a date and brief reminder of their merit.[13]

Now, besides the 1588 edition of the *Essais* mentioned above, Douce owned a copy of the 1627 Rouen edition (Jean Berthelin), two editions of the translation of the *Essais* by John Florio (London 1603 and 1613), an edition of the translation by Charles Cotton (London 1776), and the first edition of the *Voyage en Italie* (Rome 1775).[14] Isaac D'Israeli, for his part, owned at least one copy of Montaigne's *Essais* in French, in the 1669 Paris edition (Laurent Rondet, Christophe Joumel, and Robert Chevillion).[15] It is also possible that the English translation of the *Essais* by Charles Cotton (London 1711), preserved at Hughenden Manor with the *ex libris* of Benjamin Disraeli, came in fact from Isaac's collection.[16] Isaac was certainly familiar with Montaigne's *Voyage en Italie*, for in a piece on 'The Recovery of Manuscripts', first published in *Curiosities of Literature* in 1794, he discusses at some length the discovery, some 20 years earlier, of the sole copy of the travel journal in 'an old worm-eaten coffer, which had long held papers untouched by the incurious generations of Montaigne' and its authentication by French scholars on palaeographical and stylistic grounds.[17]

D'Israeli's — or indeed Douce's — ownership of copies of Montaigne in both languages seems to have been fairly characteristic of the discerning book collector and educated reader. An older contemporary of theirs, the Shakespeare editor George Steevens, whose library was particularly rich in Elizabethan literature, similarly owned a copy of the 1588 edition of the *Essais* as well as the 1613 edition of Florio's translation. Douce and D'Israeli, incidentally, both bought books from Steevens' collection when it was sold by auction after his death, but not the Montaigne editions.[18] The 1813 catalogue of Lord Byron's book collection, drawn up for a sale that did not take place, listed both a French edition of the *Essais* ([Paris]: Pierre and Firmin Didot, 1802) and an English version ([London]: C. Baldwin for W. Miller, White and Cochrane, and Lackington, Allen, and Co. 1811); both were sold at auction in 1816, before their owner set out on his travels abroad.[19] Byron — who was also an admirer of D'Israeli's pen — reacquainted himself with Montaigne in the summer of 1822, reading and marking the text in the copy of Cotton's translation that (presumably) the poet and essayist Leigh Hunt had lent him.[20] Later, Lady Marguerite Blessington and James Hamilton Browne too remarked on Byron's fond reading of Montaigne.[21]

D'Israeli's interest in Montaigne, however, was not typical in every respect. Firstly, it pre-dates by several decades the boost that the essayist's reputation in Britain received from Mary Shelley's *Life of Montaigne* (1838) or William Hazlitt the younger's 1842 edition of Montaigne's *Complete Works*. Secondly, Montaigne forms part of a broad spectrum of French authors whom D'Israeli had come to appreciate, not in the least during his travels to France in about 1788–89.[22] In these early years of his literary career, in fact, D'Israeli's 'partiality for French writers' (including Racine, Voltaire, Montesquieu, and Rousseau) was at odds with the preference for English and classical literature that many of his fellow countrymen espoused, especially during the Anglo-French wars of 1793–1802. So in 1791 (but possibly a few years later), the Exeter physician Hugh Downman, D'Israeli's friend and the future dedicatee of his *Miscellanies* (1796), berated the bookman in a satirical *Epistle* for being 'more prodigal in [his] panegyric on the most eloquent French authors, than his [i.e., Downman's] taste, and more particularly his patriotism, approved':

> With polish'd manners you would join in vain
> The smut of RABELAIS, coarseness of MONTAIGNE.
>   To sage BOILEAU what *genuine* strains belong?
> From Horace, and Tassoni, flow'd his song.
> Pope from their open fountain likewise drew:
> What mighty thanks are to the Frenchman due!
> [...]
> In vain your much-loved Nation you advance;
> She ever was, and ever will be, France.
> Like Greece or Britain never can she shine;
> Ours are the great Originals divine.[23]

2. D'Israeli and 'old Montaigne'

Well aware of the criticisms levelled against Montaigne by the likes of Downman or indeed by preceding generations, D'Israeli will revisit Montaigne and 'the simplicity of this old and admirable favourite of Europe' throughout the half-century span of his literary career, from the first edition of *Curiosities of Literature* to his last substantive work, the *Amenities of Literature, consisting of sketches and characters of English literature* of 1841.[24] Montaigne is thus portrayed as 'humorous', 'plain and unadorned',[25] and (with Dryden's term) 'honest'.[26] D'Israeli concedes in 1841 (perhaps with an eye to Downman's satirical epistle) that 'in France Rabelais and Montaigne had contracted the rust and the rudeness of antiquity, as it seemed to the refinement of the following generation'.[27] D'Israeli is certainly not always in agreement with Montaigne.[28] He even accuses the sage of being inconsistent, when he refers to the manner of his death (as described by Estienne Pasquier) in the 1807 edition of *Curiosities*: '*Montaigne* and *la Fontaine*, who wrote very philosophically on *death*, did not *die* like philosophers. The first raised himself, when expiring, with fervent devotion to the host! And the other, after his death, had on a hair shirt!'[29] In effect, in 1823 D'Israeli starts his own reflections on death by evoking Montaigne's interest in the subject, though not without repeating his gentle rebuke: 'for [Montaigne] did not die as he had promised himself, — expiring in the adoration of the mass; or, as his preceptor Buchanan would have called it, in "the act of rank idolatry"'.[30] For the most part, however, we shall see that D'Israeli's references to the essayist reveal a positive, or at the very least an indulgent, attitude towards 'old Montaigne'.

To begin with, it seems that D'Israeli seeks out the more curious and light-hearted passages. In 'The Amusements of Men of Letters' (first published in 1793, and later retitled as 'Amusements of the Learned'), for instance, D'Israeli remarks that 'Montaigne found a very agreeable play-mate in his cat', although he curtails the deeper philosophical dimension of the original statement in the 'Apologie de Raimond Sebond' (II.12), where Montaigne wonders: 'Who knows if she [the cat] passes her time more with me than I do with her?'[31] Two years later, in D'Israeli's *Essay on the Manners and Genius of the Literary Character* (1795), the notion of an ailurophile Montaigne supports the affirmation that 'men of genius' just as easily find a soothing distraction in ordinary pursuits, as they are capable of virtuosic reasoning:

> When a man of letters seeks the consolations of society, he would rest a mind enfeebled with one continued pursuit; or exercise it by suffering it to take those infinite directions which the diversities of conversation offer. If it is wearied, the simplest actions please; it is a child that would sport with flowers and pebbles; if it issues in all it's force [sic], it is an athlete that leaps in the arena, and calls for an adversary. *It is Montaigne sporting with his cat*, or Johnson maintaining a thesis amidst his marvelling friends.[32]

By 1807, however, the *Curiosities* essay 'Amusements of the Learned' restores some of Montaigne's seriousness, by referring back — albeit rather gauchely — to the Frenchman's love of writing: 'Montaigne boasts of having found a very agreeable playmate in his cat, *but his pen itself seems not less to have amused him than his cat*'.[33]

It is not that D'Israeli is unable to fathom the complexities that may lie behind even passing remarks in Montaigne's *Essais*; more that to enter into any detail either does not suit his purpose or runs counter to the prevailing literary taste of his time. The defensive phrasing at the opening of 'Imaginations and Antipathies', with its thinly veiled reference to Montaigne's chapter I.21, 'De la force de l'imagination' [Of the Power of the Imagination], is telling of D'Israeli's concern with pleasing his readership: 'I have collected several uncommon instances of the force of the imagination, which are taken from good authorities; at the same time the reader will recollect, that I am only a reporter in the present article.'[34] Indeed, later in the same essay this initial statement is followed by a deliberate yet tantalizing *praeteritio*:

> Montaigne has a copious essay on 'The Force of Imagination.' He adduces a variety of singular instances; but it will not be commendable to detail them here; for most of them are of a nature which are best recommended by his own agreeable and free manner. A modern writer is not permitted to
>
> —— "Pour himself as plain,
> "As downright Shippen or as old Montaigne."
> POPE.[35]

In this extract as elsewhere, moreover, D'Israeli readily applies the Montaignian technique of using citations to advance his own point of view, in clear defiance (as D'Israeli argues in 1823) of the received opinion that 'where there is no QUOTATION, there will be found most originality'.[36] After harking back to the Ancients, 'who in these matters [the various uses of quotation] were not perhaps such blockheads as some may conceive', and who 'considered poetical quotation as one of the requisite ornaments of oratory', D'Israeli notes: 'Old Montaigne is so stuffed with [quotations], that he owns, if they were taken out of him little of himself would remain; and yet this never injured that original turn which the old Gascon has given to his thoughts.'[37] It is true that D'Israeli mistakenly attributes a criticism of Montaigne that the anonymous 'Vindication of Montaigne's Essays' (prefixing editions of Cotton's translation from 1700 onwards) had cited and rebuffed, to Montaigne himself; but even an error such as this can be put on a par with the French essayist's avowed nonchalance and forgetfulness towards his sources.[38] Indeed, as D'Israeli had already explained in his 1796 essay 'On Novelty in Literature', what fascinated him in Montaigne was precisely the interplay of borrowed materials — be they acknowledged or teasingly left to the reader to identify — and the author's own, newly created context:

> Montaigne, with honest naiveté, compares his writings to a thread that binds the flowers of others; and that by incessantly pouring the waters of a few good old authors into his sieve, some drops fall upon his paper. The good old man elsewhere acquaints us with a certain stratagem of his own invention, consisting of his inserting whole sentences from the ancients, without acknowledgement, that the critics might blunder, by giving Nazardes to Seneca and Plutarch, while they imagined they tweaked his nose.[39]

Furthermore, just as in Montaigne's own essays, D'Israeli's allusions and quotations are spyholes that invite us to look at the original and take in the broader implications of the intertext, albeit with vastly differing results. Take for example the ostensibly summary allusion to another passage from the 'Apologie de Raimond Sebond', which occurs in the 'Account of a Singular Atrabilarian or Hypochondriac', first published in 1794 in the 'Miscellanea' section of the *Curiosities*:

> Do we not every where see what excesses men are led into by their inconstancy, their fantastic hope, their perishable ambition, in a word, their madness? Are the learned exempt from this disorder? *Montaigne has said, that between wisdom and folly there is only the turn of a screw.*[40]

At first glance, D'Israeli has only retained Montaigne's metaphor 'il n'y a qu'un demy tour de cheville à passer de l'un à l'autre', treating it as an aphorism. But the reasoning that precedes the modified quotation is clearly inspired by the original context both in terms of content and style:

> Dequoy se faict la plus subtile folie, que de la plus subtile sagesse? Comme des grandes amitiez naissent des grandes inimitiez; des santez vigoreuses, les mortelles maladies: ainsi des rares et vifves agitations de nos ames, les plus excellentes manies et plus detraquées; *il n'y a qu'un demy tour de cheville à passer de l'un à l'autre.* Aux actions des hommes insansez, nous voyons combien proprement s'avient la folie avecq les plus vigoureuses operations de nostre ame. Qui ne sçait combien est imperceptible le voisinage d'entre la folie avecq les gaillardes elevations d'un esprit libre et les effects d'une vertu supreme et extraordinaire?[41]

Nonetheless, it is especially D'Israeli's early, perfunctory reference to Montaigne's (and François de La Mothe Le Vayer's) opinion of Julian the Apostate that seems to carry a world of meaning in the *non-dit*.[42] Surely, the allusion to Montaigne's lengthy discussion in II.19, 'De la liberté de conscience' [Of Freedom of Conscience] of Julian's accomplishments and virtues as a ruler in the face of an overwhelmingly negative reception based on his religious views must be read in light of D'Israeli's own Judaism (from which he later distanced himself)?[43] Yet, once more we are not on stable ground, for by D'Israeli's own admission the article entitled 'Religious Enmity' was 'drawn from Naudé'. It does indeed heavily depend on the *Naudaeana*, according to which Gabriel Naudé himself had urged the reader: 'Voyez ce que Montaigne dit à sa loüange dans ses *Essais*, et M. la Mothe-le-Vayer en son Traitté *de la Vertu des Payens*.'[44] Whether the brief essay was too derivative (not to say plagiaristic) or dealt with too sensitive a subject, 'Religious Enmity' (or, alternatively, 'Religious Enmities') would disappear from later, nineteenth-century editions of *Curiosities of Literature*. There is certainly no evidence here that D'Israeli felt an affinity with Montaigne over shared Jewish roots: French scholars only began to explore the vexed question of Montaigne's *marrano* or new-Christian ancestry, through his mother Antoinette de Louppes, in the final quarter of the nineteenth century.[45]

On occasion, D'Israeli's desire for an arresting statement or even a *bon mot* prevails over faithfulness to Montaigne's source text. Thus, in the essay 'Historical Characters are False Representations of Nature' of 1796, D'Israeli blithely omits Montaigne's own explicit reference to Plutarch in 'De l'inequalité qui est entre nous' [Of the Inequality that is Between Us], when he asserts: 'It has been boldly said, by old Montaigne, that man differs more from man, than man from beast. But speculations on human nature must not be formed on such rare instances.'[46] Similarly, in a chapter on 'The Matrimonial State' that first appeared in the enlarged edition of *The Literary Character* (1818), D'Israeli refers to Montaigne as an authority in his own take on the old chestnut of whether a man of letters should marry:

> Assuredly it would not be a question whether these literary characters should have married, had not Montaigne, when a widower, declared that 'he would not marry a second time, though it were wisdom itself' — but the airy Gascon has not disclosed how far *Madame* was concerned in this anathema.[47]

D'Israeli draws here, quite inaccurately, on Montaigne's declaration 'De mon dessein, j'eusse fui d'épouser la sagesse meme, si elle m'eût voulu' in III.5, 'Sur des vers de Virgile' [On Some Lines from Virgil]. In this text, there is, furthermore, no mention of a second marriage: just of marriage (V, p. 852). The misrepresentation of the original may or may not be due to quotation from memory, but it is unquestionably profitable, as it allows for the addition of a good-natured quip about Montaigne's spouse, Françoise de La Chassaigne.

3. Modes of transmission: a French or English Montaigne?

It will already be clear that D'Israeli is far from systematic in his choice of editions to refer to Montaigne. Certainly, he respects Cotton as 'a translator who has not ill expressed the peculiarities of his author'.[48] But D'Israeli does not shy away from offering his own rendition, as he does in his musings on 'Gaming', where he quotes in English from III.10, 'De mesnager sa volonté' [On Husbanding your Will],[49] or on the 'Influence of Names', where — predictably — he takes inspiration from I.46, 'Des noms' [Of Names].[50] He even quotes Montaigne in French, for a variety of reasons. For instance, when referring to the Preface to the *Essais* (which was omitted from Cotton's translation), D'Israeli insists that '[a]n engaging tenderness prevails in these *naive* expressions, which shall not be injured by a version'.[51] Similarly, when in 1841 D'Israeli cites, in an extensive footnote to 'The Page, the Baron and the Minstrel', Montaigne's preposterous anecdote of the woman who, whilst drowning, still insulted her husband as 'louse-ridden' (*pouilleux*) by making delousing hand gestures above her head (II.32, 'Defense de Seneque et de Plutarque'), he asserts that 'his language must not be disguised by a modern version'.[52]

In his article on 'Singularities observed by various nations in their repasts' published in the first edition of *Curiosities*, on the other hand, D'Israeli's cites an extract from I.23, 'De la coustume et de ne changer aisement une loy receue' [Of Custom, and Not Easily Changing an Accepted Law] about savages wiping their fingers on their thighs, groin, or the soles of their feet. He does so in French, because 'it is impossible to translate this passage without offending feminine delicacy'.[53] It is unlikely, though, that D'Israeli's quotation here is first-hand, since by the author's own admission the greater part of the chapter is extracted from Jean-Nicolas Demeunier's *L'Esprit des usages et des coutumes des différens peuples*, which incorporates this exact passage from Montaigne.[54] In a touched-up version of the essay, from 1833 onwards, Demeunier himself (still unnamed) is referred to as 'a philosophical compiler'; interestingly, the remark about feminine sensitivity has now disappeared, so that the quote from Montaigne leads straight onto D'Israeli's witty comment: 'We cannot forbear exulting in the polished convenience of napkins!'[55] D'Israeli's article on 'Modes of Salutation, and amicable ceremonies observed in various nations' is of a similar ilk, but seems to combine direct knowledge of Montaigne's II.17, 'De la praesumption' [Of Presumption] with an anecdote that is in turn borrowed from the chapter on greetings in Demeunier's *L'Esprit des usages*.[56]

4. Montaigne as a model for D'Israeli's essay-craft

In the light of D'Israeli's varying treatment of Montaigne, the question remains as to how much the Frenchman's style of writing influenced D'Israeli's own concept of the essay. Firstly, it is clear that D'Israeli easily moves from terms such as 'sketches', 'articles', 'characters', and 'compilations' to 'essays' featuring 'instances' and 'anecdotes'. His early *Dissertation on Anecdotes* of 1793 admittedly makes no mention of Montaigne, but in referring to his enterprise as an 'essay', D'Israeli reveals his concept of it as a literary form. An essay, it transpires, should 'not [be] destitute of connection', even if that appears to be the case at first glance. And more than consisting of 'a mere mass of loose anecdotes', the work should also include some elucidation and reflection.[57] Always closely linked to reading, the essay, for D'Israeli, can be as much about the writer himself as it is about other authors; yet its purpose is one of edification, in the first place that of the essayist himself:

> If we regard anecdotes as they are connected with the republic of letters, I do not hesitate to declare, that they offer most exquisite gratification. In literary biography, a man of genius always finds something which relates to himself. In the history of his fellow students, a writer traces the effects of similar studies; he is warned by their failures, or animated by their progress.[58]

Unsurprisingly then, D'Israeli considered Montaigne to be 'the venerable father of modern Miscellanies'.[59] The phrase occurs precisely in D'Israeli's own essay 'Of Miscellanies', a programmatic and eponymous piece heading his *Miscellanies; or, Literary Creations* of 1796. Of all of D'Israeli's chapters and articles, its 23 pages contain the most references to Montaigne, some of which we have already had occasion to discuss. Here D'Israeli defends the French essayist — and no doubt by extension himself — against the savant who labelled Montaigne 'a bold ignorant fellow', that is, the Huguenot scholar Joseph Scaliger who had allegedly called Montaigne 'un hardy ignorant'.[60] It does not prevent D'Israeli from advocating a more restrained approach to quotations and references than the number of *loci* Montaigne himself includes in his *Essais*:

> To thinking readers, this critical summary [Scaliger's comment] will appear mysterious; for Montaigne had imbibed the spirit of all the moral writers of antiquity; and although he has made a capricious complaint of a defective memory, we cannot but wish the complaint had been more real; *for we discover in his works nearly as much compilement, as reflection, and he is one of those authors who should quote rarely, but who deserves to be often quoted.* Montaigne was censured by Scaliger, as Addison was censured by Warburton; because both, like Socrates, perceived and reprobated that mere erudition, which consists of knowing the thoughts of others and having no thoughts of our own.[61]

Montaigne, D'Israeli admits, 'has also been censured for an apparent vanity, in making himself the idol of his lucubrations'.[62] Yet, unlike Montaigne's critic Pierre-Daniel Huet to whom this comment seems to allude,[63] D'Israeli shows himself touched precisely by this writing of the self[64] — an aspect he also appreciates in Abraham Cowley's essays[65] — as well as by Montaigne's friend-like appeal to his readers;[66] even though he admits elsewhere that the essayist's candid revelations might well be a pose, 'a theatrical gesture, as much as the sensibility of Sterne'.[67] And just as Byron reputedly saw some truth in Huet's qualification of the *Essais* as 'le bréviaire des honnêtes paresseux, et des ignorans studieux, qui veulent s'enfariner de quelque connoissance du monde, et de quelque teinture des Lettres' but retorted 'that Montaigne was the greatest plagiarist that ever existed, and certainly had turned his reading to the most account',[68] so D'Israeli too casts the miscellaneous nature of the *Essais* not as a flaw but as a virtue:

> Montaigne's works have been called by a Cardinal 'the Breviary of Idlers'. It is therefore the book of Man; for all Men are Idlers; we have hours which we pass with lamentation, and which we know are always returning. At those moments Miscellanists are conformable to all our humours, and often are so congruous to our mental tone, that they illuminate in many a critical moment.[69]

5. A refracted Montaigne

The impression, then, which D'Israeli gives of Montaigne is fragmented, shattered, piecemeal, and as diverse as the shards of the *Essais* that D'Israeli quotes or alludes to. Direct readings from Montaigne mingle with half- or misremembered quotes and indirect modes of reception. For, often, D'Israeli's Montaigne appears filtered: not just through Cotton's translation but also through the *ana*, particularly the *Naudaeana* and *Huetiana* (which incidentally construed Montaigne's own *Essais* as *Montaniana*); through the French editorial remarks to the first edition of the *Journal du voyage en Italie*; or through Demeunier's philosophical compilation *L'Esprit des usages et des coutumes des différens peuples*. One might equally refer to the lenses of Carlo Goldoni's comments on the pantomimical actor Sacchi ('in his impromptus they often discovered the thoughts of Seneca, Cicero, or Montaigne'),[70] Jean-Jacques Rousseau's perusal of 'Plutarch, Montaigne and Locke',[71] or — much more opaquely — Louis-Silvestre de Sacy's 'Essay[s] on Friendship' and 'on Glory'.[72] In addition to these Continental refractions and percolations of the French thinker, D'Israeli readily notes 'Montaigne-like' traits in Pope or Dryden, but also in Hobbes,[73] Antony Wood,[74] as well as arguably in the 'self-painter' Cowley.[75]

What D'Israeli himself found in Montaigne was, firstly, a treasure house of stories, musings, and a digest of ancient authors (such as Cicero, Plutarch and Seneca), which D'Israeli, with his rather poor Latin and Greek, would not necessarily have consulted in any depth himself. In this respect, D'Israeli's reading and evaluation of Montaigne was not so different from Byron's who (according to Lady Blessington) had said that 'independently of the quaintness with which [Montaigne] made his observations, a perusal of his works was like a repetition at school, they rubbed up the reader's classical knowledge'.[76] Secondly, D'Israeli manifestly did consider Montaigne's miscellaneous style as a model of essay writing (albeit one among others) — a model that he was not afraid to adapt to the taste of his own age and to his own purpose of writing, as a passionate man of letters addressing a common readership. Above all, D'Israeli's Montaigne was anything but an unread author adorning a bibliomaniac's bookshelf. Engaging much more intensely than his friend Douce with the essence of Montaigne, D'Israeli may not always have concurred with the French essayist, nor was his appreciation of him static or consistent throughout his own, ever-changing pieces of writing. But that does not take away D'Israeli's broad and long-lasting affection for Montaigne or indeed a certain emulation on his part: such, after all, is the fertile relationship between 'a writer of imagination' and 'a reader of judgment'.

Notes to Chapter 11

1. Benjamin Disraeli, 'On the Life and Writings of Mr. Disraeli' (1848), in *The Works of Isaac Disraeli*, ed. Benjamin Disraeli (London: Routledge, Warnes and Routledge, 1858–59), vol. 1, p. vii–xxxvii (p. xix).

2. On Douce, see C. Hurst, 'Douce, Francis (1757–1834)', *Oxford Dictionary of National Biography* <http://www.oxforddnb.com/view/article/7849> [accessed 21 October 2015].

3. The copy is free from any autograph correction by Montaigne to the date of his address 'To the Reader' (as manifested in at least four other copies of this edition). See Marie-Luce Demonet and Alain Legros, 'Montaigne à sa plume: quatre variantes autographes d'une correction de date dans l'avis "Au lecteur" des Essais de 1588', *Bibliothèque d'Humanisme et Renaissance*, 75.1 (2013), 113–18.

4. See my 'Michel de Montaigne, Francis Douce, Isaac D'Israeli et les *Illustrations de la Gaulle Belgique* de Jacques de Guyse (Paris, 1531–1532): à la recherché d'un livre perdu', *Montaigne Studies*, 27 (2015), 205.

5. See James Ogden, 'D'Israeli, Isaac (1766–1848)', *Oxford Dictionary of National Biography* <http://www.oxforddnb.com/view/article/7690> [accessed 21 October 2015].

6. On the eighteenth- and nineteenth-century reception of Montaigne, see Charles Dédéyan, *Montaigne chez ses amis anglo-saxons: Montaigne dans le romantisme anglais et ses prolongements victoriens* (Paris: Boivin, 1946), and François Moureau, 'Réception de Montaigne (XVIIIe siècle)', in *Dictionnaire de Michel de Montaigne*, ed. Philippe Desan (Paris: Champion, 2007), pp. 1002–04.

7. See James Ogden, *Isaac D'Israeli* (Oxford: Clarendon Press, 1969), pp. 21–26, 210–11, and Marvin Spevack, *Curiosities Revisited: The Works of Isaac D'Israeli* (Hildesheim: Olms, 2007), pp. 32–36. There is no adequate critical edition of D'Israeli's œuvre, although Stuart Heath's online edition

of *Curiosities of Literature* (2005–06, revised 2011) <http://www.spamula.net/col/> [accessed 21 October 2015] differentiates between the different instalments of articles in this work. For my own consultation of the consecutive editions of D'Israeli's *Curiosities* and other texts, I have used Eighteenth Century Collections Online and Early American Imprints (both accessed through Warwick University Library), Gallica, The Hathi Trust, Google Books, and The Internet Archive.

8. Ogden, *Isaac D'Israeli* (1969), pp. 36–39; Spevack, *Curiosities Revisited*, pp. 75, 94–95.

9. On this fashion, see Philip Connell, 'Bibliomania: Book Collecting, Cultural Politics, and the Rise of Literary Heritage in Romantic Britain', *Representations*, 71 (2000), 24–47; Neil Kenny, 'Books in Space and Time: Bibliomania and Early Modern Histories of Learning and "Literature" in France', *Modern Language Quarterly*, 61.2 (2000), 253–86; Arnold Hunt, 'Private Libraries in the Age of Bibliomania', in *The Cambridge History of Libraries in Britain and Ireland*, ed. Giles Mandelbrote and K. A. Manley (Cambridge: Cambridge University Press, 2006), vol. 2, pp. 438–58 (p. 458); Ina Ferris, 'Book Fancy: Bibliomania and the Literary Word', *Keats–Shelley Journal*, 58 (2009), 33–52; and James Raven, 'Debating Bibliomania and the Collection of Books in the Eighteenth Century', *Library and Information History*, 29.3 (2013), 196–209. Also of interest, but taking 'bibliomania' as a pejorative notion, is Marvin Spevack's anthology *Isaac D'Israeli on Books: Pre-Victorian Essays on the History of Literature* (London: British Library, 2004).

10. [Isaac D'Israeli], *Curiosities of Literature...* (London: J. Murray, 1791), pp. 19–21; *Curiosities of Literature*, 'Fourth edition' (London: H. Murray, 1794), vol. 1, pp. 58–61; emphasis original. Consulted via Eighteenth Century Collections Online.

11. Isaac D'Israeli, *Curiosities of Literature*, 5th edn (London: J. Murray, 1807), vol. 1, pp. 10–14 (p. 10).

12. *Curiosities* (1807), vol. 1, pp. 1–10 (p. 6): 'Sir Robert Cotton, Sir Hans Sloane, Dr. Birch, Mr. Cracherode, and others of this race of lovers of books, have all contributed to form these literary treasures [public libraries], which our nation owe to the enthusiasm of individuals, who have found such pleasure in consecrating their fortunes and their days to this great public object; or, which in the result produces the same public good, the collections of such men have been frequently purchased on their deaths, by government, and thus have entered whole and entire into the great national collections.' Note that the 1807 edition of *Curiosities* is dedicated to Francis Douce.

13. Isaac D'Israeli, 'On Reading', in *Miscellanies; or, Literary Recreations* (London: T. Cadell and W. Davies, 1796), pp. 189–207 (p. 202): 'Montaigne placed at the end of those books which he intended not to reperuse, the time he had read it, with a concise decision on it's merits [sic]; that, says he, it may thus represent to me, the air and general idea I had conceived of the author, in reading the work. He has obliged his admirers with giving several of these annotations.' Compare 'Des livres': 'Pour subvenir un peu à la trahison de ma memoire et à son defaut, si extreme qu'il m'est advenu plus d'une fois de reprendre en main des livres comme recens et à moy inconnus, que j'avoy leu soigneusement quelques années au paravant et barbouillé de mes notes, j'ay pris en coustume, dépuis quelque temps, d'adjouter au bout de chasque livre (je dis de ceux desquels je ne me veux servir qu'une fois) le temps auquel j'ay achevé de le lire et le jugement que j'en ay retiré en gros, afin que cela me represente au moins l'air et Idée generale que j'avois conceu de l'autheur en le lisant. Je veux icy transcrire aucunes de ces annotations' [To compensate a little for the treachery and weakness of my memory, so extreme that it has happened to me more than once to pick up again, as recent and unknown to me, books which I had read carefully a few years before and scribbled over with my notes, I have adopted the habit for some time now of adding at the end of each book (I mean of those that I intend to use only once) the time I finished reading it and the judgment I have derived of it as a whole, so that this may represent to me at least the sense and general idea I had conceived of the author in reading it. I want to transcribe here some of these annotations] (V, p. 418; F, p. 370).

14. Oxford, Bodleian Library, shelfmarks Douce M 268, Douce M 731, Douce M 421, Douce M 345–47, and Douce MM 329–31. *Catalogue of the Printed Books and Manuscripts Bequeathed by Francis Douce, Esq., to the Bodleian Library* (Oxford: Oxford University Press, 1840), p. 189.

15. *Catalogue of a considerable portion of the valuable library of Isaac D'Israeli... which will be sold by auction, by Messrs. S. Leigh Sotheby & co. ... on Friday, March 16th, 1849, and three following days* ([London]: Compton & Richie, [1849]), p. 43, no. 653.

16. Marvin Spevack, 'The Disraeli Library at Hughenden Manor', p. 507 (shelfmark C.4.17–19). National Trust Inventory Number 3025392. The Copac catalogue provides the following description: 'Armorial bookplate: The Right Honourable Benjamin Disraeli. Binding: Nineteenth-century polished calf; gilt fillets; spines gilt.'

17. D'Israeli, 'The Recovery of Manuscripts', in *Curiosities* (1794), vol. 1, pp. 12–18 (pp. 16–17). This is the only passage of D'Israeli's that seems to have retained Charles Dédeyan's attention; *Montaigne chez ses amis anglo-saxons*, vol. 1, pp. 97–98.

18. *Bibliotheca Steevensiana: A Catalogue of the Curious and Valuable Library of George Steevens, Esq. Fellow of the Royal and Antiquary Societies (Lately Deceased) comprehending an extraordinary fine Collection of Books... which will be Sold by Auction* (London: J. Barker for T. King, 1800), p. 37, nos 681, 'Essais de Montaigne. 8vo. *dorée sur les tranches Paris, chez L'Angelier* 1588' (sold to one A. Hawkins); and 682 'Montaigne's Essayes, by Jo. Florio, with the portrait of the Translator, by Hole, *folio* Lond. 1613' (sold for 5 shillings to F[rancis] G[odolphin] Waldron). The annotated (and digitized) copies of the sales catalogue, held in Oxford, Bodleian Library, class-marks Mus. Bibl. III 8° 35 and Mus. Bibl. III 8° 244, also list Douce (*passim*) and D'Israeli (pp. 79, 104, 117, 118) among the buyers.

19. 'Byron's Library: The Three Book Sale Catalogues', edited and introduced by Peter Cochran (2009), <http://petercochran.files.wordpress.com/2009/03/byrons_library.pdf> [accessed 22 October 2015].

20. See [Leigh] H[unt?], 'Passages Marked in Montaigne's Essays by Lord Byron', *The New Monthly Magazine*, 19 (1827), 26–32 and 240–45; Richard I. Kirkland, Jr, 'Byron's Reading of Montaigne: A Leigh Hunt Letter', *Keats–Shelley Journal*, 30 (1981), 47–51; and Anne Fleming, 'Byron and Montaigne', *The Byron Journal*, 37.1 (2009), 33–42. According to Peter Cochrane, it was not Hunt but Sir John Hobhouse who lent Byron his copy of Montaigne in Cotton's translation (Cochran, 'Byron's Library'). On Byron's relation with D'Israeli, see Ogden, *Isaac D'Israeli*, pp. 107–09, 115–21, 126–27.

21. Lady Blessington, 'Journal of Conversations with Lord Byron, no. X', *New Monthly Magazine* n.s. 39 (1833), 33–46 (p. 40); [John Mitford], 'Lady Blessington's Conversations (Concluded)', *New Monthly Magazine*, n.s. 1 (1834), 583–93; James Hamilton Browne, 'Voyage from Leghorn to Cephalonia with Lord Byron, and Visit to the Seat of War in Greece', *Blackwood's Edinburgh Magazine*, 35 (1834), 56–67 (p. 58).

22. Ogden, *Isaac D'Israeli* (1969), p. 16. For a critical reappraisal assigning the details of D'Israeli's residence in France to 'lost years', see Marvin Spevack, *Curiosities Revisited*, pp. 429–31.

23. Hugh Downman, 'A Poetical Epistle to ★★★ [I. D'Israeli], On his Partiality for French Writers, written in 1791, by the late Dr. DOWNMAN, of Exeter', *Gentleman's Magazine and Historical Review*, 79.2 (1809), 959–60. See Ogden, *Isaac D'Israeli* (1969), pp. 25, 32. The year 1791 does not tally with the view that Downman's and D'Israeli's acquaintance dates from 1795, as noted by Alick Cameron, 'Downman, Hugh (1740–1809)', *Oxford Dictionary of National Biography* <http://www.oxforddnb.com/view/article/7983> [accessed 22 October 2015]. The *Miscellanies'* dedication to Downman disappeared in the republished version of 1801.

24. The quotation is from Isaac D'Israeli, *An Essay on the Manners and Genius of the Literary Character* (London: T. Cadell Jr. and W. Davies, 1795), p. 149. Compare Isaac D'Israeli, 'The Literary and Personal Character', *The Literary Character, illustrated by the History of Men of Genius...* (London: J. Murray, 1818), pp. 281–94 (p. 289): 'the simplicity of this old favorite of Europe'.

25. D'Israeli, 'On Professors of Art', in *Miscellanies* (1796), pp. 24–36 (p. 27).

26. D'Israeli, 'On Prefaces', *Miscellanies* (1796), pp. 77–94 (pp. 91–92): 'Dryden has had the candour to acquaint us with his secret of prefatory composition; for in that one to his Tales, he says, "the nature of preface-writing is rambling; never wholly out of the way, nor in it. This I have learnt from the practice of honest Montaigne." There is no great risk in establishing this observation as an axiom in literature; but, perhaps, there may be some danger in following it.' [Isaac D'Israeli], 'Miseries of Successful Authors', in *Calamities of Authors; including some inquiries respecting their moral and literary characters. By the author of 'Curiosities of literature'* (London: for John Murray, 1812), vol. 2, pp. 268–93 (p. 278): 'Dryden shall answer in his own words; with all the simplicity of Montaigne, he expresses himself with the dignity that would have become Milton or Gray.'

27. D'Israeli, 'Origin of the Vernacular Languages of Europe', in *Amenities of literature, consisting of*

sketches and characters of English literature, 2nd edn (London: Edward Moxon, 1841), vol. 1, pp. 152–76 (p. 165).

28. D'Israeli, 'Salutations and Ceremonies Observed in Various Nations', in *Curiosities* (1807), vol. 2, pp. 314–20 (p. 318): 'Surely we may differ here with the sentiment of Montaigne'; 'On Erudition and Philosophy', in *Miscellanies* (1796), pp. 129–47 (pp. 131–32): 'and if, as it cannot be denied, the pursuits of letters have been often satirized, it has been owing to their laborious trifling, and impertinent information. Montaigne has declaimed against them, in various parts of his works;* and, I lament, has in this invective, involved the more amiable studies. (In footnote: *See particularly his Chapter on Pedantry.)'

29. D'Israeli, 'James I', in *Curiosities* (1807), vol. 2, pp. 282–91 (p. 290); original emphasis.

30. D'Israeli, 'The Book of Death', in *A Second Series of Curiosities of literature* (London: John Murray, 1823), vol. 2, pp. 284–98 (p. 284).

31. D'Israeli, *Curiosities* (1793), p. 100. Compare Montaigne, II.12, 'Apologie de Raimond Sebond': 'Quand je me joue à ma chatte, qui sçait si elle passe son temps de moy plus que je ne fay d'elle' (V, p. 452; F, p. 401). See also Laurie Shannon, 'Chatte de Montaigne', in *Dictionnaire Montaigne*, ed. Desan, pp. 189–90.

32. Isaac D'Israeli, *An Essay on the Manners and Genius of the Literary Character* (London: for T. Cadell Jr. and W. Davies, 1795), pp. 67–68; emphasis mine.

33. D'Israeli, 'Amusements of the Learned', in *Curiosities* (1807), vol. 1, pp. 58–64 (p. 61); emphasis mine.

34. D'Israeli, 'Imaginations and Antipathies', in *Curiosities* (1794), vol. 2, 'Miscellanea', pp. 472–83 (p. 472).

35. D'Israeli, *Curiosities* (1794), vol. 2, pp. 478–79. The quotation from Pope will re-occur in D'Israeli's *Quarrels of Authors* of 1814: 'Political Criticism on Literary Compositions', in *Quarrels of Authors; or, Some memoirs for our literary history, including specimens of controversy to the reign of Elizabeth* (London: printed for John Murray, 1814), vol. 3, Appendix, pp. 273–311 (p. 286). For more on 'De la force de l'imagination', see Kate Tunstall's essay in the present volume.

36. D'Israeli, 'Quotation', in *A Second Series of Curiosities* (1823), pp. 75–85 (p. 85).

37. D'Israeli, 'Quotation', p. 77.

38. Anon., 'A Vindication of Montaigne's *Essays*', in *Essays of Michael seigneur de Montaigne*, trans. Charles Cotton (London: printed for Daniel Brown *et al.*, 1711), vol. 1, pp. 1–13 (p. 3): 'These angry Gentlemen [the enemies of Montaigne] do likewise pretend, that what is most admir'd in *Montaigne* is stoln from some ancient Authors, and that if those Quotations and the little Stories he tells us about his Temper and Inclinations were taken out of his Book, the rest would be very little or nothing at all.' The 'Vindication' is in fact a translation of Charles Sorel's 'Des *Essais* de Michel de Montaigne', in *La Bibliothèque françoise* (Paris: Compagnie des Libraires du Palais, 1667), pp. 80–91 (for our quotation, see p. 82). I owe thanks to Professor Warren Boutcher for drawing my attention to this point.

39. D'Israeli, 'On Novelty in Literature', in *Miscellanies* (1796), pp. 310–38 (p. 318). Compare III.12, 'De la phisionimie' [Of Physiognomy]: 'Comme quelqu'un pourroit dire de moy que j'ay seulement faict icy un amas de fleurs estrangeres, n'y ayant fourny du mien que le filet à les lier' [Even so someone might say of me that I have only made a bunch of other people's flowers, having furnished nothing of my own but the thread to tie them] (V, p. 1055; F, p. 984). I.26, 'De l'institution des enfans' [On Educating Children]: 'Je n'ay dressé commerce avec aucun livre solide, sinon Plutarque et Seneque, où je puyse comme les Danaïdes, remplissant et versant sans cesse. J'en attache quelque chose à ce papier; à moy, si peu que rien' [I have not had regular dealings with any solid book, except Plutarch and Seneca, from whom I draw like the Danaïds, incessantly filling up and pouring out. Some of this sticks to this paper; to myself, little or nothing] (V, p. 146; F, p. 129). 'Des livres': 'Ez raisons et inventions que je transplante en mon solage et confons aux miennes, j'ay à escient ommis parfois d'en marquer l'autheur, pour tenir en bride la temerité de ces sentences hastives qui se jettent sur toute sorte d'escrits, notamment jeunes escrits d'hommes encore vivants, et en vulgaire, qui reçoit tout le monde à en parler et qui semble convaincre la conception et le dessein, vulgaire de mesmes. Je veux qu'ils donnent une nazarde à Plutarque sur mon nez, et qu'ils s'eschaudent à injurier Seneque en moy' [In the reasonings and inventions that I transplant into my soil and confound with my own, I have

sometimes deliberately not indicated the author, in order to hold in check the temerity of those hasty condemnations that are tossed at all sorts of writings, notably recent writings of men still living, and in the vulgar tongue, which invites everyone to talk about them and seems to convict the conception and design of being likewise vulgar. I want them give Plutarch a fillip on my nose and get burned insulting Seneca in me] (V, p. 408; F, pp. 359–60).

40. D'Israeli, 'Account of a Singular Atrabilarian or Hypochondriac', *Curiosities* (1794), vol. 2, 'Miscellanea', pp. 520–25 (p. 525); emphasis mine.

41. 'Apologie de Raimond de Sebond' [Of what is the subtlest madness made, but the subtlest wisdom? As great enmities are born of great friendships, and mortal maladies of vigorous health, so are the greatest and wildest manias born of the rare and lively stirrings of our soul; it is only a half turn of the peg to pass from the one to the other. In the actions of the insane we see how neatly madness combines with the most vigorous operations of our soul. Who does not know how imperceptibly near is madness to the lusty flights of a free mind and the effects of supreme and extraordinary virtue?] (V, p. 492; F, pp. 440–41).

42. 'The ancient Fathers have said every thing they could imagine to depreciate the character of Julian the Apostate. Though they had not done this, had he not proved an apostate and a persecutor of the Christians; they do not in the slightest manner notice his many eminent qualities. He was rigorously just, a man of strict morals, and a great politician. *See what Montaigne and La Mothe le Vayer observe of him*; and particularly his character, elaborately delineated by Mr. Gibbon'; D'Israeli, 'Religious Enmity', in *Curiosities* (1791), pp. 187–91 (p. 188); emphasis mine.

43. V, pp. 669–71. For a discussion of 'De la liberté de conscience', see Richard Scholar, *Montaigne and the Art of Free-Thinking* (Oxford: Peter Lang, 2010), especially pp. 118–33. Montaigne also makes reference to Julian in I.16, 'De la punition de la couardise' [Of the Punishment of Cowardice] (V, p. 70) and I.42, 'De l'inequalité qui est entre nous' [Of the Inequality That Is Between Us] (V, pp. 266–67). François de La Mothe Le Vayer discussed the example of Julian the Apostate in his controversial *De la vertu des païens* of 1641/47: La Mothe Le Vayer, *De la vertu des payens* (Paris: François Targa, 1642 [in fact 1641]), especially pp. 319–67, and in the second, augmented edition (Paris: Augustin Courbé, 1647), pp. 263–304.

44. Gabriel Naudé, *Naudaeana et Patiniana, ou Singularitez remarquables prises des conversations de Mess. Naudé & Patin*, 2nd edn [ed. A. Lancelot] (Amsterdam: François vander Plaats, 1703 [1702?]), p. 98.

45. See Daniel Ménager, 'Juifs — Judaïsme', and Jean Balsamo, 'Louppes, Antoinette de', and 'Louppes, famille', in *Dictionnaire Montaigne*, ed. Desan, pp. 630–32, 699–700, and 700–01; and Elisabeth Mendes da Costa, 'Aspects of Tolerance of the Jew in Selected French Texts in the Later French Renaissance (1550–1615)', PhD thesis, King's College London, 2007, pp. 141–87, especially pp. 145–48.

46. D'Israeli, *Miscellanies* (1796), pp. 59–76 (p. 75). Compare 'De l'inequalité qui est entre nous': 'Plutarque dit en quelque lieu qu'il ne trouve point si grande distance de beste à beste, comme il trouve d'homme à homme. [...] Mais, à propos de l'estimation des hommes, c'est merveille que, sauf nous, aucune chose ne s'estime que par ses propres qualitez' [Plutarch says somewhere that he does not find so much difference between one animal and another as he does between one man and another. [...] But apropos of judging men, it is a wonder that, ourselves excepted, nothing is evaluated, except by its own qualities] (V, pp. 258–59; F, p. 229).

47. [Isaac D'Israeli], 'The Matrimonial State', in *The Literary Character, illustrated by the history of men of genius, drawn from their own feelings and confessions. By the author of 'Curiosities of literature'* (London: J. Murray, 1818), pp. 250–72 (p. 258). For more on Montaigne and marriage, see Chimène Bateman's essay in this volume.

48. D'Israeli, 'Cicero', in *Curiosities* (1794), vol. 1, pp. 85–87 (pp. 86–87). See also his 'Anecdotes of Fashion', in *Curiosities* (1807), vol. 1, pp. 93–120 (pp. 387–88), quoting Montaigne's 'De l'institution des enfans' (V, p. 172) in Cotton's translation: 'I have never yet been apt to imitate the *negligent garb* which is yet observable among the young men of our time; to wear my *cloak on one shoulder*, my *bonnet on one side*, and *one stocking* in something *more disorder than the other*, meant to express a manly disdain of such exotic ornaments, and a contempt of art' (D'Israeli's italics). D'Israeli's topic (fashion) leads to the excision of Montaigne's qualifying statement: 'but I find that negligence of much better use in the form of speaking'.

49. D'Israeli, 'Gaming', in *Curiosities* (1807), vol. 1, pp. 313–19 (p. 315): '[Eckeloo, author of *De Alea, sive de curanda ludendi in pecuniam cupiditate*, 1569] had not the good sense of old Montaigne, who gives us the reason why he gave over gaming. "I used (says he,) to like formerly games of chance with cards and dice; but of that folly I have long been cured; merely because I found that whatever good countenance I put on when I lost, I did not feel my vexation the less." A man of letters to be a gambler is one of the most undubitable [sic] follies he can practise.' Compare V, p. 1014: 'J'aymois autrefois les jeux hazardeux des cartes et dets; je m'en suis deffaict, il y a long temps, pour cela seulement que, quelque bonne mine que je fisse en ma perte, je ne laissois pas d'en avoir au dedans de la piqueure.' I have compared the wording with Florio's and with Charles Cotton's, in the 1711 and 1776 editions.

50. D'Israeli, 'Influence of Names', in *Curiosities* (1807), vol. 2, pp. 408–26 (pp. 415–16): 'Some nations have long cherished a feeling that there is a certain elevation or abasement in proper names. Montaigne on this subject says, "A gentleman, one of my neighbours, in overvaluing the excellencies of old times, never omitted noticing the pride and magnificence of the *names* of the nobility of those days: Don *Grumedan, Quadragan, Argesilan*, when fully sounded, were evidently men of another stamp, than *Peter, Giles*, and *Michel*."' Again, I have compared D'Israeli's English phrasing with Florio's and with Charles Cotton's in the 1711 and 1776 editions.

51. D'Israeli, 'Of Miscellanies', in *Miscellanies* (1796), pp. 6–23 (p. 7).

52. D'Israeli, 'The Page, the Baron and the Minstrel', in *Amenities of Literature*, vol. 1, pp. 111–27 (p. 125).

53. D'Israeli, 'Singularities Observed by Various Nations in their Repasts', in *Curiosities* (1791), 'Historical Anecdotes', pp. 264–71 (pp. 265–66).

54. Jean-Nicolas Demeunier, 'Cérémonies et politesse à tables. Manieres de manger', in *L'Esprit des usages et des coutumes des différens peuples* (London: Pissot, 1776), vol. 1, pp. 22–32 (p. 26). D'Israeli gives only the title of the work, not the author's name.

55. Isaac D'Israeli, 'Singularities Observed by Various Nations in their Repasts', in *Curiosities of Literature* (Boston: Lily, Wait, Coldman and Holden, 1833), vol. 1, pp. 233–36 (p. 234). The same change is also present in the London edition of 1834.

56. D'Israeli, 'Modes of Salutation, and Amicable Ceremonies, Observed in Various Nations', *Curiosities* (1794), vol. 2, 'Historical anecdotes', pp. 388–95 (p. 393): 'The Chinese are singularly affected in their personal civilities. [...] If two persons meet after a long separation, they both fall on their knees, and bend the face to the earth, and this ceremony they repeat two or three times. Surely we may differ here with the sentiment of Montaigne, and confess this ceremony to be ridiculous. It arises from their national affectation. They substitute artificial ceremonies for natural actions.' Compare Demeunier, 'Manieres de s'aborder, de saluer. Révérences. Compliments', in *L'Esprit des usages*, vol. 3, 'Usage domestiques', pp. 29–48 (p. 39): 'Si deux personnes se rejoignent après une longue separation, elles tombent toutes deux à genoux, et baissent la tête jusqu'à terre; et elles répetent deux ou trois fois la même cérémonie'; and II.17, 'De la praesumption' [Of Presumption], V, p. 633: 'Il y en a d'autres, artificiels, dequoy je ne parle point, comme les salutations et reverences, par où on acquiert, le plus souvent à tort, l'honneur d'estre bien humble et courtois: on peut estre humble de gloire. Je suis assez prodigue de bonnettades, notamment en esté, et n'en reçoys jamais sans revenche, de quelque qualité d'homme que ce soit, s'il n'est à mes gages. Je desirasse d'aucuns Princes que je connois, qu'ils en fussent plus espargnans et justes dispensateurs: car, ainsin indiscrettement espandues, elles ne portent plus de coup. Si elles sont sans esgard, elles sont sans effect' (see F, pp. 582–83).

57. Isaac D'Israeli, *A Dissertation on Anecdotes* (London: Printed for C. and G. Kearsley and J. Murray, 1793), p. iv: 'I am even desirous, that this Essay may not be considered as destitute of connection, because at the first glance it may thus appear. The work consists not of a mere mass of loose anecdotes; these are given as sketches of the manner in which various topics may be conducted; and elucidate those reflections on the nature of anecdotes, which if they shall be found to be pertinent, is all of which I am solicitous.'

58. D'Israeli, *A Dissertation on Anecdotes* (1793), p. 31. See also p. [1]: 'A writer should correct others, or correct himself: I therefore hazard this essay.'

59. D'Israeli, 'Of Miscellanies', in *Miscellanies*, pp. 1–23 (p. 5). The expression long pre-dates the common epithet of 'the father of the modern essay', which seems to go back to the second half of the nineteenth century.

60. Although the colourful quotation appears to be apocryphal, it had become something of a winged expression. See Alan Boase, *The Fortunes of Montaigne: A History of the Essays in France 1580–1669* (New York: Octagon Books, 1970), p. 17. The phrase does not occur in any of the printed editions of the *Scaligerana*. It is first attested in Charles Sorel's *La Bibliothèque françoise* (Paris: La Compagnie des libraires du Palais, 1664), p. 70, and is reported in Antoine Teissier's comments on the obituary notice on Montaigne culled from Jacques Auguste de Thou's *History of his Own Times* (A. Teissier, *Les Éloges des hommes savans tirez de l'histoire de M. de Thou* (Geneva, J. H. Widerhold, 1683), vol. 2, p. 179).

61. D'Israeli, 'Of Miscellanies', in *Miscellanies* (1796), pp. 1–23 (pp. 5–6). William Warburton's critique of the essayist and poet Joseph Addison can be found in his 'Notes [to the] Prologue to the Satires', in *The Works of Alexander Pope*, ed. William Warburton (London: Printed for J. and P. Knapton, 1757), vol. 4: *The Satires*, pp. 27–29, and 'Notes [to the] Imitations of Horace', in *The Works of Alexander Pope*, vol. 4, pp. 173–76 (especially p. 175).

62. D'Israeli, 'Of Miscellanies', in *Miscellanies* (1796), pp. 1–23 (p. 7).

63. Pierre-Daniel Huet, 'Essais de Montagne', in *Huetiana, ou Pensées diverses de M. Huet, evesque d'Avranches* (Paris: Jacques Estienne, 1722), pp. 14–17.

64. D'Israeli, 'Of Miscellanies', in *Miscellanies* (1796), pp. 1–23 (pp. 7–8): 'Those authors who appear sometimes to forget they are writers, and remember they are men, will be our favourites. He who writes from the heart, will write to the heart; every one is enabled to decide on his merits, and they will not be referred to more learned heads, or a more distant period.'

65. D'Israeli, 'Cowley. Of his Melancholy', in *Calamities of Authors* (1812), vol. 1, pp. 81–100 (pp. 85–86): 'All of Cowley's tenderest and undisguised feelings have therefore not perished. These Essays now form a species of composition in our language, a mixture of prose and verse — the man with the poet — the self-painter has sat to himself, and, with the utmost simplicity, has copied out the image of his soul.'

66. D'Israeli, 'Of Miscellanies', in *Miscellanies* (1796), pp. 1–23 (p. 18): 'The readers of Montaigne, had they met with him, would have [...] found a friend complaining like themselves of his infirmities, and smiling with them, at the folly of his complaints.'

67. D'Israeli, *An Essay on the Manners and Genius of the Literary Character* (1795), p. 149.

68. See *Huetiana*, p. 15; [Mitford], 'Lady Blessington's Conversations (Concluded)', p. 592 (slightly misquoting Huet's phrase).

69. D'Israeli, 'Of Miscellanies', in *Miscellanies* (1796), pp. 1–23 (p. 19). D'Israeli apparently conflates Cardinal Du Perron's designation of the *Essais* as 'le bréviaire des honnêtes gens' with the comment made by Huet, who was Bishop of Avranches.

70. D'Israeli, *Curiosities of Literature* (1823), vol. 4, p. 188.

71. D'Israeli, 'The Man of One Book', in *A Second Series of Curiosities* (1823), vol. 3, pp. 120–26 (p. 125).

72. D'Israeli, *An Essay on the Manners and Genius of the Literary Character* (1795), pp. 23–24. Louis de Sacy's *Traité de l'amitié* was first published in 1703 and translated into English the following year; his *Traité de la gloire* first appeared in 1715.

73. Isaac D'Israeli, 'Hobbes and his Quarrels', in *Quarrels of Authors; or, Some memoirs for our literary history, including specimens of controversy to the reign of Elizabeth* (London: J. Murray, 1814), vol. 3, pp. 3–85 (p. 70): '[Hobbes] disperses, in all his works, some Montaigne-like notices of himself'.

74. D'Israeli, 'Laborious Authors', *Calamities of Authors* (1812), vol. 1, pp. 231–73 (p. 247).

75. See n. 65 above. Compare Montaigne, 'Au Lecteur', V, p. 3: 'car c'est moy que je peins'.

76. Blessington, 'Journal of Conversations with Lord Byron, no. X', p. 40.

CHAPTER 12

'Le Demi-sourire de Montaigne': Flaubert and the *Journal de voyage*

Timothy Chesters

ITALIE: Donne lieu à bien des déceptions, n'est pas si belle qu'on dit.[1]

Passing through the streets of Rome in the winter of 1581, Montaigne stops to observe a Jewish circumcision ceremony. He watches the guests assemble with their gifts; the Rabbi cuts the child, discards the flesh, and sucks the wound. Later, back in his lodgings, he recalls the occasion in his travel diary, adding this observation: 'Le cry de l'enfant est pareil aux nostres qu'on baptise.'[2] When Gustave Flaubert comes to read Montaigne's *Journal de voyage* sometime in the middle years of the nineteenth century, he singles out this remark in his notebook, where we find it introduced with the following commentary: 'belle phrase d'une simplicité toute naïve ou d'une ironie profonde, peut-être ensemble l'un et l'autre pour qui connaît Montaigne: "le cry de l'enfant est pareil aux nostres qu'on baptise"'.[3]

Two voices merge in one. On the one hand, *of course* the child's cry resembles that of Christian infants: distressed young children sound alike, whatever the acculturating rites imposed on them by adults. In its humanity as well as its 'simplicité naïve' the sentence would be worthy of Félicité, the 'simple heart' of Flaubert's *Trois contes*. On the other, Montaigne's may be a disingenuous simplicity — a knowing shot aimed at religious rituals in general, with their inflated sense of their own distinction. This detection of 'une ironie profonde' revives an eighteenth-century tendency to claim Montaigne as a precursor of anticlericalism; the essayist is drawn close to Voltaire's *ingénus* abroad; mock innocence levels the world's religions to a single, superstitious plane. And yet the Montaigne initiate ('qui connaît Montaigne') knows that in truth we cannot separate this second, ironic voice from the first, naïve one. Ultimately, the beauty of this 'belle phrase' lies in what Flaubert calls elsewhere 'le demi-sourire de Montaigne' — the same serene inscrutability to which the novelist aspired his whole career.[4]

1. At the sign of the bear

Flaubert certainly knew his Montaigne. Writing to Louise Colet in October 1853 he recalls his first, teenage, encounter with the *Essais*:

> C'est singulier comme je suis plein de ce bonhomme-là! Est-ce une coïncidence,
> ou bien est-ce parce que je m'en suis bourré toute une année à 18 ans, où je
> ne lisais *que lui*? Mais je suis ébahi, souvent, de trouver l'analyse très déliée de
> mes moindres sentiments! Nous avons mêmes goûts, mêmes opinions, même
> manière de vivre, mêmes manies.[5]

Flaubert's intensely identificatory mode of reading Montaigne gives rise to scores
of quotations and allusions in his *Correspondance*, the majority clustered between
1838 — the period recalled here — and the appearance of *Madame Bovary*, his first
published novel, almost 20 years later; three unpublished *récits* from this period also
carry epigraphs and 'moralités' taken from the *Essais*.[6] These letters and juvenilia
formed the basis for important studies by Bruneau, Fairlie, and Vatan, all of whom
emphasize the role of Flaubert's 'père nourricier' in his literary education.[7] Since
the appearance of these studies, further traces have emerged. Steps to digitize
Flaubert's library in Canteleu-Croisset have made available his copy of Joseph-
Victor Le Clerc's 1836 edition of the *Essais*, and more than 350 sidelines pencilled in
its margins.[8] And now supplementing these is an extensive *cahier* of his reading notes
on Montaigne, which recently resurfaced in a British private collection. Sixty of
its pages concern the *Essais* — excerpts for the most part, with the occasional terse
commentary.[9] On the final 18 pages of this document, inserted as a separate sheaf
and written in a later hand, appear his notes on the *Journal de voyage*. These notes,
so far unknown to scholarship, are the focus of what follows.

An outline of the document will offer a preliminary flavour. Flaubert records
having read the work in the two-volume duodecimo edition produced by Meusnier
de Querlon a few years after its discovery in the early 1770s.[10] His notes on other
works tend to omit detailed notations of format and imprint, but here an exception
has been made, probably because he was reading a library copy.[11]

The manuscript tracks Montaigne's transit through southern France, Switzerland,
Germany, and Italy in two distinct modes. The first is represented in the main
body of the document (14 pages) featuring, as is customary for Flaubert's reading
practice, a mix of excerpts and summaries with just the occasional gloss, as when
he defends Montaigne from Querlon's charge of 'égoïsme'. Aside from these scarce
commentaries (to which I shall return), the interest of this portion lies in the silent
triage of selection and omission. There is a marked bias towards the Italian stages
of the journey (12 pages) as compared to a relative lack of interest in the German
leg (two pages), and complete indifference to the Swiss (no pages). As one might
expect, Flaubert is attentive to the succession of different voices in the text ('ici finit
la dictée de Montaigne — Le livre est maintenant à la 1ère personne' [p. 10] — 'à la
p. 178 cesse le français. Le reste est écrit en italien' [p. 13] — 'Montaigne reprend le
français' [p. 14]). The encounters that tend to loom largest in Montaigne scholarship
today are conspicuously absent. The essayist's conversations with religious and
intellectual luminaries such as Juan Maldonado, Felix Platter, François Hotman, or
Theodor Zwinger, the manuscripts of Aquinas and Virgil in the Vatican library,
and his brush with the Papal censors are passed over without comment. Instead
Flaubert's focus seems more broadly anthropological, falling on customs governing
dress and etiquette at table, on the execution of a criminal witnessed in Rome, or

on Montaigne's introduction to an unlettered poetess he meets in Bagno della Villa. These are the notes of one observer on another.

The second mode of note-taking adopts an alternative perspective on the journey. On the front and back pages enclosing the main portion of the notes (four pages in total), Flaubert has compiled under the heading 'Itinéraire du voyage de Montaigne' a list of all 154 stops on Montaigne's trail [pp. 16–18, 1] (see Figure 1). This apparatus anticipates a feature of some modern editions.[12] The layout suggests that he completed this task only after the main body of the notes, filling up the back pages only to run out of space and use the blank leaf at the front. Some of the entries are annotated. Occasionally he marks the date at which Montaigne leaves a particular location (e.g. 'Rome, en part le 3 avril' [p. 17]), especially where this departure follows a significant time interval (Bagno della Villa, Pavia, Florence): as well as highlighting those places in which Montaigne lingers longest, these hint at an interest in the rhythms of the journey. A handful of other annotations supply materials omitted in the main body of the notes. For example, beside Vitry-le-François he writes: 'C'est là où M. entend parler des 2 hermaphrodites cités dans ses essais' [p. 16].[13] Next to 'Donremy [sur Meuse]', where Montaigne visits the birthplace of Joan of Arc, a rough quotation from the *Journal* sounds a distinctively Flaubertian note of historical melancholy: 'le devant de la maisonette de la Pucelle où elle naquit est toute peinte de ses gestes; mais l'aage en a fort corrompu la peinture' [p. 16].[14] Unlike many of the notes in the main section, all these refer to a person or event specific to a given place ('c'est là que...', 'y est visité par...', etc.).

Before coming to a more detailed account of Flaubert's notes, we would be entitled to ask why he troubled to read the *Journal de voyage* at all. Its unpopularity in France during the nineteenth century is notorious.[15] Despite the upturn in Montaigne's reputation during the Restoration, furthered by mid-century 'Montaignologues' such as Jean-François Payen, Gustave Brunet, and Alphonse Grün, no new edition followed Querlon's until 1889.[16] The embarrassment that had greeted its discovery before the Revolution — at Montaigne's fixation on his kidney stones, at the anti-philosophical piety he shows at the shrine of Loreto — had not subsided, and if anything the aesthetic landscape of the early 1800s had proven even less hospitable.[17] Stendhal, an enthusiastic reader of the *Essais*, was famously unable to forgive Montaigne's indifference to Italian art.[18] Chateaubriand further complained of a corresponding insensibility to natural landscape, as when Montaigne writes these deathless lines on the countryside around Rome, the setting for the first six books of the *Aeneid*: 'Montaigne lui-même à qui certes l'imagination ne manquait pas, dit: "nous avons loins sur notre main gauche l'Appenin, le prospect du pays malplaisant, bossé, plein de profondes fendasses [...], le terrain nud, sans arbres, une bonne partie sterile".'[19] Such criticisms were widely repeated.[20]

Even extracts were difficult to find. The editor of Flaubert's copy of the *Essais*, Joseph-Victor Le Clerc, includes 10 of Montaigne's letters and the whole of La Boëtie's *Discours de la servitude volontaire*, and yet mentions the *Journal de voyage* just twice, in footnotes to the *Essais*.[21] This indifference seems especially pronounced when compared with the text's warm reception in England. William Hazlitt's early Victorian edition includes an unabridged translation; Mary Wollstonecraft

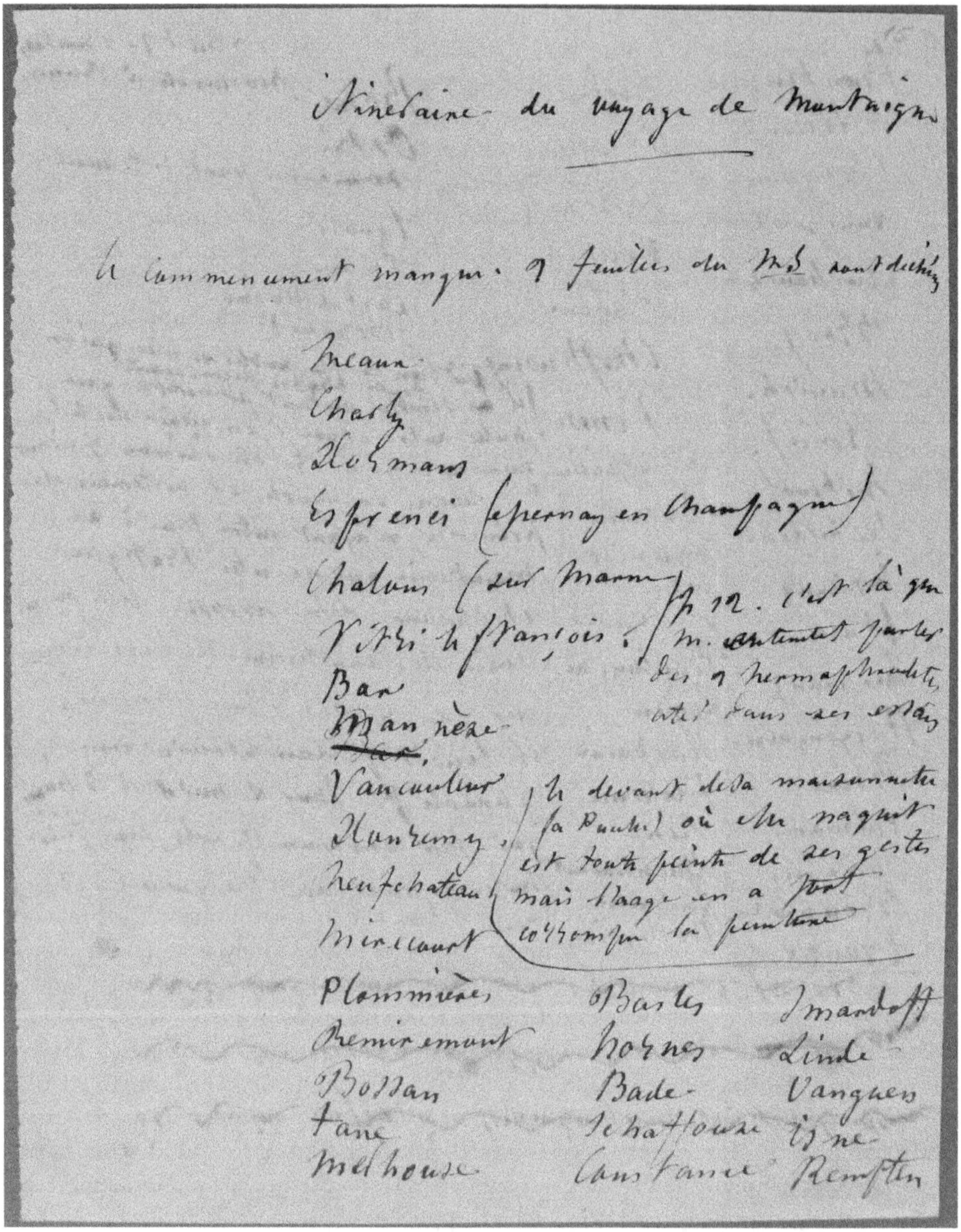

FIG. 1. Gustave Flaubert, [Notes sur le Journal de voyage de Montaigne], p. 16. With permission, Camellia Collection, UK.

Shelley finds the *Journal* 'singularly interesting', not least for its descriptions of Rome ('short, but drawn with a master's hand — graphic, original, and just'); and the radical journalist Bayle St John, the author of the first full-length biography of Montaigne, devotes well over 100 pages to the work.[22] St John, who spent much of his short life in Paris, remarks on French hostility to Montaigne's travel diaries. He recalls once asking a bookseller whether he thought they might be reprinted: 'He answered with some indignation, using, I believe, the words of the "Manuel du Libraire," — "No, sir: they are of very little value." '[23]

Flaubert's reading notes on the *Essais* can be dated to his late adolescence at the end of the 1830s; the date and context of those on the *Journal de voyage* are harder to establish.[24] Possibly the impetus was paternal. In the late summer of 1840, he visited southern France and Corsica in the company of Jules Cloquet, a family friend. Shortly before he set off, his father, Achille-Cléophas Flaubert, wrote to him invoking Montaigne's advice in I.26, 'De l'institution des enfans' [On Educating Children]:

> Profite de ton voyage et souviens-toi de ton ami Montaigne qui veut que l'on voyage pour rapporter principalement les humeurs des nations et leurs façons, et pour 'frotter et limer notre cervelle contre celle d'aultruy'. Vois, observe, et prends des notes; ne voyage pas en épicier ni en commis-voyageur.[25]

Achille-Cléophas here displays a level of sympathy for his son's tastes — as reader and traveller — with which literary historians have not always credited him.[26] Gustave the sexual adventurer would soon take literally this paternal license to 'rub up' against exotic Others — on this trip the Toulon innkeeper Eulalie Foucauld, later and further afield the bardashes of Cairo, or the Egyptian courtesan Kuchuk-Hanem. But alongside and in tension with this physical proximity also appears a recognizably Flaubertian instruction to stand back and *see* — not in the gawping, second-hand mode of the petit-bourgeois *épicier*, but as active observer and note-taker.

The insistence on note-taking is especially striking placed so close to the reference to Montaigne. In urging his son to take the essayist as his model, might Achille-Cléophas have had in mind the *Journal de voyage*? Did Flaubert read the text at his father's instigation? The idea is pleasing, not least because it would echo a possible genesis of the *Journal* itself: that in keeping it Montaigne was following the example of the 'papier journal' kept by *his* father, Pierre, of his travels in Italy years before.[27] In any event, Gustave followed his father's instruction to take notes. The travel journal now known as *Pyrénées-Corse* records how, while in Bordeaux public library, he handled 'le manuscript de Montaigne avec autant de vénération qu'une relique'.[28]

As attractive as this thesis may appear, the *Journal de voyage* probably caught his attention only later, perhaps as he prepared for one of the trips he undertook to Italy in 1845 or 1851. Support for this later dating is provided by the handwriting, which most resembles that found in preparatory notes for the first *La Tentation de Saint-Antoine* (1849). Also intriguing, if hardly conclusive, is Flaubert's underlining of the name of a hostel visited by Montaigne and his party. The otherwise unremarkable note on this passage reads: 'à Rome 'Nous vinmes loger à l'Ours.' (avait logé à Kempten à la même enseigne)' [p. 5].[29] Readers of Flaubert's letters from the 1840s may recognize this bear:

> Je ne vais nulle part, ne vois personne et ne suis vu de personne; [...] comme dit le sage ancien: 'Cache ta vie et abstiens-toi.' — Aussi trouve-t-on que j'ai tort, je devrais aller dans le monde, je suis un drôle d'original, un ours.[30]

In tandem with Epicurus's motto 'Cache ta vie', the bear becomes an emblem of Flaubert's increasing self-seclusion throughout his twenties and thirties.[31] His letters of the period repeatedly evoke the lure of the cave:

> Je suis ours et veux rester ours dans ma tanière, dans mon antre, dans ma peau, dans ma vieille peau d'ours, bien tranquille et loin du bourgeois et des bourgeoises.[32]

> J'ai même envie d'acheter un bel ours (en peinture), de le faire encadrer et suspendre dans ma chambre après avoir écrit au-dessous: Portrait de Gustave Flaubert, pour indiquer mes dispositions morales et mon humeur sociale.[33]

Coupled with the strong tendency towards identification with Montaigne, Flaubert's newly adopted insignia may well explain his attention to the hostel signs in Kempten and Rome, especially if his notes were dated to the mid 1840s onwards.[34]

2. Interlude: Henry and Jules

Questions of travel and travel-writing preoccupied Flaubert around the middle of the 1840s, as the democratization of tourism (the chemin de fer had reached Rouen in 1843, much to his dismay) was visibly beginning to transform both. How should one travel? And what should be the literary yield: a travel journal, poetry, a novel? A passage in the 1845 Éducation sentimentale shows him weighing the alternatives as he contrasts the conduct of his two protagonists, Henry and Jules, on their trip to Italy:

> Henry se levait de grand matin, courait par les rues, dessinait les monuments, compulsait les bibliothèques, inspectait tous les musées, visitait tous les établissements, parlait à tout le monde. Jules [...] porté au hasard, où le poussait son caprice, perdu dans ses songeries [...], retournait dix fois voir la même figure dans un tableau, et il s'en allait ensuite sans connaître la galerie. Il aurait passé sa vie entière à voir ce qu'Henry voyait en un seul jour, et ce qui fournissait dix lignes à celui-ci, il lui aurait fallu tout un volume pour le dire; Henry rapporta un journal complet, Jules seulement de temps à autre écrivait quelques fragments de vers, avec lesquels il allumait son cigare.[35]

Adrianne Tooke points out that although this passage may mock both types of traveller — the 'Conscientious Tourist' and the 'Poet-Dreamer' — Flaubert himself combined elements of each.[36] Like Henry he returned with 'un journal complet' from all his excursions in this period: as well as the earlier Pyrénées-Corse (1840), the texts now referred to as Voyage en Italie (1845), Par les champs et par les grèves (the Loire valley and Brittany, with Maxime Du Camp, 1847), and Voyage en Orient (Egypt, Athens, and Rome, 1851). Also like Henry he was an assiduous museum- and gallery-goer. The voyage to Italy in the summer of 1845, undertaken with his parents as they accompanied his sister on her honeymoon, included visits to collections in Lyon ('deux Rubens'), Avignon, Arles, Marseille, Turin ('musée nul'), the Biblioteca and Pinacoteca Ambrosiana in Milan, and, most famously, the

Palazzo Balbi in Genoa (Breughel's *Temptation of Saint Anthony*).

The happiest visits were those he made alone, although solitude was difficult to find. Writing to Alfred Le Poittevin from Marseille he complains that the presence of his family, like that of 'le Docteur Cloquet' five years earlier, has caused him to miss all the best sites:

> Je voulais voir Aigues-Mortes et je n'ai pas vu Aigues-Mortes, la Sainte-Baume et la grotte où Madeleine a pleuré, le champ de bataille de Marius, etc. Je n'ai rien vu de tout cela parce que je n'étais pas seul, je n'étais pas libre. Voilà deux fois donc que je vois la Méditerranée en épicier.[37]

Even when managing to break loose from the family party he is never entirely alone, and still less safe from *épicier* intrusions. Hence certain museums in the *Voyage en Italie* appear as memorable for their tour guide as for their exhibits:

> L'observatoire. mine ébahie et lourde du montreur.[38]

> Musée. Le Silène sans tête, cuisse molle, ventre flasque [...] — tête de Cybèle sans nez; jolis tumulus. Le guide: 'J'ai des dictionnaires latins, grecs'.[39]

Guides are not the only figures who interpose themselves between the traveller and the objects of his gaze. The *Voyage en Italie* frequently triangulates Flaubert's own responses to art or landscape with those of other tourists:

> Excursion à ARONA: bateau à vapeur, presque rien que des gens du pays. Vieille anglaise prenant des notes et regardant dans son livre le nom de chaque coin de terre.[40]

> Pendant que je regardais la *Tentation* de Breughel il est venu un monsieur et une dame qui sont partis à peine entrés; leur mine devant ces toiles était quelque chose de très profond comme bêtise. — Ils accomplissaient un devoir.[41]

At first glance *bêtise* may seem to arrive entirely from without, in others; in reality, as elsewhere in Flaubert, the horror and fascination it provokes is always partly self-directed. Both the note-taking 'vieille anglaise' and the dutiful sightseers embody modes of travelling that come dangerously close to resembling his own. *Bêtise* becomes an emanation of the tourist gaze *tout court*.

Reluctant to adopt the role of tourist, Flaubert could also exhibit a Jules-like reverie bordering on indolence. Writing of their voyage to Egypt in 1849–51, Maxime Du Camp would recall years later that they had scarcely arrived in Cairo when he began to notice his companion's 'lassitude' and 'ennui'. 'Flaubert n'avait rien de mon exaltation, il était calme et vivait en lui-même', he remembers, 'Le mouvement, l'action lui était antipathiques.'[42] While Du Camp tore around the desert with his camera — a tireless Henry — Flaubert sat and smoked.

The same antipathy extended to activity of travel-writing itself, a genre Flaubert despised. Although he kept travel diaries, he refused to publish them — principally out of distaste for the kind of descriptive striving he felt the genre made unavoidable. Thus when his friend Ernest Feydeau confides his ambition to write up an account of his adventures abroad, he receives this reply: 'Je repousse absolument l'idée que tu as d'écrire ton voyage. 1° parce que c'est facile; 2° parce qu'un roman vaut mieux. As-tu besoin de prouver que tu sais faire des descriptions?'[43] Novels transform experience; descriptions merely transpose it.[44] As early as *Pyrénées-Corse*, Flaubert eschews descriptive facility for its own sake. Here his account of a ride through the forest of Marmano is self-consciously cut short:

> Nous avons monté depuis le matin et nous entrons dans la forêt de Marmano. Le chemin est raide et va en zigzag à travers les sapins, dont le tronc a des lueurs du soleil qui pénètre à travers les branches supérieures et éclaire tout le pied de la forêt; l'air embaume de l'odeur du bois vert. Il ne faut pas écrire tout cela.[45]

The later Italy accounts retreat still further into what Francis Claudon, discussing the *Voyage en Italie*, calls Flaubert's 'mutisme volontaire'.[46] About to remark on the view from the Simplon Pass, he writes simply: 'Indescriptible, il faut rêver et souvenir'.[47] Where he does transcribe his impressions, what prevail are evanescent *choses vues* akin to Jules's 'fragments de vers':

> Un moine a passé, dans la lumière, maigre, à plis flottants, tout blanc, allant vite; mouvement pour tourner dans l'escalier [...]

> Grand homme barbu, enfants à l'air maudit marchant à pied à côté des charrettes. Comme nous les regardions avec nos lorgnons, ils ont poussé de grands cris.[48]

> Cimetière, figure pâle du fossoyeur, homme maigre sous son bonnet de laine grise.[49]

Unlike Henry's completed journal these sketches suggest preparatory rather than finished work, as if their transfiguration into art were intended to come later. But of course deferral carries its own risks. Jules may steer clear of otiose description only to succumb, like his more famous avatar Frédéric Moreau, to 'l'étourdissement des paysages'.[50] His future projects may prove as insubstantial as cigar smoke — the traveller's experience not transfigured, but diminished to a blank.

3. A sensibility on tour

The Montaigne of the travel journal is neither Jules nor Henry, yet similar concerns govern Flaubert's notes on that text: with different modes of looking and seeing, with the mediating presence of others, and with the uncertain connection between the fragmentary labours of note-taking and a future, finished work. Seldom does the focus fall on Italy itself, and only then insofar as it illuminates what Francis Steegmuller, writing of Flaubert's own travels, calls a 'sensibility on tour'.[51]

On the question of seeing, the notes are most eloquent in their omissions. Almost none of Flaubert's excerpts show Montaigne adopting the posture of the sightseer, still less that of the aesthete. Whatever Stendhal's criticisms, the *Journal* itself is far from lacking in such moments.[52] While in Florence Montaigne is shown a number of Michelangelo busts; but Flaubert, who worships Michelangelo in his letters, ignores them. The admiration Montaigne expresses for the fountains and water gardens at Castello and Pratelino, and for many other examples of hydraulic and architectural ingenuity, is likewise passed over. 'Deux belles pages sur la campagne de Rome' do receive a mention (in silent contradiction of Chateaubriand's view of the same passage), yet no excerpts have been made. Similarly, Montaigne's reflections on the ruins of Rome are only acknowledged in the most perfunctory fashion: rather than excerpt them, Flaubert simply notes his 'pages éloquentes inspirées par la mélancolie du ruine' (Querlon, vol. 1, pp. 305–10). Ruins especially tend to evoke in Flaubert the Romantic 'pittoresque' (particularly when coupled with eloquence), and so were to be strenuously avoided.[53]

In one of the rare instances where Montaigne takes up an explicitly contemplative posture — this time before the landscape at Montefiascune — the moment of contemplation is over before it has begun. Couched amid pages of unremarked material, it appears transcribed in Flaubert's notes: 'Montefiascune. "Il (Montaigne) s'y fut arresté p^r la beauté du lieu, mais son mulet qui aloit devant estoit déjà passé outre"' [p. 5].[54] As he dictated to his secretary that evening, it is curious that Montaigne's thoughts should have turned to this abortive act of looking. Flaubert, for his part, must have found it irresistible. He always declaimed as he read, even if only internally, and beside the obvious bathos of the baggage train the rhythm might have struck his ear. 'Mais' cuts across not just the view but a line of alexandrine verse ('il s'y fut arresté pour la beauté du lieu'). The prosaic tread of the mule takes revenge on poetry.

To read over Flaubert's shoulder is to be made aware just how many interruptions and impediments obstruct Montaigne's view. Hardly has the party crossed into Germany when the essayist offers a rueful summary of how *not* to travel, digested in the manuscript as follows:

> Montaigne regrettait trois choses de n'avoir emmené avec lui un cuisinier 'p^r l'instruire de leurs façons et en pouvoir un jour en faire voir la preuve chez lui'. de n'avoir pas un valet allemand 'car de vivre à la mercy d'un belistre de guide il y sentoit une grande incommodité'. De n'avoir pas lu les livres sur les pays qu'il alloit voir, tels que la cosmographie de Sebastien Munster. [pp. 3–4][55]

The lack of preparatory reading (Montaigne owned a 1556 edition of Munster's *Cosmographia*, but had clearly omitted to consult it), the missing cook, and the 'belistre de guide' all result in a journey either insufficiently mediated by others or too much. Impatience with such figures sometimes reached a violent climax. Besides having to contend with his guide, on the road from Foligno, Montaigne lashes out at his driver (*vetturino*), resulting in a fear of reprisals and an abrupt change of itinerary. Flaubert's note reads:

> Montaigne ne derogeait pas en voyage à sa basse coutume de donner des soufflets à ses valets. en ayant donné un à son vetturino 'qui est un grand excès selon l'usage du païs temoin le veturin qui tua le prince de Tresignano ne me voyant plus suivre au dict veturin et en estant tout à part mais un peu en humeur qu'il fit des informations ou autres choses je m'arrestai contre mon dessein (qui etoit d'aller à Tolentino) à souper à Valchimara.' [p. 10][56]

The reference to Montaigne's 'coutume' of slapping his servants may be a memory of a passage in II.31, 'De la colere' [Of Anger].[57] Just once the notes pick out an instance of unmediated pleasure: 'sur les courses de chars à Florence. "ce spectacle me fit plus de plaisir qu'aucun de ceux que j'eusse vu en italie par la ressemblance que j'y trouvois avec les courses antiques"' [p. 13].[58] Whereas the Roman ruins were able to give rise only to humanist melancholy, here historical distance is abolished: Montaigne joins the company of the Ancients. But such instants are short-lived. In another summary, of the essayist's visit to the Janiculum in Rome, the manuscript reports nothing of what he found there, only that 'Montaigne y perdit sa bourse' [p. 8].[59]

Of all the obstacles to the traveller's enjoyment the greatest were his kidney stones. Montaigne records in notorious detail their size, shape, and consistency, as well as their agonizing passage through his urinary system. For some early critics of the work this fastidiousness also proved a major obstacle to readerly enjoyment, a common complaint being that the *Journal* seemed to offer the 'égoïsme' of his *Essais* without any of their compensating wisdom. Thus Querlon's footnote to one such passage reads:

> Nous ne demandons point grâce pour tous ces détails, qui ne sont ni ragoûtans ni curieux. On les pardonnera, si l'on veut, à Montaigne; mais on voit qu'ils entroient si bien dans son genre d'égoïsme, qu'il en a semé ses *Essais*. Nous ne pouvions donc les supprimer, sans altérer le compte qu'il se rend à lui-même.[60]

Flaubert does not disregard this dimension of the text. 'Montaigne s'inquiète par tout des eaux minerales dont il prend pour ses reins. — il donne souvent des détails intimes sur sa santé', reads one note; another records his interest in the benefits of sleep and 'les bienfaits de la diète'. Elsewhere, though, he registers an onset of self-consciousness: 'Montaigne semble lui-même se gourmander de faire si attention à sa santé "c'est une sotte coutume de conter ce qu'on pisse" [p. 12] (see Figure 2).[61] And further on another, more outspoken commentary seeks explicitly to defend Montaigne from the charge of 'égoïsme' made in Querlon's footnote. It appears in response to the celebrated moment across the page in which he is suddenly overcome with the memory of his friend Étienne de La Boëtie:

> 'le jeudi matin j'en rebus cinq livres, creignant d'en estre mal servi et ne les vuider. Elles me firent faire une selle, uriner fort peu, et ce même matin escrivassant à M. Ossat je tumbe en un pansement si pénible de M. de la Boëtie et y fus si longtamps sans me raviser, que cela me fit grand mal.' — on etait alors en 1581, — la Boétie etait mort en aout 1563, depuis 18 ans!! Je souhaite aux natures sentimentales qui traictent celle de Montaigne d'égoïste de penser de cette façon à leurs amis après dix huit ans que la mort est venue; et de placer la douleur qu'ils en ressentent tout naturellement parmi les souffrances physiques c'est à dire parmi les tangibles et les mordantes. [pp. 12–13][62]

Early nineteenth-century admirers of the *Essais* often rebuffed attacks on Montaigne's sangfroid by appealing to his friendship with La Boëtie. Even Alphonse de Lamartine, who grew to dislike the *Essais*, still acknowledged the depth of feeling shown in I.28, 'De l'amitié' [On Friendship].[63] But Flaubert's challenge to '[les] natures sentimentales' takes this argument one stage further, distinguishing Montaigne's sensibility from mere sentimentality by placing it on a continuum with physical pain. Here the essayist's own syntax points the way, as the peculiar connective *et* ('et ce même matin escrivassant...') seamlessly conjoins the laxative effects of the spa waters with those brought on by the thought of his dead friend. Some later editors amend this conjunction and the surrounding punctuation, finding it unnatural. Flaubert, a writer whose own idiosyncratic *et* would one day

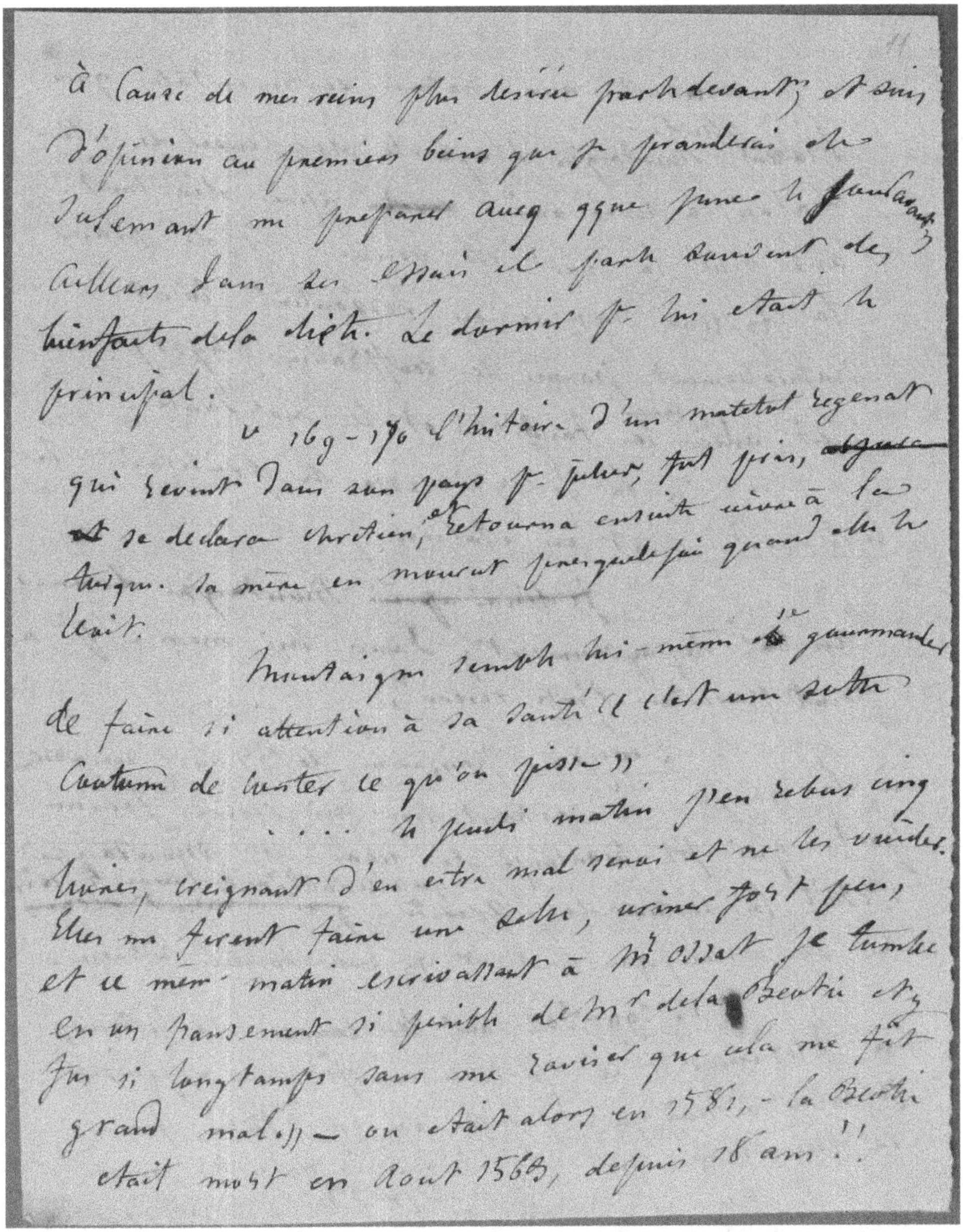

FIG. 2. Gustave Flaubert, [Notes sur le Journal de voyage de Montaigne], p. 12.
With permission, Camellia Collection, UK.

provoke literary-critical debate, was well placed to appreciate its impact.[64] Whereas the *Essais* — and certain of their readers — idealize the friendship with La Boëtie, the *Journal* embodies its effects.

The portions of the manuscript considered so far build an impression of Montaigne as passionate traveller — not in the mode of the swooning, Stendhalian Italophile but prone to bouts of irascibility, pain, grief, and, just occasionally, pleasure. Not all the notes are of this sort, however. Many show Montaigne in more familiar guise as a detached observer of foreign manners.

In Germany he expresses admiration for the local crockery ('assiettes de bois polies à la verité et très belles' [p. 4]) in preference to the steel crockery used back home in Montaigne. Reflecting a preoccupation of his fiction, Flaubert records the presence of this and further 'détails culinaires sur les services des tables d'Allemagne' [p. 3]; elsewhere he remarks the 'ceremonial et etiquetes [sic] des repas' [p. 8] and, when Montaigne is invited as a guest of the Roman governor, the luxury and '[la] pittoresque des festins du 16e siècle' [p. 9].[65] Montaigne's remarks on Catholic ceremony recur throughout the notes: what Flaubert calls the 'formes toutes particulieres' [p. 6] of Christmas Mass in St Peter's, where the gospel is read first in Latin and then in Greek; the instrument for drinking from the chalice, 'pour prouvoir la sûreté du poison' [p. 6]; and his conclusion that 'ces ceremonies semblent plus magnifiques que devotieuses' [p. 6].[66] As with Montaigne's observation on the Jewish circumcision, the passages excerpted on religious customs are gently deflationary: on the resentment of the townspeople of Kinsief towards the Jesuits for their dissolute lifestyle, or on Montaigne's audience with Gregory XIII, the pope whose life and morals harboured 'rien de fort extraordinaire ny en l'une ny en l'autre part, toutesfois inclinant beaucoup plus sur le bon' [p. 7].[67] Away from religious matters, Montaigne registers the cost of Italian post horses and, in Venice, of hiring a gondola. Above all, like Flaubert on his travels, he notices the women:

> Siene. 'Les fames portent des chapeaus en leur teste, la pluspart. Nous en vismes qui les ostoient par honneur comme les hommes à l'endroit de l'elevation de la messe.' [p. 5][68]

> Femmes — beauté italienne comparée à la beauté française, plus majestueuse les hommes au contraire manières plus communes. [p. 9][69]

> trouva que les femmes n'y sont pas plus belles qu'ailleurs 'et au demeurant que comme à Paris la beauté plus singulière se trouvoit entre les meins de celles qui la mettent en vante'. [p. 7][70]

A long annotation attached to Flaubert's 'Itinéraire', detailing the number and sheer ostentatiousness of the Venetian courtesans, completes this sequence.[71]

A further category of notes remarks on Montaigne's interactions with individual characters — whether in paint, through hearsay, or in person. His recollection of the portrait of the precocious Pico della Mirandola resembles some of Flaubert's own commentaries on paintings in his *Voyage en Italie*. Formal aspects are passed over, giving way to a rapidly sketched but suggestive physiognomy:

> Urbin au palais. 'je vis là l'effigie au naturel de Picus Mirandula. un visage blanc, très beau, sans barbe de la façon de 17 ou 18 ans, le nez longuet, les yeux dous, le visage maigrelet, le poil blon qui lui bat jusques sur les espaules et un

estrange accoustrement'. [p. 10][72]

Pico is the only Renaissance cultural celebrity featured in Flaubert's notes; but he is not the only prodigy. He notes Montaigne's meeting with Divizia, the literary autodidact introduced to him in Bagno della Villa; completely illiterate, she learned the art of poetry from an uncle's recitations of Ariosto, and now recites verses of her own. Montaigne notices a boil on her neck; Flaubert has underlined her name. He notes the story Montaigne hears of one Giuseppe, a renegade sailor who is captured by the Turks and converts only to be recaptured, reconverted and returned to his mother 10 or 12 years later. Flaubert's abridged summary picks out the cataclysmic effect of this reunion, the shock of which kills the mother not long afterwards. Finally, he notes the 'amitié et familiarité' Montaigne strikes up in Plombières with the Seigneur d'Andelot, who tells of how a portion of his beard suddenly turned white with grief on hearing of his brother's death:

> il avait un endroit de sa barbe tout blanc et un costé du sourcil; et recita à Mr de Montaigne que ce changement lui estoyt venu en un instant, un jour estant chez lui plein d'ennuy pour la mort d'un sien frère que le duc d'Albe avoit faict mourir comme complice des comtes d'Eguemont (Egmont) et de Hornes; qu'il tenoit sa teste appuyé sur sa main par cet endroit de façon que les assistants penserent que ce fust de la farine qui lui fust de fortune tombée là. [p. 3][73]

An early chapter of the *Essais* (I.2, 'De la tristesse' [On Sadness]) had already signalled Montaigne's interest in the stupefying effects of extreme grief or joy. Here the somatic force of Andelot's emotion recalls both the fate of Giuseppe's mother and Montaigne's memory of La Boëtie. All three episodes testify to the prodigious force of human attachments, and the pain caused when they are undone.

Even here, though, the extent of Montaigne's emotional commitment to the story is heavily underspecified: as so often in the *Journal*, no commentary is offered. To this extent Montaigne's 'sensibility' remains opaque, such that what emerges more forcefully is a certain kind of voice. It is the voice of the circumcision scene, and can be heard again in the execution of the bandit Catena in Rome, or at least as it appears in Flaubert's abridged excerpt:

> Envoi d'un condamné au supplice — 'il (M) rencontra qu'on sortoit de prison Catena un fameux voleur et capitaine des banis qui avait tenu en creinte toute l'italie et duquel il se contoit des meurtres enormes et notamment de deux capucins auxquels il avait fait renier Dieu promentant sur une condition leur sauver la vie et les avoit massacrés après cela sans aucune occasion ny de commodité ny de vengeance [...] il fit une mort commune, sans mouvemens et sans paroles; estoit homme noir, de trente ans ou environ.'[74]

In the full text of the *Journal*, Montaigne's own focus falls mainly on the formal procedures of the execution (here omitted with '[...]'): notably the continuous presentation of the image of Christ, masking the condemned man's face from the crowd, right up until the moment of death. By leaving out this aspect, Flaubert brings into closer proximity the exceptional crimes that Catena is purported to have committed ('*il se contoit* des meurtres enormes') and the actual banality of his death on the scaffold. The abruptness of this shift from 'meurtres enormes' to 'mort commune', and especially the deadpan final line, recalls Montaigne's remark on the cries of the circumcised child. Here too, at the other end of a life, the solemnity of ritual violence is quietly exploded in the shift from assumed distinction to the human norm, from the narrative elaborations of others to inarticulate pain.

Conclusion

> Il n'y a que les lieux communs et les pays connus qui soient d'une intarissable beauté.[75] (Flaubert, letter to Louis Bouilhet, 23 May 1855)

A few years after Flaubert's death in 1880, Du Camp recalls his friend's practice of note-taking:

> Sa méthode de travail était peu pratique; sous prétexte de prendre des notes, il copiait les livres écrits sur les matières qu'il avait à étudier; or il copiait machinalement, en pensant à autre chose; le résultat était une fatigue physique et une accumulation de paperasses sans valeur.[76]

Du Camp's recollection returns us to the sometimes obscure relation between note-taking and future acts of writing. Montaigne's motives in keeping his *Journal* are unstated but relatively clear. Though never meant for publication, the episodes he records there were still turned to productive account in the *Essais*. They fed into exactly the same storehouse of *loci communes* as was nourished by his reading; from that storehouse the fates of Marie Germain, or Catena on the scaffold, are gathered up, juxtaposed, and made the objects of his judgement no less than an *exemplum* found in Aulus Gellius or Plutarch.[77] If Du Camp is to be believed, Flaubert's reading notes stand in stark contrast to this commonplacing practice. The novelist is likened rather to Bouvard and Pécuchet, cheerfully yoked to their copydesks but producing nothing of their own. This is not the moment to revisit the story of how, as the age of Renaissance *inventio* gave way to that of mechanical reproduction, the once fertile *lieu commun* — the fount of invention — took on the debased guise of the *idée reçue*.[78] But perhaps Du Camp, and indeed this story, paint too bleak a picture. It should not be forgotten that for Flaubert *bêtise* can be a beatific state. He may never have had occasion to re-use the succession of 'places' that parade past as he read the *Journal de voyage*; and in this narrow sense they leave no trace. But perhaps they had other ways of reappearing — in the half-smile of *Bouvard et Pécuchet* or, much earlier, in the visitations of Saint Antoine.

'Des paperasses sans valeur': these words should serve as a warning to genetic critics everywhere. And yet even the most vacant note-taker, provided he or she does not copy everything, will still betray *relative* patterns of attention. This essay has sought to bring out the most prominent of Flaubert's: on the art of travel itself, on an eye for people over places, and on the persistent hesitation between empathy and detachment and, correspondingly, the distinctive note of Montaigne's narrative voice. These are of course Flaubertian themes, every one, and yet another instance of the essayist's ability to provoke identificatory responses across a whole range of readers. But fortunately Flaubert is not just any reader. Like the most incisive and generous of teachers, he shows us something in Montaigne that we would not have seen without him.

Notes to Chapter 12

1. [ITALY: Very disappointing, isn't as beautiful as people say]; Gustave Flaubert, *Le Dictionnaire des idées reçues*, ed. Anne Herschberg Pierrot (Paris: Livre de Poche, 1997), p. 95. All translations from French are mine unless otherwise stated; translations from Montaigne are taken from Frame.

2. [The boy's outcry is like that of ours when they are baptized] (F, p. 1153); Michel de Montaigne, *Journal de voyage*, ed. François Rigolot (Paris: Presses universitaires de France, 1992), p. 103. Subsequent references to this edition are marked Rigolot.

3. Gustave Flaubert, [*Notes sur le Journal de voyage de Montaigne*], p. 9. Subsequent references to this manuscript are included in square brackets in the main text. The manuscript is quoted by kind permission of Camellia Collection, UK.

4. Gustave Flaubert, [*La Première*] *Éducation sentimentale* (1845), in *Œuvres complètes* (henceforth OC), vol. 1: *Œuvres de jeunesse*, ed. Claudine Gothot-Mersch and Guy Sagnes (Paris: Gallimard, 2001), p. 1033.

5. [It's extraordinary how full I am of that fellow! Is it a coincidence, or is it because I stuffed myself with him for a whole year at the age of 18, when I read *nothing but him*? I'm often astonished to find the most detailed analysis of my slightest sentiments! We have the same tastes, same opinions, same way of life, same obsessions]; Gustave Flaubert, *Correspondance* (henceforth Corr.), ed. Jean Bruneau and Yvan Leclerc (Paris: Gallimard, 1973–2007), vol. 2, p. 459; emphasis original.

6. OC, vol. 1, pp. 112, 185, 757.

7. Jean Bruneau, *Les Débuts littéraires de Gustave Flaubert: 1831–1845* (Paris: Armand Colin, 1962), pp. 17–38; Alison Fairlie, 'Flaubert and the Authors of the French Renaissance', in *The French Renaissance and its Heritage: Essays Presented to Alan M. Boase*, ed. Donald R. Haggis (London: Methuen, 1968), pp. 43–62; Florence Vatan, 'Un livre pour vivre: Flaubert lecteur des *Essais*', *Montaigne Studies*, 10 (1998), 151–67. See, more recently, Philippe Jousset, 'Flaubert lecteur de Montaigne', *Flaubert: revue critique et génétique*, 2 (2009) <http://flaubert.revues.org/848> [accessed 23 October 2015].

8. Michel de Montaigne, *Essais de Michel de Montaigne avec les notes de tous les commentateurs*, ed. Joseph-Victor Le Clerc (Paris: Lefèvre, 1836); see Alessandra Preda, 'Flaubert et son exemplaire des *Essais*: être et disparaître en suivant Montaigne', in *Le Letture/la lettura di Flaubert*, ed. Liana Nissim (Milan: Cisalpino, 2000), pp. 99–120. Flaubert's digitized copy of the *Essais* can be accessed through the website of the Centre Flaubert at the University of Rouen, <http://flaubert.univ-rouen.fr> [accessed 23 October 2015].

9. See Timothy Chesters, 'Flaubert's Reading Notes on Montaigne', *French Studies*, 63.4 (2009), 399–415.

10. Michel de Montaigne, *Journal du voyage de Michel de Montaigne en Italie, par la Suisse & l'Allemagne en 1580 & 1581. Avec les notes de M. de Querlon*, 2 vols (Rome [Paris]: Lejay, 1774). Where appropriate, quotations from Flaubert's notes will be accompanied by the corresponding page number in this edition (marked Querlon). On the manuscript's discovery and publication, see Concetta Cavallini, *'Cette belle besogne': Étude sur le 'Journal de voyage' de Montaigne* (Fasano: Schena, 2005), pp. 19–110.

11. The catalogue of the novelist's library, drawn up following the death of his niece Caroline in 1931, makes no reference to the *Journal de voyage*. Flaubert may have consulted one of the three copies still held in the Bibliothèque Villon in Rouen: two of these were acquired in 1838, the third in 1847. My thanks to the librarian, Mme Christel Valières, for the dates of accession.

12. See for example Rigolot's edition (pp. x–xi) and Frame's translation (pp. 1052–54).

13. Querlon, pp. 12–15; *Journal de voyage*, ed. Rigolot, pp. 6–7. [It is there that M. hears tell of the 2 hermaphrodites mentioned in his essays.] The reference is to I.21, 'De la force de l'imagination' [Of the Power of the Imagination] (V, p. 99).

14. Querlon, p. 17; Rigolot, p. 8. [The front of the little house where she [the Pucelle] was born is all painted with her exploits; but age has greatly damaged the painting]; F, p. 1061. On Flaubert's fascination with paintings that have become degraded over time, see Adrianne J. Tooke, *Flaubert and the Pictorial Arts: From Image to Text* (Oxford: Oxford University Press, 2000), pp. 115–17.

15. On Montaigne's reputation in the nineteenth century, see Donald Murdoch Frame, *Montaigne in France: 1812–1852* (New York: Columbia University Press, 1940); on the reception of the *Journal de voyage*, see Concetta Cavallini, 'État et perspectives de la recherche sur le *Journal de voyage de Montaigne*', *Studi di letteratura francese*, 29–30 (2004–05) [= *Il viaggio francese in Italia*], 31–51.

16. The edition included by Jean-Alexandre C. Buchon in his 1837 *Œuvres* (Paris: Desrez) is simply a reprint of Querlon, minus the Italian portion of the text.

17. On the initial reception of the *Journal*, see Maturin Dréano, *La Renommée de Montaigne en France au XVIIIe siècle* (Angers: Éditions de l'Ouest, 1952).

18. Stendhal, *Promenades dans Rome* (Paris: Delaunay, 1829), vol. 2, p. 381.

19. [Montaigne himself, who was not lacking in imagination, says: 'we have on our left-hand-side in the distance the Appenines, the prospect of the country unpleasant, bumpy, full of deep crevices [...], the landscape bare, without trees, for the most part infertile']; François-René de Chateaubriand, *Mémoires d'Outre-Tombe*, ed. Jean-Paul Clément (Paris: Gallimard, 1997), pp. 1985–87, 2000.

20. See Frame, *Montaigne in France*, pp. 123–24.

21. The otherwise exhaustive editions of Éloi Johanneau (1818, 5 vols) and Amaury Duval (1820–22, 6 vols) each devote only a summary 'Notice' to the travels in Italy.

22. Michel de Montaigne, *The Complete Works*, ed. William Hazlitt (London: Templeman, 1842), pp. 527–629; [Mary Wollstonecraft Shelley], *Lives of the Most Eminent Literary and Scientific Men of France* (London: Longman, 1838–39), vol. 1, p. 18; Bayle St John, *Montaigne the Essayist: A Biography* (London: Chapman and Hall, 1858), vol. 2, pp. 127–228.

23. St John, *Montaigne the Essayist*, p. 194; the allusion is to Jean-Charles Brunet, *Manuel du libraire et de l'amateur de livres* (Paris: Silvestre, 1843), vol. 3, art. 'Montaigne': 'ce journal ne présente aucun intérêt, aussi n'a-t-il point eu de succès' ['this journal is of no interest, hence it has had no success'].

24. See Chesters, 'Flaubert's Reading Notes on Montaigne', p. 401.

25. [Profit from your journey and remember your friend Montaigne, who wants us to travel in order to bring back principally the ways and temperaments of nations, and to 'rub and polish our brains by contact with those of others'. See, observe, and take notes; don't travel like a shopkeeper or a sales representative]; *Corr.*, vol. 1, p. 68.

26. Most notably Sartre's *L'Idiot de la famille*. For a more balanced view, see Geoffrey Wall, *The Enlightened Physician: Achille-Cléophas Flaubert 1784–1846* (Bern: Peter Lang, 2013), pp. 33–34.

27. 'Et si [Pierre Eyquem] avoit eu fort longue part aux guerres delà les monts, desquelles il nous a laissé, de sa main, un papier journal suyvant poinct par poinct ce qui s'y passa'; II.2, 'De l'ivrognerie' [On Drunkenness]; V, p. 344. [And yet he had taken a very long part in the Italian wars, of which he has left a diary in his own hand, following what happened point by point].

28. [Montaigne's manuscript with much veneration as a relic.] The reference is to the *Exemplaire de Bordeaux*; *OC*, vol. 1, p. 653.

29. [In Rome 'We took up lodgings at The Bear' (had lodged in Kempten at the same sign).]

30. [I go nowhere, see no one and am seen by no one; [...] as the ancient sage says: 'Hide your life and refuse to commit.' — People think that I'm wrong, that I should go out and about, I'm an oddball, a bear]; Letter to Ernest Chevalier, 31 December 1841; *Corr.*, vol. 1, p. 89.

31. Flaubert repeatedly misattributes the slogan 'Cache ta vie' to Epictetus; e.g. *Corr.*, vol. 1, p. 77, vol. 2, pp. 214, 218, 301, 508; he may have encountered it (correctly attributed) in II.16, 'De la gloire' [On Glory].

32. [I'm a bear and wish to stay a bear in my hidey-hole, in my cave, in my skin, in my old bearskin, nice and calm and far from the bourgeois and the bourgeoise]; Letter to Caroline Flaubert, 20 December 1843; *Corr.*, vol. 1, p. 201.

33. [I even want to buy a lovely bear (in a painting), to have it framed and hung in my room, having written underneath: *Portrait of Gustave Flaubert*, so as to indicate my moral dispositions and social temperament]; Letter to Ernest Chevalier, 15 June 1845; *Corr.*, vol. 1, p. 238.

34. A letter to Colet of 16 September 1853 suggests the probable *terminus ad quem*. Colet was at that time preparing her *Enfances célèbres*, a volume on precocious children that would appear the following year (Paris: Hachette, 1854). One of her chosen prodigies was Pico della Mirandola, about whom Flaubert recalls a passage in Montaigne, only to find himself unable to track it

down (*Corr.*, vol. 2, p. 431). This reference puzzled the editor of the *Correspondance*, who assumed (as Flaubert must have done) that the reference to Pico was to be found in the *Essais*, and duly failed to locate it (*Corr.*, vol. 2, p. 1204). In reality it appears in the *Journal de voyage*, where Montaigne describes a portrait of Pico hanging in the palace of Urbino. Flaubert has excerpted the passage in his notes.

35. [Henry would get up in the early morning, run through the streets, draw the monuments, examine the libraries, inspect all the museums, visit all the establishments, talk to everyone. Jules [...] carried along by chance, wherever his whims took him, lost in his reveries [...], would go back ten times to see the same figure in a painting, only to wander off afterwards without seeing the gallery. It would have taken him a whole lifetime to see what Henry saw in just one day, and that which furnished Henry with ten lines Jules would have needed a whole volume to express. Henry brought back a complete journal; Jules wrote only a few fragments of verse from time to time, which he would use to light his cigar]; *OC*, vol. 1, p. 1066.

36. Tooke, *Flaubert and the Pictorial Arts*, pp. 11–12.

37. [I wanted to see Aigues-Mortes and I didn't see Aigues-Mortes, the Sainte-Baume and the cave where Madeleine wept, the Marius battlefield, etc. I didn't see anything of all that because I wasn't alone, I wasn't free. So that's twice I've seen the Mediterranean as a shopkeeper]; *Corr.*, vol. 1, p. 223.

38. [The observatory. Heavy, stupefied face of the exhibitor]; *OC*, vol. 1, p. 1085.

39. [Museum. The headless Silenus, soft thighs, flabby belly [...] — head of Cybele with nose missing; attractive barrow. The guide: 'I have Latin dictionaries, Greek']; *OC*, vol. 1, p. 1088.

40. [Excursion to ARONA: steam boat, virtually nobody but locals. An old Englishwoman taking notes and looking up the name of every last parcel of land in her book]; *OC*, vol. 1, p. 1112.

41. [While I was looking at Breughel's *Temptation* a gentleman and lady arrived who left almost as soon as they came in; their faces as they stood before those paintings was something very profound in the way of *bêtise*. — They were fulfilling a duty]; *OC*, vol. 1, p. 1099.

42. Maxime Du Camp, *Souvenirs littéraires*, ed. Daniel Oster (Paris: Aubier, 1994), p. 314.

43. [I completely reject your idea of writing up your journey. 1. because it's facile; 2. because a novel would be better. Do you really need to prove that you know how to write descriptions?]; *Corr.*, vol. 3, p. 96.

44. See Geneviève Bollème, *La Leçon de Flaubert* (Paris: Julliard, 1964), pp. 121–37.

45. [We have climbed since morning and are entering the forest of Marmano. The path is steep and zigzags through the pines, the trunks of which glisten in the sunlight coming in through the higher branches and lighting up the leafbed of the forest; embalmed air scented with greenwood. One mustn't write all this]; *OC*, vol. 1, p. 710.

46. Francis Claudon, 'À propos des voyages de Flaubert: le voyage en Italie et en Suisse (1845)', in *Flaubert et Maupassant: écrivains normands* (Paris: Presses universitaires de France, 1981), pp. 91–109 (p. 99).

47. [Indescribable. We must daydream and remember]; *OC*, vol. 1, p. 1113.

48. *OC*, vol. 1, p. 1088.

49. *OC*, vol. 1, p. 1094.

50. 'Il voyagea./ Il connut la mélancolie des paquebots, les froids réveils sous la tente, l'étourdissement des paysages et des ruines, l'amertume des sympathies interrompues./ Il revint' [He travelled the world. He tasted the melancholy of packet ships, the chill of waking under canvas, the boredom of landscapes and monuments, the bitterness of broken friendship. He returned home]; Gustave Flaubert, *L'Éducation sentimentale* (1869), ed. Samuel Silvestre de Sacy (Paris: Folio, 1965), p. 450; *A Sentimental Education*, trans. by Robert Baldick (London: Penguin, 2004), p. 449.

51. Francis Steegmuller, *Flaubert in Egypt: A Sensibility on Tour: A Narrative Drawn from Gustave Flaubert's Travel Notes and Letters* (London: Bodley Head, 1972).

52. See Richard A. Sayce, 'The Visual Arts in Montaigne's *Journal de voyage*', in *'O un amy!' Essays in Honor of Donald M. Frame*, ed. Raymond La Charité (Lexington, KY: French Forum, 1977), pp. 219–41.

53. 'RUINE: Font rêver, et donne de la poésie à un paysage' [RUIN: Makes you dream, and lends poetry to a landscape]; *Dictionnaire des idées reçues*, p. 118. Compare this reaction of Sainte-Beuve's: 'Rome inspire Montaigne et l'élève jusqu'à elle. Quel langage auguste et magnifique!

quelle haute idée!' [Rome inspires Montaigne and lifts him up to its level. What august and magnificent language! What a lofty conception!]; Charles-Augustin de Sainte-Beuve, 'Montaigne en voyage', in *Causeries sur Montaigne*, ed. François Rigolot (Paris: Champion, 2003), pp. 201–16 (p. 214).

54. Querlon, vol. 1, p. 270; Rigolot, p. 89. [He [Montaigne] had stopped to admire the beauty of the place, but his mule had already gone on ahead.]

55. Querlon, vol. 1, pp. 92–93; Rigolot, p. 32. [Montaigne regretted three things: not having taken a cook with him 'to instruct him in their ways and have him one day attempt the same thing back home'. Not having a German valet 'since he felt greatly discomfited living at the mercy of an idiot guide'. Not having read books about the places he was going to see, such as Sebastian Munster's cosmography.]

56. Querlon, vol. 2, p. 94; Rigolot, p. 137. [While travelling, Montaigne did not disdain his custom of slapping his valets. Having slapped his driver, 'which is a great outrage according to the usage of the country — witness the driver who killed the prince of Tresignano — seeing myself no longer followed by the said driver, and being privately a little concerned that he might lodge a complaint against me or cause some other trouble, I stopped, contrary to my plan (which was to go to Tolentino), for supper at Valchimara']; F, p. 1183.

57. 'Je conseille qu'on donne plustost une buffe à la joue de son valet, un peu hors de saison, que de geiner sa fantasie pour representer cette sage contenance' [I advise that we rather give our valet a slap on the cheek out of season than strain our inclination to represent this wise bearing]; V, p. 719; F, p. 660. In his notes on the *Essais*, Flaubert remarks of this passage, 'Montaigne assez enclin a être emporté' [Montaigne quite inclined to lose his temper]; Gustave Flaubert, [*Notes sur les Essais de Montaigne*], p. 33.

58. Querlon, vol. 2, pp. 299–302; Rigolot, p. 254. [I enjoyed this spectacle more than any other I had seen in Italy for its resemblance to the ancient type of race]; F, p. 1226.

59. Querlon, vol. 1, p. 304; Rigolot, p. 99. [Montaigne lost his purse there.]

60. Querlon, vol. 2, p. 174. [We owe no apology for all these details, which whet neither appetite nor curiosity. Some will be happy to forgive Montaigne; but it is clear that they fit so well his brand of egoism, that he scattered them all over his *Essays*. Therefore we cannot suppress them without altering the account he gives of himself.]

61. Querlon, vol. 2, p. 174; Rigolot, p. 162. [Montaigne himself seems to chastise himself for paying so much attention to his health: 'it is a stupid habit to keep count of what you piss']; F, p. 1207.

62. Querlon, vol. 2, p. 175; Rigolot, p. 162. ['They made me have one stool and urinate very little and this same morning, writing to Monsieur d'Ossat, I was overcome by such painful thoughts about Monsieur de La Boétie, and I was in this mood so long, without recovering, that it did me much harm.' — this was 1581, — La Boétie had died in August 1563, 18 years previously!! I would like to see those sentimental natures who call Montaigne's *égoïste* thinking like this about their friends eighteen years after death has come; and to place the pain it makes them feel quite naturally amidst physical suffering, that is to say pain that is tangible and biting]; F, p. 1207, adapted.

63. See Frame, *Montaigne in France*, pp. 16–27.

64. 'La conjonction "et" n'a nullement dans Flaubert l'objet que la grammaire lui assigne'; see Marcel Proust, 'À propos du "style" de Flaubert', reprinted in Albert Thibaudet, *Reflexions sur la littérature*, ed. Antoine Compagnon (Paris: Gallimard, 2007), pp. 1639–54 (p. 1644).

65. On feasting in Flaubert, see Jean-Pierre Richard, 'La Création de la forme chez Flaubert', in *Littérature et sensation: Stendhal, Flaubert* (Paris: Seuil, 1954), pp. 137–252 (pp. 137–38).

66. Querlon, vol. 1, p. 284; Rigolot, p. 93. [These ceremonies seem to be more magnificent than devout]; F, p. 1144.

67. Querlon, vol. 1, p. 291; Rigolot, p. 96. [Nothing very extraordinary about them one way or the other, but incline much more to the good]; F, p. 1146.

68. Querlon, vol. 1, p. 264; Rigolot, p. 87. [The women mostly wear hats on their heads. We saw some who took them off out of reverence, like the men, at the point of the elevation during Mass]; F, p. 1138.

69. Querlon, vol. 1, pp. 319–20; Rigolot, p. 104. [Women — Italian beauty compared to French beauty, more majestic the men by contrast more vulgar in their manners.]

70. Querlon, vol. 1, p. 284; Rigolot, pp. 93–94. [He found that the women there are no more beautiful than elsewhere 'and moreover that, as in Paris, the most singular beauty was found among those who put it on sale']; F, p. 1144.

71. Querlon, vol. 1, pp. 207–08; Rigolot, p. 69.

72. Querlon, vol. 2, pp. 129–30; Rigolot, p. 148. [I saw here a portrait from life of Pico della Mirandola: a pale, very handsome face, beardless, seeming about seventeen or eighteen, a longish nose, gentle eyes, rather thin face, blond hair falling down to his shoulders, and a strange costume]; F, p. 1194.

73. Querlon, vol. 1, pp. 23–34; Rigolot, p. 10. [One part of his beard was all white, and part of one eyebrow; and he told Monsieur de Montaigne that this change had come upon him in an instant, one day when he was at home full of grief for the loss of a brother of his whom the duke of Alva had put to death as an accomplice of the counts of Egmont and Horn; and that this part of his face had been resting on his hand, so that those present thought it was some flour that by chance had fallen on him just there]; F. p. 1063.

74. Querlon, vol. 1, pp. 297–98; Rigolot, pp. 97–98. [It happened that they were taking out of prison Catena, a famous robber and bandit captain who had kept all Italy in fear and to whom some monstrous murders were ascribed, especially those of two Capuchins whom he had made to deny God, promising on that condition to save their lives, and then massacred without any reason either of advantage or of vengeance [...] he made an ordinary death, without movement or word; he was a dark man of thirty or thereabouts]; F. 1148.

75. [Only commonplaces and known lands are inexhaustibly beautiful]; Corr., vol. 2, p. 575.

76. [His working method was impractical; on the pretext of taking notes, he copied out books written on the subjects he needed to study; the thing is that he would copy them mechanically, while his mind was elsewhere; the result was physical exhaustion and a heap of worthless papers]; Du Camp, Souvenirs, p. 195.

77. In I.21 ('De la force de l'imagination') and II.11 ('De la cruauté' [Of Cruelty]).

78. See Ruth Amossy, 'Introduction to the Study of Doxa', Poetics Today, 23.3 (2002), 369–94.

CHAPTER 13

A Disagreeing Likeness:
Michel de Montaigne, Robert Burton,
and the Problem of Idiosyncrasy

Kathryn Murphy

1. Persons singular

At the end of the first paragraph of 'Democritus Junior to the Reader', the satirical and pseudonymous preface to *The Anatomy of Melancholy*, Robert Burton addressed his reader directly, signalling at once his debt to and difference from Montaigne: 'Thou thy selfe art the subject of my Discourse.'[1] In its skewing of a phrase in Montaigne's address 'Au lecteur', 'Je suis moy-même la matière de mon livre' (V, p. 3), Burton's appropriation suggests both a recognition of kindred preoccupations, and the establishment of different priorities.[2] The phrases indicate, at least grammatically, a joint concern with the singular: with the particular human being identified by 'je' and 'thou'. At the same time, the alteration from first to second person suggests a fundamentally different orientation of attention, from self-exposure to therapeutic and pastoral concern.[3]

Both the *Essais* and the *Anatomy* are late humanist copious texts, composed of the weaving together of fragments of a common cultural archive, fretted with the contrary imperatives of synthesis and analysis: on the one hand the desire to accumulate and incorporate the widest variety of material, and demonstrate erudition and copious invention; on the other, the urge to reduce that burden of variety to method and order.[4] Particularly in its length, digressiveness, miscellaneity, and Burton's inveterate habits of expansion, the *Anatomy* has several particular analogies with the *Essais*. Moreover, it has long been known that Burton read Florio's translation of Montaigne.[5] Comment has however focused on Burton's direct citations, of which there are eight in a work which, in its final posthumous edition, ran to 771 folio pages.[6] William Hamlin's recent study of the reading of Florio's translation uses Burton as an exemplar of what he calls 'instrumental' or 'opportunistic borrowing', raiding the *Essais* as a treasure house of anecdote, a source of exotic instances to spice one's own writing.[7] The ways in which the *Essais* appear both formative and transformed in the *Anatomy* are however inevitably missed when Montaigne's importance for Burton is understood as a source of textual ornament.

Establishing an account of a more fundamentally emulative relationship between the *Anatomy* and the *Essais* is however problematized by one of the main features they have in common: the patchwork composition of their texts, and their participation in what Eric MacPhail calls 'the endless irresolution of commonplace culture', which he claims reaches 'a sort of paroxysm [...] with [...] *The Anatomy of Melancholy*' and its 'tribute to Montaigne and the waning tradition of humanism'.[8] Montaigne and Burton are preoccupied with discerning the difference between what is idiosyncratic and what common in writing. Both works repeat and refute the calumnies directed at commonplacing: charges of repetitiousness, banality, and theft. 'These rapsodies of common places', Montaigne writes in III.12, 'De la phisionimie' [Of Physiognomy], 'serve not greatly but for vulgar subjects', while 'there is a great and incomparable preferrence, betweene the honour of invention, and that of allegation [*sc.* quotation]' (Fl. p. 629; V, p. 1056). Burton weaves the objections into the fabric of his own text: 'wee skim off the Creame of other mens Wits, pick the choyce Flowers of their tild Gardens to set out our owne sterill plots [...]. They lard their leane bookes with the fat of others Workes' (vol. 1, p. 9). Burton anticipates readerly complaint at the *Anatomy*'s redundancy: 'an unnecessary worke, [...] the same againe and againe in other words' (vol. 1, p. 8).[9] The reincorporation of material from others leads to repetitiousness: 'we weave the same Web still, twist the same Rope againe and againe' (vol. 1, p. 10), compiling 'Tautologies, Apish imitation, a Rapsody of Rags gathered together from severall Dung-hills' (vol. 1, p. 12).

In response to such anticipated accusations, both writers offer defences that rely not on claiming the originality of their commonplace material, but on their deployment of it. Montaigne demands: 'Let no man busie himselfe about the matters [of his book], but on the fashion I give them' (Fl. p. 236; V, p. 408). He acknowledges that 'some might be said of me: that here I have but gathered a nosegay of strange floures, and have put nothing of mine vnto it, but the thred to binde them'. Such 'borrowed ornaments' are not intended to 'cover and hide' Montaigne's idiosyncrasy; instead, he wishes to 'make a shew of nothing that is not mine owne, yea and mine owne by nature' (Fl. p. 629; V, p. 1055). Such propriety can indeed be exhibited by the gathering and arrangement represented by the 'thred':

> to iudge in [an author] the partes most his owne and best worthy, togeather with the force and beauty of his minde; t'is very requisite, we know first what is his owne, and what not: and in what is not his owne, what we are behoulding to him for, in consideration of his choise, disposition, ornament, and language he hath thereunto furnished. (Fl. p. 563; V, p. 940)

What is proper to the writer is paradoxically demonstrated in the treatment of material whose source is elsewhere, as Montaigne articulates aptly by reworking a familiar trope:

> The bees do heere and there sucke this, and cull that flower, but afterward they produce the hony, which is peculiarly their owne, then is it no more Thyme or Marjoram. So of peeces borrowed of others, he may lawfully alter, transforme, and confound them, to shape out of them a perfect peece of worke, altogether his owne. (Fl. p. 71; V, p. 152)

Though often identified with Seneca, the image of the bee for the transformative and sweetening work of writing is so ubiquitous that it is less borrowed or plundered than drawn from common stock. The specificity of thyme and marjoram, however, make Montaigne's rendering of the trope memorable and local; in a paradoxical reversal of the metaphor, the worn image of the bee-blent honey resolves into its elements to make a figure that is Montaigne's own.[10]

Similar paradoxes of appropriation preoccupy Burton. The first two editions of the *Anatomy* carried a motto on their frontispiece which read 'Omne meum, nihil meum'. The phrase also appears in a passage which exemplifies the patchwork of commonplacing culture:

> I have only this of *Macrobius* to say for my selfe, *Omne meum, nihil meum*, 'tis all mine and none mine. As a good hous-wife out of divers fleeces weaves one peece of Cloath, a Bee gathers Wax and Hony out of many Flowers, and makes a new bundle of all,
>   *Floriferis ut apes in saltibus omnia libant*,
>   I have laboriously collected this *Cento* out of divers Writers, and that *sine injuriâ*, I have wronged no Authors, but given every man his owne [...]. The matter is theirs most part, and yet mine, [...] which nature doth with the aliment of our bodies, incorporate, digest, assimilate, I doe *conquoquere quod hausi*, dispose of what I take. [.... T]he method onely is myne owne, I must usurpe that of *Wecker è Terentio, nihil dictum quod non dictum priùs, methodus sola artificem ostendit*, we can say nothing but what hath beene said, the composition and method is ours onely, and shewes a Schollar. (vol. 1, p. 11)

Burton uses a translated paraphrase of a quotation of a quotation from Terence to insist that his words have already been in the mouths of others, and yet are his. The prose shifts frenetically between inherited tropes: weaving, honey-making, the *cento*, the process of digestion. As the Clarendon edition notes, his attribution of the phrase 'Omne meum, nihil meum' to Macrobius is wrong — it is drawn from Lipsius's *cento*, the *Politica* — proving that Burton has not quite given every man his own.[11] The individuality of his 'composition and method', here, lies less in apian transformation, than in the magpie-minded mosaic of his sentences.

Such defences of the transformation of borrowed material make an argument about Burton's debt to Montaigne more difficult to mount: citations have no shaping role in the 'composition and method' of a work, and in any case Burton quotes very many sources, some far more frequently than the *Essais*. Nonetheless, I will argue that the similarities between the *Essais* and the *Anatomy* are more than accidental — indeed that it is precisely in their treatment of similarity, accident, and idiosyncrasy that Burton's 'tribute' to Montaigne consists.

2. The abridgement of infinity

Montaigne's announcement that he is the matter of his book is followed immediately by a paradoxical recommendation that the reader stop reading: 'It is then no reason thou shouldest employ thy time about so frivolous and vain a subject' (sig. A6v). This is another of the tropes of Montaigne's 'Au lecteur' which Burton adopts: the *Anatomy* is 'not worth the reading, I yeeld it, I desire thee not to loose time in perusing so vaine a subject' (vol. 1, p. 12). The blithe modesty topos conceals a more fundamental epistemological problem: a gulf between the singularity of 'je' and 'thou', and the discourse that Montaigne and Burton supposedly base upon them.

The problem for Burton is obvious: addressing unknown and unknowably various readers, how can he claim that his sprawling and diverse work applies equally and entirely to each?[12] Montaigne's 'je', speaking of personal experience, seems immune to this problem, but a similar difficulty applies. It was an axiom of the Aristotelian tradition of logic that there can be no knowledge of individuals, or discourse on them. Instead, warrantable knowledge began with the abstraction from particulars to species and genera, and the neglect of their accidents and circumstances. Francis Bacon — normally no friend to Aristotelian principles — wrote in the *Advancement of Learning* (1605) that 'it is the dutie and vertue of all knowledge to abridge the infinitie of indiuiduall experience [... T]hat knowledge is worthiest, which is charged with least multiplicitie.'[13] The individual objects of sense experience are too various and changeable to be compassed by the human intellect, too subject to infinitely variable circumstances and accidents. As Ian Maclean observes, on an ancient analogy with the letters that make up words, 'communicability is only possible through common signs. If all individual characters expressed themselves through unique signs equivalent to proper names, then there would be no communication'.[14] Some abstraction, some abridgement, is necessary to make the particular intelligible.

Introducing the classificatory procedures of logical division and definition, the Neoplatonic philosopher Porphyry explained that, while genera and species were finite, the particulars which belong to them are innumerable, and thus not available for discussion: '[Plato] tells us to leave the infinites alone, for there will be no knowledge of them'.[15] But any form of knowledge founded on sense experience, or on what Montaigne called the 'wonderfull, vaine, diverse, and wavering subject' (Fl. p. 2; V, p. 9) of man, could not eschew particulars. A popular definition of art, attributed to Porphyry, was *de infinitis finita disciplina* or *finita scientia*: the finite discipline of the indeterminate, the reduction of the infinity of possible particulars to a teachable, repeatable way of reasoning and acting on such reasoning.[16] Law, for example, faces the infinite variety of human circumstance and behaviour, such that the abstraction of legal principle could never hope to legislate for every possible case. For medicine the problem is idiosyncrasy in a technical sense: the Galenic tradition rested on the notion that each individual was constituted of a unique temperament of humours and affected in unpredictable ways by their peculiar circumstances and the six 'non-naturals', thus giving rise to infinitely various symptoms and possibilities of treatment.[17] Maclean has made his own the study of the dialectical procedures available to such disciplines which had to 'grapple with the problem of the infinite variability of their subject matter and the need to make this intelligible and to classify individual cases under given rules'.[18]

Despite the disciplinary development of complex strategies to handle variety, however, many writers in the early modern period questioned the capacity of human reason to aptly abridge the infinite variety of experience. Maclean and Pierre Force have argued that much of what is identified as sceptical in Montaigne and his contemporaries derives not from the rediscovery of the works of Sextus Empiricus, but from longer traditions of querying how experience and natural particulars might be incorporated in a theory of knowledge and of eclectic approaches to philosophy.[19] These reach a crisis in the early modern period. Francis Bacon's whole project of an *Instauratio magna*, a great restoration of learning, could be said to rest on an insistence that the abridgement of experience had hitherto been pursued wrongly, and that particulars had suffered a neglect, which led to a useless philosophy. Others exhibited a doubt that the incorrigible plurality of the natural world and human vicissitude could ever be compassed by knowledge.[20] Rudolph Agricola, in his *De inventione dialectica*, acknowledged the challenge that the infinite variety of things presented: 'Things are immeasurable in number, and correspondingly immeasurable are their properties and diversity. For this reason, no speech or power of the human mind can compass everything either belonging to individuals or setting them apart from one another.'[21] It was common to argue that, since it was impossible to compass the infinite variety of experience available to the senses, perfect enumeration and inductive knowledge were impossible: any general statement would be stalked by the possibility of a lurking exception.[22] Burton himself, in direct contradiction of the Porphyrian dictum, asserted that 'finitum de infinito non potest statuere' (vol. 1, p. 174) — it is not possible to establish the finite from the infinite, placing the possibility of art in doubt.

3. The elk's horn

These problems, and the validity of solutions to them, preoccupy Montaigne and Burton. They exhibit the anxiety of variety: copiousness designed less for the plea-sures of abundance and invention than for dismay at the unruly and teeming world. Montaigne's 'Of Drunkennesse' (II.2, 'De l'yvrongnerie') begins '[t]he world is nothing but varietie, and dissemblance' (Fl. p. 197; V, p. 339). Despite a title that asserts similarity as a badge of lineal descent, chapter II.37, 'De la ressemblance des enfans aux peres' [Of the Resemblance betweene Children and Fathers], and thus the second book, ends with a statement of radical unlikeness: 'never were there two opinions in the world alike, no more than two haires, or two graines. *Diversitie is the most vniversall qualitie*' (Fl. p. 450; V, p. 786; emphasis original). This is again Montaigne's theme in a sequence of maxims in 'Of Experience' (III.13, 'De l'experience'):

> No qualitie is so vniversall in this surface of things, as varietie and diversitie [...]. Dissimilitude doth of it selfe insinuate into our workes, no arte can come neere vnto similitude [...]. Resemblance doth not so much make one, as difference maketh another. (Fl. p. 634; V, p. 1065)

The abstraction of particulars into species and genera involves the forgetting of accidental difference, in favour of a single salient similarity which holds a class together, and distinguishes it from all others. Montaigne denies that some qualities or accidents are thus privileged; all differences instead are salient, and all things *sui generis*.

Similar tropes abound in 'Democritus Junior to the Reader', in an enactment of what has been called information overload.[23] The texture of Burton's prose suggests a hopscotching of attention that makes of the sentence a capacious receptacle for quotation and paraphrase, alternating between the common stock of literature and moments of self-disparagement and confession. The sentence is a different kind of receptacle in Burton's lists. From the secluded 'Minerva's Towre' of Christ Church, Oxford, he hears:

> new newes every day, & those ordinary rumors of War, Plagues, Fires, Inund-
> ations, Thefts, Murders, Massacres, Meteors, Comets, Spectrums, Prodigies
> [...], Battels fought, so many men slain, Monomachies, Shipwracks, Piracies,
> and Sea-fights [...]. New bookes every day, Pamphlets, Currantoes, Stories,
> whole Catalogues of Volumes of all sorts, new Paradoxes, Opinions, Schisms,
> Heresies, Controversies in Philosophy, Religion, &c. (vol. 1, pp. 4–5)

The prodigies of catastrophe lose their sting and their separate interest in Burton's heap, while the list of controversial literature subdues individual issues to a generalized mob of textual voices. As he confesses elsewhere, 'examples are infinite' (vol. 1, p. 196). His pages are peppered with et cetera: the repeated '&c.' is a gesture to the impossibility of perfect induction. Burton associates the 'roving humor' which causes him to behave 'like a ranging Spaniell, that barkes at every bird he sees' (vol. 1, p. 4) with Montaigne:

> I had a great desire [...] to have some smattering in all, to be *aliquis in omnibus,*
> *nullus in singulis,* [...] *to have an Oare in every mans Boat, to tast of every dish, and*
> *sip of every Cup,* which saith *Montaigne,* was well performed by *Aristotle* and his
> learned Country-man *Adrian Turnebus.* (vol. 1, pp. 3–4; emphases original)

Montaigne acts here as both endorsement and subtle undermining of this centrifugal scatter.[24]

Both Montaigne and Burton also undermine the disciplinary strategies of law and medicine to manage idiosyncrasy and variety. Montaigne takes the epistemological basis of legal reasoning to task in 'Of Experience'. The 'hundred thousand kindes of particular cases [...] hath no proportion, with the infinite *diversitie* of humane accidents',[25] Montaigne complains, and thus 'the multiplying of our inventions shall never come to the variation of examples':

> Adde a hundred times as many vnto them, yet shall it not followe, that of events
> to come, there be any one found, that in all this infinite number of selected and
> enregistred events, shall meete with one, to which hee may so exactly joyne and
> match it, but some circumstance and diversitie will remaine, that may require
> a diverse consideration of judgement. (Fl. p. 634; V, p. 1066)

Without distinguishing between proper and accidental circumstances, each event is *sui generis*, scuppering the generalizations necessary to the functioning of communicable knowledge: Montaigne refuses the abridgements necessary in legal logic.

In 'Of the Resemblance betweene Children and Fathers', medicine is susceptible to the same critique. Montaigne stages a thought experiment, in which someone attempts to find a cure for epilepsy: 'I imagine man,[26] heedfully viewing about him the infinite number of things, creatures, plants, and mettalls. I wot not where to make him beginne his Essay'. Montaigne speculatively suggests that the seeker might fall by chance on the curious remedy of 'an Elkes-Horne'. But this offers no remedy to the problem of variety. Among infinite possibilities it is impossible to find out

> what this Horne is: Amongest the numberlesse diseases that are, what an Epilepsie is; the sundrie and manifolde complexions in a melancholy man; So manie seasons in Winter; So diverse Nations amongest French-men; So many ages in age; So diverse coelestiall changes and alterations, in the conjunction of *Venus* and *Saturne*; So severall, and many partes in a mans body, nay in one of his fingers.[27]

The idiosyncrasy of the individual and the vagaries of circumstance exponentially multiply. If a single finger is various enough to take up the physician's whole attention, how can an art proceed?

This is the prevailing condition of the *Anatomy*. The 'sundrie and manifolde complexions' of melancholy, the infinity of symptom and circumstance, is the substance of Burton's book. That diseases were infinite was a commonplace of medical literature, but Burton makes of it a peculiarly modern phenomenon:

> How many diseases there are, is a question not yet determined. *Pliny* [...] saith *morborum infinita multitudo*, their number is infinite: Howsoever it was in those old times, it boots not; in our dayes I am sure the number is much augmented. (vol. 1, p. 129)

Moreover, Burton characterizes melancholy as the universal blight of mankind and 'the Character of Mortalitie' (vol. 1, p. 136), whose chief symptom is variety. 'Who can sufficiently speake of these symptomes, or prescribe rules to comprehend them?', Burton laments:

> if you will describe melancholy, describe a phantasticall conceipt, a corrupt imagination, vaine thoughts and different, which who can doe? The foure and twenty letters make no more variety of words in divers languages, then melancholy conceipts produce diversity of symptomes in severall persons. They are irregular, obscure, various, so infinite, *Proteus* himselfe is not so divers, you may as well make the *Moone* a new coat, as a true character of a melancholy man; as soone finde the motion of a bird in the aire, as the heart of man, a melancholy man. (vol. 1, p. 407)

The notion of 'sufficient speech' suggests an exhaustive account, enumerating all accidents and circumstances without abridgement. When Burton declares that his task is to 'describe melancholy', he is using a technical term in dialectic: description is a form of definition which uses accidents as well as proper differences to specify a thing.[28] The *Anatomy* and the *Essais*, in all their bulk, are testaments at once to the fantasy of sufficient speech on any given topic, and the impossibility of ever achieving it.

What is required instead is some kind of elk's horn: a way to begin in spite of perplexity. As Maclean has shown, disciplines which could not hope for perfect definitions, or divisions which left no remainder and threatened no exception, looked to dialectic and topical logic, which aimed only at probable knowledge, true for the most part. Topical logic utilized topoi or 'places' which grouped moves in argument under headings, ready to be consulted to find the most fertile and persuasive approach for whatever subject presented itself. Such strategies allowed for pragmatic, ad hoc, and 'intuitive dissimilarity/similarity decisions'.[29] Topical divisions, definitions, and descriptions were not intended to be exhaustive, and could include matters of circumstance and accident. Though not, in their dialectical form, intended to encourage endless expansion, in their rhetorical mode — especially in Erasmus's *De copia* — topical strategies could foster a potentially endless generation of text. Peter Mack has called the topics of argument 'a technique of verbal association'.[30] The result is a horizontal rather than a vertical mode of thinking: one based on experience without resorting to the abridgement of infinity.

Montaigne's phrase 'I wot not where to make him beginne his Essay' insinuates that the strategies of managing variety in medicine and allied arts are associated with the kind of writing he is himself undertaking. Montaigne's 'homme', casting about for a remedy, requires a place — a topos — from which to begin. So too those who write of particulars. Each chapter faces the problem of how to broach its topic. The first sentence of I.46, 'Des noms' [Of Names] suggests that a title supplies a minimal and nominalist notion of commonality: 'What diversitie there-be in hearbs, all are shuffled-vp together vnder the name of a sallade'. This ad hoc division applies also to his writing: 'Even so, vpon the consideration of names, I wil here huddle-vp a galiemafrie of divers articles' (Fl. p. 148; V, p. 276).[31] Montaigne's chapters indulge in the kind of lateral adhoccery that moves by association rather than logic, and maintain their coherence by the title they are given rather than through internal organization.[32] He claims he has 'no fashion, but hath varried according to accidents' (Fl. p. 642; V, p. 1080).[33] Burton, likewise, states that his book was 'writ with as small deliberation as I doe ordinarily speake' (vol. 1, p. 17), and shares the features of copious expansion and apparent digression. And like Montaigne, he demonstrates problems in grasping the elk's horn. Although 'Democritus Junior to the Reader' is 78 pages long in the sixth edition, it ends 'I will beginne' (vol. 1, p. 113).

4. *Similitudo dissimilis*

Ending 'Democritus Junior to the Reader' by beginning is only the first example of a trope which is one of the most salient features of the *Anatomy*. Burton repeatedly presents incorrigible, proliferating variety, only to make a contingent but pragmatic gesture of division. Immediately following the passage on melancholy's Protean variability, Burton asks 'who can distinguish these melancholy symptomes so intermixt with others, or apply them to their severall kindes, confine them into method?' The question expects the answer 'no one', yet Burton steps up: ''Tis hard I confesse yet I have disposed of them as I could, & will descend to particularize them according to their species' (vol. 1, p. 408). The bathos is most extreme at the opening of the section on religious melancholy, where Burton lays out 'a stupend, vast, infinite Ocean of incredible madnesse and folly' (vol. 3, p. 331):

> The parties affected are innumerable almost, and scattered over the face of the earth, farre and neere, and so have beene in all precedent ages, from the beginning of the world to these times, of all sorts and conditions. For methods sake I will reduce them to a twofold division. (vol. 3, p. 337)

Despite the bafflement of variety, Burton effects a quasi-miraculous parting of the infinite ocean.

The subsection 'Symptomes or Signes in the Minde' makes this strategy explicit. Burton concludes a discussion of bizarre phenomena — melancholics who believe they are made of glass, butter, cork, or feathers, or 'have naught but bag-pipes in their braine' — with the anxiety of variety:

> [Melancholics] will act, conceave all extreames, contrarieties, and contradictions, and that in infinite varieties. [... S]carce two of two thousand, that concurre in the same symptoms; The tower of *Babel* never yeelded such confusion of tongues, as this Chaos of melancholy doth variety of Symptomes. (vol. 1, p. 395)

Melancholy is not a disorder, but disorder itself. Yet, with no signal of transition — no concessive adverb, no paragraph break — the complaint is followed by a remedy:

> There is in all melancholy *similitudo dissimilis*, like mens faces, a disagreeing likenesse still; And as in a River we swimme in the same place, though not in the same numericall water: [...] so the same disease yeelds diversity of Symptomes. Which howsoever they be diverse, intricate, and hard to be confined, I will adventure yet in such a vast confusion and generality, to bring them into some order, & so descend to particulars. (vol. 1, pp. 395–96)

Despite the Babel and Chaos, there is nonetheless in melancholy a subterranean commonality: a ground on which classification can proceed and a body of knowledge be assembled.

The hinge between the two parts is the phrase *similitudo dissimilis*, or 'disagreeing likenesse', a strategic dismissal of the surface dissimilarities of things. The principle had purchase in various fields as a principle of composition, interpretation, or logical analysis.[34] As the physician John Cotta argued, '[i]t is a chiefe point in all learnings truly to discerne between differing similitudes and like differences', to avoid creating distinctions between things really alike, or bringing together things which have only an accidental similarity.[35] Burton's turn to *similitudo dissimilis* however raises bathos and irony. The bulk of the subsection takes pleasure in heaping up curious examples of melancholic delusion, undecided between the pleasures and anxieties of variety. The mismatch between the scale of Burton's examples, and the two-sentence turn to order, suggests that neither pleasure nor anxiety is adequately 'confined' by Burton's abrupt shift to division.

Burton's mention of 'mens faces' gestures to a common trope, and to a discipline in which questions of similarity and difference were particularly complex.[36] Montaigne likewise uses the disagreeing likeness of physiognomy as a topos. Many of the quotations which illustrate his concern with universal difference and the individuality of written style come from 'Of the Resemblance betweene Children and Fathers' and 'Of Physiognomy', chapters which, despite their apparent digressions from the titular theme, circle around ideas of semblance, originality, and the problems of abridging experience. In 'Of Experience', Montaigne discusses his own observation of his friends: he observes them, he says, '[n]ot to marshall or range this infinite varietie of so diverse and so distracted actions to certaine Genders or

Chapters [genres et chapitres], and distinctly to distribute my parcels and divisions into formes and knowne regions' (Fl. p. 640; V, p. 1076). Montaigne implies that such strategies are not his business: 'I leave it to Artists and I wot not whether in a matter so confused, so several and so casuall, they shall come to an end, to range into sides, this infinite diversitie of visages; and settle our inconstancie and place it in order' (Fl. pp. 640–41; V, p. 1076). Montaigne's dismissive gesture to 'Artists' scorns Porphyry's notion of an art as the delimitation of infinity.

Yet 'genres et chapitres' suggest that the procedures of logical classification are associated with the literary form of the *Essais*, and shortly after this passage, Montaigne too offers a principle of *similitudo dissimilis*:

> As no event or forme doth wholy resemble an other, so doth it not altogether differ one from another. [...] *If our faces were not like, we could not discerne a man from a beast: If they were not unlike, we could not distinguish one man from another man.* All things hold by some similitude: Every example limpeth. [...] Comparisons are neverthelesse joyned together by some end [par quelque coin]. (Fl. p. 636; V, p. 1070; emphases original)

Like Burton facing the unmanageable variety of things, Montaigne appeals to a disagreeing likeness, and grasps his subject by some corner.

5. 'Our stile bewraies us'

Montaigne and Burton, then, share a preoccupation with tropes of the anxiety of variety, and a concern with ways of solving it, through the looser, topical models of textual generation. But rather than using such strategies to abridge the infinity of individual experience, their writing strives instead to preserve it. Both works allow the possibility of infinite proliferation, and deploy a principle of *similitudo dissimilis* which aspires at the same time to be a *dissimilitudo similis*.

This returns us to the questions of literary method and influence with which this essay began. The idiosyncrasy which Montaigne and Burton assert is a problem in giving accounts of their works. There is a danger of stressing the *similitudo* over the *dissimilitudo*, so that their particularity is abridged. I have suggested that Burton's debt to Montaigne is more than a matter of superficial borrowings and opportunistic raids on a stock of example and exotica. But to say so is paradoxically untrue to the emphasis in Montaigne on personal idiosyncrasy, and to Burton's repeated insistence on the originality of appropriation.

Of course, this in itself is a commonality: Burton and Montaigne are paradoxically alike in their refusal to be alike. This chimes with one of the ways in which Montaigne characterizes his book, in the chapter appropriately entitled 'Of the Inconsistency of our Actions' (II.1, 'De l'inconstance de nos actions': 'We are all framed of flappes and patches, and of so shapelesse and diverse a contexture, that everie piece, and everie moment playeth his part. And there is as much difference found betweene vs and our selves, as there is betweene our selves and others' (Fl. pp. 196–97; V, p. 337). We are all the same in being constituted of difference. This characterization of self is equally apt for the *Essais* and the *Anatomy*. It suggests a procedure of atomic composition, local and temporalized, which would make the textual patchwork of each work discrete portions of the same mosaic surface, locally contradictory and various, made coherent only by the covers of the book, like the green leaves corralled into a class by the name of salad.

Montaigne's 'difference between us and ourselves' recalls his famous statements of self-inconsistency, like the opening sentences of 'Of Repenting', which cast his portrait of 'a particulare' man as a study of his own changeability, varying minute by minute, a 'historie [...] fitted to the present': 'It is a counter-roule of diuers and variable accidents, and irresolute imaginations, and sometimes contrarie: whether it be that my selfe am other, or that I apprehend subiects, by other circumstances and considerations' (Fl. p. 483; V, pp. 804–05). The notion of self-alienation across time is also evident in Montaigne's accounts of his own reading of the *Essais*. In 'Of the Affection of Fathers to their Children' (II.8, 'De l'affection des peres aux enfans'), he remarks of his book that '[h]e may know many things, that my selfe know no longer, and hold of me what I could not hold myselfe: and which (if neede should require) I must borrow of him as of a stranger' (Fl. p. 233; V, p. 402). The 'je' that writes the book becomes a 'thou' that reads it.

This begins to clarify Burton's transformation of Montaigne's 'Je suis moi-même' into 'Thou thy selfe'. 'Democritus Junior to the Reader' begins with a reluctance to expose what lies beneath the pseudonym, urging the reader 'Seeke not after what is hid', since 'I would not willingly be knowne' (vol. 1, p. 1). This appears a wilful reversal of Montaigne's 'Au lecteur', especially the claim that he will display himself naked and entire. Burton turns disclosure into concealment. Nonetheless, he flirts with the identification of the book's matter with himself. He offers his credentials by insisting that, while other authors '*get their knowledge by Bookes, I mine by melancholizing*, Experto crede ROBERTO' (vol. 1, p. 8; emphasis original). In a typical irony, Burton's insistence that his knowledge is not literary but experiential is expressed by a quotation: the 'I' is that of the consul Gaius Marius in Sallust's *Bellum iugurthinum*, though adapted from soldiery to melancholy.[37] This is still more poignant in Burton's self-reference: the phrase 'experto crede Roberto' ('believe Robert, who has experienced this') was proverbial, and the coincidence of the proper name mere chance. At these points, Burton's first-person singular speaks simultaneously on behalf of himself, and as a focal point through which tradition is vocalized.

This is also the sense of Burton's 'thou' in his first paragraph. The sentence emerges out of a refutation of any suspicion that he writes a 'ridiculous Treatise' based on paradox and prodigy, and is preceded by a translation of an epigram from Martial:

> No *Centaures* here, or *Gorgons* looke to finde,
> My subject is of Man, and humane kind.
> Thou thy selfe art the subject of my Discourse. (vol. 1, p. 1)

The singular emerges as the realization of the human possibilities of kind: idiosyncratic, but also common and exemplary. When Burton moves to 'particularize' the illimitably various symptoms of melancholy 'according to their species', he states that though he has 'expatiated in more generall lists or termes, speaking promiscuously', there is an important caveat: 'Not that [the symptoms] are all to be found in one man, for that were to paint a monster or Chimera, not a man; but some in one, some in another, and that successively or at severall times' (vol. 1, p. 408). Like the *Essais*, the *Anatomy* is a portrait of its subject in successive moments, under different circumstances and aspects; considering them simultaneously effects a monstrous distortion which can only be resolved in attention to the particular in the moment.

For all his insistence on individuality and resistance to essentialism, Montaigne too repeatedly insists that 'men be all of one kind [espece]' (Fl. p. 127; V, p. 51). This does not imply a self-contradictory emphasis on the sameness of human beings. Rather than offering the common as a minimal and bland abstraction of universal principles, to render the species for Montaigne is to offer a various, copious, and capacious exhibition of common human potential. In II.10, 'Des livres' [Of Bookes], Montaigne unexpectedly claims that he seeks knowledge of man in general, despite the stress on idiosyncrasy elsewhere. But Montaigne seeks this knowledge in history, which, like medicine and law, is a study of particulars. Knowledge of man in general is offered 'more lively and perfectly' in history than elsewhere, since it offers 'the varietie and truth of [man's] inward conditions, in grose and by retale [*sc.* detail]: the diversitie of the meanes of his collection and composing, and of the accidents that threaten him' (Fl. p. 240; V, p. 416).[38] Anecdotes harbour what Montaigne calls 'a trick of humane capacitie' (Fl. p. 45, V, p. 105): a realization of one facet of the infinite variety of human possibility. History, with its anecdotes and examples, is the crucible in which idiosyncrasy sublimates into universality, or universality precipitates into the particular.

Burton's 'thou' and Montaigne's 'je' thus amount to the same thing: the singular participating precisely by means of its idiosyncrasy in the species of man. This is not 'some corner' of similarity by which we can group Burton and Montaigne together: it is something Burton learned from reading the *Essais*. Shortly after warning his reader not to waste time on his vain subject, Burton anticipates censure from readers:

> I have assay'd, put my selfe upon the Stage, I must abide the censure [...]. It is most true, *stylus virum arguit*, our stile bewraies us, and as Hunters find their game by the trace, so is a mans *Genius* descried by his workes [...] I have layd my selfe open (I know it) in this Treatise, turned mine inside outward, I shall be censured[.] (vol. 1, p. 13)

Burton declares that he has 'assay'd': that is to say, essayed, exposed himself to trial in imitation of Montaigne.[39] 'Stylus virum arguit' is Burton's own articulation of a commonplace, expressed with his typical ambivalence: style reveals the writer, but the pen, or stylus, also betrays him, running beyond his conscious control. That Burton expresses this in the plural — 'our stile bewraies us' — articulates again the simultaneity of idiosyncrasy and commonality. What is revealed is 'a mans *Genius*': like Montaigne scrutinizing his friends' 'productions', the style of a work reveals an idiosyncratic constitution. But Roman Genius was a tutelary deity who presided at once over 'an individual's innate qualities', and those forces, like the drive to procreate, which belong to the species and are least within the individual's control.[40] Again what is most idiosyncratic is intimately linked to what is most common.

A final example confirms Burton's association of simultaneous idiosyncrasy and commonality with Montaigne. In 'Of Exercise or Practise' (II.6, 'De l'exercitation'), Montaigne justifies the discussion of his own experience by insisting that it is not doctrine, not the abstracted principles of art, but instead only something for himself to study, which might, by accident, chime with the reader:

> Now as *Plinie* saith, every man is a good discipline unto himselfe, alwayes provided he is able to prie into himselfe. This is not my doctrine, it is but my studie; And not another mans lesson, but mine owne. Yet ought no man to blame me if I impart the same. What serves my turne, may happily [*sc.* by chance] serve another mans: otherwise I marre nothing, what I make use of, is my owne. (Fl. p. 219; V, p. 377)

In the subsection 'A Consolatory Digression', Burton uses this passage to return to question of borrowed words: 'what can any man say that hath not beene said?' How to avoid cliché in words of comfort? Burton again faces the problem of addressing the unknowably individual reader. He resolves the difficulty by writing to and of himself:

> though it be the same againe, I will say it [...] *Non meus hic sermo*, 'tis not my speech this, but of *Seneca, Plutarch, Epictetus, Austin, Bernard, Christ and his Apostles*. If I make nothing, as *Montaigne* said in like case, I will marre nothing, 'tis not my doctrine but my study, I hope I shall doe no body wrong to speake what I thinke, and deserve not blame in imparting my minde. (vol. 2, p. 216)[41]

The paradoxes pursued throughout this essay are particularly sharp here: though professing to 'speake what I thinke', Burton does so in a range of voices not his own. '['T]is not my speech this' is at once a pleonastic truism, as a translation of a line from Horace's *Satire* II. 2. 2, and a performative contradiction, since, spoken in the first person, these are Burton's words. This dilemma Burton recognizes as also Montaigne's, adapting his words 'in like case': the first person of '[i]f I make nothing [...] I will marre nothing' is at once Montaigne and Burton, speaking in common about the preservation of idiosyncrasy.

Burton closes his adapted quotation from Montaigne with another pragmatic continuation of writing, despite the discursive problems idiosyncrasy generates: 'If it be not for thy ease, it may for mine owne: be it as it may, I will essay' (vol. 2, p. 126). What Burton found in the *Essais* was an example of how to preserve the particular from abridgement while nonetheless articulating something common, allowing the paradoxes of singularity and universality to operate in the play between 'je', 'thou', and man in general. For Burton, to 'essay' is to write, self-exposingly, as oneself, and thus by accident to reveal what is common. Without being doctrine, the study of Montaigne had indeed served another man's turn.

Notes to Chapter 13

1. Robert Burton, *The Anatomy of Melancholy*, ed. Thomas C. Faulkner, Nicolas K. Kiessling, and Rhonda L. Blair (Oxford: Clarendon Press, 1989–2000), vol. 1, p. 1. All references hereafter will be to this edition and in the text.
2. 'Thus gentle Reader my selfe am the ground-worke of my booke', in the translation by John Florio. See Michel de Montaigne, *The Essayes, or Morall, Politike and Millitarie Discourses*, trans. Florio (London: By Valentine Sims for Edward Blount,1603), sig. A6v. Since this is the version

of Montaigne that Burton read, quotations will be taken from it and references given in the text using the abbreviation 'Fl.'.

3. On Burton's concern with reading as therapy and pastoral care, see Mary Ann Lund, *Melancholy, Medicine, and Religion in Early Modern England* (Cambridge: Cambridge University Press, 2010).

4. On copious texts in general see the special issue 'Copious Texts' in *Renaissance Studies*, 28.2 (2014), including my 'Robert Burton and the Problems of Polymathy', 279–97; and Terence Cave, *The Cornucopian Text: Problems of Writing in the French Renaissance* (Oxford: Clarendon Press, 1979).

5. It is possible Burton and Florio were acquainted: William Vaughan's *The Golden Fleece* (London: Printed for Francis Williams, 1626) contains a fictional dialogue between Vaughan, Florio, and 'Democritus Junior' (pp. 23–30). The most sustained attention to their literary relationship appears in Fritz Dieckow, 'John Florios englische Übersetzung der *Essais* Montaignes und Lord Bacons, Ben Jonsons, und Robert Burtons Verhältnis zu Montaigne', PhD dissertation, Strassburg, 1903. For briefer comparisons, see Angus Gowland, *The Worlds of Renaissance Melancholy: Robert Burton in Context* (Cambridge: Cambridge University Press, 2006), p. 299 *et ad indicem*; Lund, *Melancholy, Medicine, and Religion*, pp. 47–50, 142–43, 196; and Eric MacPhail, *Dancing Around the Well: The Circulation of Commonplaces in Renaissance Humanism* (Leiden: Brill, 2014), pp. 89–91.

6. See the index of the Clarendon edition at vol. 6, p. 388. Christopher Grose, in '*Theatrum libri*: Robert Burton and the Failure of Encyclopaedic Form', in *Books and Readers in Early Modern England*, ed. Jennifer Andersen and Elizabeth Sauer (Philadelphia: University of Pennsylvania Press, 2002), pp. 80–96, claims that Burton's reference to '*Zisca's* drumme' (vol. 1, p. 24) is a further unacknowledged borrowing (see *Essayes*, p. 7). This is possible, though Žižka's drum was a commonplace. For further discussion, see Lund, *Melancholy, Medicine, and Religion*, p. 1.

7. William Hamlin, *Montaigne's English Journey* (Oxford: Oxford University Press, 2013), pp. 91, 93.

8. MacPhail, *Dancing Around the Well*, pp. 89, 91.

9. This may be an unnoticed gesture to Rudolph Agricola's *De inventione dialectica* (Strasbourg: Johannes Knoblouch, 1521): 'Est & alia ratio dicendi copiose, quae sit, cum unam eandemque rem iterum atque iterum enumeratis dicimus uerbis', sig. 116v.

10. Montaigne concludes the quoted passage 'pour en faire un ouvrage tout sien: à sçavoir son jugement', equating the work to which imitation amounts with the student's judgement. Florio, translating from the de Gournay edition of 1595, follows its punctuation to compress the reference to judgement into the succeeding sentence, thus making a different point: 'altogether his owne; always provided, his judgement, his travel, studie, and institution tend to nothing, but to frame the same perfect.' For discussion of Montaigne's interimplication here of free-thinking and judgement, scepticism, and imitation, see Richard Scholar, *Montaigne and the Art of Free-Thinking* (Oxford: Peter Lang, 2010), pp. 54-63, esp. 62-63.

11. See the commentary at Burton, vol. 4, p. 26.

12. See Lund, *Melancholy, Medicine, and Religion*.

13. Francis Bacon, *The Advancement of Learning*, ed. Michael Kiernan (Oxford: Oxford University Press, 2000), pp. 84–85.

14. Ian Maclean, 'The Logic of Physiognomony in the Late Renaissance', *Early Science and Medicine*, 16.4 (2011), 275–95 (p. 289).

15. Porphyry, *Introduction*, ed. and trans. Jonathan Barnes (Oxford: Oxford University Press, 2003), p. 7. See also Aristotle, *Metaphysics*, 1007a15 and 1027a20–21.

16. For this phrase from Porphyry, see (briefly) Ian Maclean, *Logic, Signs, and Nature in the Renaissance: The Case of Learned Medicine* (Cambridge: Cambridge University Press, 2001), p. 273, and *Interpretation and Meaning in the Renaissance: the Case of Law* (Cambridge: Cambridge University Press, 1992), pp. 25 and 113–14; and Gowland, *The Worlds of Renaissance Melancholy*, p. 57.

17. The 'non-naturals' are diet, '*Retention, and Evacuation*', air, exercise, sleep, and the passions, to each of which Burton devoted a subsection of the *Anatomy*.

18. Maclean, *Logic, Signs, and Nature*, p. 164. See, in addition, Maclean, *Interpretation and Meaning*; 'Logic of Physiognomony'; 'Evidence, Logic, the Rule and the Exception in Renaissance Law

and Medicine', *Early Science and Medicine*, 5.3 (2000), 227–56; 'White Crows, Graying Hair, and Eyelashes: Problems for Natural Historians in the Reception of Aristotelian Logic and Biology', in *Historia: Empiricism and Erudition in Early Modern Europe*, ed. Gianna Pomata and Nancy Siraisi (Cambridge, MA: MIT Press, 2005), pp. 147–79.

19. See Maclean, 'The Sceptical Crisis Reconsidered: Galen, Rational Medicine, and the *libertas philosophandi*', *Early Science and Medicine*, 11.3 (2006), 247–74; and Pierre Force, 'Montaigne and the Coherence of Eclecticism', *Journal of the History of Ideas*, 70.4 (2009), 523–44.

20. See Kathryn Murphy, 'The Anxiety of Variety: Knowledge and Experience in Montaigne, Burton, and Bacon', in *Fictions of Knowledge: Fact, Evidence, Doubt*, ed. Yota Batsaki, Subha Mukherji, and Jan-Melissa Schramm (Basingstoke: Palgrave Macmillan, 2012), pp. 110–30.

21. 'Res [...] numero sunt immensae, et proinde immensa quoque proprietas atque diversitas earum. Quô fit, ut omnia, quae singulis conveniant aut discrepent, singulatim nulla oratio, nulla vis mentis humanae possit complecti'; Rudolph Agricola, *De inventione libri tres/Drei Bücher über die Inventio dialectica*, ed. and trans. Lothar Mundt (Tübingen: Max Niemeyer, 1992), p. 18.

22. For examples see Maclean, 'Evidence, Logic, the Rule and the Exception', and 'White Crows', and Murphy, 'Anxiety of Variety'.

23. See the essays gathered in *Early Modern Information Overload*, ed. Daniel Rosenberg, special issue of the *Journal of the History of Ideas*, 64.1 (2005); Ann Blair, *Too Much to Know: Managing Scholarly Information before the Modern Age* (New Haven, CT: Yale University Press, 2010); and Murphy, 'Robert Burton'.

24. Florio's Montaigne describes Aristotle as one who 'hath an oare in euery water, and medleth with all things' (Fl. p. 6; V, p. 17). Hamlin, failing to see Burton's irony, argues that Burton 'completely misrepresents' Montaigne, and that this is an example of Burton's 'tendentious instrumentality' (*Montaigne's English Journey*, p. 80). The French has merely 'Aristote, qui remue toutes choses'. Neither Montaigne nor Florio mention Turnebus at this point.

25. Florio's 'humane accidents' misses the legal pun on senses of 'action' in 'l'infinie diversité des actions humaines'.

26. The French has 'l'homme'.

27. Fl. p. 448; V, p. 782. Florio mistranslates: 'parmy cette infinité de choses que c'est cette corne; parmy cette infinité de maladies, l'epilepsie; tant de complexions, au melancolique; tant de saisons, en hyver; tant de nations, au François; tant d'aages, en la vieillesse; tant de mutations celestes, en la conjonction de Venus et de Saturne; tant de parties du corps, au doigt'.

28. See Peter Mack, *Renaissance Argument: Valla and Agricola on the Traditions of Rhetoric and Dialectic* (Leiden: Brill, 1993), p. 154.

29. Maclean, 'Evidence, Logic, the Rule and the Exception', p. 237.

30. Mack, *Renaissance Argument*, p. 130; see also Cave, *The Cornucopian Text*, pp. 12–18.

31. Cf. Fl. p. 642, V, p. 1079: 'all this galiemafrie which I huddle-vp here, is but a register of my lives-Essayes'.

32. Maclean points out Montaigne's reliance on the topoi of arguments à similis, à circumstantiis, and à causâ. Maclean, *Montaigne philosophe* (Paris: Presses universitaires de France, 1996), pp. 46–48; see also Maclean, 'Montaigne and the Truth of the Schools', in *The Cambridge Companion to Montaigne*, ed. Ullrich Langer (Cambridge: Cambridge University Press, 2005), pp. 142–62. Peter Mack traces the topical structure of Montaigne's essays in *Reading and Rhetoric in Montaigne and Shakespeare* (London: Bloomsbury Academic, 2010).

33. Without mentioning the topical tradition, Ann Hartle observes Montaigne's movement through 'the accidental similarity of discrete and fragmentary stories': *Montaigne and the Origins of Modern Philosophy* (Evanston, IL: Northwestern University Press, 2013), p. 25.

34. In music theory, *similitudo dissimilis* described patterns of modified similarity between different phrases; in hermeneutics the foundation of typological relationship; in scholastic ontology, a way of accounting for the similarity that obtains between different members of a species, or between a thing and the cognized image of that thing. See, respectively, Emmanuela Kohlhaas, *Musik und Sprache im gregorianischen Gesang* (Stuttgart: Steiner, 2001), pp. 303–09; Karl F. Morrison, *History as a Visual Art in the Twelfth Century Renaissance* (Princeton, NJ: Princeton University Press, 1990), pp. 104, 107; and Leen Spruit, *Species Intelligibilis: From Perception to Knowledge* (Leiden: Brill, 1994–95), vol. 1, p. 202.

35. John Cotta, *A short discoverie of the unobserved dangers of severall sorts of ignorant and unconsiderate practisers of physicke in England* (London: For William Jones and Richard Boyle, 1612), p. 17; cited in Maclean, *Logic, Signs and Nature*, p. 137 and Gowland, *The Worlds of Renaissance Melancholy*, p. 114. Burton cites Cotta, though not this passage, at vol. 1, p. 253.

36. See Maclean, 'Physiognomony'.

37. See the commentary at Burton, vol. 4, p. 20.

38. Again Florio's doublets and over-literal translation of the French make matters more obscure: 'the diversitie of the meanes of his collection and composing' renders 'la varieté des moyens de son assemblage'.

39. Montaigne also describes his work as a skeleton, at Fl. p. 220; V, p. 379.

40. See *Brill's New Pauly*, s.v. 'Genius', <http://referenceworks.brillonline.com/entries/brill-s-new-pauly> [accessed 17 August 2015]; and Giorgio Agamben, 'Genius', in *Profanations*, trans. Jeff Fort (New York: Zone Books, 2007), pp. 9–12.

41. Discussed in Gowland, *The Worlds of Renaissance Melancholy*, p. 272.

CHAPTER 14

Montaignian Moments:
Shakespeare and the *Essays*

Colin Burrow

Most people who write about Shakespeare's relationship to Montaigne begin by saying that Shakespeare's only incontrovertible allusion to the *Essays* is in *The Tempest*. Everyone agrees that Gonzalo's speech about his imaginary commonwealth, the latter end of which 'forgets its beginning', has its roots in John Florio's translation of Montaigne's essay I.31, 'Des cannibales' [Of the Caniballes] because the two passages share a lot of words.[1] After that statement, studies of this subject tend to divide in their approach. They might go abstract and say that Shakespeare was part of a wider 'Montaignian moment' which heralded the emergence of self-consciousness,[2] or that 'Montaigne' in various ways represents a subject-position in relation to which Shakespearean drama can usefully be explored;[3] or they might go enumerative and philological and list the words which are in Florio's Montaigne and which are not found in Shakespeare's works before about 1603 (the tastier items on that list include 'bellyful', 'copulation', 'bastardizing', 'derogate', 'marble-hearted', 'sterility', and 'disnatur'd');[4] or they might go cultural historical and say that the two writers shared a common background in rhetorical training and intellectual foundations,[5] or argue (as Warren Boutcher has done in an extremely persuasive essay) that Montaigne 'was used by scholars and advisers to furnish the real aristocracy and by playwrights to furnish the staged aristocracy with matter for topical philosophical discussion — as Gonzalo does Alonso'.[6] On the whole they then go on to say that it is impossible to locate instances of influence outside *The Tempest* which are incontrovertible — although there has been a little flexibility in recent years over what 'incontrovertible' means in this context. It is now routinely accepted that Prospero's claim that 'the rarer action is/ In virtue than in vengeance' (v. I. 27–28) derives from II.11, 'De la cruauté' [Of Crueltie],[7] and some scholars are now willing to agree that the connections between Montaigne's essay II.8, 'De l'affection des pères aux enfans' [Of the Affection of Fathers to their Children] and *King Lear* are strong enough to warrant thinking about that play as quizzically investigating Montaigne's benevolent notion that fathers should hand over much of their estate to their children before their death.[8]

This diversity of approach is naturally a source of delight. But it does provoke a question. Why has this relationship prompted so much disagreement?

Two reasons might be singled out. The first is a general one: literary criticism has historically not been well equipped with a vocabulary or a method for writing about relationships between two authors where thinking, rather than direct verbal borrowing, might be involved.[9] The category 'source' as it is generally deployed in writing about Shakespeare is horribly tricked out with the defence mechanisms of empirical scholarship. The only evidence that will pass the test imposed on 'sources' by a knuckle-headed (and often also knuckle-fisted) empiricist is an exact verbal parallel. The idea that 'exact verbal parallels' might be intrinsically alien to some of the ways in which writers respond to what they read is not one that carries much weight with traditionalists. As a result critics with intelligent things to say about the relationship between Shakespeare and Montaigne tend now to 'finesse the question of direct influence',[10] where 'finesse' is a delicate way of indicating that they will avoid discussing it while implying that Shakespeare shared so many premises with Montaigne that it would be strange to suppose them to be the result of coincidence.

The second reason that critics cannot agree what to do with the relationship between Shakespeare and Montaigne derives from the distinctive history of the category 'source' as it has come to be thought of in relation to Shakespeare. The main reference work still used by scholars when they want to know where a given play came from is Geoffrey Bullough's eight volumes of *Narrative and Dramatic Sources of Shakespeare.*[11] As their title indicates, these volumes contain chiefly the plays, poems, and *novelle* that gave Shakespeare what we now call narrative or plot. This interest in where the playwright got his stories from has its roots in Charlotte Lennox's collection of Shakespeare's sources called *Illustrations of Shakespeare* (1753–54).[12] Lennox was a novelist, and her aim was to make Shakespeare accessible to a female readership familiar with narrative fiction. Although she has a lot to say about probability and plausibility in narrative fiction (and about Shakespeare's failure to provide it) she has nothing to say about the origins of passages of argumentation in Shakespeare's works. She reproduces *novelle* by Cinthio and Lodge as Shakespeare's 'sources', but does not include works by Seneca or Cicero (or indeed any classical texts, since she believed Shakespeare did not read them) or Montaigne. Bullough makes disparaging reference to Lennox in the preface to the first volume of *Narrative and Dramatic Sources*,[13] but his volumes are a monument to the long-term success of her belief that to understand the genesis of Shakespeare's plays you need to read texts which offer precise parallels to those plays in plot and action. Bullough, however, also includes, as Lennox does not, a scattering of works of which there are verbal echoes in Shakespeare's plays. Hence he includes among 'narrative' sources texts such as Golding's translation of Medea's speech from Ovid's *Metamorphoses*, which has words in common with Prospero's address to the 'elves of hills, brooks, standing lakes and groves' (v. 1. 33), despite the fact this is clearly not a 'narrative' source at all.[14] Bizarrely, he chose not to print Florio's translation of 'Of the Caniballes', although it clearly meets the criterion of indisputable verbal echo. Other passages of Montaigne that Shakespeare read and with which his works clearly engage — 'Of the Affection of Fathers to their Children', or 'Of Crueltie' — also drop through the cracks between a 'narrative' source and a verbal source. Given that Shakespeare appears to have drawn words from Florio within a year or so of the publication in 1603 of the *Essays*, and, given that several other English dramatists were borrowing passages from Florio from about 1603–04 onwards, the omission of this material is hard to defend except on the pragmatic grounds that eight volumes of 'narrative and dramatic sources' are probably enough.

To these two reasons why critics have been cautious about how far to press the relationship between Shakespeare and Montaigne we might add a third, even more specific to Shakespeare. Shakespeare tends to position Montaigne-like moments within his drama in a distinctive way. Where Marston and Webster tend to put phrases from Montaigne into the mouths of sophisticates and cynics,[15] Shakespeare is prone to make people who are crazy sound like Montaigne. Crazy people in Shakespeare tend not only to fracture their own discourse but that of other people too. When Lear is wandering and mad he meets the blind Gloucester and delivers a diatribe on justice:

> What, art mad? A man may see how this world goes with no eyes; look with thine ears. See how yon justice rails upon yon simple thief. Hark in thine ear: change places, and handy-dandy, which is the justice, which is the thief? ...
>
> > Thou rascal beadle, hold thy bloody hand.
> > Why dost thou lash that whore? Strip thy own back.
> > Thou hotly lusts to use her in that kind
> > For which thou whip'st her. (Folio text IV. 5. 146–59)

It has been suggested[16] that this diatribe lifts off from a passage printed in italic in Florio's English translation of Montaigne's essay III.9, 'De la vanité' [Of Vanitie]:

> *Of the same paper, whereon a judge writ but even now the condemnation against an adulterer, hee will teare a scantlin[g], thereon to write some love-lines to his fellow-judges wife. The same woman from whom you came lately, and with whom you have committed that unlawfull-pleasing sport, will soone after, even in your presence, raile and scolde more bitterly against the same fault in her neighbour, than ever* Portia *or* Lucrece *could. And some condemne men to die for crimes, that themselves esteeme no faults.* (Florio, p. 592)

Despite the mad scrambling, in which the mental state of the speaker diffuses the 'source' text and supplements it with rage, it is entirely reasonable to suppose that Montaigne fragmentarily underlies Lear's meditation on justice. This is the only use of 'handy-dandy' (a game where you hide something in one hand and ask a child to guess which one it is) in Shakespeare. That phrase crops up in the chapter which immediately precedes the putative source, III.8, 'De l'art de conferer' [Of the Arte of Conferring] (which is partly also concerned with the undue respect accorded to foolish kings, which is clearly a question of interest to Lear), and it does so in a sentence which is rare in Florio for being short and punchy as well as showing his general penchant for the tangily vernacular: 'Handy-dandie, what is this?' (Florio, p. 562). The jumbling, the maddening of Montaigne's anecdote, its widening into a general principle about justice, makes the 'source' seem distant because it was not a set of words that Shakespeare quoted but a span of text and body of argument to which he responded and which he then warped to make it suit the voice of a dispossessed monarch.

*   *   *   *   *

We can edge forward from this observation. It may or may not be the case that there was a 'Montaignian moment' in England around 1600, in which a shared body of rhetorical principles and texts, a growing interest in the difficulty of connecting individual experiences with general precepts, and a desire among many readers to read texts which appeared to enact thought and display personal experience all issued in a deep change in the collective mentality. It may or may not be the case that Shakespeare was caught up in such a wider moment. But I shall suggest that several of Shakespeare's plays after about 1600 contain some rather more precise kind of Montaignian moments. What are those moments?

In order to answer that question it helps to ask a prior and even more flat-footed question. How might we expect an essay to influence a play? Montaigne's kind of writing is most likely to help a dramatist at certain kinds of theatrical moment. These might be relatively 'plotless' or motionless moments — occasions which lie beyond the orbit of the traditional search for Shakespeare's 'Narrative and Dramatic Sources' because they are not scenes which represent action, let alone bed-tricks or other narrative devices which can be traced to a particular version of a story. This is illustrated by the echoes of Montaigne's 'Of the Caniballes' in Gonzalo's commonwealth. These occur during a scene of awful stasis. The Neapolitan courtiers are wrecked and arrested in a journey, and so are quite literally 'in transit' without much prospect of ever arriving at their destination. King Alonso has lost his son as a result of having sought a marriage for his daughter on a distant shore rather than nearer to home, and is slumped in misery. It is a scene in which there is nothing to say or do except fill in time. This kind of theatrical moment — where there is no 'narrative' going on because no one can do anything, but where there is a huge weight of affect — is characteristic of a kind of scene in later Shakespeare which could reasonably be called a Montaignian moment. It is a scene which poses the problem of what a dramatist or a set of characters can do when there is no possibility of action. The courtiers are deliberately associated through a series of allusions to Virgil's *Aeneid* with the traditional *amechania* of epic heroes in the aftermath of a shipwreck. That moment of stasis is broadly analogous to many of the scenes in *Hamlet*, that great play of overwhelming affect and deadlock of action, in which critics have repeatedly found echoes of Montaigne. It is also analogous to the scenes in the hovel and on the way to Dover in *King Lear*, in which fragments of Montaigne reverberate between the voices of a mad king, a fool, and someone who is pretending to be mad. When you have strong reason to experience and articulate emotions but where circumstances prevent any action, you have to speak about something, if only to fill in time; and on these theatrical occasions the tricks and turns of the *Essays* — either directly imitated or reconstructed as a style of thinking and writing — are particularly helpful to a dramatist, and especially to one like Shakespeare after 1599, who was attempting to attract fashionable readers of the *Essays* of Francis Bacon (the first selection of which first appeared in 1597) and of William Cornwallis (first printed in 1600) to the Globe Theatre. The discursive, learned, and assimilative form of the *Essays* is at such moments a powerful theatrical resource. It allows for the representation of learned thinking in process and in response to occasion, and it allows also for that kind of talking to be fully and marvellously ineffective — and indeed a bit gratuitous, even foolish.[17]

To this very obvious remark about the theatrical occasions on which it is possible to make use of Montaigne we should add an equally obvious qualification. There is no final distinction between discourse and action on the stage. That is, when someone starts sounding like Montaigne onstage because there just isn't much else to do, other people start responding to what they say in the light of their own preoccupations, and so the abstract discussion tends to become 'action' in the form of interpersonal drama. Gonzalo has read Montaigne and is trying to cheer Alonso up, but he is a bit of a fool. He is so not just in the morally judgemental sense; he is structurally akin to a fool in that he is in this scene taking on the main theatrical function of Shakespeare's fools: he talks to fill in time and cheer up his master, although he does so by philosophical rather than comical discourse. His monologue on an ideal commonwealth is constructed in such a way as to invite sardonic marginal commentary from the other courtiers, and he finally and disastrously prompts Sebastian and Antonio to mention marriage: 'No marrying 'mong his subjects?' This harps on the string which Gonzalo has already insensitively set buzzing by his repeated references to 'the marriage of the King's fair daughter' (II. 1. 74–75) and 'I wore it at your daughter's marriage' (II. 1. 110). It prompts King Alonso finally to tell them to shut up, with 'Prithee, no more. Thou dost talk nothing to me'. He does this because he is grieving over his son, whom he believes has been drowned as the direct result of his having chosen to travel in order to marry off his daughter. For his courtiers to make a Montaignian disquisition on the golden age which recurs to the theme of marriage is, in the circumstances, more than a little tactless. This suggests a more general principle. When Montaigne is transposed into a theatrical setting he suffers a sea change. His currents of abstract philosophizing are directly and awkwardly thrown up against personal circumstances and experiences. Stuck in transit the courtiers may be; but even in that becalmed state the process of filling in time by philosophical banter always becomes interpersonal, and, as we say, 'dramatic'.

Above the level of reactions by particular characters to the abstract ideas which seep into the play from Montaigne's *Essays* there are signs in the action of *The Tempest* that this 'non-dramatic' source, in a play which notoriously lacks a single main 'narrative' source, is generating possibilities for action.[18] Gonzalo's Montaignian moment has consequences at the level of what we now call 'narrative'. There may be a deliberate wryness to the way that an exchange based on Montaigne's 'Of the Caniballes' leads more or less instantly to a section of its aristocratic audience, Gonzalo and Alonso, falling asleep;[19] but there is also a direct comment on Montaigne's utopianism in the way that Sebastian and Antonio immediately after hearing about the golden world of Gonzalo's commonwealth set about attempting to kill their king, even though they have little reason to believe that they will ever return to the kingdom which they are attempting to acquire through usurpation and murder. The 'non-narrative' source, that is, feeds back in complex ways into the action of the play, perversely generating the kind of plot development that would be expected in a more conventional political drama — a plot development which is then itself arrested by the intervention of Ariel. A 'non-narrative' source can therefore have surprisingly deep relationships to the action of a play, and a Montaignian moment can extend beyond a passage of direct allusion and influence what characters do.

★　★　★　★　★

That observation may help us to clarify the nature of Montaigne's role in some of Shakespeare's slightly earlier plays. Critics have periodically argued over the nature and extent of Montaigne's presence in *Measure for Measure*, which was performed at court in 1604. This play contains several Montaignian echoes, and has been persuasively presented as resting on a Montaignian form of scepticism about authority.[20] It also contains some more debatably Montaignian moments. When Claudio is imprisoned he finds himself in a particularly extreme form of narrative stasis. Being in a prison cell awaiting execution radically narrows one's options for participating in a narrative, and from at least Boethius onwards has provided a space and a time for philosophical reflection.[21] The duke, disguised as a friar, tells Claudio to 'Be absolute for death' (III. 1. 5), and delivers a sermonical tissue of commonplaces against the fear of dying. Claudio's response to this advice in his discussion with Isabella is effectively 'yes, but what happens when you put my body in the place of this abstract case?' — or, to put that more poetically, as Shakespeare of course does:

> Ay, but to die, and go we know not where;
> To lie in cold obstruction, and to rot;
> This sensible warm motion to become
> A kneaded clod, and the dilated spirit
> To bath in fiery floods, or to reside
> In thrilling region of thick-ribbèd ice. (III. 1. 118–23)

Hovering behind the whole action of *Measure for Measure* is both a legal argument about how particular cases can be subsumed under the general principles of the law and a corporeal argument about the ways in which the appetites and the senses rage against the principles of reason — themes which lead the play towards what Ian Maclean in his groundbreaking study *Montaigne philosophe* termed 'le champ de la singularité', experiences which appear to resist being subsumed by universal concepts.[22] For Claudio the palpably experienced fear of death will not be silenced by philosophical reflection. Curiously (and perhaps coincidentally, but it is a striking coincidence if that is indeed what it is) those concerns are very close to the argument which Montaigne explores in the very sentence before he discusses the case of the corrupt judge who pens notes to his mistress in 'Of Vanitie', which was italicized in Florio and transformatively echoed in *King Lear*:

> To what purpose are these heaven-looking and nice points of Philosophie, on which no humane being can establish and ground it selfe? And to what end serve these rules, that exceed our use and excell our strength? I often see, that there are certaine Ideaes or formes of life proposed unto us, which neither the proposer nor the Auditors have any hope at all to follow; and which is worse, no desire to attaine. (Florio, p. 592)

Claudio does not simply state this human perspective. When Montaigne's habitual mingling of personal experience and principle is transposed into a theatrical setting his delicate blend of abstract principle and personal example splits into several different elements: one character rages against death from his own particular theatrical situation, while another philosophizes about it from his present role as a friar and confessor. That is to say, the twists and turns between general principle and individual experience which characterize many of the *Essays* tend to become disentangled in a theatrical medium, and the personal instance before our eyes tends to stand much more vehemently as an exception to a rule than it generally does in Montaigne. And this in turn helps to explain why Shakespeare's relationship to Montaigne is hard to identify without question. In this particular case the duke's speech in his persona as a friar sounds like a string of *sententiae* culled from a commonplace book, with the result that scholars have argued that it is impossible to say that this scene is specifically influenced by Montaigne, by the essay 'Que philosopher c'est apprendre à mourir' [That to Philosophise is to Learn how to Die] (I.20; I.19 in Florio) in particular or by any other of Montaigne's many meditations on death.[23] They may be right to do so. But we should also remember that the process of transforming an essay into theatre almost necessarily has the effect of unstitching its component elements — of, as it were, reverse engineering the commonplace book from which Montaigne's *Essays* may have arisen. Different currents in a given essay end up being separated into more or less adversarially related strands spoken by different characters. This process of disassembly puts great pressure on critics' established criteria for detecting influence, and explains why those writing about relationships between Montaigne and the prison scenes in *Measure* have either argued that Shakespeare drew on a digest of commonplaces about death or from some Senecan epigone, or (as Fred Parker has suggested in an extremely perceptive essay) that Shakespeare is here arguing with Montaigne and is resisting his philosophizing with a carnal urgency.[24] Montaignian moments in Shakespeare tend to turn into interpersonal drama, with the result that 'Montaigne' is more often than not dissolved into dialogue and transformed into several different voices. That makes Shakespeare a particularly valuable reader of Montaigne, since there are times when his drama can appear to pick apart the contexture of commonplaces, abstract principles, and personal experiences from which so many of the essays are so delicately woven. It is almost as though Shakespeare can sometimes allow one to see behind the *Essays*, and, as it were, allow his audience to glimpse their genesis.[25]

★　★　★　★　★

I have already suggested that characters in Shakespeare often respond to Montaignian arguments when they connect with their own peculiar perspectives and experiences. Alonso is presumably listening to his courtiers when their conversation turns to marriage, but before that moment an actor could legitimately play him as being lost in his own world of grief while Gonzalo delivers his fantasy on a theme from Montaigne. Asking if Shakespeare listened to Montaigne in the same situated way is obviously about as naïve a critical question as it is possible to ask. Even the very simple claim that William Shakespeare was an historical agent who read books and had different thoughts about those books at different times is, in our strange world, contentious; the notion that his drama can give evidence of those personal experiences is doubly or trebly so. But critics have frequently suggested that there is something prickly and adversarial, as well as something sportively liberating, about the places in which Montaigne turn up in Shakespeare: fake friars, ineffectual courtiers, spikey satirists, mad kings, bastards, bastard-makers, dispossessed princes with problems telling hawks from handsaws, prisoners, and people with nowhere to go: these are the kinds of person and occasions in which able readers of Shakespeare and of Montaigne are most likely to find parallels between the two writers. The notion that an early modern reader might have a distinct interpersonal attitude to a particular writer is often dismissed as merely fantastical or speculative, but it is not at all an anachronistic notion. As Montaigne says in II.10, 'Des livres' [Of Bookes], reading is a matter of descrying the 'private humours' of an author: 'For (as I have saide else-where) I am wonderfull curious, to discover and know, the minde, the soule, the genuine disposition, and naturall judgement of my Authors' (Florio, p. 239). In that essay he gives a number of examples of his own idiosyncratic judgements on the writers he principally admires. William Hamlin has recently drawn our attention to the wide variety of responses to Florio's translation of Montaigne among early modern readers, which range from shocked orthodoxy to quirky idiosyncrasy.[26]

There can be no certainty about how or when Shakespeare read Montaigne. But there are a few things about which we can be reasonably certain even in this world of doubt. We know that Shakespeare was called William. It is reasonable to suppose that he liked a joke and was interested in names.[27] We also know that in 1596 he or his father applied to be granted a coat of arms. Those modest facts can be used to imagine, at least, a situated and resistant reading of Montaigne's essay I.46, 'Des noms' [Of Names], an essay in which there is a lot to catch Shakespeare's eye — not least his own name, since 'Will' and 'William' recur repeatedly in this essay as the type of a common name, and are printed in italic type, as was usual in this period. As Hamlin has shown, readers of Florio's Montaigne were particularly prone to notice passages that were italicized, and we have already encountered an example which suggests the same may have been true for Shakespeare.[28] And by 1603 at least one capitalized rather than italicized noun in this essay might have caught the eye of the author of a play called *Hamlet*:[29] 'It is an ill custome, and of exceeding bad consequence in our countrie of *France*, to call every man by the name of his Towne, Mannor, Hamlet, or Lordship' (Florio, p. 150), declares the author who calls himself Michel de Montaigne. The socially mobile William Shakespeare, whose acquisition of coat of arms in 1596 was to become a point of dispute among heralds and possibly also the object of mockery by Ben Jonson,[30] might have grimaced as Montaigne, apparently so sure and settled in his estate and status, went on to deplore 'Some silly-upstart purchaser of Armes' who might adopt Montaigne's heraldic insignia as his own.[31] Whether or not this piece of social needling piqued the attention of a glover's son turned gentleman-playwright, the passage that follows seems to have done so:

> Who letteth [prevents] my horse boy to call himselfe *Pompey* the Great? But after all, what meanes, what devises, are there that annex unto my horse keeper deceased, or to that other who had his head cut-off in *Aegypt*, or that joyne unto them this glorified, and far-renowmed word, and these pen dashes, so much honored, that they may thereby advantage themselves? (Florio, p. 151)

The supposedly 'sourceless' subplot of *Measure for Measure* (which Charlotte Lennox in her introduction to the play's principal 'narrative' source, Cinthio's tale of Juriste and Epitia, dismissed as 'all Episode' which 'has no Dependance on the principal subject')[32] includes a tapster/bawd-turned-executioner called Pompey. Shakespeare had also played games with the pompous name of Pompey in *Love's Labour's Lost*.[33] But Pompey in *Measure for Measure* is not simply named Pompey (surname Bum). Characters do *not* cry out to him from his first appearance 'How now, brave Pompey?' His name emerges only when he is asked to reveal it by Escalus, in Act II scene 1. Before and after that moment his name in the Folio speech-headings appears as various abbreviations of 'Clown'. Pompey is once addressed by Mistress Overdone as 'Thomas Tapster' (I. 2. 104). Then he is called 'Hannibal', the editors say in error for 'cannibal', by Elbow (II. 1. 167), although it is possible that Elbow, who is confused about more or less everything, has confused his classical warriors. The moment when Escalus asks the name of the character previously just thought of as generic 'Clown' or as Thomas Tapster is therefore theatrically significant. It is as though the act of questioning by an authority within the play prompted Shakespeare to give the character a name. And he used exactly the name which Montaigne presented as an example of the most inappropriate possible name for a lower-class character: Pompey. Once Pompey's name is out there it becomes a running joke. Even the sober Escalus just can't stop using it:

> I advise you, let me not find you before me again upon any complaint whatsoever; no, not for dwelling where you do. If I do, Pompey, I shall beat you to your tent, and prove a shrewd Caesar to you; in plain dealing, Pompey, I shall have you whipped. So, for this time, Pompey, fare you well. (II. 1. 235–40)

When Pompey is next arrested Lucio also cruelly reiterates the name: 'How now, noble Pompey? What, at the wheels of Caesar? Art thou led in triumph? (III. 1. 311–12). The incongruous name of Pompey is then, like most of Shakespeare's jokes, folded into the argument of the play. When Pompey is imprisoned he is then drafted as the executioner's assistant (IV. 2). This means that the person who gets employed to chop off other people's heads is named after the most famous Roman general to have had his own head chopped off. But more than this is going on. Pompey becomes part of the play's larger concern with the delegation of authority to people who might be no better than the law-breakers they punish. And in developing him in this way Shakespeare is very likely to have recalled a passage from Montaigne's favourite author Plutarch, in his syncrisis of Pompey the Great with Agesilaus: 'Neither can any man matche Pompeis with the like: who, to shew his frends what power he was of, did break the lawes which him selfe had made.'[34] From this tissue of Montaignian reading, Pompey grows into a tiny replica of Angelo, one of those justices who think the abstract principles of the law do not apply to their own circumstances — handy-dandy, which is the justice and which is the thief?

And then, as though to mark his genealogy in the essay 'Of Names', Pompey goes on to become one of the most active name-givers in Shakespeare. In his new role as executioner he produces a list of names which suddenly fills the jail of Vienna with people (in the words of the late Anne Barton) 'like a drop of pond water upon which a microscope has just been focused'.[35] He creates a whole world of bit-parts, who have the instantly characterizing kinds of name which were typical of early Jacobean city comedies: they include Master Rash, Master Caper, Master Three-pile, young Dizie, Master Deep-vow and Master Copperspur and Master Starve-Lackey and Drop-heir and Master Forthright and Shoe-tie and Half-can (IV. 3. 1–17). Montaigne's essay 'Of Names' turns Pompey almost into the creator of a little commonwealth; and it also suggests that Shakespeare's reading of this particular essay, which principally argues that names are arbitrary pen-marks, was reactive and resistant reading. The names Pompey recites necessarily suggest an intrinsic link with the moral or physical characteristics of those who bear them, since the names are all we ever know of any of these people. Shakespeare's reading of Montaigne can provoke banter among courtiers, byplay among fools and madmen in *King Lear*. It also generated the prison population of Vienna in *Measure for Measure* and a rich set of connections between the subplots and the main plot of that play.

★   ★   ★   ★   ★

Montaigne in 'Of Bookes' (II.10, 'Des livres') took contemporary dramatists to task for their slavish dependency on plots from Terence and Plautus:

> It hath often come unto my minde, how such as in our daies give themselves to composing of comedies (as the Italians who are very happie in them) employ three or four arguments of *Terence* and *Plautus* to make up one of theirs. In one onely comedie they will huddle up five or six of *Bocaces* tales. That which makes them so to charge themselves with matter, is the distrust they have of their owne sufficiency, and that they are not able to undergoe so heavie a burthen with their owne strength. They are forced to finde a body on which they may rely and leane themselves: and wanting matter of their owne wherewith to please us, they will have the storie or tale to busie and ammuse us: whereas in my Author it is cleane contrary. (Florio, pp. 237–38)

What Shakespeare, the author of *The Comedy of Errors*, which welds together a scenario from Plautus's *Menaechmi* with elements from the *Amphitruo*, and a plunderer of plots from Boccaccio through William Painter and other intermediaries, would have made of this remark we can only imagine. But it is a salutary reminder that over-dependence on narrative devices from earlier plays was something to which educated readers in this period could object. Montaigne's observations, when combined with the examples explored in this essay, help us to reassess the question of what a 'source' was for Shakespeare. The works which Lennox institutionalized as Shakespeare's 'sources' and which came to be called Shakespeare's 'narrative sources' — *novelle*, plays, and historical works which provided the outlines of stories — represent only one element in the overall genesis of a play. What I have termed reactive reading of discursive texts was another major element. Because of the range of reactions which a discursive text might prompt — disagreement, the recognition of an underlying logical structure, chance overlaps with personal concerns, the provision of commonplaces or *sententiae*, or a provocation to thinking — the discursive texts to which an early modern playwright reacted and the nature of the reaction to them require care, tact, and a degree of courage to reconstruct. It is not an exercise in empirical discovery so much as an act of critical exploration. The cumulative effect of a narrative about such a connection between two writers, however, might be to create a persuasive case: repeated arguments about a similar theme, perhaps coupled with connections which might be as slight as a single word, combined with a plausible account of how one author situated in a particular way might be expected to react to the words of another author presented to him in a particular way, might make it reasonable to believe that (for example) Shakespeare did not simply read Montaigne from at least 1603, but reacted to him as Montaigne reacted to his own reading: with the kind of resistant eclecticism that comes of treating a book as akin to a person with whom you might argue. Shakespeare, indeed, seems to have 'conferred' with Montaigne rather than simply reading him:

> The studie and plodding on bookes, is a languishing & weake kinde of motion, and which heateth or earnesteth nothing; whereas conference doth both learne, teach and exercise at once. If I conferre with a stubborne wit, and encounter a sturdy wrestler, he toucheth me to the quick, hits me on the flanks, and pricks me both on the left and right side: his imaginations vanquish & confound mine. (Florio, p. 553)

The other, wider implication of this essay is perhaps even more tendentious. As far as we can tell from the surviving records, one of the major things that Shakespeare and his contemporaries did to drama at the end of the sixteenth and at the start of the seventeenth century was to slow it down, and sickly it o'er with a pale cast of thought. The drama of the most successful theatrical company of the 1580s, the Queen's Men, has been aptly described as 'literal' in style, and relied on visual elements and stage business as much or more than it did on verse.[36] Surviving play-texts from the Queen's Men tend to contain relatively little deliberative rhetoric, argumentation, or overt reflection. Where Shakespeare is known to have worked on plots which were also the subject of plays put on by the Queen's Men he consistently increased the level of deliberative rhetoric and foregrounded the abstract implications of the action. In these cases he might be said to have Montaignianized his 'narrative' sources.

So if *King Lear* is placed beside its principal 'dramatic source', the anonymous Queen's Men play *The True Chronicle History of King Leir*, two points instantly stand out. The Shakespearean play brings to the story of King Lear the abrasive tones of Senecan drama and many reflections drawn from Senecan philosophy,[37] it doubles up its meditations on the relationship between children and parents by adding the Gloucester subplot, and it brings in a rich layer of sometimes abstract, sometimes carnal and confused, meditations on justice. The relationship between *Measure for Measure* and its principal 'source' play *Promos and Cassandra* is more complex, because George Whetstone's drama was never performed, and, given Whetstone's circle of associates, was in all likelihood written with an audience of lawyers in mind, and because the surviving text of *Measure* is generally agreed to contain elements by Thomas Middleton. Nonetheless the thematic interweaving of the main plot and the incidents of the subplot in *Measure for Measure* — making Pompey shadow Angelo, and making the whole play explore how angelic the person who carries the name of Angelo might be — is one of the features that distinguishes Shakespeare's play from its source, and from the *novella* by Cinthio from which it ultimately derived. Creating a play which appeared to be as much an interconnected argument as a narrative (and we should remember that for those versed in the classical rhetorical tradition a *narratio* was one element in the process of proving a case) was one of the things that Shakespeare aimed to do, and that aim became more pronounced in the plays written after the establishment of the Globe Theatre on the South Bank of the Thames in 1599. Generating for plays written in this period what I have termed 'Montaignian moments' — which punctuate the action with scenes in which characters reflect, joke, philosophize, explore the awkward misrelation between general principle and personal experience, and open out alternative perspectives on the main action — was one of the ways in which Shakespeare broadened the range of his drama and differentiated it from that of the immediately preceding generation. Montaigne was by no means the sole driver of this process; but Montaigne and the wide range of deliberative authors on whom he drew, from Plutarch to Seneca and Cicero, comprised a core of texts from which Shakespeare also drew, with which he argued, and with which he played (catlike), or order to fashion drama that both provoked and represented thinking in his own Montaignian moments.

Notes to Chapter 14

1. *The Tempest*, II. I. 149–76. Cf. Montaigne, I.31, numbered I.30 in Florio. References are to William Shakespeare, *The Complete Works*, ed. Stanley Wells and Gary Taylor (Oxford: Clarendon Press, 1986). References to Montaigne are to Michel de Montaigne, *The Essays or Morall, Politike and Millitarie Discourses*. trans. John Florio (London: Valentine Sims for Edward Blount, 1603). I have retained Florio's italics (see note 28), but modernized i/j and u/v.
2. Robert Ellrodt, 'Self-Consciousness in Montaigne and Shakespeare', *Shakespeare Survey*, 28 (1975), 37–50.
3. Hugh Grady (*Shakespeare, Machiavelli, and Montaigne: Power and Subjectivity from Richard II to Hamlet* (Oxford: Oxford University Press, 2002), p. 24) argues for 'an alternative "Montaignian" theory of early modern subjectivity, one based much more on themes of Adorno, Horkheimer, Lacan, and others to be identified below as the discussion develops, rather than the "Machiavellian" French poststructuralism that has set the agenda for much previous cultural materialism'.
4. Work on this began with George Coffin Taylor, *Shakspere's Debt to Montaigne* (Cambridge, MA: Harvard University Press, 1925), and some highlights are in William Shakespeare, *King Lear*, ed. Kenneth Muir (London: Methuen, 1972), pp. 235–39.
5. Peter Mack, 'Montaigne and Shakespeare: Source, Parallel or Comparison?', *Montaigne Studies*, 23 (2011), 151–80, argues that Montaigne should be read in comparison with Shakespeare rather than as a source, and Mack's *Reading and Rhetoric in Montaigne and Shakespeare* (London: Bloomsbury Academic, 2010) offers such comparative readings.
6. Warren Boutcher, 'Marginal Commentaries: The Cultural Transmission of Montaigne's *Essais* in Shakespeare's England', in *Shakespeare et Montaigne: vers un nouvel humanisme*, ed. Pierre Kapitaniak and Jean Marie Maguin (Paris: Société francaise Shakespeare, 2003), pp. 13–29 (p. 21).

7. The echo of 'Of Crueltie' was noted by Eleanor Prosser in 'Shakespeare, Montaigne, and "the Rarer Action"', *Shakespeare Studies*, 1 (1965), 261–64, and even accepted by the conservatively inclined Kenneth Muir in *The Sources of Shakespeare's Plays* (New Haven, CT: Yale University Press, 1978), p. 281. Further connections between this essay and Jacques in *As You Like It* have been proposed: see William Shakespeare, *As You Like It*, ed. Richard Knowles and Evelyn Mattern (New York: Modern Language Association of America, 1977), p. 74, and Lars Engle, 'Shame and Reflection in Montaigne and Shakespeare', *Shakespeare Survey*, 63 (2010), 249–61 (p. 255). Jacques talks of age '[s]ans teeth, sans eyes, sans taste, sans every thing' (II. 7. 166), while Florio describes 'the soules of the gods, sanse tongues, sanse eyes and sanse eares, have each one in themselves a feeling of that which the other feele' (p. 396), noted in *As You Like It*, ed. Knowles, p. 137.

8. The case was made by in an essay reprinted in Leo Salingar, *Dramatic Form in Shakespeare and the Jacobeans: Essays* (Cambridge: Cambridge University Press, 1986), 'King Lear, Montaigne and Harsnett', pp. 107–39. For its development, see for example Mack, *Reading and Rhetoric*, pp. 158–61.

9. Richard Scholar, 'French Connections: The *Je-Ne-Sais-Quoi* in Montaigne and Shakespeare', in *How to Do Things with Shakespeare: New Approaches, New Essays*, ed. Laurie E. Maguire (Oxford: Blackwell, 2008), pp. 11–33, and Terence Cave, 'When Shakespeare Met Montaigne', in *Thinking with Shakespeare: Comparative and Interdisciplinary Essays*, ed. Richard Scholar and William Poole (Oxford: Legenda, 2007), pp. 115–19. Both address this question, which underlies the series of penetrating articles by Lars Engle cited in the following note.

10. Lars Engle, 'Sovereign Cruelty in Montaigne and *King Lear*', in *Shakespearean International Yearbook 6*, ed. Graham Bradshaw, Thomas Bishop, and Peter Holbrook (Aldershot: Ashgate, 2006), pp. 119–39 (p. 119). See also Engle's 'Shame and Reflection', and his '*Measure for Measure* and Modernity: The Problem of the Sceptic's Authority', in *Shakespeare and Modernity: Early Modern to Millennium*, ed. Hugh Grady (London: Routledge, 2000), pp. 85–104.

11. Geoffrey Bullough, *Narrative and Dramatic Sources of Shakespeare* (London: Routledge & Kegan Paul, 1957–75). A team headed by Terence Hawkes is presently re-editing these volumes. I have argued in 'Shakespeare's Authorities', in *Shakespeare and Authority*, ed. Angus Vine and Katie Halsie (forthcoming, Palgrave) that the title and contents of these volumes needs radical rethinking.

12. On Lennox's achievement, see Margaret Anne Doody, 'Shakespeare's Novels: Charlotte Lennox Illustrated', *Studies in the Novel*, 19 (1987), 296–310; on her influence on Samuel Johnson and the sophisticated conception of probability which she brought to the project, see Jonathan Brody Krammick, 'Reading Shakespeare's Novels: Literary History and Cultural Poetics in the Lennox–Johnson Debate', *Modern Language Quarterly*, 55 (1994), 429–53. For a clear and balanced account, see Ann Thompson and Sasha Roberts, 'Charlotte Lennox (née Ramsey) 1729?–1804', in *Women Reading Shakespeare, 1660–1900: An Anthology of Criticism* (Manchester: Manchester University Press, 1997), pp. 15–21.

13. 'She unwisely tried to show that Shakespeare spoiled many of his stories by complicating the intrigue and introducing absurdities'; Bullough, *Narrative and Dramatic Sources*, vol. 1, p. ix.

14. Bullough, *Narrative and Dramatic Sources*, vol. 8, pp. 314–15.

15. Peter Mack, 'Marston and Webster's Use of Florio's Montaigne', *Montaigne Studies*, 24 (2012), 67–82.

16. Salingar, *Dramatic Form*, p. 130.

17. On the general association of philosophy with folly in Shakespeare, see Jonathan Bate, 'Shakespeare's Foolosophy', in *Shakespeare Performed: Essays in Honor of R. A. Foakes*, ed. Grace Ioppolo (Newark: University of Delaware Press, 2000), pp. 17–32. Mack (*Reading and Rhetoric*, p. 171) suggests that 'Montaigne is here being joked with'.

18. 'No source has been discovered for the main plot of *The Tempest*'; Muir, *Sources*, p. 278.

19. Compare the marginal note recorded in William M. Hamlin, *Montaigne's English Journey: Reading the Essays in Shakespeare's Day* (Oxford: Oxford University Press, 2013), p. 1: 'Montaign hath the Art above all men to keep his Reader from sleeping'.

20. See the list of verbal parallels indexed in William Shakespeare, *Measure for Measure*, ed. Mark Eccles (New York: Modern Language Association of America, 1980), p. 543; for persuasive

exploration of links with Montaigne's treatment of the law, see Engle, 'Measure for Measure and Modernity'.

21. See Rivkah Zim, *The Consolations of Writing: Literary Strategies of Resistance from Boethius to Primo Levi* (Princeton, NJ: Princeton University Press, 2014), pp. 21–47.

22. Ian Maclean, *Montaigne philosophe* (Paris: Presses universitaires de France, 1996), pp. 53–58.

23. Alice Harmon, 'How Great Was Shakespeare's Debt to Montaigne?', *PMLA*, 57 (1942), 988–1008 (p. 1000). She argues against John M. Robertson, *Montaigne and Shakespeare: And Other Essays on Cognate Questions* (London: A. and C. Black, 1909), pp. 86–88.

24. Fred Parker, 'Shakespeare's Argument with Montaigne', *Cambridge Quarterly*, 28 (1999), 1–18, especially p. 13. Compare Engle, 'Shame and Reflection', p. 261: 'Shakespeare's response to Montaigne needs to be recognized as ambivalent rather than assumed to be celebratory and directly appropriative.'

25. Writers of essays in the period occasionally drew on 'Montaignian moments' from Shakespeare's plays: William Drummond, *A Midnight's Trance*, ed. Robert Ellrodt (Oxford: Luttrell Society, 1951), pp. 11–12 quotes Hamlet Q2 (although Drummond subsequently cut those borrowings), as well as drawing elsewhere in *A Midnight's Trance* on Montaigne. See Dermott Cavanagh, 'William Drummond of Hawthornden as Reader of Renaissance Drama', *Review of English Studies*, 66 (2015), 676–97.

26. Hamlin, *Montaigne's English Journey*, pp. 1–34.

27. I forbear footnoting the first of these claims, but in support of the second see in particular Laurie E. Maguire, *Shakespeare's Names* (Oxford: Oxford University Press, 2007) and Anne Barton, *The Names of Comedy* (Oxford: Clarendon Press, 1990).

28. Hamlin, *Montaigne's English Journey*, pp. 143–44.

29. Engle ('Shame and Reflection', p. 257) suggests that the name of Touchstone derives from a similar typographical quirk in Florio, p. 507.

30. Samuel Schoenbaum, *William Shakespeare: A Documentary Life* (Oxford: Clarendon Press, 1975), pp. 166–73.

31. Montaigne's aristocratic self-presentation was of course less secure than might appear to a reader of Florio's translation: see most recently Philippe Desan's biography, *Montaigne: une biographie politique* (Paris: Odile Jacob, 2014).

32. Charlotte Lennox, *Shakespear Illustrated* (London: A. Millar, 1753–54), vol. 1, p. 27.

33. v. 2. 542–57, also with a Clown playing Pompey.

34. *Plutarch's Lives of the Noble Grecians and Romans*, ed. George Wyndham (London: D. Nutt, 1895), vol. 4, p. 294. Montaigne refers to this syncrisis in his defence of Seneca and Plutarch, II.32, 'Defense de Seneque et de Plutarque' (Florio, p. 416).

35. Barton, *The Names of Comedy*, p. 35. On p. 107 she cites Montaigne on his horse boy, and goes on: 'But then there is nothing either — as the Shakespeare who christened Mistress Overdone's servant "Pompey Bum" would readily have agreed — to stop the bearer of such an incongruous title, or his associates from constantly holding the name up against the person, in ways crucial to an understanding both of how that person views himself and how he is perceived by others.'

36. Scott McMillin and Sally-Beth MacLean, *The Queen's Men and their Plays* (Cambridge: Cambridge University Press, 1998), pp. 128–32.

37. See Colin Burrow, *Shakespeare and Classical Antiquity* (Oxford: Oxford University Press, 2013), pp. 195–201, and Kathy Eden, 'Liquid Fortification and the Law in *King Lear*', in *Shakespeare and the Law: A Conversation among Disciplines*, ed. Martha Craven Nussbaum, Bradin Cormack, and Richard Strier (Chicago, IL: University of Chicago Press, 2013), pp. 203–21.

AFTERWORD

Ian Maclean

This is not just an afterword to the contributions to this volume; nor even to the stimulating workshop which took place in Oxford in September 2014, at which the first versions of these papers were discussed; nor even to the conference on transforming the early modern republic of letters held in the spring of that year, at which many of the contributors to this volume were present; nor even to the long series of informal encounters in various places in Oxford, including the Maison Française, the Old Library in St Edmund Hall, and the hospitable rooms of Richard Scholar in Oriel, at which (so far) the early chapters of the *Essais* have been discursively explored over sandwiches by a fluid group of Montaigne scholars of various ages. My Afterword's origins go back to an earlier time in Oxford of which the *Essays in Memory of Richard Sayce* which I edited with Ian McFarlane in 1982 are a material record, and which has been evoked in the generous final paragraph of Terence Cave's essay in this volume. Even before that, I was fortunate enough to have Richard Sayce as my supervisor in the late 1960s. His *The Essays of Montaigne: A Critical Exploration* (London: Weidenfeld & Nicolson, 1972) remains a very important contribution to my own understanding of Montaigne, and his meticulous work on early editions of the *Essais*, completed after his death by David Maskell, is a groundbreaking study in material bibliography from which I and many other contributors to the volume have benefited. For all my time at Oxford, the University has been fortunate in having a nucleus of committed Montaignistes, in the midst of whom the three editors of this volume (to whom heartfelt thanks are due) play prominent roles. The number of those attending has recently been swollen by distinguished scholars from the Faculty of English, who have, as the contributions of Colin Burrow and Kathryn Murphy show here, their own particular take on Montaigne studies. As well as appreciating the French, they view the text through the interpretative lens (or prism) of Montaigne's English translator John Florio, who sees the *Essais* from what Montaigne himself might have called a 'veuë oblique'. In this volume, his inventive approach is investigated also by Warren Boutcher and by Valerie Worth-Stylianou.

Those informal lunchtime gatherings of Montaignistes in Oxford over recent years have been joined by Montaigne scholars from London, Cambridge, Warwick, and even Durham. They have mulled over the chapters in sequence in a deliberately unstructured way, which always involves very close reading of cruces in the text through terminological, syntactic, and rhetorical analysis, with the aim of releasing its manifold energies. During these very enjoyable occasions, the particular bugbears (an appropriate term here, given Valerie Worth-Stylianou's contribution) of the various participants become apparent. My own arises from Montaigne's asseverations about his scholarly and linguistic competence. He claims not to have any specialist or higher-level knowledge, and confesses to only the most superficial acquaintance with the various fields of knowledge of his day:

> [J]e voy, mieux que tout autre, que ce ne sont icy que resveries d'homme qui n'a gousté des sciences que la crouste premiere, en son enfance, et n'en a retenu qu'un general et informe visage: un peu de chaque chose, et rien du tout, à la Françoise. Car, en somme, je sçay qu'il y a une Medecine, une Jurisprudence, quatre parties en la Mathematique, et grossierement ce à quoy elles visent. Et à l'adventure encore sçay-je la pretention des sciences en general au service de nostre vie. Mais, d'y enfoncer plus avant, de m'estre rongé les ongles à l'estude d'Aristote, monarque de la doctrine moderne, ou opiniatré apres quelque science, je ne l'ay jamais faict; ny n'est art dequoy je sceusse peindre seulement les premiers lineamens [...]. Je n'ay dressé commerce avec aucun livre solide, sinon Plutarque et Seneque[.] (V, p. 146)[1]

> [I myself see better than anyone else that these are nothing but reveries of a man who has tasted only the outer crust of sciences in his childhood, and has retained only a vague general picture of them: a little of everything and nothing thoroughly, French style. For to sum up, I know that there is such a thing as medicine, jurisprudence, four parts in mathematics, and roughly what they aim at. And perhaps I also know the service that the sciences in general aim to contribute to our life. But as for plunging in deeper, or gnawing my nails over the study of Aristotle, monarch of modern learning, or stubbornly pursuing some part of knowledge, I have never done it; nor is there an art of which I could sketch even the outlines [...]. I have not had regular dealings with any solid book, except Plutarch and Seneca[.]] (F, p. 129)

I have permitted myself to doubt this claim in various pieces that I have written, where I set about showing how both the context of Aristotelian philosophy and the study of civil law jurisprudence (as opposed to the experience of the courts as a magistrate) might shed light on Montaigne's philosophical enterprise. Knowledge of the former could have been acquired through the ubiquitous arts course to which Montaigne might have been exposed during or after his humanist education at the Collège de Guyenne. The scholastic approach to knowledge could also have been picked up from secondary texts, such as Cornelius Agrippa von Nettesheim's *De vanitate omnium scientiarum et artium*, which, at one point in the 'Apologie de Raymond Sebond' (II.12, V, pp. 540–41), Montaigne quotes verbatim and at length, and whose savage satire of the pretentions of human reason the essayist is happy to reproduce. As for civil law, Montaigne might have encountered it in Toulouse at the time when he was there to hear the local jurist Jean de Coras talk about the famous case of Martin Guerre (V, p. 1030). Montaigne's allusion to that visit gave rise to a 'myth' of university study, according to Roger Trinquet;[2] but recently, Ingrid De Smet's and Alain Legros's publicization of a manuscript owned by Montaigne comprising a student's transcription of François Baudouin's Paris lectures on Roman law of 1561 has added credence to our author's technical interest in jurisprudence,[3] as do a significant number of verbal echoes in the *Essais*, culminating in the incisive and sustained critique of legal interpretation at the beginning of the ultimate chapter of the *Essais* (V, pp. 1066–73). Such an interest would make Montaigne aware of the linguistic procedures and terms of art of Roman law, which did not form part of the school curriculum of classical texts to which he makes frequent allusion.

It is also well known that Montaigne claims about Latin that '[il] m'est comme naturel, je l'entens mieux que le François' [it is like a native tongue to me; I understand it better than French] (V, p. 810; F, p. 746), that he attempted to write Latin poetry (with poor results, if we are to believe what he himself says about it: V, p. 635), and that if he had assessed his enterprise more highly, he would have composed the text in that language: 'Si ç'eust esté une matiere de durée, il l'eust fallu commettre à un langage plus ferme' [If it had been durable matter, it would have had to be committed to a more stable language] (V, p. 982; F, p. 913). This led me to wonder whether his vocabulary and use of language might not have been influenced by his strong grasp of Latin, which he derived even before the Collège de Guyenne from the German tutor whom his father employed to instil that language in him (V, p. 173). My dogged pursuit of echoes in the French text from Latin terms and phrases became an occasion for some good-humoured persiflage in the informal lunchtime sessions, whose *sanior pars* rightly identified the principal linguistic thrust of the *Essais* to be French, not Latin, even if Montaigne's exquisite sensitivity to that ancient language contributed much to the text through quotation, and enabled him to engage in several sophisticated acts of stylistic analysis.

The contributions of Emma Herdman and Valerie Worth-Stylianou in this volume are formal examinations of Montaigne's bilingual practices as a humanist and the transits between authors and readers that they enable and enact. As well as this, there is another aspect of Montaigne's bilingualism which has, as a general problem, exercised me throughout my engagement with intellectual history. It is addressed by Lucien Febvre in the second chapter of his *Problème de l'incroyance au seizième siècle: la religion de Rabelais* (Paris: Albin Michel, 1942). He asks himself how Frenchmen of that century could think clearly, articulately, and analytically without any of the terms that are only attested later in the history of the language, such as 'absolu', 'relatif', 'virtuel', 'insoluble', 'intentionnel', 'intrinsèque', 'inhérent', 'occulte', 'primitif'. His associated notion of 'outillage mental' (to which Rowan Tomlinson makes reference in her essay) places conceptual limits on thinkers of the past. My own sense of Renaissance authors such as Girolamo Cardano and Montaigne is that they did not encounter insurmountable barriers when seeking to find ways of exceeding the perceived limits of a given language, but found ways to pass into the 'pays au-delà' (V, p. 146).[4] Montaigne himself refers to such cognitive moments, but he also confesses that the resources of French might be felt to be inadequate for the complete articulation of one's thoughts, and in need of support from ancient, more stable, languages (V, p. 874). As a consummate Latinist, he had access to terms, oppositions, and concepts missing in French, and that fact emboldened me in my search for semantic echoes from Latin. A perceived restriction on the linguistic expressiveness of French gives rise to another feature of his writing, which Richard Sayce highlighted: namely, his predilection for word pairs which reinforce the sense that he himself aspires to express.[5] These have various effects, among them disambiguation, rhetorical emphasis, and amplification, and the enrichment of an epithet by a change of register, and can help identify possible sources or parallels of the usage in question.

It seems to me appropriate here to evoke one of our lunchtime discussions to illustrate these features of the text. In I.11 'Des prognostications' [On Prognostications], we encountered the following passage:

> Le demon de Socrates estoit à l'advanture certaine impulsion de volonté, qui se présentoit à luy, sans attendre le conseil de son discours. En une ame bien espurée, comme la sienne, et preparée par continuel exercice de sagesse et de vertu, il est vray semblable que ces inclinations, quoy que temeraires et indigestes, estoyent tousjours importantes et dignes d'estre suyvies. Chacun sent en soy quelque image de telles agitations d'une opinion prompte, véhemente et fortuite. C'est à moy de leur donner quelque authorité, qui en donne si peu à nostre prudence. Et en ay eu de pareillement foibles en raison et violentes en persuasion: ou en dissuasion, qui estoient plus ordinaires en Socrates, ausquelles je me laissay emporter si utilement et heureusement qu'elles pourroyent estre jugées tenir quelque chose d'inspiration divine. (V, p. 44)

> [The daemon of Socrates was perhaps a certain impulse of the will that came to him without awaiting the advice of his reason. In a well-purified soul such as his, prepared by a continual exercise of wisdom and virtue, it is likely that these inclinations, although *temeraire* [weak] and undigested, were always important and worth following. Everyone feels within himself some likeness of such stirrings of a prompt, vehement, and accidental opinion. It is my business to give them some authority, since I give so little to our wisdom. And I have had some as weak in reason as violent in persuasiveness — or dissuasiveness, as was more ordinary in Socrates — by which I let myself be carried away so usefully and fortunately that they might be judged to have in them something of divine inspiration.] (F, p. 35; adapted)

I was struck by the occurrence in successive sentences of the words 'temeraire', 'véhemente', and 'violente'. In a Roman law context, 'praesumptio temeraria' ('weak' as opposed to other, stronger, forms of presumption: 'probabilis', 'violanta', and 'necessaria') is a term of art, as is 'vehemens', which is associated with evidence ('indicia') and its effect on the mind of the judge.[6] The former collocation occurs in a passage from I.27, 'C'est folie de rapporter le vray et le faux à nostre suffisance' [It Is Folly to Measure the True and False by our Own Capacity]:

> Combien y a il de choses peu vray-semblables, tesmoignées par gens dignes de foy, desquelles si nous ne pouvons estre persuadez, au moins les faut-il laisser en suspens: car de les condamner impossibles, c'est se faire fort, par une temeraire presumption, de sçavoir jusques où va la possibilité. Si l'on entendoit bien la difference qu'il y a entre l'impossible et l'inusité, et entre ce qui est contre l'ordre du cours de nature, et contre la commune opinion des hommes, en ne croyant pas temerairement, ny aussi ne descroyant pas facilement, on observeroit la regle de: Rien trop, commandée par Chilon. (V, p. 180)

> [How many things of slight probability are there, testified to by trustworthy people, which, if we cannot be convinced of them, we should at least leave in suspense! For to condemn them as impossible is to pretend, with *temeraire* [weak] presumption, to know the limits of possibility. If people rightly understood the difference between the impossible and the unusual, and between what is

contrary to the orderly course of nature and what is contrary to the common opinion of men, neither believing *temerairement* [rashly] nor disbelieving easily, they would observe the rule of 'nothing too much', enjoined by Chilo.] (F, p. 162; adapted)

The sentiment expressed here is very close to the view expressed by Pietro Pomponazzi about miracles: 'non sunt autem miracula quia sint totaliter contra naturam et praeter ordinem corporum coelestium, sed pro tanto dicuntur miracula, quia insueta et rarissime facta et non secundum communem naturae cursum sed in longissimis periodis' [miracles are not miracles because they are totally against nature and against the determination of celestial bodies, but they are called miracles to the extent that they are unusual, happening very rarely and not in the common course of nature, unless this is seen over very long periods of time].[7] But it would be going too far to claim this as an unacknowledged source for Montaigne, although he did call himself a 'naturaliste' (V, p. 1056), an epithet used to describe Pomponazzi and his application of the Albertine maxim 'de naturalibus naturaliter'.[8] Montaigne is very insistent that anyone can have a thought arising from his own mental processes and without a necessary precedent (V, pp. 152, 1056); there has to be compelling evidence that the essayist is borrowing something from another thinker to identify him as a direct unacknowledged source, as in the case with the verbatim passage from Agrippa's *De vanitate*. An example of the difficulty of attribution is Montaigne's evocation of the phrase 'suum cuique tribuere' (D I.I.I: part of the tripartite definition of justice): 'la justice qui distribue à chacun ce qui luy appartient' [justice that distributes to everyone what is his due] (V, p. 499; F, p. 346). In Cicero's *De natura deorum* (III. 38), we find the phrase 'iustitia quae suum cuique distribuit'. This is closer to Montaigne's text than Justinian's Digest, but I don't think that even that greater degree of proximity of is sufficient to classify Cicero's phrase as a direct source.

Usage of the word group 'temeritas', 'temerarius', and 'temere' is not rare in the Corpus Juris Civilis, having connotations of moral rashness and weakness (of proof);[9] but on reflection, having looked into the broader context thanks to the open access electronic text and search engine of the Montaigne Project of the University of Chicago, I am no longer convinced that the legal context is established by these words occurring in close proximity. Cicero's employment, for example, of 'temeritas' associates it with chance, rashness, and unreflectiveness, and opposes it as a vice to the virtue of prudence (as does Augustine, and later Aquinas).[10] If we look from these contexts to Montaigne, who is quite fond of the word group (it occurs 65 times), we find that even if my intuition of a discipline-specific usage is not borne out, his awareness of the Latin usage may well be. The essayist's pairings of 'temeraire' and 'temerité' are not only with words indicating imprudence (V, pp. 1030, 1035), presumption (V, pp. 320–21), obstinacy (which is equivalent to heresy in some contexts: V, pp. 68, 592, 938), over-confidence in one's mental powers, precipitateness or rashness, disorderly or irrational thought (V, pp. 181, 560, 715, 741),[11] but also, quite frequently, chance, as in V, p. 44 cited above ('d'une opinion prompte, véhemente et fortuite'), in the phrase 'le changement temeraire et fortuite de nos opinions' [the heedless and accidental change in our opinions] (V, p. 441; F,

p. 390; also V, pp. 460, 471) and the collocation of 'temerité' and 'fortune' at V, pp. 62 and 580. That Montaigne should have retained this association is not surprising, given the number of chapters which cast doubt on the efficacy of human judgement and prudence as a factor in reaching successful outcomes, and attribute these much more to chance and fortune (see for example I.10, I.24, I.31, and I.34).

A last echo in Montaigne worthy of mention links temerity to love (for women) in comparison with friendship:

> [D]'y comparer l'affection envers les femmes, quoy qu'elle naisse de nostre choix, on ne peut, ny la loger en ce rolle. Son feu, je le confesse, [...] est plus actif, plus cuisant et plus aspre. Mais c'est un feu temeraire et volage, ondoyant et divers, feu de fiebvre, subject à accez et remises, et qui ne nous tient qu'à un coing. [...] Qui plus est, en l'amour, ce n'est qu'un desir forcené apres ce qui nous fuit [...]. Aussi tost qu'il entre aux termes de l'amitié, c'est à dire en la convenance des volontez, il s'esvanouist et s'alanguist. La jouyssance le perd, comme ayant la fin corporelle et sujecte à sacieté. (V, p. 186)

> [To compare this brotherly affection with affection for women, even though it is the result of our choice — it cannot be done; nor can we put the love of women in the same category. Its ardor, I confess — [...] — is more active, more scorching, and more intense. But it is a *temeraire* [weak] and fickle flame, undulating and variable, a fever flame, subject to fits and lulls, that holds us only by one corner. [...] What is more, in love there is nothing but a frantic desire for what flees before us: [...]. As soon as it enters the boundaries of friendship, that is to say harmony of wills, it grows faint and languid. Enjoyment destroys it, as having a fleshly end, subject to satiety.] (F, pp. 166–67)

This passage reminded me of a sentence in Erasmus, who in a famous hendiadys denounces heterosexual love in the following terms: 'at praepostera res est amor, ac temeritas, brevisque voluptatis lenocinio pertrahunt hominem in perpetuos et inexplicabiles angores' [but love is preposterous and rash, and it drags a man, lured by the prospect of short-lived pleasure, into an endless and inextricable labyrinth of vexation][12] (one might think here of Chimène Bateman's contribution). This wry comment from a cloistered 'inexpertus' is clearly not a source for Montaigne, who mentions Erasmus only once (V, p. 810); but the similarity of the *Essais* with the outlook and literary processes of the *Adages* has struck many Montaignistes, who have wondered why Montaigne refers so little to his illustrious predecessor. It is not impossible that Montaigne (unlike the Gallican Church of his time) toed the Roman Inquisition's line on the Dutch humanist, and abstained from mentioning an author whose works were unacceptable 'donec corrigantur'. It should not be forgotten here that his *Adages* were only allowed to appear without the name of the author in lands that accepted the authority of the Roman Index.[13]

★   ★   ★   ★   ★

What I have so far written has been closer to a *flux de caquet* inspired by the *esprit d'escalier* than a peroration to the volume. The editors have already shown the links the contributions share in respect of the theme of transit; there are other connections between these articles that can be discerned. All of the essays devote themselves in different ways to making it possible for Montaigne's book to be taken up and read with pleasure and insight by readers in the present, at the same time as being consummate exercises in historical contextualization, some using the 'triangulation' of a source shared by Montaigne and a subsequent writer, who reacts to both (Kate Tunstall and Timothy Chesters). It is not possible to give accounts of these rich contributions without devoting almost as much space to them as they themselves take up. I shall venture a few comments about them, but cannot hope to be fair to all of them. Some are reports on ongoing projects, such as that of Warren Boutcher to produce an edition of Florio's translation of the work which will make visible the Ciceronian distribution of the text to readers not versed in Renaissance stylistics through typographical processes and *mise en page*. He does this in the wake of André Tournon's remarkable edition of the essays using Montaigne's own punctuation and use of majuscules,[14] and Kathy Eden's identification of periodic structures in the sentences of the *Essais*.[15] A radical reassessment of the text from a different perspective is undertaken by Terence Cave, who attributes its enduring appeal to its haptic quality and the cognitive force of imaginative writing. For him, the *Essais* give rise to a complex psychosomatic event discovered by repositioning the text in a metacognitive context (which brings to mind the phrase quoted by Frank Lestringant: 'plaisirs intellectuellement sensibles, sensiblement intellectuels' [pleasures [...] intellectually sensual, sensually intellectual] (V, p. 1107; F, p. 1035).[16] The classical and humanist background to the text is richly explored in different ways by Kathy Eden, Valerie Worth-Stylianou, Emma Herdman, and Rowan Tomlinson; Colin Burrow, Kathryn Murphy, John O'Brien, Timothy Chesters, Kate Tunstall, and Ingrid De Smet investigate its reception and use by dramatists, thinkers, and writers. Broadly thematic approaches are adopted by Chimène Bateman and Frank Lestringant, and investigated also by Kathryn Murphy through an intertextual study of the problem of the general and the contingent particular in Burton and Montaigne. All these contributions are sensitive to what may have been lost in transmission, and evince a complex and productive range of critical responses that show how, since the days of Pierre Villey, the 'allongement du questionnaire' [expansion of the questionnaire], to use Paul Veyne's term,[17] has broadened and enriched the understanding of the *Essais*, as has the 'hermeneutics of suspicion': in the wake of Friedrich Schleiermacher's claim that the historian can know an author better than he knew himself, interpreters now can attempt to see what Montaigne didn't see or chose to hide about his text.[18] These will include unacknowledged borrowings, but also the latent energies in his use of language that can be released by subsequent critics, whether they are there intentionally or not.

What finally unites all of the contributors as well as the three editors is their appreciation of the enduring appeal of the *Essais*. Montaigne could not have been more wrong when he wrote 'j'escris mon livre à peu d'hommes et à peu d'années' [I write my book for few men and for few years] (V, p. 982; F, p. 913). What is closer to the truth is found in two passages: the former is one of the opening sentences to III.9, 'De la vanité' [On Vanity], quoted here by Frank Lestringant: 'qui ne voit que j'ay pris une route par laquelle, sans cesse et sans travail, j'iray autant qu'il y aura d'ancre et de papier au monde?' [who does not see that I have taken a road along which I shall go, without stopping and without effort, as long as the is ink and paper in the world?] (V, p. 982; F, p. 876). His critics have also benefited from this infinite productivity (in both the economic and the mathematical sense). The other passage that comes to mind, which is fitting to provide an end to this Afterword, has intimations of mortality, but at the same time records the benefits of infinite enquiry:

> ce n'est rien que foiblesse particuliere qui nous faict contenter de ce que d'autres ou que nous-mesmes avons trouvé en cette chasse de cognoissance; un plus habile ne s'en contentera pas. Il y a tousjours place pour un suyvant, ouy et pour nous mesmes, et route par ailleurs. Il n'y a point de fin en nos inquisitions; nostre fin est en l'autre monde. (V, p. 1068)

> [It is only personal weakness that makes us content with what others or we ourselves have found out in this hunt for knowledge. An abler man will not rest content with it. There is always room for a successor, yes, and for ourselves, and a road in another direction. There is no end to our questionings; our end is in the other world.] (F, p. 996; adapted)

Notes to the Afterword

1. In this collection of essays, this passage is evoked by John O'Brien's Christoph Besold.
2. Roger Trinquet, *La Jeunesse de Montaigne* (Paris: Nizet, 1972), pp. 513–20.
3. Ingrid De Smet and Alain Legros, 'Un manuscrit de François Baudouin dans la librairie de Montaigne', *Bibliothèque d'Humanisme et Renaissance*, 75 (2013), 105–11.
4. See my 'The Process of Intellectual Change: A Post-Foucauldian Hypothesis', in *Cultural History after Foucault*, ed. John Neubauer (Berlin: Walter de Gruyter, 1999), pp. 163–76.
5. See R. A. Sayce, 'The Style of Montaigne. Word-Pairs and Word-Groups', in *Literary Style: A Symposium*, ed. Seymour Chatman (London: Oxford University Press, 1971), pp. 383–405, and *The Essays of Montaigne, A Critical Exploration* (London: Weidenfeld & Nicolson, 1972), pp. 301–08.
6. The four-term classification is first encountered in the thirteenth-century jurist Tancredus of Bologna; see Hans Joachim Musielak, *Die Grundlagen der Beweislast im Zivilprozess* (Berlin: de Gruyter, 1975), p. 256. See also Baldus de Ubaldis, *In vij,viij, ix x et xi Codicis libros commentaria* (Venice: heirs of Giorgio Varisco, 1615), fol. 208r: 'suspicio [est] aliqualis applicatio animi ad aliquid cum vehementi titubatione [...] praesumptio [est] similitudo sufficiens ad rem dubiam, de qua creditur, credenda [...] indicium [...] semiplenum [dubitatum] vel plenum seu indubitatum [quae est] demonstratio rei per signa sufficentia per quae animus in aliquo tanquam in existente quiescat [...] argumentum [est] propositio ex aliquibus existentibus resultans ad propositum ostendendum seu concludendum [...] adminiculum [est] vel vehemens vel non vehemens [quod est] aliqualis confirmatio rei probabilis, vel est aliqualis confirmatio veri tendens ad aliquid suspendendum de defectu probationis.' Also Prospero Farinacci, *Tractatus de haeresi* (Rome: Andreas Phaeus, 1616), fol. 325r; Henri Boguet, *Discours des sorciers, avec six advis en faict de sorcellerie* (Lyon: Pierre Rigaud, 1610), pp. 53, 76; and Julius Clarus, *Liber quintus receptarum sententiarum*, in *Opera omnia* (Frankfurt: Wolfgang Richter, 1604), p. 137 (q. 20, n. 2): 'et sic habes in hac materia suspiciones, praesumptiones, indicia, semiplenam probationem, et plusquam semiplenam probationem [...] in hac materia indiciorum non potest dari certa regula, sed multum iudicis arbitrio committitur'. See also Jean Bodin, *De la demonomanie des sorciers* (Paris: Jacques Du Puys, 1580), fol. 186–87: 'or il y a des presomptions temeraires, les autres probables, les autres violentes'.
7. Pietro Pomponazzi, *Opera* (Basel: Henricus Petri, 1567), p. 294; translation mine.
8. See my article 'The Sceptical Crisis Reconsidered: Galen, Rational Medicine and the Libertas philosophandi', *Early Science and Medicine*, 11 (2006), 249–74 (pp. 262–63).
9. See D 19.1.13.1 (reference to a 'temerariam indicationem'); D 22.5.3.6; D 22.5.3.6; D 38.2.19; D

39.4.12pr; D 47.2.9.3; D 47.12.3.8; D 48.16pr; D 48.16.1.5; D. 49.19.28.3; D 50.17.64 ('ea quae raro accidunt non temere in agendis negotiis computantur').

10. Cicero, *De natura deorum*, II. 31. 56; *De divinatione*, II. 41. 85; for other loci, see Jonathan Zarecki, *Cicero's Ideal Statesman* (London: Bloomsbury, 2014), p. 144. Aquinas cites Augustine's determination of 'temeritas' in *Contra Julianum*, IV. 3 as a contrary of 'prudentia' in *Summa Theologiae* 2a 2ae 53,1; see also 2a 2ae 21,4. Rudolph Goclenius (*Lexicon philosophicum* (Frankfurt: widow of Matthias Becker for Peter Musculus and Rupert Pistorius, 1613), pp. 1120–21) rejects the association with chance, and reserves the use of 'temere' for cases arising from a moral disposition.

11. An important theological context is referred to by Montaigne at V, p. 320: 'ce n'est pas sans grande raison, ce me semble, que l'Eglise defend l'usage promiscue, temeraire et indiscret des sainctes et divines chansons que le Sainct Esprit a dicté en David'. It is possible that Montaigne is here referring to the fourth of the rules authorized by Pius IV concerning the use of the Bible by the laity and its translation into vernacular languages: *Index librorum prohibitorum cum regulis confectis per Patres a Tridentina Synodo delectos auctoritate* [...] *Pii IIII comprobatis* (Rome: Paulus Manutius, 1564), sig. B2r–D8v. See also V, p. 321 (on the Lutheran interpretation of the Bible through that sect's use of 'cette science verbale et vaine, nourrice de presumption et de temerité'). Montaigne may also be referring to the fourth session of the Council of Trent of 8 April 1546, where the following ordonnance is to be found: '[sacrosancta Synodus Tridentia] temeritatem illam reprimere volens, qua ad profana quaeque convertuntur et torquentur verba et sententiae Sacrae Scripturae, ad scurrilia scilicet, fabulosa, vana, adulationes, detractiones, superstitiones, impias et diabolicas incantationes, divinationes, sortes, libellos etiam famosos, mandat et praecipit, ad tollendam huiusmodi irreverentiam et contemptum, et ne de cetero quisquam quomodolibet verba Scripturae Sacrae ad haec et similia audeat usurpare, ut omnes huius generis homines, temeratores et violatores verbi Dei, iuris et arbitrii poenis per Episcopos coerceantur.'

12. Erasmus, *Christiani matrimonii institutio*, in *Opera omnia*, ed. Jean Leclerc (Leiden: van der Aa, 1703–06), vol. 5, p. 642; translation mine.

13. The relevant expurgated edition has as its title *Pauli Manutii Adagia quaecumque ad hanc diem exierunt, ab omnibus mendis vindicata*; it was published by the Giunti presses in Florence in 1575.

14. Montaigne, *Essais*, ed. André Tournon (Paris: Imprimerie nationale, 1998). For a discussion of the merits of this and other innovative recent editions of the *Essais*, see John O'Brien, 'Are We Reading What Montaigne Wrote?', *French Studies*, 58 (2004), 527–32, and my review article 'Versions of Michel de Montaigne', *Times Literary Supplement*, 5480 (11 April 2008), pp. 255–56.

15. Kathy Eden, 'Cicero's Portion of Montaigne's Acclaim', in *Brill's Companion to the Reception of Cicero*, ed. William H. F. Altman (Leiden: Brill, 2015), pp. 39–55.

16. For a different approach to this phrase, see my *Montaigne philosophe* (Paris: Presses universitaires de France, 1996), pp. 116–19.

17. Paul Veyne, *Comment on écrit l'histoire* (Paris: Seuil, 1978), pp. 141–56.

18. Paul Ricœur, *Le Conflit des interprétations* (Paris: Seuil, 1969), p. 326; Friedrich Schleiermacher, *Hermeneutik und Kritik*, ed. Manfred Frank (Frankfurt: Suhrkamp, 1977); Jean Grondin, *L'Herméneutique* (Paris: Presses universitaires de France, 2006), p. 82.

INDEX OF NAMES

INDEX OF CHAPTERS OF THE *ESSAIS*

❖

www.ingramcontent.com/pod-product-compliance
Lightning Source LLC
Chambersburg PA
CBHW080837250626
47160CB00009B/2965